Martin Luther's Theology

Martin Luther's Theology

A CONTEMPORARY INTERPRETATION

Oswald Bayer

Translated by Thomas H. Trapp

William B. Eerdmans Publishing Company
Grand Rapids, Michigan / Cambridge, U.K.

First published 2003 in German as *Martin Luthers Theologie. Eine Vergegenwärtigung.*
© 2003 J. C. B. Mohr (Paul Siebeck) Tübingen. This translation is based on the third
edition, 2007

Published 2008 by
Wm. B. Eerdmans Publishing Co.
2140 Oak Industrial Drive N.E., Grand Rapids, Michigan 49505 /
P.O. Box 163, Cambridge CB3 9PU U.K.

Printed in the United States of America

13 12 11 10 09 08   7 6 5 4 3 2 1

Library of Congress Cataloging-in-Publication Data

Bayer, Oswald.
   [Martin Luthers Theologie. English]
   Martin Luther's theology: a contemporary interpretation / Oswald Bayer;
   translated by Thomas H. Trapp.
      p.   cm.
   ISBN 978-0-8028-2799-9 (pbk.: alk. paper)
   1. Luther, Martin, 1483-1546.   I. Title.

   BR333.3.B3913   2008
   230.41 — dc22

                           2008003818

www.eerdmans.com

Contents

B. INDIVIDUAL THEMES (SPECIFIC ELEMENTS OF DOGMATICS AND ETHICS)

Translator's Preface

I wish to begin by expressing my deepest gratitude to Dr. Robert Kolb, who teaches at Concordia Seminary in St. Louis. He read every part of this translation and provided me wonderful guidance. Both Dr. Bayer and I turned to Bob for consultation in translating this work. I will be forever grateful to Bob for his ready help. Bob is indeed a unique Christian scholar, always ready to squeeze in the time necessary to work with others on their projects while continuing to do his own. He is most gracious in the process.

This book presents a series of lectures given to university-level students at the University of Tübingen. I sought to arrive at a translation that will satisfy scholars who know the subject matter. But I also aimed to find English words that would bring the novice into the unique dimensions of Luther's theology. Because Dr. Bayer based many observations on sections from Luther's Small Catechism and Luther's hymns, I chose at times to make literal translations and not just cite already extant translations. Hymns are particularly difficult to cite in translation and then use in a detailed discussion. Since Dr. Bayer was basing his observations on Luther's writings and the *Book of Concord,* I chose to translate everything afresh from the German in the body of the text, rather than to cite other translations. The original German documents are referenced in the footnotes, followed by a notation for an English translation when such is available. This makes for a smoother flow of the text and of the argument. I thank Tom Raabe of Eerdmans for his considerable help with bibliographical notations in the footnotes. It made the project considerably easier.

I will share just a few examples of the challenges of choosing the right word in English. What is one to do with *reformatorisch?* Dr. Bayer seeks to discover what is really "reformational" about the Reformation. This goes beyond what happened in the Reformation in general. Was there a unique turning point, a unique insight, on which the Reformation as such hinges? For Dr. Bayer, that is rooted in *promissio*. My spell-check does not like "reformational," but it is the best I could use.

What about *Anfechtung?* I determined that one word would not do. I decided "agonizing struggle" was the best overall term. It is more than just external temptation and deeper than a momentary struggle with an issue.

What about *was Christum treibet,* with its mix of the Latin accusative and the German? Some Luther scholars easily resolve this with "what drives Christ," but that leaves open the possibility for me that it points to what motivates Christ to do what he does for our salvation. At first I thought "what manifests Christ" would work, though it was weak. I follow Bob Kolb's suggestion to use "what drives Christ home," as what demonstrates that all Scripture is finally about Christ and the act of salvation.

What was to be done about God's two *Regimente?* For me, the English word "regiment" conjures up soldiers on horses. "Two kingdoms" was definitely out! "Two governments" had possibilities. "Two types of authority," "two ways of ruling," and "two ways of governing" were all given serious consideration. I finally settled on the "two realms." But that brought up the further issue of how to describe the two. I settled on "spiritual" and "temporal." It is common for translators to use "sacred" and "secular," but our English word "secular" seems to convey anything but the reign of God on earth. "Temporal" seemed preferable in the end to "worldly."

One final example must suffice. What to do about *leibliches Wort?* This has been translated as "bodily word." I could not get a picture of what that meant. Was it Christ as the "Word made flesh"? The parallel Latin term suggests that the "external Word" is best, stated in opposition to those who would think that God communicates internally within the individual human being apart from the physical Word of the Scripture.

No one term is ever completely adequate because each person has different experiences with the words we use. It is my hope that what Dr. Bayer sought to convey to his students will come through. I am honored that I was asked to do this translation. I have profited mightily in my own pastoral and teaching ministries from this in-depth work with Luther, as explained and articulated by Dr. Bayer. I appreciate my wife Kathy's patience during the many hours that I devoted to this project during a sabbatical that was intended to give me time to relax a bit. Another time!?

I pray that the book will bring great benefit to all who read it and evaluate their own fiercely held ideas, in light of the gospel. The book will help the reader to know which ideas are to be held just as tightly as before and which are to be abandoned as deficient.

THOMAS H. TRAPP
Professor of Theology at Concordia University,
St. Paul, Minnesota
Pastor at Emmaus Lutheran Church,
St. Paul, Minnesota

Preface

1. Luther — a Systematic Theologian?

Martin Luther did not write a systematic work that was comparable to a theo logical summa — as Thomas Aquinas wrote. Nor did he set forth theological *"Loci,"* as Melanchthon did. The reality is that presenting one's thinking as a system was foreign to him, though it had been standard operating procedure for philosophers and theologians for two hundred years already. Those who think within a systematic framework are obsessed with unity and consistency; without exception everything has to fit together seamlessly for them. Luther's theology raises fundamental questions about that entire enterprise, though, by contrast, it is a common postulate for us to think in this way.

Luther took his professorship in theology, a post he was granted in 1512, with such utter seriousness that he turned his attention to biblical texts with a unique measure of concentration and intensity. He was primarily what one would call an "Old Testament theologian"; the majority of his lectures deal primarily with books of the Old Testament. His academic activities furnish thereby a clear indication of the unique character of his theology. In addition, his work was embedded in the practice of praying the psalms daily, a practice that was integral to the life of an Augustinian eremite monk. Luther devoted his scholarly attention in particular to the psalms. The church and the lecture hall were thus closely and specifically intertwined. In addition, in his role as a monastic priest, he was required to preach. Even after he became a professor he continued to preach, right up to his death, in the widest variety of settings, chiefly at the Wittenberg town church and before the large gathering of those who ate with him at home.

Luther spoke and wrote using the widest variety of forms, in the widest possible variety of circumstances, to widely different types of people, to both individuals and groups — generally in response to very specific questions. Correspondingly, the sources yield a whole library of the most widely different types of texts — lectures, sermon transcription notes, written polemics, letters of consolation, prefaces — chiefly on the books of the Bible — theses from disputations, table talks, fables, and hymns; they lift the spirit, teach, admonish, comfort, rebuke, and scold. These addresses and occasional writings cannot be assembled neatly into a systematic compendium. In spite of that, they are all related to a specific setting in life, as is paradigmatically pointed out by the title of his first reformational writing, in a series of theses that appeared in early spring 1518: *Pro veritate inquirenda et timoratis conscientiis consolandis (For the Inquiry into Truth and for the Comfort of Troubled Consciences)*. This is a wonderful title, because Luther does not separate the academic disputation that seeks to ascertain truth from comforting the troubled conscience. Intellectual knowledge about faith is not separated from the affective experience of faith; the art of disputation serves the task of caring for souls.

2. Foundational Motif

The chief concern in Luther's theology, to sharpen and comfort consciences of those who face the last judgment — throughout the widest variety of his writings — corresponds to the *central* core: the foundational motif of his theology. This central core admittedly cannot be summarized by pointing to a *single* isolated concept. Just the fact that it must be examined from many different perspectives calls for one to describe the subject in its many different facets.

One can start by saying that the whole of Luther's theology is expressed by the motto "You are called to *freedom!*" (Gal. 5:13). What kind of freedom is meant? In the biblical and reformational context, the concept of freedom is to be understood in terms of the *distinction between law and gospel*. This is a second way to articulate the foundational motif that runs throughout Luther's theology. And yet, this phraseology does not appear explicitly in all the important texts either. A third signature theme is *"justification by faith alone."* Luther never tires of identifying this teaching as the center of Holy Scripture, and it thus plays an important role in his theology as well. But even "justification" is in danger of being distorted if used without considering the impact of the breadth and depth of his theology of creation, as well as when its eschatological implications are not taken seriously.

Luther's theology is too lively and too complex to be summarized by a single concept. It was not conceived a priori as a system, but maintains its internal coherence only because of the way it is concerned to articulate, at every stage, the dynamic that differentiates the gospel — the promise *(promissio)* of God — from the law. One might say that the interrelationship between law and gospel forms the chromosomal structure within every cell of Luther's theology. Whether he is teaching about the living Scripture, which interprets itself by the power of the Holy Spirit, or the christologically based happy exchange that involves sinful man and the God who justifies, whether it concerns the basic structure of humanity that directs its look outward, or the church, or finally whether one speaks of his way of dealing with ethical issues, using a few basic principles but applying them in a highly flexible way — in every aspect of Luther's theology one detects a dynamic flow that keeps one from arranging his teachings in a linear progression.

3. Development

The difficulties noted here are reflected in various articulations of Luther's theology that have appeared up to the present — with some concentrating on unfolding the historical development of his thought and others oriented toward arranging his thinking within a systematic framework.

This present exposition cannot deny, nor claims to deny, that the effort is problematic. This study is arranged in such a way that an introduction ("The Rupture between Ages"), which sets the stage for the entire enterprise *in nuce* already at the outset, and the prolegomena (A: chapters 1–4) identify the essence of the dynamic of Luther's theology thematically. The central elements of the prolegomena are treated in four segments: "Theological Understanding," "The Subject of Theology," "Identification of What Is 'Reformational,'" and "Scriptural Authority." The rest of the book (B: chapters 5–15) unfolds the foundational motif in greater detail. This latter part of the book is divided into two sections: the first begins with a discussion of creation and ends with the question about evil, and the second begins with the topic of how evil is overcome and ends by examining the consummation of the world and the triune nature of God, the divine Trinity. The dividing point between these two sections identifies the decisive turning point, corresponding exactly to Luther's great Reformation hymn of deliverance: "Dear Christians, One and All, Rejoice," according to which the journey into hell that is experienced when one comes to know oneself undergoes a surprising and undeserved turn of events because of God's mercy. As it is distributed, this mercy, which was acquired once for all, is experienced again and again by the person who has been redeemed. That the confrontation between the sinful human being and the holy God does not end in death is the result of the inconceivable upheaval that occurs within God himself (Hos. 11:8): God is mercy and love in his Son, our Lord. God's unearned grace in Christ is the foundation for that which follows: discussion about the Holy Spirit, the church, the new life of the Christian, and finally the eschaton and the incontestable revelation of the triune God as love.

At the same time, the trinitarian structure of the creed is manifested within the sequence of themes: God appears as Father and Creator, as Son and Savior, as Spirit and Consummator — but not in such a way as to suggest that the course of salvation history is transparent from the outset or that it fits together so exactly at the conclusion that we can see already now how it fits together seamlessly. Therefore the chapter "Consummation of the World and God's Triune Nature" is followed by an epilogue that is called for within the structure of the whole presentation, which reflects on our contemporary existence with the prayerful awareness that we are still on this journey of faith and do not yet live in the realm where we can see clearly (2 Cor. 5:7).

To be sure, not only the systematic outline of the creed but also the more comprehensive arrangement of the entire catechism determines the structure of the exposition. Every part of the Small Catechism — the Decalogue, the creed, the Lord's Prayer, the sacraments, the Baptismal Booklet and Marriage Booklet, and the Table of Duties — is thoroughly interwoven throughout.

Last but not least, a conscious decision was made in presenting this study to integrate ethical issues organically into the discussion, so that ethical matters are not left to be an addendum that comes only after the dogmatic materials have been presented. Within the confines of the study, it is not possible to set forth an intensive discussion of various specific ethical topics in a comprehensive way — topics such as marriage and family, economics and politics — and yet the perspectives are identified.

4. Method

The whole presentation is based on an analysis of and meditation upon representative portions of texts from Luther.[1] To be sure, at times passages are in-

---

1. Even when the specific historical questions concerning the development of Luther's theology are not discussed explicitly, one can assume that such issues have been taken into account and included.

cluded that offer summaries and surveys, but the substance of the whole study is fed at every turn by work on those specific texts that most clearly articulate a particular concept.

Corresponding to the multiform nature of Luther's theology, the widest variety of genres is incorporated: sermons, treatises, written polemics, table talks, lectures, and disputations; predominant are the three genres of catechism, prefaces to biblical books, and hymns. Working with texts thus does not just provide ornamental trappings or merely initial work leading to that which is "truly systematic." The work with the texts corresponds, more properly, to the task of systematic theology: to listen and to probe, to mull over and to allow one's conclusions to be put into question. In short, one is to give shape to one's thinking and one's judgments by measuring one's ideas against texts that might seem to state the opposite viewpoint. Whoever thinks he already knows it all or claims, with the unsubstantiated intuition of the moment, to understand clearly is what Luther described as being "like fruit that falls out of season before it is even half ripe." The readers of this book are thus invited to delve more deeply into the wider contexts of what Luther writes, so as to allow the fruits of their own judgment to ripen.

5. A Contemporary Interpretation

The following account strives to present a "contemporary interpretation" as a re-presentation in the double sense of the phrase. In the first place, the *historical subject matter* needs to be brought anew into the modern consciousness — since our present is, in a certain sense, always dependent upon and determined by this subject matter, even though the intervening time has witnessed reshaping, rearranging, and distorting. And yet the interests of every theologian, not just the systematician, need to go beyond mere historical reconstruction. The question must be posed: What is true? Likewise: What has enduring value within the river of historical changes?

When we contemporize Luther with a *systematic intention* — namely, posing the question about what is true — we discover that he speaks to our contemporary situation at the same time; we might say that he imposes himself upon us. This does not happen primarily because of his forceful personality, but because of what his theology urges upon us. We cannot get away from the fact that our own contemporary existence must be examined in light of the same questions that occupied Luther for his entire life: What is the correct way to talk about God and his relationship to human beings? How do salvation, life, and blessedness enter into a world of sin, the devil, and death? How does one become confident about this salvation, precisely at the time when things happen every day to contradict it? Is the church necessary, and if so, who needs it? How does the Christian live in a world that is viewed apocalyptically? These questions were clearly not resolved by the transition from the Middle Ages to the present age and on into the postmodern world. Despite the many ways that views about how to think and how to live have been recast, these questions are still posed for our contemporary world, just as they were at the time of Luther.

My own approach to being involved with systematic theology grew out of the highly controversial task of trying to relate Luther's theology to contemporary problems; I have provided an account of this effort in my introduction to *Leibliches Wort. Reformation und Neuzeit im Konflikt* (Tübingen, 1992) (*The External Word: Reformation and Modernity in Conflict*). The present study is imbued with the same characteristics, as the truths discovered by Luther are clarified by comparing and contrasting them with other views. Luther is therefore brought into conversation — and into polemical disputation when necessary — with truth seekers such as Kant, Hegel, Schleiermacher, and others. This approach is not anachronistic; it focuses on the struggle for truth that reaches across ages; it cannot be relegated to the past and resolved by treating certain issues as part of the history of another age.

6. "A Documentary Film"

This book reflects forty years of investigative work about and with Luther. It is comparable to a film archive; past work has served as a repository from which material was extrapolated for fifteen double-hour lectures for a general studies course taught at Tübingen in the Winter Semester 2001/2002. The sequential nature of the book arose from the way the course was presented. The "splices" can be seen in some places — as also in the various levels of the presentation. All in all, what has resulted may be likened to a documentary film that comes at the topic from multiple perspectives, which hopefully does not err on the side of too much detail, but which also does not suffer because it leaves gaps that are too large.

For their wonderful cooperation in bringing this study into print, I warmly thank Markus Frank, Gerda Scheytt, Dr. Johannes Schwanke, and Samuel Vogel. I am also indebted to the publishing house Mohr Siebeck, above all to Dr. Henning Ziebritzki, for fruitful cooperative efforts.

I offer special thanks to Dr. Martin Abraham for an ongoing *mutuum colloquium*. He was the one who tirelessly searched through that "film archive" and energetically recommended the most important clips. The book profited greatly from his ecclesiological expertise.

With great thanks I dedicate this book to my friend and brother-in-law, Gerhard Hennig, who gave me my first impulse into deeper occupation with Martin Luther's theology.

O.B.   *Tübingen, July 31, 2003*

The entire text was examined carefully as both the second and third editions were prepared. Errors were corrected and minor additions have been included.

The acceptance of the book to this point — as can be seen particularly in the way it has been evaluated in volume 1 of *NZSTh* 2006 — shows that the "Contemporary Interpretation" has been understood as it was intended: not as a shortcut actualization and also not as a "utilization" of Luther to solve contemporary problems. Instead, it is a conversation with Luther, in which one is ready to listen and ready to engage critically, which applies to issues that are shared in common.

O.B.   *Tübingen, January 21, 2004*
                                                                      Hennef, October 31, 2006

I would like to take the opportunity in this preface to express my profound thanks to Eerdmans Publishing House — especially Tom Raabe for his very helpful commitment and his patience editing the English version of this book. Above all I am deeply thankful to Thomas H. Trapp, who has translated this book with an extraordinary and passionate effort.

OSWALD BAYER   *Hennef, April 22, 2008*

Abbreviations

LuJ	*Luther-Jahrbuch*
LW	*Luther's Works*, American Edition
MJTh	Marburger Jahrbuch Theologie
MPG	Migne, Patrologia Graeca
MPL	Migne, Patrologia Latina
NRSV	New Revised Standard Version
NTD	Neues Testament Deutsch
NZSTh	*Neue Zeitschrift für systematische Theologie*
PF	Pädagogische Forschungen
PhB	Philosophische Bibliothek
RGG	*Religion in Geschichte und Gegenwart*
SA	Smalcald Articles
SC	Small Catechism (Luther)
STh	*Summa Theologiae*
TBT	Theologische Bibliothek Töpelmann
ThEx	Thcologische Existenz heute
ThLZ	*Theologische Literaturzcitung*
ThSt	Theologische Studien
ThStKr	*Theologische Studien und Kritiken*
TRE	*Theologische Realenzyklopädic*
TRev	*Theologische Revue*
WA	Weimar Ausgabe
WA BR	Weimar Ausgabe, Briefe
WA DB	Weimar Ausgabe, Deutsche Bibel
WA TR	Weimar Ausgabe, Tischreden
WdF	Wege der Forschung
WUNT	Wissenschaftliche Untersuchungen zum Neuen Testament
ZevKR	*Zeitschrift für evangelisches Kirchenrecht*
ZThK	*Zeitschrift für Theologie und Kirche*

Introduction The Rupture between Ages

*God is with us in the muck and in the work
that makes his skin steam.*

1. Between the New and Old Aeon

"He senses the huge rupture between ages / and he tightly grasps his Bible's
pages." That is how it was stated poetically by Conrad Ferdinand Meyer in
1871, in "Hutten's Last Days."[1] With a tightly held Bible, in a defiantly heroic
pose, standing tall, in a flowing gown, even in that era he was placed on a ped-
estal: Luther the German. And "the huge rupture between ages" is perceived
even today as a way to pose the question whether Luther and his work belong
to the modern age or rather to the Middle Ages.

And yet this question does not go deep enough. To be sure, it attempts to
profile a particular observation, and on those grounds it certainly deserves
mention. But something else is more decisive: the huge rupture between ages
is, in reality, that between the old and the new aeon, which takes place on the
cross of Jesus Christ. That is the rupture between the old world that has come
to an end, that of the fallen creation, and the renewed creation, the new
world, which is so new that it will never again become old; it is eternally new.
One can attribute the really new actuality to *this* new age: the present age, the
present age of the Spirit.

It is this rupture between ages that gave shape to Luther's life and work,
moved him in his innermost being, made him who he was in every way possible, as Michael Mathias Prechtl appropriately depicted him: "Martin Luther,

---

1. Conrad Ferdinand Meyer, *Huttens letzte Tage. Eine Dichtung* (1871), XXXII: "Luther"
(end of the section) (Stuttgart: Reclam 6942, 1975), 39.

1

from deep within, a full figure."[2] Once again, as said by Meyer's Hutten: "His spirit is the field of battle between two aeons / it surprises me not that he sees demons!"[3]

2. In Spite of Evil

Demons! The evil of the old world that came to an end on the cross rears up one last time: right in front of the gospel that has overcome and still overcomes evil. "For this reason, we really get to know the devil rightly for the first time from the gospel," said Luther in his New Year's Day sermon of 1535.[4] Luther's insights, gained from an intimate struggle with evil, were not surpassed by such masters of the hermeneutics of suspicion as Marx, Freud, and Nietzsche. Luther is admittedly not a calm observer who describes what is going on from a discreet distance. Instead, he is passionately involved, body and soul, skin and hair. His passion does not make him blind, but rather makes him see — with sight that admittedly comes only through the words of Holy Scripture, which for him is much more than words to read on paper, but a powerfully effective Word that gives life.[5]

More than anywhere else, it was in Luther's ongoing activity with the psalms that he learned that and how I am at enmity with myself, that and in what forms others are at enmity with me — even that and how God is at enmity with me and how God becomes for me a demon, as long as I do not look to the Crucified One. God is at enmity with me as the dark, utterly distant

---

2. Prechtl adapts a picture of Luther as an old man, sketched in 1545 by the Reformer's assistant, Johann Reifenstein. Cf., e.g., Martin Brecht, *Martin Luther*, vol. 3, *The Preservation of the Church, 1532-1546* (Minneapolis: Fortress, 1999), 234. His conceptualization of the aged Luther is overlaid by the figure of Luther from the central panel of the triptych at the altar of the city church at Weimar (by Lucas Cranach the Elder, 1553). Prechtl takes Luther's face from Reifenstein's sketch; from Cranach's portrait he takes the collar with conspicuous streaks of cardinal red, the way the hands are positioned around the open Bible, and the figure of the Crucified that Cranach positioned separately from Luther but which is positioned "inside" the body of Luther by Prechtl, along with the stream of blood that spurts from the wound in the Lord's side. Prechtl's watercolor leaves the pages of the open Bible blank. In Cranach's portrait they have writing on them and can be read by anyone who looks at the scene depicted by the altar. Luther's index finger points to Heb. 4:16 (cf. below, n. 19): "Let us therefore approach the throne of grace with boldness [= freedom, sincerity; Greek: παρρησία], so that we may receive mercy and find grace to help in time of need."

3. Cf. n. 1 above, 40.

4. WA 41:3.26.

5. Cf. chap. 4 below.

Michael Mathias Prechtl, "Martin Luther, An Inherently Full Figure"
Watercolor, 1983. The title cites Dürer: "A good painter is an
inherently full figure."

and, at the same time, utterly close power — consuming, burning, oppressively near. God hides himself within that almighty power that works in life and death, love and hate, preserving life and removing life, fortune and misfortune, good and evil, in short, working everything in everyone, and we cannot extricate ourselves from having a relationship with him.[6] "God cannot be God; to begin with he must become a devil."[7]

That is just one of Luther's comments that includes such an observation: "God cannot be God; to begin with he must become a devil" — a demon such as the one that fell upon Jacob at the ford of the Jabbok during the night and wrestled with him until dawn appeared. Jacob fought and "said, I will not let you go, unless you bless me" (Gen. 32:26). He obtained the blessing, was accorded a new name, and was known from then on as "Israel": "Striver with God" — "for you have striven with God and with humans" (Gen. 32:28).

Luther's insight into evil allows him to understand the world realistically. That distinguishes him sharply from the inoffensive view of modern theologians of love, who take the foundational Christian confession that God is love and make love into an epistemological and organizational principle for a dogmatic system that they consider internally consistent and complete. They can accomplish this only by minimizing the enemies that fight against those who pray the psalms, turning them into paper tigers and making them disappear, as they press their theory to its limits.

By contrast, Luther's life and work is marked through and through by agonizing struggle with this enemy and by the battle against it. For example, one need only glance at his commentary on Psalm 119 to see that he treats this psalm's repeated motif concerning the "enemies" of the Word of God by powerfully intensifying it, carrying it still further, and sharpening its application for the present — most especially in his polemic against the Roman papacy as the embodiment of the Antichrist[8] and against the Enthusiasts. That Luther erred horribly in his identification of the enemies of the Word of God in his

6. Cf. chap. 9 below.

7. WA 31I:249.25f.; cf. *LW* 14:31 (on Ps. 117, 1530).

8. Luther's judgment of the papacy as Antichrist is no longer accurate with respect to the modern papacy. But at that time it did apply, insofar as the papacy was destroying God's order in the world because of a false understanding of the church, marriage, and family, and of economic and political matters as well: WA 39II:39-91. The complete title of this circular disputation, dated May 9, 1539 (on Matt. 19:21), shows precisely in what sense Luther regarded the pope as Antichrist: *De tribus hierarchiis: ecclesiastica, politica, oeconomica et quod Papa sub nulla istarum sit sed omnium publicus hostis (Concerning the Three Hierarchies: The Ecclesiastical, Political, Economic, and That the Pope Is Not to Be Located within Any One of Them, but Is Rather the Public Enemy of All of Them)*; cf. especially WA 39II:52.6–53.14, and chap. 6 below.

later[9] writings against Jews — with fatal results when applied at a much later time — causes consternation and pain.

Luther's understanding of the world, the age, and the Word, when surveying the overall picture of time that stretches from the beginning of the world to its end, concentrates on the present — not in a mystical or actual directness that surrenders to the "moment," but rather in a way that is completely engaged with what is happening at his time and with a critique of such events. Prechtl thus correctly gets to the heart of the matter when his painting of Luther depicts knights with lances fighting against peasant farmers who wield threshing flails, as he portrays the Peasants' War and the general situation in 1525, which Luther viewed as the onset of the demise of the world. But at that same end of time, "to spite" the devil,[10] Luther took God's creative will seriously when he married and established a family: these are signs of faith in God the Creator, in the midst of the apocalyptic lightning bolts. "And if I can make it happen, to spite him [the devil], I still plan to take my Käte in marriage, before I die. . . . I hope that they [the peasants] are not able to take from me my courage and [my] joy. . . . In just a little while the righteous judge will come,"[11] the final one, who brings the world to its completion with his judgment. The meaning of that which affected Luther and what struck him so deeply within, which stretched far beyond the unique historical events of that time, comes clear when it catches our attention that one of the soldiers portrayed by Otto Dix is depicted as a farmer, and we are reminded of the hell that was Verdun, as well as the entire horror of the wars and their terrors that have been fought since then. On the other side, one might consider Albrecht Dürer's portrayal of the band of knights in his *Four Horsemen of the Apocalypse* and *Knight, Death, and Devil;* however — by means of citations from Hieronymus Bosch's "depictions of evil" — they are elevated into the mythical realm; one of the knights, with a blood-smeared sword, has a body with scales: Behemoth and Leviathan.

9. WA 53:579-648 (*Of Shem Hamphoras and the Lineage of Christ,* 1543), but above all *LW* 47:137-306 (*On the Jews and Their Lies,* 1543); the early treatise is quite different: *LW* 45:199-229 (*That Jesus Christ Was Born a Jew,* 1523). For a particularly helpful analysis of the differences, cf. Peter von der Osten-Sacken, *Martin Luther und die Juden. Neu untersucht anhand von Anton Margarithas "Der gantz Jüdisch glaub"* (1530-31) (Stuttgart: Kohlhammer, 2002). Cf. further chap. 15 below, n. 24.

10. WA 18:277.35 (*A Christian Writing for Walter Reissenbusch, Encouraging Him to Marry,* 1525).

11. WA BR 3:482.81-83, 93f.; to Rühel on May 4 (5?), 1525.

3. The Crucified One and the Message from the Cross

Into the midst of this meat grinder, within this history of the world as a battle of everyone against everyone else, in a life-and-death struggle for mutual recognition, God himself has entered through his Son, sacrificed him, given him up even to death, to death on a cross. God is human. He is "with us in the muck and in the work that makes his skin steam," as Luther preached about the name of Christ, "Immanuel," "God is with us."[12] By the power of his love, the Crucified One, God endured and overcame the night of sin, of death, and of hell.[13]

Such images and scenes about life as a battle exert power in our earthly life to the last moment and aim to block our view of anything else. But in the Crucified One, who "was tempted just as we are, by the image of death, of sin, and of hell,"[14] you are able "to regard death from the viewpoint of life, sin from that of grace, hell from that of heaven."[15] The sign and image of the cross will make you victorious and you will live, even if you die.

As the artist makes it clear to see, the Crucified One does not simply remain merely a figure in the picture, but lets himself be heard; he has something to say: he comes in the Word of the Bible that is preached. The ray cast forth by his blood opens the meaning of Holy Scripture, opens the testament, as the message from the cross, which bequeaths to us eternal communion with God by means of forgiveness, in the midst of our hellish personal history and our world's history.

Luther, as the servant of the divine Word, points to this message from the cross, promises the forgiveness of sins in the name of God, offers it, imparts it. The Bible is not somehow — bound up tightly — a closed document, not a weapon of fundamentalism, but it is open — opened by the One who alone can open it: opened by the Crucified One, who lives (Luke 24:30-32).

Luther's pointing finger rests on a very specific passage in the opened Bible. On which one? One might think of Romans 3:25: it speaks of the one who "SVNDE VERGJBT" ("forgives sin").[16] In the entire Bible this is the only se-

---

12. WA 4:608.32–609.1.

13. Cf. chap. 10 below.

14. WA 2:691.25f.; cf. *LW* 42:107 ("A Sermon on Preparing to Die," 1519).

15. WA 2:688.35f.; cf. *LW* 42:103. Cf. WA 11:141, on lines 22/29: "media vita in morte kers umb media morte in vita sumus" [in the midst of life we are in the midst of death] (sermon on Luke 1:39-56; July 2, 1523). Cf. WA 43:219.37 ("media morte in vita sumus" [in the midst of death we are in the midst of life]): WA 40III:496.16f.; WA 12:609.17f.

16. On this subject, cf. Martin Schloemann, "Die zwei Wörter. Luthers Notabene zur 'Mitte der Schrift,'" *Luther* 65 (1994): 110-23.

quence of words that Luther writes in capital letters and identifies in a marginal note as "the foremost passage" and the "central passage in this epistle and in the entire Scripture."[17]

The stubborn nature and the comfort of the evangelical faith rest in the reliance on taking the statement of the promise of the forgiveness of sins literally.[18] Luther can even speak about it by saying that we should "lay claim to" God's promises for ourselves, that we should step forth before him, having claimed his promises.[19] Corresponding to this, one reads in a passage from the extensive lectures on Genesis, which virtually presents a theological testament:

> I am baptized; I am absolved; I die trusting this. No matter whatever challenges this, no matter what brings this into question, such as temptations and cares; that will never cause me to waver. For the one who has said: "Whoever believes and is baptized will be saved" and "Whatever you loose on earth, is loosed in heaven" and "This is my body, this is my blood, which is poured out for you, for the forgiveness of sins," that one cannot deceive and lie. That is most certainly true.[20]

In another passage, in the great Galatians commentary, it reads: "That is the reason why our theology is trustworthy: because it tears us away from ourselves and places us outside of ourselves — in such a way that we do not rely on our own powers, our conscience, our senses, our person, our works, but it supports us instead on that which is outside of ourselves *(extra nos)*, namely, on the promise and truth of God, which cannot deceive."[21]

---

17. D. Martin Luther, *Biblia: das ist: Die gantze Heilige Schrifft: Deudsch, Wittenberg 1545,* on Rom. 3:23ff.; cf. Luther's definition of the theme of theology in *LW* 12:311 (on Ps. 51, 1532). On the subject, cf. chap. 2 below.

18. Cf. chap. 3 below.

19. This is demonstrated in an instructive way in the interpretation of Heb. 4:16 (cf. n. 2 above), dated March 1518, in connection with the reformational change in Luther's theology: "This faith alone makes one pure and worthy, which does not rely on such works but relies on the completely pure, trustworthy, and solid Word of Christ, who says: 'Come to Me, all of you who labor and are weighed down: I will give you rest' [Matt. 11:28]. In short: one must approach in the arrogance of what is stated by these words [*In praesumptione igitur istorum verborum*], and those who approach in this way will not be confounded" (WA 57III:171.4-8; cf. *LW* 29:172-73, scholium on Heb. 5:1). Cf. Oswald Bayer, *Promissio. Geschichte der reformatorischen Wende in Luthers Theologie,* 2nd ed. (Darmstadt: Wissenschaftliche Buchgesellschaft, 1989; original 1971), 206-12, especially 208f.

20. WA 44:720.30-36; cf. *LW* 8:193-94 (*Lectures on Genesis,* chaps. 45–50, 1544, on Gen. 48:21).

21. WA 40I:589.25-28; cf. *LW* 26:387 (*Lectures on Galatians,* chaps. 1–4, 1535, on Gal. 4:6; 1531). What follows immediately after this reads: "The pope knows nothing of this."

4. Personal Story and the World History

It is thus clear why Luther considered his teaching, not his person, to be important. Already in 1522 in his "Earnest Admonition to All Christians, to Keep Themselves from Rebellion and Insurrection," he sought that

> each person ought to refrain from mentioning my name, and not call oneself a Lutheran, but rather, a Christian. What is Luther? Is it not true that the teaching is not mine! In the same vein, I have been crucified for no one. Saint Paul [1 Cor. 3:4] would not allow it that the Christians would be called Pauline or Petrine, but just Christians. How did it happen to me that I, a poor, stinking sack of maggots, should have someone call the children of Christ after my unworthy name? Not so, beloved friends! Let us eliminate the names that identify various parties and just call ourselves Christians, because of Christ, whose teaching we have. . . . I am and wish to be master of no man. I have, along with the community, the one, universal teaching of Christ, who alone is our master [Matt. 23:8].[22]

Luther's interest in the story of his own life and in the history of the world, in the course of his own existence and in the course of the world, is totally immersed in his interest in the path forged by the Word of God, in the *cursus euangelii*,[23] the course of the gospel, an interest he had in common with the book of Acts. When it does come to speaking about his life, about his biography, and when actions taken throughout the Reformation need to be summarized, from such historical observations, what ends up being described concerns "what happened to me in connection with the beloved Word of God, what had to be suffered because of so many and powerful enemies in these last fifteen years."[24]

The following comment to the reader, with which Luther closes his preface to the first volume of his Latin writings (1545), is not conventional, flowery language, but identifies the controlling frame of reference within which his life and work were to be appropriately evaluated: "Pray for the growth of the Word against Satan, for he is powerful and evil; he rages and raves now

---

22. WA 8:685.4-16. WA 23:17-37 in particular indicates that Luther was not concerned for his person, but only for his teaching (*Luther's Answer to the Lampoon of the King of England*, 1527).

23. WA TR 4:311.25–312.1 (no. 4436, 1539): "They want to prevent us from spreading the gospel [cf. 2 Thess. 3:1], which is not under our control anyway, just as we cannot stop a field from getting green or growing." Cf. *LW* 2:334 (on Gen. 13:4): *fortuna verbi* (the fate of the Word).

24. WA 38:134.6-8 ("Preface to the Catalogue or Register of All the Books and Writings of Luther," 1533).

with his final fury, since he knows that he has only a short time left. But may God strengthen within us what he has accomplished, and may he complete his work, which he has begun in us, to his honor. Amen."[25] This setting in which history is experienced, in which one's own journey through life is inextricably bound up with the journey of the Word of God, which encounters contradiction and is rejected and is fought against, but which is marked concurrently as a time of passionate laments and petitions that the Lord will return and carry out his final judgment, can hardly be called anything other than "apocalyptic."[26]

5. Apocalyptic and Courage to Live

Luther's apocalyptic understanding of creation and history bars the door to him, so that he cannot search for a way to explain history from a comprehensive historical-philosophical perspective, particularly as such a view is expressed in the modern concept of progress.[27] The rupture between the old and the new world, which occurs in what happened on the cross of Christ and which marks each one biographically in baptism, ruptures metaphysical concepts of an overall unity as well as historical-theological thinking that one can achieve perfection.

Baptism is the point of rupture between the old and new aeon. Ethical advances can come only in the return to one's baptism. Progress, because of which we are enabled to promise ourselves what is really good, in fact what is best, comes in repentance and in a return to one's baptism and thereby to an awareness of the world in which the alternatives of optimism and pessimism, a horrific fear of the future versus a euphoric hope for a further evolution of the cosmos and an expansion of its opportunities, are destroyed — since what is real is that God the Creator makes things unceasingly new.

Luther's own courage to go on living — beyond either optimism or pessimism — because he is rooted in baptism, comes not from an expression that he himself formulated but from a proverb that certainly captures his own way

25. WA 54:187.3-7; cf. *LW* 34:338 ("Preface to the Complete Edition of Luther's Latin Writings," 1545). The citations are from Acts 12:24; 19:20; Rev. 12:12; and Phil. 1:6.

26. The term used here does not denote a specific literary genre. It accentuates a fundamental and determinative consciousness of the Christian faith, which goes deeper than any of the distinctions drawn by form-critical studies and tradition-historical studies, consciousness that we are at present anticipating the judgment of the world as the consummation of the world.

27. Cf. chap. 13.3 below.

of thinking: "If the world should come to an end tomorrow, I will still plant a little apple tree today!"[28]

Within this proverb one sees interwoven both the belief in God the Creator and the hope for the downfall of the perverted world as that which comes when grace wins its final victory — in such a way that fragmentary observations are not yet completely clarified and epochal changes need not be understood as necessary, where contradictory elements need not ultimately make sense. Guilt and forgiveness are not linked together in a way that will appear immanent within world history; continuity is expected solely because of the faithfulness of the one who does not abandon the work of his hands.[29] I am then delivered from the necessity of speaking a final judgment about myself and others, and I am not forced to think, with Hegel, that the history of the world is the judgment of the world.

Even today the evangelical church and evangelical theology expend much effort in domesticating Luther's teaching, depicted so appropriately in Prechtl's painting: it thinks that the downpour from such a theology ought to be controlled in as pleasant a way as possible, as it runs off. And yet Christendom is thereby rendered of no significance and tedious; it loses its worldliness and its realistic insight into the human heart, whose musings and aspirations are evil.

We will really become conscious of how Luther is significant for today when we pay attention to his — apocalyptic — view about time, when we pay attention to that rupture in the ages between the new and the old aeon that took place once for all on the cross of Jesus Christ. Luther's understanding of time finds its decisive point in the interweaving of times when judgment, consummation of the world, and creation are dealt with all at once: the future of the world comes from within God's present reality. His new creation shows that the world that does not live in harmony with him is really the "old" world, whereas he is reinstating the one that existed originally. The present salvation that is being imparted — because of the Crucified One — includes within it the coming consummation of the world and lets stand the contradiction of the suffering and sighing creature rooted in the old world, to be experienced with anguish, over against the promised creation, the world as it began.

---

28. Cf. Martin Schloemann, *Luthers Apfelbäumchen? Ein Kapitel deutscher Mentalitätsgeschichte seit dem Zweiten Weltkrieg* (Göttingen: Vandenhoeck & Ruprecht, 1994).

29. Cf. chap. 15 below.

6. Hidden and Revealed God

Believers have to live with this particular contradiction, as long as they are still on their journey through life, in agonizing struggle. The greater the promise and expectation, the deeper and more passionate the lament and question: "Why?" (Ps. 22:1). In light of the contradiction experienced every day by one who takes seriously God's promise of life that is offered to all creatures, with great force the question arises concerning whether God holds to that which he once promised and promises still. In direct contradiction to the promise to hear, the problems of the world cry out in anguish: injustice, undeserved suffering, hunger, murder, and death.

This situation of the agonizing struggle, in which God withdraws and hides himself, is not downplayed and rendered unimportant by Luther; instead, he takes it seriously, right down to its uttermost depth and severity. Experiences of suffering are not ignored. But Luther refuses to go so far as to attribute to them ultimate significance. For this reason he flees from the God who hides himself — and toward the God who became human and who reveals himself in a most hidden way on the cross. It is appropriate "to press on toward and to call to God against God":[30] toward the revealed God against the hidden one.[31]

When Luther makes this differentiation and articulates the relationship between the "hidden" and "revealed" God, this does not involve some speculative thought process, trying to make what is unbearable bearable, and does not attempt to have suffering appear to make sense. Discussion about the "hidden" God has much more to do with a very specific "setting in life": it is extracted from within the agonizing struggle in the form of a lament.

But lament does not happen all by itself. It requires some message that has preceded it, some authoritative statement. "My heart holds you to your word: 'You are to seek my face.' Therefore I do indeed seek your face, Lord" (Ps. 27:8). Laments and petitions are uttered only because of the promise: "Call on me in the day of trouble; I will deliver you" (Ps. 50:15). God is the one who addresses the human being, hears him, and has heard him, even before he calls to him: "Before they call I will answer" (Isa. 65:24).

Only by the power of the Word that has been spoken already, yes, in light of the answer that has come already, can such agonizing struggle teach one to pay attention to the Word. Because of the answer that has been given already, the lament in the midst of the agonizing struggle drives one to take hold of

---

30. WA 19:223.15f.; cf. *LW* 19:72 (*Lectures on Jonah*, 1526, on Jon. 2:3).
31. Cf. chap. 9 below.

the oppressive, incomprehensible God at the point where he allows himself to be comprehended and understood: in the Word of his promise.

In a most concentrated way his promise is given so as to be heard and savored in the Lord's Supper. The Lord of the meal is the Crucified One. He has "tasted death" (Heb. 2:9), and, as the Living One, by virtue of his death, he gets the final word. Thus, suffering and death are not excluded from the midst of life, as one can ascertain in this communal meal. They are part and parcel of one's daily bread. The gifting words of this meal, in which God gives himself just as completely as in any other preaching[32] of the gospel, thereby awaken the "Eucharist": the thanks and the jubilation. From that meal comes a new focus toward fellow creatures, with a proper courage to live life. The faith as a "lively, risk-taking confidence in God's grace . . . makes one happy, bold, and joyful in relation to . . . all creatures."[33] Faith is the courage to expect the rescue of all things, through and beyond judgment and death. In the promise of this courage, the God who frees is incomprehensibly revealed: as the Crucified One, who lives.

32. Cf. chap. 12 below.

33. Heinrich Bornkamm, ed., *Luthers Vorreden zur Bibel,* 3rd ed. (Göttingen: Vandenhoeck & Ruprecht, 1989), 183 (= WA DB 7:10.16-19; cf. *LW* 35:370-71 ["Preface to the Epistle of St. Paul to the Romans," 1546/1522]).

A. BASIC THEMES (PROLEGOMENA)

Chapter 1 Every Person Is a Theologian:
Luther's Understanding of Theology

We are all called theologians,
just as [also we are] all [called] Christians.

1.1. What Is a Theologian?

"Shema Israel — Hear!" (Deut. 6:4). "The ears alone are the organs of a
Christian."[1] And *what* is to hear — to hear at the first and at the last? Answer:
the gospel preamble to the Decalogue: "I am the Lord, your God!" (Exod.
20:2). Luther understands faith on the basis of this address and promise —
and not in some sense the other way around: the Word of address on the basis
of faith. For then the Word of God would simply be a way to express our religious predilections.

No, in the way Luther organizes the subjects in the catechism,[2] it is crucial that the creed follows after the Decalogue, that the creed needs to come
after its gospel preamble and must be related to it. This is what is stated in the
programmatic statement by Luther, which is of utmost significance for the
unique systematic of Luther's theology, "that faith is nothing other than a response and confession of the Christian, given in response to the first commandment."[3]

From this starting point one can also understand theology in a more precise sense: actually, one can understand the theologian more precisely. We are
admittedly used to asking: "What is theology?" and we think thereby that we
are able to ask about the subject matter "in and of itself." Luther, by contrast,

1. WA 57III:222.7; cf. *LW* 29:224 (on Heb. 10:5, 1518): "Solae aures sunt organa Christiani
hominis."
2. Cf. Oswald Bayer, *Theology the Lutheran Way* (Grand Rapids: Eerdmans, 2007), 67-74
("Catechetical Systematics"), and the list, WA TR 5:574-81 (no. 6287).
3. *BSLK* 647.36-38; cf. LC II, 10, in *BC*, 432.

asks first about the theologian, meaning that the question is more specifically about the unique individual's life story, where one lives, what is unique about each individual, and what is happening at that time.

But if we wish to get to the heart of the matter when we ask the question: "What is a theologian?" we have to transform that question into the following form: "Who are you?" That is because the evangelical understanding considers every human being to be a theologian, and every believing person to be a Christian theologian.[4] Faith causes one to reflect: not only the professional theologian — so identified in a special sense — but every time a woman or man is asked the question: "Who are you?" the answer that follows is: I am the one to whom it is said: "I am the Lord your God." I am the one who came into existence only through this Word. So it has happened and continues to happen as the individual subject is constituted. Such existence is not simply assumed, as if one can follow Descartes and start with one's own subjectivity when asking about where one comes from. What is true instead is that the subject *receives,* in ever new ways, an *address,* which determines one's existence. The subject and that person's freedom are to be characterized therefore as a response, not as something that takes place somehow in absolute spontaneity. The question "Who am I?" can be answered adequately and appropriately only when I speak of God as the author of my life history and of the history of the world — as my poet and the poet of the whole world,[5] so that one certainly must start not with speaking *about* him, but *to* him, must start with answering him. Such activity takes place in prayer, in the *oratio:* in praise and in lament — in the speaking of the heart with God in petition and intercession, with thanks and adoration.

Within the arena of life and time thus described, which has been created through the address of the Creator and within which the answer of the created person belongs, whether from within faith or from unbelief, within that setting the "What is?" question has its validity. In and of itself, the "What is?" question is always bound up in abstractions, as has been shown most clearly in Anglo-Saxon linguistic analysis. The "What is?" question leads one astray so that one assumes an objective reality, characterized in general by the existence of things. That leads one to think that the question about the "essence" of theology — "What is theology?" — can be posed without considering the *personal* element. But the personal characteristic is constitutive. One can thus

4. Cf. n. 8 below.

5. "'Nos sumus ποίημα poëma Dei.' Ipse poëta est, nos versus sumus et carmina quae condit" ["We are God's work" [Eph. 2:10], his poem. He himself is the Poet; we are the verses and songs that he makes and creates]; WA 44:572.26f.; cf. *LW* 7:366 (*Lectures on Genesis,* chaps. 38–44, 1544 [on Gen. 44:17]).

speak of "theology" only because each woman or man is constituted as a theologian: namely, by the address of God, who has summoned me and all creatures to be alive.

How can one characterize the theological nature of each individual subject? In a table talk, Luther gave a brief but comprehensive answer to that question: "Quae faciant theologum: 1. gratia Spiritus; 2. tentatio; 3. experientia; 4. occasio; 5. sedula lectio; 6. bonarum artium cognitio."[6] What makes each person a theologian? (1) The grace that is worked through the Holy Spirit; (2) the agonizing struggle; (3) experience; (4) opportunity; (5) constant, concentrated textual study; (6) knowledge and practice of the academic disciplines.

To be sure, this list focuses initially only on the identifying criteria that apply to the development of *professional* theologians, starting with the divine gifts of the Spirit (1) and ending with human intellectual efforts (6). But closer examination will show that religion, education, and the narrative of one's life story are part of the life of *every* Christian and, as we shall see, of every human being. This observation also holds true as regards Luther's famous three rules for studying theology: *oratio, meditatio, tentatio* (see below, chap. 2.1); they are singled out as the most important of what Luther describes in his more expansive discussion of the six identifying characteristics in this table talk.

1.1.1. *Gratia Spiritus* (Grace of the Spirit)

The first of the six identifying characteristics deals with how the theologian is constituted within the framework of a theology of creation and according to one's fundamental view about what it means to be human. What makes a theologian a theologian? First of all: the *gratia Spiritus*, as the grace of the Spirit *creator*. No self-empowerment, no self-confidence, not what one has in one's memory bank makes the theologian a theologian; it comes only through the Spirit, that is, by the *creatio ex nihilo* (creation out of nothing) that comes through his Word, by which we are given the divine breath, the "Spirit of his mouth" (Ps. 33:6), including being gifted with our ability to use our reason to communicate (Gen. 2:19-20).

It is important that one note *first of all* that being a theologian is situated initially within a fundamental understanding of what it means to be human. All the other identifying characteristics would otherwise be left hanging in

6. WA TR 3:312.11-13 (no. 3425).

the air. For this reason *gratia Spiritus* is correctly placed first. For only when understood within this framework can one deal in a theologically appropriate way with the legitimate questions about the subjectivity of the theologian, about connectedness in terms of one's own life story and one's place in the world, and find answers.[7]

Only one who is clear about the fact that the true nature of the theologian is grounded in an understanding of what it means to be human can properly assess the way one must apply the sixth and final identifying characteristic, the *bonarum artium cognitio,* in its true sense. The *professional* theologian, who undergoes training by the arts faculty, and is thereby trained in the academic discipline of *quaestio* and *disputatio,* is really not to be distinguished from any other Christian, in fact, not even from any other human being who has also been given the ability to reason. An academically trained theologian is to be differentiated from other Christians, who as Christians have all already begun to be theologians as well,[8] only in the fact that — and this is his professional calling — he is to be asked to give an account of the Christian faith by formulating intellectual statements; this means he is to craft statements that attain to the highest possible level of accuracy. And yet, theology does not simply have as its task a responsibility to academe. In a primary way and in its essence, it has a responsibility to speak to the world.

With this distinction between "academic task" and "world-oriented task" I follow a linguistic usage employed by Kant.[9] The "*school* task" as understood in philosophy is handled professionally in the school, the academy, the university — which articulates concepts with terminology unique to each discipline. The appropriate way to use such terminology, school speech, can be learned and understood only within a relatively narrow circle and is a specific form of life in itself.[10] By contrast, the *world-oriented* task, as framed by that philosophical usage, is oriented toward that which every human being encounters as a human, what happens without fail to each person; it deals with

---

7. Cf. the well-known statement: "I, the Christ, am myself the subject of knowledge for the theologian" (Johann Christian Konrad von Hofmann, *Theologische Ethik* [Nördlingen, 1878], 17).

8. "Omnes dicimur Theologi, ut omnes Christiani" [We are all called theologians, just as (also we are) all (called) Christians]. WA 41:11.9-13 ("Sermon on Ps. 5:17," January 1535).

9. Immanuel Kant, *Logik,* in Kant, *Schriften zur Metaphysik und Logik, Werke,* ed. Wilhelm Weischedel, 10 vols. (Darmstadt: Wissenschaftliche Buchgesellschaft, 1968), 5:446-50.

10. Cf. Pièrre Hadot, *Exercices spirituels et philosophie antique,* 2nd ed. (Paris: Etudes Augustiniennes, 1987) (= *Philosophie als Lebensform. Geistige Übungen in der Antike* [Berlin: Gatza, 1991]).

the ultimate goal of the human, with each individual's place in the world, with what each person plans for himself: "What is a human being? For what reason am I in this world anyway? What is my own eternal destiny within time?"

Theology, as well, has more than just an academic task, with accompanying rules and methods — such as historical-critical, empirical, ideological-critical; it operates within the realm of the *quaestio* that has been refined over the last one thousand years: the questioning, testing, and decision making that have developed as this craft has been firmly institutionalized by university theological faculties since the High Middle Ages. The world-oriented task of theology is to be distinguished from this activity of the guild and from the life-form that it takes there, from the scholastic theological terminology. This latter task orients itself — as does the world-oriented task in philosophy — toward that which affects every human being as a human.

Each and every person is affected by basic impulses — such as astonishment and lament — which suggest that such elementary questions need to be stated and which provoke one to pose them. That most elementary questioning is ultimately grounded in God's self-revelation "I am the Lord, your God!" and in the point of conflict brought about when it must be further stated: "You shall have no other gods besides me!" From this most basic point of conflict, which involves Word and faith, a secondary point of conflict arises that motivates the intellectual questions.[11]

Such a differentiation between the academic task and the world-oriented task as it relates to theology can be discerned and put into practice when interacting with Luther — most especially in that which is most important, in what relates to the world-oriented task, based on his already-mentioned three basic rules for theological study: *oratio, meditatio, tentatio* (prayer, [scriptural] meditation, experience of agonizing struggle). *A theologian is one who, driven by agonizing struggle, enters with prayer into the Holy Scripture and interprets what is set forth within it, in order to give insight to others who are engaged in agonizing struggle, so that they in a like manner — with prayer — can enter into the Holy Scripture and can interpret it.*[12]

If it is true "that we are such creatures with whom God wishes to speak in eternity and for all time, whether it takes place in wrath or by grace,"[13] then

11. Cf. Bayer, *Theologie,* 505-11 and 528f.

12. That, and in what sense, I am interpreted by Holy Scripture, as God addresses me through it, is articulated in greater detail below, in chap. 4.1. Cf. further, Oswald Bayer, *Autorität und Kritik. Zu Hermeneutik und Wissenschaftstheorie* (Tübingen: Mohr, 1991), especially 1-82.

13. WA 43:181.32-35; cf. *LW* 5:76 (*Lectures on Genesis,* chaps. 26–30, 1542ff. [on Gen. 26:24-25]); cf. chap. 15.1.2 below.

every human lives by meditation: in interaction with God's Word. *Or else* one lives in the *distorted sense* of this interaction — *in statu corruptionis* (in a state of corruption); one exists then in a *distorted, blundering* "meditation" that names as god what in reality is not God.[14] Unbelief wastes its chance most especially with regard to the *cross,* since it certainly does *not* expect God *there.*

Luther's understanding of *meditatio,* staying for a moment with this rule from among his three, is so stated that it precludes one from walking away from the issue, though that is characteristic of our present situation: walking away into academic theology, into a professional type of public religion, and into silent private piety. What is resolved by going in two separate directions, when one solves the dilemma in such a fashion, remains interrelated in Luther's concept of *meditatio.* It is worthwhile to inject this concept of meditation into the discussion and to bring out the full force of its meaning once again, in serious discussion with modern thinking — "postmodernism" as some call it, whereby what is proposed by or what seeks to be explained by "postmodernism" can be interpreted only as a serious *metacriticism* of the modern era.

1.1.2. *Tentatio* (Agonizing Struggle)

Agonizing struggle and temptation — their meanings cannot be differentiated theologically in a hard-and-fast sense, especially since the Greek Bible and the Latin Bible each use only one root word for both (πειρασμός, *tentatio*). Both convey in their deepest severity, as stated in the New Testament and in Christendom in general, that there is a horrific possibility that one can face a final destruction, but yet one that will never come to an end, which is even more horrific than the destruction of the whole world and all of humanity: eternal death as existing eternally apart from God, the breakdown of a communal relationship with God, the divorce from God as the evil one, plain and simple.

This agonizing struggle is thus more powerful than the most radical intellectual doubt, grabbing hold in the fear one faces when being shaken to the depth of one's being, grabbing hold as well when one faces danger and the loss of trust in oneself and in the world. It brings one into the situation in which "everything disappears / and I see nothing but my nothingness and destruction,"[15] in which I become an enemy to myself and the entire world be-

---

14. Cf. chap. 6.2 below on Jon. 1:5.

15. *EG,* #373, 5 (Johann Heinrich Schröder, "Jesu, hilf siegen, du Fürste des Lebens").

comes my enemy; yes, even God himself causes agony for me, in that he confronts me as the one who breaks his own Word and contradicts what he himself has said (Gen. 22).[16]

In this situation it is appropriate, against one's own "conflicting thoughts [that] will accuse or perhaps excuse" (Rom. 2:15), against the verdict of one's own conscience, against calling into question the "very good" (Gen. 1:31) creation because of sickness, defamation, injustice, suffering, pain, and death, but in the bitterest moment even against the God who is contradictory and most horribly hidden, who acts "as if he does not care about you,"[17] that one flee instead to the God who not only cares about you but also speaks on your behalf and intervenes — to the Father who, through the Son in the Holy Spirit, provides the goodness and the righteousness of his creation beyond all doubt: this is the one who has overcome the agonizing struggle in its every form and continues to do so still, in that he creates the certainty of salvation (Rom. 8:26-39).

Certainty of salvation is much more than cognitive knowledge. When Luther accentuates *tentatio*, for him it involves the excess of *certainty* on the part of the one who knows, over against one's capacity to know in a propositional sense; said another way: experience over against knowledge. For the agonizing struggle "teaches you not only to know and understand, but also to experience how right, how true, how sweet, how lovely, how mighty, how comforting" not something such as your faith is, but what "God's *Word* is."[18] Luther's translation of Isaiah 28:19 matches this way of thinking: "For agonizing struggle alone teaches one to pay attention to the Word."

1.1.3. *Experientia* (Experience)

When Luther refers to "experience," he does not refer primarily to an *actio* but to a *passio*, not primarily to the experiences that I am in charge of, but in connection with that which I suffer. It is — to take it to the highest level — the experience that is mine in the agonizing struggle with the Word of God. This is the real point of Luther's famous statement: "sola experientia facit

16. On this matter, cf. Luther's exposition in *LW* 4:91-98 (*Lectures on Genesis*, chaps. 21–25, 1535-45).

17. *EG*, #361, 9 (Paul Gerhardt, "Befiehl du deine Wege" = "Entrust Your Days and Burdens"; cf. *LSB*, #754).

18. "Preface to the Wittenberg Edition of Luther's German Writings (1539)," in *Martin Luther's Basic Theological Writings*, ed. Timothy F. Lull (Minneapolis: Fortress, 1989), 66, italics added. Cf. chap. 2.1.3 below.

theologum" [only experience makes a theologian],[19] which is admittedly most generally applied incorrectly, since *it is not experience as such that makes one a theologian, but experience with the Holy Scripture.*

The characteristic "experience" is thus not to be understood in some diffuse, general sense. Instead, experience is constituted by means of a definite text-based world, which might appear to be narrow because it is based on definite written material but is wide-ranging in every sense of the word. The existence of an individual Christian, and thereby of a professional theologian as well, in fact that of every human being, insofar as that individual experiences agonizing struggle — no matter what form it may take — is a pathway of experience, and it takes time to walk that pathway. The reformational turning point in Luther's own life and theology did not happen all at once, even for him, in the blink of an eye; instead, it happened in the midst of "meditating day and night."[20] Luther emphasizes that he was one "of those, who, as Augustine writes about himself, made progress when writing and teaching, not one of those who became the greatest without effort, in one fell swoop, even though such a one is really nothing, having neither labored intensely nor suffered in agonizing struggle, nor having had experience, but rather is one who has thought to master the entire spirit of the text after a single glance at Scripture."[21]

1.1.4. *Occasio* (Opportunity)

By taking the aspect of time into account, which we have just discussed, the fourth characteristic is identified already. Luther, who also makes mention at other times in his table talks of the *occasio* as a characteristic of theological existence,[22] is likely guided in his understanding of time most particularly by Qoheleth, the Preacher, on which he commented in a lecture in 1526.[23] Qoheleth speaks of time that comes to me, is allotted to me, presents a decisive moment for me: everything has its own time; not everything has its own time at the same time.

Luther emphasizes that the *temporal* moment is even more important

---

19. "Experience alone makes the theologian." WA TR 1:16.13; cf. *LW* 54:7 ("Table Talk Recorded by Veit Dietrich," no. 46, 1531).

20. WA 54:186.3; cf. *LW* 34:337 ("Preface to the Complete Edition of Luther's Latin Writings"); cf. Ps. 1:2.

21. WA 54:186.26-29; cf. *LW* 34:338; cf. Augustine, *Epistolae* 143.2 (MPL 33:585).

22. Especially WA TR 6:358-60 (no. 7050).

23. WA 20:1-203.

than actual locality, personality, and individuality.[24] But "the word *tempus* (time) is too general. I take it that the etymology is *a cadendo*, as when one speaks of a chance event." The *occasio* (occasion) is what is "chance" time for me, a favorable opportunity, which I myself cannot arrange for and cannot make happen by my effort, but which is preserved contingently for me instead and at the same time has a summons within it: "Use the hour, and that which the hour brings with it";[25] *Carpe diem!*[26] Whoever fails to seize opportunity by the forelock, whoever does not take advantage of the *kairos*, grabbing the youngster by the hair on his forehead, will have to watch as the bald part on the back of his head disappears.[27] "The occasion greets you and offers you its hair to grab, as if it would say to you: Look, now you have me, grab hold of me! Oh, you think, it will certainly come again. Well, then, it says, if you do not want to, then grab me by the rear in the backside!"[28] It is thus important to seize the moment that is given, that "little moment,"[29] with utmost seriousness: to see the opportunity and to grasp it energetically, fully conscious of what you are doing, at that moment.

Particularly impressive in regard to the *occasio* is the little speech Luther makes in the document *To the Councilmen of All Cities in Germany That They Establish and Maintain Christian Schools* (1524):

> Beloved Germans, buy, as long as the market is in front of the door, gather together, as long as the sun shines and there is good weather, make use of God's grace and Word, as long as it is there. For you ought to know this: God's Word and grace is a swiftly passing downpour, which does not come back again to where it once was. It came to the Jews — but gone is gone. They now have nothing. Paul brought it to the country of Greece. Gone is also gone. They are controlled now by the Turks. Rome and the Latin-speaking lands have had it as well — gone is gone. Now they have the pope. And you Germans need not bother thinking that you will have it forever, for thanklessness and scorn will not allow it to remain. Therefore, get at it. . . .[30]

24. Cf. WA TR 6:359.14f. (no. 7050).

25. WA TR 6:359.16f., 19.

26. Horace, *Odes* 1.11.8.

27. "Fronte capillata post haec occasio calva" (WR TR 6:358.33 [no. 7050]; the quotation is from Cato Dionysius).

28. WA TR 6:358.31-34.

29. WA 19:226.20; cf. *LW* 19:226.20 *(Lectures on Jonah);* WA DB 10II:11.1, and often.

30. WA 15:32.4-13.

"Get at it, because it is high time. Now, now, while it is still now!"[31] "O that today you would listen to his voice . . . !" (Ps. 95:7-8; Heb. 3:7-15).

The urgency of taking the *occasio* seriously is urgent in the most important sense when considered in light of the promise of the gospel. Its *kairos* (2 Cor. 6:2; cf. Isa. 49:8) is bound up in the risky appropriation of Word that has its unique application, together with each individual's responsibility to pass on what one has received. Every time it is applied to the present moment, it is always something new, because it is focused of necessity on a specific new time and situation. The gospel needs to be freshly stated, again and again, without anything really new — anything really different — being spoken, because indeed *that* new message is to be spoken anew, which will never be old again. For this reason the gospel must indeed be articulated anew, over and over again; but, in contrast to myth, it never permits itself to undergo development without losing that which makes it definitive.

The gospel thus remains gospel only when it is differentiated from law. One is a theologian only if one recognizes what time it is: whether it is time for the law *(tempus legis)* or for the gospel *(tempus euangelii)*.[32] *As regards the correct perception of what is determinative concerning each* occasio, *it is most necessary that one can concretely perceive the specific difference between law and gospel.*

This recognition of the difference between law and gospel cannot be guaranteed by constructing a narrative that tells the story of salvation; the art of distinguishing the two elements is not shaped by a chronological description but by a kairological approach. To encounter the differentiation in a concrete way cannot be taught by articulating a method; it happens for me rather as a happy moment that comes by chance, because it is purely the work of God himself, the work of the Holy Spirit[33] — a skill[34] that comes as favor, as the favor of the hour of God.

Seizing the *occasio*, the *kairos*, is thus not an interpretation of the signs of the times achieved by using one's own powers; what is decisive comes when one is enlightened by the Holy Spirit. For this reason the fourth characteristic, the *occasio* — as well as all the other characteristics — is to be interpreted in light of the first, the *gratia Spiritus* (the grace of the Spirit). So in regard to the coming of the Holy Spirit, I can do nothing else but pray. One thus has to return once again to the first of those three rules: to the *oratio* (prayer).

---

31. WA TR 6:359.36f.
32. Cf. *LW* 26:117, 342, 343 (*Lectures on Galatians*, chaps. 1–4, 1535).
33. Cf. *LW* 54:127 (no. 1234; 1531); WA 36:13.22-27 ("Sermon on Gal. 3:23-29," 1532).
34. WA 36:9.28f.; *LW* 26:342; WA TR 6:142 (no. 6716).

1.1.5. *Sedula Lectio* (Constant, Concentrated Textual Study)

If what is decisive, the enlightenment of the dark heart, the transformation of existence as the activity of the grace of the Spirit, can be sought only in prayer, then what can *sedula lectio* achieve: the study of Holy Scripture that proceeds according to a plan; that is devoted methodically to the task; that is observant, passionate; and that works in a constant, concentrated manner throughout one's life? One cannot help but notice how a significant tension appears when discussing these last two characteristics, a tension between divine gifts of the Spirit and human academic activities.

The work of the Holy Spirit, and thereby the work of the triune God, that is prayed for and expected, and does not happen because of the hard work of human effort and academic development, does not somehow preclude human effort and careful observation; instead, it actually frees one to engage in such pursuits. The *gratia Spiritus* (grace of the Spirit) frees the human who has the capacity to reason so that such reason can be used in a way that adequately matches what it was created to be: for use in dominion over the earth (*dominium terrae;* Gen. 1:28), for tilling and keeping (Gen. 2:15), for learning and working, for giving shape to the spheres of earthly life that Luther conceptualizes when he teaches about the three estates.

The Word is fundamental for the activity in which humans go about the work of developmental learning, for which the divine gracious gift of the Spirit sets one free: hearing and speaking, reading and writing; "there is no more powerful or more honorable task for a human being than speaking, since the human being is most specifically to be distinguished from other animals by the ability to speak (Gen. 2:19f.), more than by means of the bodily form or other actions."[35] Thus, in the first place, the *sedula lectio* admittedly refers most specifically to the daily activity of the "regularly called" theologians, who "publicly teach or preach or administer the sacraments in the church";[36] it refers to constant, concentrated interaction with the biblical texts, to the lifelong practice of careful meditation on the texts: "that is: not only in the heart, but also publicly speaking the words and a constant pursuing and scouring, reading and rereading, diligently noticing with great care and reflecting on the literal Word in the book, to discern what the Holy Spirit means to convey."[37] But this *sedula lectio* is necessary for *every Christian.*

---

35. Heinrich Bornkamm, ed., *Luthers Vorreden zur Bibel,* 3rd ed. (Göttingen: Vandenhoeck & Ruprecht, 1989), 66; cf. *LW* 35:254 ("Second Preface to the Psalms," 1528).

36. *BSLK* 69.3f.; cf. CA XIV, in *BC,* 46.

37. WA 50:659.22-25; cf. "Preface to the Wittenberg Edition," 66. Cf. chap. 2.1.2 below.

Though one must concede the necessity of distinguishing the Word and Book of eternal life from the books that are useful for temporal life, this means that the existence of *every human being* is constituted in a setting where one hears and reads: each person is addressed and receives communication in written form, so that each one can answer — in response to reading and hearing — but also because each one must answer for oneself.

Luther's passionate appeal, particularly in the address to the German nobility that has been mentioned, that care be taken to teach language and speaking, has fundamental-anthropological and fundamental-ethical import; in that sense he was one with the humanists.[38] Learning languages has fundamental, elementary meaning not only for spiritual matters and concerning eternal life, but also for worldly and temporal existence; languages are not only necessary "in order to understand Holy Scripture," but also "in order to exercise dominion within the world."[39]

1.1.6. *Bonarum Artium Cognitio* (Knowledge and Practice of the Academic Disciplines)

The sixth characteristic is the least significant aspect for the "world-oriented task" of theology. This characteristic is appropriate only insofar as every human being has the ability to use the language of reason, and, in one way or another, either is educated properly or, instead, is educated improperly and in a distorted way. The importance attached to this concluding characteristic concentrates on the *schooling* aspect of theology. Without the knowledge of and practice in *(cognitio)* the seven liberal arts *(septem artes liberales),* which are divided into the trivium (grammar, dialectic, rhetoric) and the quadrivium (arithmetic, geometry, music, astronomy), the theologian is not prepared for carrying out his or her calling.

What Luther clearly and distinctively accentuates in the canon of educational development that had been passed on from ancient times is competence in the languages.[40] Thus, the contamination of the *bonae litterae* (fine arts) and the *artes liberales* (liberal arts) in the identification of this last characteristic did not happen by chance; instead, it is informative for making

38. Helmar Junghans, "Die Worte Christi geben das Leben," in *Wissenschaftliches Kolloquium "Der Mensch Luther und sein Umfeld"* (May 2-5, 1996, at the Wartburg), ed. Wartburg-Stiftung Eisenach, Wartburg-Jahrbuch, Sonderband (Regensburg and Eisenach: Wartburg-Stiftung, 1996), 154-75.

39. WA 15:36.17f.

40. Cf. especially *LW* 45:357-66.

sense of Luther's intention. The point is that one can use the arts of grammar, dialectic, and rhetoric to determine the meaning of the text of Holy Scripture; one can make sense of it and teach it to others in the schools and institutions of higher learning — thus serving to articulate the external clarity of Scripture, which "is employed in service to the Word."[41]

Luther gives pride of place in the trivium to grammar: "Among all the academic disciplines that have been developed by human beings, in a most important way grammar is most useful for the advancement of theology";[42] "we will want to pay attention, first of all, to grammatical matters — this is what is really theological."[43] In Luther's assessment of what is important, rhetoric follows grammar, along with the "poets and historians";[44] grammar and rhetoric are more important for him than dialectic,[45] which drifts along emptily, without language or history, and leads one astray. For this reason Luther strongly urges that one ought to teach and attend to grammar and rhetoric *before* learning dialectic. For the reality is that "the Sophists did not take what has been logical from time immemorial into account, that is, they did not think it important that grammar and rhetoric need to be taught first. For whenever one seeks to know about logic before one knows grammar, and where one would rather teach than hear, would rather judge than speak, nothing correct is going to follow therefrom."[46] But if one can assume knowledge of and correct use of grammar and rhetoric, the knowledge and practice of dialectic, along with its proper application in an academic disputation for clarification of a theological controversy, make it indispensable. Luther himself masterfully practiced the art of disputation and went so far as to write his own "dialectic" — for his son Hans.[47]

1.2. *Habitus* θεόσδοτος (God-given Skill)

The sequence of the six characteristics is pertinent. It delineates the arc that originates with the divine gift of the Spirit and ends up with human educa-

---

41. WA 18:609.5; cf. *LW* 33:28 *(The Bondage of the Will)*. Cf. chap. 4.6.1 below.

42. WA 6:29.7f. ("15 Thesen zur Frage, ob philosophische Bücher dem Theologen nützlich oder unnütz sind" [15 Theses on the Question as to Whether Philosophical Books Are Useful or Useless to the Theologian], 1519?).

43. WA 5:27.8f.; cf. *LW* 14:286 (on Ps. 1, 1519).

44. WA 15:46.18; cf. WA 51:23–52:24.

45. WA 15:46.19-21; cf. *LW* 45:376.

46. WA 26:443.8-12; cf. *LW* 37:301 *(Confession concerning Christ's Supper,* 1528).

47. WA TR 4:647-49 (no. 5082b; 1540). The longer version in WA 60:140-62 is an expanded version of this table talk; it is highly unlikely that it originates with Luther.

tional activities. Two different types of movements, one describing the path of the gifts that come through the Spirit of God and the other describing the path of educational development that is acquired by humans, are held together to form one unity. Corresponding to this, the Lutheran theologian Johann Gerhard (1582-1637) used paradoxical language to attribute to the theologian a "*habitus* θεόσδοτος,"[48] that is, a *habitus* that comes as a gift from God. *Habitus* is a term that appears in Aristotelian ethics and refers to readiness that can be acquired as one engages in methodical practice; it describes in that setting the development that a human being sets in motion on one's own, in which one can realize one's potential. But the provocative nature of what is implicit in Gerhard's paradoxical description cannot be ignored. And yet, it is not to be assumed that his terminology applies merely to the school-oriented aspect of theology; it is involved in the world-oriented aspect as well. For all human educational activity is a result of a divine gift of God, even when it is not so perceived.

48. Johann Gerhard, *Loci theologici* (Jena, 1610-22), "Prooemium: de natura theologiae," par. 31.

Chapter 2

The Topic of Theology: The Sinning
Human Being and the Justifying God

Theology is an unending wisdom,
because it can never be learned completely.

What has been mentioned already about Luther's concept of theology can be
unfolded and taken to a deeper level if one examines Luther's exposition of
three main topics for theology from an academic, theoretical perspective,
three issues that were posed to Luther for discussion by the Tübingen theology professor Gabriel Biel.[1] These are not examined merely because of historical interest; more important, this exposition can provide conclusive and
fruitful help when examining the central academic and theoretical problems
that are still under discussion today.

The "topic of theology" — the sinning human being and the justifying
God — will be discussed not as a topic in and of itself, but deliberately as part
of the larger context within which one examines the concept of theology. For
only when one places Luther's specific concept of theology within the larger
framework of his specific concept of time and experience, and within his
theological understanding that results in his pastoral interest to comfort the
troubled conscience, does it become clear that justification is no timeless
principle but is an occurrence that happens in a dramatic way.

In discussing the following three issues independently, we do not intend
for them to be three separate blocks of material that can be isolated one from
the other; dividing them into these parts is intended simply as a way to aid in
painting the whole picture and achieving understanding. To state it somewhat differently: what is involved concurrently, each of the three times an as-

1. Gabrielis Biel, *Collectorium circa quattuor libros Sententiarum*, vol. 1, ed. Wilfrid Werbeck
and Udo Hofmann (Tübingen: Mohr, 1973), 8. On the subject cf. Oswald Bayer, *Theologie*, HST 1
(Gütersloh: Gütersloher Verlagshaus, 1994), 31f. and 36-55.

29

pect of the issue is discussed, deals with wisdom, as the type of wisdom related to experience, as wisdom is related to justification, and as wisdom is related to faith — even though these three issues are discussed separately, one after the other.

2.1. *Sapientia Experimentalis* (Experiential Wisdom)

In response to the question posed to him about what type of knowledge is involved in theology, Luther opted for an understanding of theology according to which it is more wisdom *(sapientia)* than science *(scientia)* — already the early Luther spoke of theology as a *sapientia experimentalis* (an experiential wisdom), as a wisdom that comes by experience,[2] and he stays with that understanding; *scientia* is not utterly distinct from *sapientia* but is included within it. Wisdom reflects on the relationship of what science can contribute to understanding the connection of the academic with the preacademic world of life.

Since the time of Aristotle, academic disciplines have been guided by necessary, basic principles, *principia,* and at its deepest level, by one single *principium;* according to the Aristotelian scientific system, that deepest principle is rational theology, theo-logic.[3] Scientific endeavors carried out within the framework of this philosophical concept of God are part of a closed system. Wisdom, by contrast, in a non-Aristotelian sense, deals in the realm of experience. Without getting too far afield already at the outset,[4] one notes that experience does not take place in a closed system. If *sapientia* (wisdom) is part of a larger arena, within which *scientia* (knowledge) is discovered, then *scientia* itself cannot verify its own claims; it must allow its conclusions to be

2. WA 9:98.21 (marginal notes on Tauler's sermons, ca. 1516).

3. Cf. *Metaphysica* 12: one must obviously keep in mind that, for Aristotle, "every matter can be demonstrated only on the basis of its own unique causes" (*Analytica posteriora* 1.9.75b), so that "every academic discipline has its own principles" (Otfried Höffe, "Einführung in die Wissenschaftstheorie der Zweiten Analytik," in *Aristoteles, Lehre vom Beweis oder Zweite Analytik,* PhB 11 [Hamburg: Meiner, 1990], xxv). "Viewed from the perspective of the history of academic study," this is "a most significant insight. It departs from the pursuit of system thinking and the philosophical quest for unity of all knowledge, and prepares the way for each area of study to engage in scientific research." But Höffe also asserts at the same time that this insight does not cause the *prima philosophia* to be rejected; it assumes that it is the "foundational science." But this raises the question about how the large number of the individual sciences — each with its own way of doing scientific research and with its own principles — are to relate to that *one* principle of the *prima philosophia,* the principle of theo-logic.

4. On the distinction between *experientia vaga* and *experientia ordinata,* cf. Dietz Lange, *Erfahrung und die Glaubwürdigkeit des Glaubens* (Tübingen: Mohr, 1984), 17.

relativized by setting them within the larger framework of life lived in the world outside academe.

Aristotle eliminated this distinction between *scientia* and *sapientia*. He reconciled philosophy and theology by making *sapientia* the highest form of *scientia*. Such a solution admittedly excludes from the concept of theology everything historical, everything empirical, every experiential moment. Theology, when viewed as "theo-logic," is purely rational theology. In this form it is the highest science, the science of principles, indeed, the science of a single principle — the divine, which moves everything, but which is itself not moved and which does not suffer.

Luther goes about it very differently. He maintains that the knowledge about God, in fact knowing God himself, is something that is eminently going to occur within time. He thus understands theology not as learning on the basis of principles but as learning that takes place within history and experience. Aristotelian ears detect a contradiction when they hear the two words *sapientia experimentalis* (experiential wisdom). For Aristotle the historical, the empirical, the experiential cannot be the subject of, and certainly not the basis for, scientific knowledge. By contrast, Luther states: "Theology is an unending wisdom, because it can never be learned completely."[5]

A remarkable understanding of theology as experience and as wisdom is expressed in this sentence and within its context,[6] stating that the human being hears and learns, but also loses such understanding, time and again, from the ears and from the heart, thus distorting what has been learned, which is learned all over again from within the duress of agonizing struggles and afflictions. In this sense theology is understood as having an open-ended history — virtually as unending history. Constitutive for theology is time that is lived and experienced: time that is wasted versus time that is used to the full, time that is qualified — obviously at this point not only time in the sense of a particular "moment," not as an event that cannot be extended, not as a point in time, but rather in the arena of remembrance and of the future, as it is created by God's promise and allows itself to be heard in the here and now. In this way one is guided by an "apocalyptic" understanding of history, time, and existence, which we discussed already in the introductory chapter. It deals with an experience in which I am experienced, probed, tested, tried, a type of experience that I thus do not primarily "design" but "suffer." I am not a lord over such experience, either by means of an *actio* or a *contemplatio*.[7]

---

5. WA 40III:63.17f. (on Ps. 121:3; 1532f.).
6. WA 40III:63.18–64.7.
7. Cf. chap. 2.3 below ("*Vita Passiva:* Faith").

The revolution that took place in Luther's understanding of faith and theology, over against the Aristotelian understanding of scientific knowledge and reality, includes within it a radical criticism of the Aristotelian understanding of God. Plato's argument is determinative for Aristotle. It would lower the importance of the self for a person to become something other than, something worse than, something less than what that individual is already. The purest activity of God would thus be to see himself and to reflect about himself. Luther's pithy judgment about such an understanding of God reads as follows: "The Primeval being sees [only] himself. If he were to look outside of himself, he would see the suffering of the world. At this point he [namely, Aristotle] negates God without saying a word."[8] The god of Aristotle's metaphysic sees nothing but himself in his perfection; he participates with no one else, gives of himself to no one. He does not love and thus he does not suffer either. He does not submit himself to time and to change. He is not historical. Luther states the opposite: "If God were like this, he would see only himself, and would not see the suffering of the world that is beyond him himself, in order to be concerned about it, which means he would be no *ens perfectissimum,* but rather an *ens miserrimum*":[9] no most complete being, but only a most deplorable being.

The way Luther goes into more detail to define theology as *sapientia,* in fact more specifically as wisdom gained through experience, *sapientia experimentalis,* is set forth most clearly in his "three rules" for the correct way to study theology: *oratio, meditatio, tentatio:* prayer, meditation on the text, agonizing struggle. He writes about this in the preface to the first volume of his German writings (1539)[10] and bases his comments on Psalm 119, which praises God's Word.

2.1.1. *Oratio* (Prayer)

In the first place, you should know that the Holy Scripture is a book of such a type that it makes the wisdom of all other books into foolishness, since no book teaches about eternal life except this book alone. For this reason, you should immediately despair of using your own mind and reason. For with such tools you will not succeed, but with such presumptuousness you yourself and others with you will plunge from heaven (as happened to Lucifer) into the abyss and into hell. Instead, kneel down in your

---

8. WA TR 1:57.44f. (no. 135; 1531). Cf. (73f.) 73.22-24 (no. 155; 1532).
9. WA TR 1:73.32.
10. WA 50:657-61; *LW* 34:283-88, interpreted in detail by Bayer, *Theology the Lutheran Way* (Grand Rapids: Eerdmans, 2007), 42-65.

little chamber and pray with proper humility and earnestness to God, that he would desire to give you his Holy Spirit through his beloved Son, who will enlighten you, lead you, and give you understanding.

As you can see, David prays repeatedly in the above-named psalm, "Teach me, Lord, instruct me, guide me, show me," and he uses many similar words. Even though he knew the texts from Moses and from other books better, and heard and read them daily, he still wanted to have the proper master of Scripture for himself, so that he would not fall because of reason and would himself seek to become its [that is, the text's] master. For from such activity come the mob spirits [that is, the Schismatics], who fool themselves into thinking that Scripture is placed under their control and can be understood easily with their own reason, as if Scripture has the character of Marcolphus or Aesop's Fables, for which they need neither the Holy Spirit nor prayer.[11]

Though Luther is willing to give pride of place to reason in "this life," and though he praises it in this regard as "almost something divine,"[12] he is ruthless in his sharp critique of the capacity of reason to comprehend "eternal" life and thus to arrive at knowledge of God and the self. His judgment in this regard is absolutely negative. When it comes to consciousness of my godlessness and of sin, with respect to the God who judges and justifies, and when it comes to being able to trust him completely, then it remains the case that one should "immediately despair of using [one's] own mind and reason." For one's own mind and reason can lead only into error, seeking God in those places where he does not allow himself to be comprehended, and missing the mark in those situations where he does allow himself to be comprehended. It is only the blundering thoughts of one's own mind and reason, of deluded reason at that, that play "blindman's bluff" with God. Luther is drastic with his mockery of the scholastic theologians of reason: "If they bore up into the

---

11. WA 50:659.5-21. The citations in this section that are not specified stem from this initial citation. As a summary of what Luther has in mind with the triadic formula *oratio, meditatio, tentatio,* cf. WA TR 2:67.32-40 (no. 1353) = *The Table Talk of Martin Luther,* ed. Thomas Kepler (New York: World, 1952), 6: "We ought not to criticize, explain, or judge the Scriptures by our mere reason, but diligently, with prayer, meditate thereon, and seek their meaning. The devil and temptations also afford us occasion to learn and understand the Scriptures, by experience and practice. Without these we should never understand them, however diligently we read and listen to them. The Holy Ghost must here be our only master and tutor; and let youth have no shame to learn of that preceptor. When I find myself assailed by temptation, I forthwith lay hold of some text of the Bible, which Jesus extends to me; as this: that he died for me, whence I derive infinite hope."

12. WA 39I:175.9f.; cf. *LW* 34:137 (*The Disputation concerning Man,* thesis 4, 1536).

heavens with their heads and look around in heaven, they will find no one there, since Christ lies in the crib and in the lap of the woman; they thus fall headlong back down again and break their neck."[13]

If one who studies theology goes no further than to take seriously the way he humbles himself, this coming down and this humility of God, then he loses the desire to comprehend what is above; he begins down below — humble, not arrogant. *No interpretation of Holy Scripture will try to get around the way that God presented himself. The humiliation involved in the way God gave of himself will correspond to the humility with which one engages in interpretation.* Thus the highest form that the first rule takes is: "Kneel down in your little chamber [Matt. 6:6] and pray with proper humility and earnestness to God, that he would desire to give you his Holy Spirit through his beloved Son, who will enlighten you, lead you, and give you understanding."

2.1.2. *Meditatio* (Meditation on the Text)

In the second place you should meditate, that is, not only just within your heart but also in an external way by using your voice and by examining and working, by reading and rereading the literal word in the book, with arduous notation and reflection about what the Holy Spirit means here. And take care that you do not get bored or think that you have done enough if you have heard it, read it, or spoken it a time or two and that you have made complete sense of it all thereby. For no theologian of note will develop with this minimal effort, and you will be like fruit that falls out of season, before it is even half ripe.

From this vantage point you can see in the same psalm how David continually boasts that he wishes to talk, write poetically, speak, sing, listen, and read day and night and keep on doing it — though about nothing else except what comes from God's Word and commandments. For God will not give you his Spirit apart from the external Word; you are to use it to give you guidance. For his was no idle talk when he expressly commanded one to write, preach, read, listen, sing, speak, etc.[14]

With this second rule, with impressive phraseology, Luther turns outward what he had specifically accented as the inner aspect. In spite of all his emphasis on prayer being tied to work with Scripture, Luther feared that what

---

13. WA 9:406.17-20 ("Sermon on Gen. 28," 1520). On "playing blindman's bluff" with God, see chap. 6.2.2 below.

14. WA 50:659.22-35.

had been said about *oratio* could be used in a spiritualizing way that would seek inner enlightenment and could thus be misunderstood as one's own speculation.[15] He makes the point, in a sharp, almost harsh way, that the text of Holy Scripture, as it has been written and as it reads, is to be used not only in the heart, but also externally. It is hard to miss the fact that the adjective "external"[16] is placed both at the beginning and at the end of this two-paragraph citation that deals with *meditatio*.

Luther uses the word "meditation" in an uncommon way when he specifically refers to meditation upon the external Word. He does not just hasten to use some chance brainstorm. Instead, he harkens back to an insight of the ancient church and to its practice, which has faded away more and more as time has passed, if it has not indeed been relegated to what has been forgotten altogether. This involves the practice of reading and praying out loud and, what is still more important, that such activities are practiced with regard to Scripture, particularly that one would have an especial acquaintance with the Psalter. Such meditation does not just involve gazing at one's navel; it does not eavesdrop on the inner self. It does not probe deeper into the self but goes outward from the self. One's innermost being lives outside itself only when it is within the Word of God. That is where it is described as it really is; it is "the heart essentially in the Word."[17] Meditation thus cannot go deeper to what is behind the text of Holy Scripture, back to a time when there was so direct a relationship that communication was not necessary, concerning which the text of Holy Scripture would then merely be an "expression" of what is deeper yet. Meditation moves instead within the realm of the Word that has been received; it is interaction with what is written and heard.

2.1.3. *Tentatio* (Agonizing Struggle)

In the third place there is *tentatio,* agonizing struggle. This is the touchstone. This does not teach you simply about knowing and understanding, but also about experiencing how correct, how true, how sweet, how lovely, how powerful, how comforting God's Word is, wisdom above all wisdom.

---

15. At the end of the preceding section of the preface (line 18), Luther had accorded them the name *Rottengeistern,* who get together as a mob and split the church.

16. In contrast to present-day usage of "external," at Luther's time the word did not merely denote what is on the outside, but what is separate from something *(externum):* Jacob Grimm and Wilhelm Grimm, *Deutsches Wörterbuch,* vol. 1 (Leipzig: S. Hirzel, 1854), 1035.

17. WA 10I/1:188.6; cf. *LW* 52:46 (on John 1:1-14, "The Gospel for the Main Christmas Service," 1521-22).

For this reason you see how David, in the psalm to which reference has been made, complains so often about all manner of enemies, about wicked princes or tyrants, about false spirits and hosts under which he had to suffer, because he meditated, which means that he went back and forth with God's Word (as mentioned) in all sorts of ways. For as soon as the Word of God permeates you, the devil will seek to afflict you so as to make you a real doctor and will teach you by his temptations to seek the Word of God and to love it. For I myself (since I, mouse droppings, mix myself in with the pepper) have many of my papists to thank, that they have so smitten me, oppressed me, and alarmed me through the blustering of the devil that they have produced a rather good theologian, which I would otherwise never have become. And what, by contrast, they have won because of me, I am most happy to let them have: the honor, the victory, and the triumph, for that is what they wanted.[18]

Whoever meditates must suffer. Nothing remains untouched in this open warfare, which Luther perceives within a horizon for time that is apocalyptic, but which also, concurrently, deals with the depths to which each individual must sink; the battle is universal. This same universal scope, which is a distinguishing mark for Luther's understanding of meditation, is the identifying mark of the third rule as well. The battle does not simply go on at the level of the pastor in his particular office, but assails every Christian, indeed, every human being.

As regards the agonizing struggle, about which Luther would gladly have written a book, it is really wrapped up within the importance of what is stated in the first commandment. God's unity, along with the unity of reality and how reality is experienced, does not stand steadfast as an eternal and necessary principle that is never attacked; instead, questions are raised about all these issues in actual and practical ways, as well as in an "external" way. Whoever meditates upon the first commandment is entangled thereby in the battle between the one Lord and the many lords. One cannot extricate oneself from this entanglement by holding to a speculative idea about the unity of God. It is not enough just to know about the unity and thus about the almighty nature of God; it is not enough for the spiritual eye to hold onto such realities as timelessly present; each person must in a more real way also experience such realities. But such experience takes time; it sets one forth on a journey that brings with it times of testing, that takes one farther than one wishes to go, even to the point that it insists on being experienced.

Agonizing struggle is not the touchstone that validates the authenticity of

18. WA 50:660.1-16.

faith, as if to demonstrate the veracity and the credibility of the believing person. Instead, agonizing struggle is the touchstone that shows the Word of God itself to be credible and mighty within such struggle and when opposing it. "For agonizing struggle alone teaches one to take the Word of God into account." Luther articulates this most decisive point for his understanding of the entire Scripture and theology with this unforgettable application of Isaiah 28:19 — which is based not on the Hebrew text but follows instead the rendering of the Vulgate.

Luther's famous statement "Only experience makes the theologian" excludes flighty musings, speculations, and with it purity of knowledge; but it does not advocate in its place some principle of pure experience, which could offer instead the principle of some indeterminate openness and open-endedness.

It is not experience as such that makes the theologian a theologian, but rather experiencing Holy Scripture.

2.2. *Subiectum Theologiae* (The Subject of Theology)

The second major question Biel addressed to Luther deals with what makes any academic area of study a unity. One would expect that the unity of a discipline would result from the unity of its *subiectum*. So what does Luther say is the unified subject matter of theology? What makes all its philological, historical, philosophical, rhetorical, and pedagogical efforts part of one unity?

For some the subject of theology, simply and unconditionally, is "God"; "God" is "the actual subject of theology."[19] Each element that theology identifies as a topic for study is set forth "with respect to its relationship to God *(sub ratione Dei)*"; from this point of view, theology could be termed "the study of God."[20]

By contrast, a definition that seems to be intolerably narrow would be appropriate for anyone who sides with Luther by viewing the subject — the *subiectum* — of theology as a study of "the *sinning* human being and the *justifying* God."[21] In the sense that Luther identifies the proper subject matter, it

---

19. Wolfhart Pannenberg, *Wissenschaftstheorie und Theologie* (Frankfurt, 1973), 300.

20. Pannenberg, *Wissenschaftstheorie und Theologie*, 300 (with reference to Thomas Aquinas, *Summa Theologiae*, Latin text and English translation, vol. 1, trans. Thomas Gilby [New York: McGraw-Hill, 1964], I, q. 1, art. 7, pp. 24f.). Cf. Pannenberg, *Systematische Theologie*, vol. 1 (Göttingen: Vandenhoeck & Ruprecht, 1988), 15.

21. WA 40II:328.1f.; cf. *LW* 12:311 (on Ps. 51). Cf. the introduction above, n. 17, and Bayer, *Theology the Lutheran Way*, 16-21 and 97-106.

is necessary to see the verbal adjectives (the *sinning* human and the *justifying* God) not as accidental and incidental, but rather as essential and determinative of the essence of the matter. According to this viewpoint, the human being, when considered strictly from a theological point of view, is essentially the one accused and acquitted by God. Stated in the opposite way, concerning that which is most decisive, God is the one who both accuses and acquits the human being. Questions of a cosmological and political nature, and the like, become the proper subject of theology only as they are related to what has been identified already as appropriate to the topic. If this viewpoint is correct, it has consequences that cannot be overestimated. Every theological statement is affected by the precision of this definition. Thus Luther's teaching about creation, his teaching about Christology, and his teaching about the judgment of the world as the consummation of the world are each articulated within the framework of his teaching about justification.

It is not by chance that Luther's answer to the question about the subject of theology is articulated in his interpretation of Psalm 51, which tradition has counted among the penitential psalms; it has particular importance for the history of Luther's theology. The wording of the psalm forces one to speak of sin and grace; as a consequence, Luther's theology has no other theme. Admittedly, it is possible to discourse about the topics of sin and grace philosophically — "metaphysically," "morally," or "historically." The "rule" by which Luther identifies and assesses what is theological about theology reads as follows: "by means of the divine promises and laws, not by means of a human rule, which results in one being able to say: 'so that you are justified in what you say' [Ps. 51:4]."[22] To speak theologically of sin and grace means to speak of God's *promissio* and of his *lex,* about the law that accuses as well as kills and about the gospel that comforts as well as makes alive.

Concerning the story of David as the exemplary sinner, who experiences the justifying God, Psalm 51 speaks extensively "about the whole of sin and its roots,"[23] both concerning its radical nature and concerning its universal applicability. Its universal nature applies both as it affects all of humanity and in regard to the breadth and depth of the existence of each individual. Being a sinner, or, more specifically: the confession of one's sins, makes each person an individual, makes each one a unique being. "Against you, you alone [O Lord], have I sinned" (*Tibi soli peccavi;* Ps. 51:4). Without a confession of sins such as this, each human being would simply be one example of the human

---

22. WA 40II:373.5-7; cf. *LW* 12:342. On Luther's rejection of a "metaphysical," "moral," or "historical" understanding, cf. Bayer, *Theology the Lutheran Way,* 17 n. 6 (216).

23. WA 40II:319.8f.; cf. *LW* 12:305 (on Ps. 51).

species, not an individual. Such an act of confession brings into view the anthropological depth of the definition of theology and concurrently provides the basis for a theological anthropology.

This depth of the definition of theology is disclosed and even developed in a specific medium, by means of the Word. The theological nature of the *subiectum theologiae* calls for a specific way that words are used, for specialized language. *God and humans coexist in the Word: in the Word of the confession of sins and in the Word of the forgiveness of sins.* Luther's statement of definition is cast in the third person. But this statement of assertion is a derivative statement. It is easy to go back to more fundamental first- and second-person statements, to statements of address and response. That such statements were originally in this form, which all dogmatic statements have to take into account as the proper original setting, means that they are statements of divine address and human response, statements of prayer, and statements that are doxological and confessional, in which God is given the glory and is seen to be in the right, as in the doxology that praises his judgment in Psalm 51:4: "Against you, you alone, have I sinned, and done what is evil in your sight, so that you are justified."

This is how the individual prays, as one who sees that God is in the right, that very God who credits righteousness to him and attributes it to him. Such a specific setting for prayer is the "setting in life" in which one acknowledges God's attributes and his unique qualities. The copula *et* in Luther's definition of theology *(homo peccator et Deus iustificans)* is thus placed there to describe the dialogue between God and the human being. The sinning human and the justifying God coexist when they are in dialogue.

That God and the human being interact with one another in a communicative sense certainly cannot be assumed as obvious. What is surprising about this is clear when one looks at the contrasting statement: in sharp contrast to the way God and the human being associate when they coexist, Luther speaks of how they dissociate in the setting in which they are separated from one another — divorced, divorced to the death. When this dissociation takes place, "the naked God is there with the naked human being."[24] The "naked God" is God "in his absolute majesty," *Deus absolutus*.[25] One cannot have anything "to do" with him, one cannot "associate" with him, cannot "have dealings," cannot "speak"; one cannot believe in him. But being dissociated from him does not allow the naked human being to come somehow to some state of rest. He experiences the naked God as enemy. Thus the dialogue between the

24. WA 40II:330.1. (The exact translation is missing in *LW* 12:312.)
25. WA 40II:330.12 and 17; cf. *LW* 12:312.

sinning human being and the justifying God commences as a battle, in which the question revolves around which one is in the right — a life-and-death battle that calls for each to acknowledge respect for the other. Such a dialogue is not some harmless effort to find a way to square knowledge of God with knowledge of self. That is because it is not completely clear at the outset just who the opponent is, this one who stands opposite the individual human being. Is it God or the devil? Did Jacob wrestle at the Jabbok during the night with a demon or with Yahweh (Gen. 32)?

The story of Jacob's battle at the Jabbok shows most clearly what is involved when the human being as sinner has an encounter with the justifying God. When Luther emphasizes that "Christ is within,"[26] inside this battle, he identifies more specifically thereby the way in which he intervenes: it is the office and work of Jesus Christ to interject himself within this collision between the naked God and the naked human being and to be victorious over this deadly confrontation, so that God speaks to the sinner and saves him mercifully — from death, not the least of which means deliverance from being turned in on oneself, which is the origin of all idolatry. This relationship between God and the human being, which does not bring destruction but rather coexistence, where communication takes place, is a coexistence in the Word; it takes place as a *dialogue in the Word*. When Christology is discussed, the following issues will be treated with greater specificity: who is next to whom, on account of whom, and in what medium; stated more explicitly yet: who comes to the other one and who is brought in to be with the other one.

Whether the opponent, the one who is opposite the human, is God or the devil is determined by what the Word specifically says, and thus on the basis of what Christology thereby implies. Only from this starting point can issues concerning Word and faith be introduced as subjects for and topics of theology. "God never had anything else to do with the human being, nor does he have anything else to do with him now, apart from the Word of the promise. Stated the other way, we can never have anything else to do with God apart from faith in the Word of his promise."[27]

For God and the human being to coexist in a salutary way in dialogue does not thus happen simply when a harmless way is found to get along and to interact; instead, it is the good situation that ends the deathly confrontation between God and the human being, an end that certainly could not have been anticipated. It is a wonder, about which I can never be astonished sufficiently. In no way can it be assumed — using positivistic thinking —

---

26. WA 40II:329.7. (The phrase does not appear in *LW* 12:312.) Cf. chap. 10 below.
27. WA 6:516.30-32; cf. *LW* 36:42 (*The Babylonian Captivity of the Church*, 1520).

that this was to be expected as the normal course of events, so that theology can obviously commence with its work from this starting point. That this outcome is not obvious at the outset is integral to how the chief topic of theology is defined, which applies also in regard to one's hope for meaning. If this uncertain outcome were removed from one's hope for meaning, so that one would no longer remember one's yearning for meaning and the terrors that come with it — that primal dread — then the rest of the definition is dead. But if the sinning human being and the justifying God — one can say it a different way but can mean the same thing: when the Word of the law that kills and the Word of the gospel that makes alive — provide the substance of theology, then this subject is not something one can look at positively and make fine assumptions, nor is it a dead object, about which one can make appropriate observations and offer proper utterances. The subject is a living, dramatic event that is just as difficult to depict as a bird in flight — but it must be taught anyway.

Since the sinning human being and the justifying God coexist in the Word and in faith, theology cannot be treated in alternate ways, so that some teaching is about the Word and other teaching is about the faith — even though, to accentuate the greater import of the Word over that of the faith, it is more appropriate to speak of teaching the Word than of teaching the faith. Correspondingly, it cannot be ignored that the subject matter is constituted specifically with respect to the text.

Since the subject of theology is constituted as that which happens through speaking, one can express it negatively: theology is not primarily focused on a body of knowledge (the theoretical misunderstanding) or on a body of action (the moral misunderstanding). It also does not deal with something that is more original and that is actually behind the Word, providing a foundation for it (the psychological misunderstanding). It focuses instead on those elementary speech acts in which law and gospel happen in a concrete way. This unique liveliness and the embodied nature of its subject bring theology to the point that it has its own special understanding of the nature of the subject as subject, which does not direct one to choose between the common alternatives of subject-object and some ideal of unity. This unique way to understand the subject for theology — sinning human being and justifying God — takes shape when three elements are considered in this theological thinking, which are not related to each other in any more basic way and which cannot be integrated as parts of some overarching concept — such as the self-revelation of God. The dramatic event in which this "subject" happens takes place *within* these three settings, namely:

a. in the conflict with the *law* that judges me, that convicts me with regard to my sins, that accuses me, and that delivers me over to the final judgment of death;[28]

b. in the promise of the *gospel,* in which God himself speaks by means of Jesus Christ on my behalf, indeed takes my place;[29] and

c. in the assault of the *hiddenness of God,*[30] which cannot be understood merely as the effect of the law and which so radically contradicts the gospel in an oppressive and incomprehensible way.

2.3. *Vita Passiva:* Faith

Biel's third and last question, "whether theology is practical or theoretical,"[31] is the best one for disclosing Luther's concept of theology, since it can be answered by stating what he understands *faith* to be, which is foundational for his concept of theology.

Luther goes at the question in such a way that he demolishes the tradition passed on from Aristotle that suggests a dualistic pattern that differentiates between *theoria* and *praxis,* between *contemplatio* and *actio* — "so that the *vita activa,* with its deeds, and the *vita contemplativa,* with its speculations, do not lead us astray."[32] Luther thus does not subsume either the theology of *actio* or the theology of *contemplatio.*[33] The third way that he finds is a unique procedure and a way for which Luther coined the term *vita passiva.*

The decisive aspect of the *vita passiva* is that it is linked to a specific experience: to an experience for which I am not the prime initiator, but which instead I suffer: "He becomes a theologian in that he lives, yes, even more so, in that he dies and delivers himself to hell, not in that he knows, reads, or speculates."[34]

---

28. Cf. chap. 3, n. 27 below, and chap. 8.

29. Cf. chap. 10 below.

30. Cf. chap. 9 below.

31. Cf. n. 1 above.

32. WA 5:85.2f. (= AWA 2:137.1f. [*Psalmenvorlesung,* 1519-21; on Ps. 3:4]).

33. It is most important for Luther's polemic that both aspects be linked together as one. He regards a "practical" reflection, such as "I have dealt badly; I am damned," as "speculative": WA TR 2:56.20-22 (no. 1340; 1532). Cf. *LW* 12:312-14 (on Ps. 51).

34. WA 5:163.28f. (= AWA 2:296.10 [*Lectures on the Psalms,* 1519-21; on Ps. 5:12]). Luther is clearly exaggerating, for he does not want to exclude knowing and reading, as a comparable statement with respect to this famous sentence shows (WA 39I:421.4f. [*Foreword to the Second Disputation against the Antinomians,* 1538]). Reading and knowing are certainly described in a positive sense in that passage!

The righteousness of faith[35] is passive, "in that we allow God alone to work in us and we ourselves, with all our powers, do not do anything."[36] "Faith is a divine work within us that changes us and brings us to a new birth from God [John 1:13] and kills the old Adam; he makes of us a completely different human being in the heart, mood, mind, and in all powers"[37] (cf. Deut. 6:5). Faith is thus the work of God, through and through, with nothing accomplished by the human being; rather, it can only be received and suffered. The righteousness of Christ is set in complete opposition to the righteousness of works; it is passive. We can only receive it. We do nothing, but instead suffer its coming from another, who works in us: God. The world cannot understand this.[38] It is hidden from the human being who is caught up in the self, who seeks to perform on his own, who not only wants to make something of himself by his deeds and actions, but also wants to be self-made.

Luther's revolutionary new way to conceive of faith as a *vita passiva* found Luther sharing something in common with a particular form of mysticism, which he came to know in Tauler's preaching and which he had learned to esteem highly. His consideration of such views is admittedly critical. For though it would seem that mystical contemplation appears to be passive, the opportunity lurks within that one can make advances in one's speculations and renunciations. That which alone is passive, the righteousness of faith (*iustitia passiva*), which can only be suffered, by contrast, happens when all thinking that one can justify oneself, in a metaphysical sense, as well as when all acting, in a moral sense, together with the desire to unite the two efforts, are radically destroyed. *Faith is not knowledge and not action, neither metaphysical nor moral, neither* vita activa *nor* vita contemplativa, *but* vita passiva.

---

35. It should be noted that Luther does not oppose the Aristotelian definition of "righteousness" (*Nichomachean Ethics* 5) as such, but only when it is brought into the discussion of the teaching about sin and grace. With respect to ethics, Luther allows what Aristotle writes in his *Ethics* and *Politics* to stand.

36. WA 6:244.3-6.

37. Heinrich Bornkamm, ed., *Luthers Vorreden zur Bibel*, 3rd ed. (Göttingen: Vandenhoeck & Ruprecht, 1989), 182; cf. *LW* 35:370 ("Preface to the Epistle of St. Paul to the Romans," 1546 [1522]).

38. WA 40I:41.2-6; cf. *LW* 26:4-12 (*Lectures on Galatians,* The Argument, 1535). "But the kind of righteousness that comes forth from us is not the righteousness of the Christian; we do not become righteous thereby. The righteousness of the Christian is the exact opposite: passive righteousness, which we can only receive, about which we do nothing but only suffer it, for another one works in us, namely, God. This is not understood by the world: '[It is] hidden in secret' [1 Cor. 2:7]."

Chapter 3 What Does "Evangelical" Mean?
The Reformational Turning Point
in Luther's Theology

I do not wish to become a heretic
in that I contradict
that through which I have become a Christian.

The Protestant churches, particularly the confessional churches that name themselves after Luther, affirm by the very fact that they exist that the reformational turning point in Luther's theology is correct. And yet the reality of their existence, as such, does not thereby bring with it any normative power. For this reason, taking seriously their obligation to exercise a critical function within and over against the church, both historical theology and systematic theology must of necessity examine the appropriateness of the way these churches make their claim, including the way they use the adjectives "evangelical" and "reformational." But that poses the question: *Which* matters are appropriately designated by this term? Asked another way: What is "reformational" in Luther's theology?

I would like to answer this question in four stages — so I will begin by fully examining the perspective from which the question as such is posed, in order to lead to the decisive point, which is centered in a specific concept of promise. This concept will be described in detail in the second phase. In the third phase the profile of the concept of promise will be sharpened, to demonstrate how the gospel as a promise that is given will be clearly distinguished from the law, which makes demands and convicts one of sins. Finally, it will be necessary to discuss the confidence that is granted by the Holy Spirit in regard to the practical way in which law and gospel are to be distinguished.

3.1. Perspective of the Question[1]

Only an initial, vague hint concerning what is being asked in the question about what is reformational is provided by the term *reformatio* itself. It refers to grasping backward to something original, as an attempt to make something original important once again or to make it applicable once again. And yet, a study of its usage before, at the time of, and after Luther cannot convey the uniquely specific nature of the content that has to be identified with respect to the meaning of a term. One must go further than just identifying a phenomenon within church history and world history in general, including its effect upon the present; it needs to serve a normative function as well. This normative function should completely guide the person who works totally within this framework; the individual should be able to apply the confessional writings, defend them, consider oneself duty-bound to them, and allow oneself to be bound by them — as at one's ordination into the pastoral office. Such a concept proclaims thereby that the reformational turning point in Luther's theology is not just a random starting point for a process that continues to unfold even today, in which the "reformational" aspect comes into its own only gradually. Instead, it proclaims that what is meant by it has been articulated in a very specific, verbal way and that it was set within a very critical time in history that involved systematic questions and theological controversies.

The way this concept is understood is admittedly not frozen in stone, so it cannot move. For this reason, the nature of what is "reformational" has to be examined repeatedly, so that one knows if it is being used correctly, and to determine whether what it states to be true really is — particularly in light of the welcome discussions since Vatican II that deal with Roman Catholic and evangelical Lutheran theology. It is an unavoidable presupposition that earnest and meticulous effort must be expended to examine controversial theological issues before one can try to reach any ecumenical understanding.

How then might one determine what is "reformational" in the texts when the term is already being used in a specific way before one even starts to analyze it? Can it be defined by a formula, such as "at the same time justified and sinner" *(simul iustus et peccator)*?

Not much is accomplished when one canonizes a formula, which itself needs to be interpreted, and which thus cannot function as a criterion. The fewest difficulties are presented when one seeks to determine what is "reformational" in a *textual context* that is as clear as possible and is part of a

---

1. For a more detailed discussion, cf. Oswald Bayer, "Die reformatorische Wende in Luthers Theologie," *ZThK* 66 (1969): 115-50.

discrete textual unit, which has not been canonized capriciously, but which provides the criterion because of its actual historical setting. It needs to demonstrate its ability to test the spirits and needs to have been created in the midst of a situation that involved a theological controversy. The treatise known as *De captivitate Babylonica ecclesiae praeludium (On the Babylonian Captivity of the Church)* from 1520 is without doubt just such a discrete textual unit. Luther's own position is stated in it in an unmistakable way — which cannot be said of writings such as the Heidelberg Disputation (1518), with its articulation of the *theologia crucis* (theology of the cross). At the same time, this treatise caused a sharply negative reaction from the Roman Church, which — to summarize polemic that lasted decades — resulted in the most important decisions made at the Council of Trent. These decisions included definitions concerning how the sacraments are to be understood, the decree on justification, and in the most negative reaction of all, the statement concerning this treatise and its impacts. Thus, in terms of its content, this treatise articulates the way to understand the relationship between *promissio* and *fides,* between promise and faith; what is "reformational" in Luther's theology is thus set forth with a specificity that is unequaled in any other of his writings.

If one wishes to use this text to articulate the criterion of what is unique, then the question is posed immediately about how this text relates to the earlier Luther texts. What is "reformational" has to be viewed as a discovery, not as something that is seen as happening necessarily — in the historical and philosophical sense of the term — not even in retrospect; it has to be identified as something that happened in a surprisingly contingent way. That does not mean that the result is disconnected from what provided the stimulus; it just means that one ought to question and reject the idea that it is possible to follow a clear rectilinear line of development. It ought not be possible for one to interpret the early texts in an organic sense that uses the pattern of a "bud developing step by step into a plant." One is on the right track when using such a pattern if the intention is to keep from tearing apart the early from the later theology. But a radical change of direction and a turning point cannot be understood just as a development, nor as a necessary event as a movement unfolds — even when what is old relates to what is new as a question relates to its answer. To be sure, a question narrows the horizon of what is being discussed; only a certain number of answers are possible. But *any particular* answer does not have to come by necessity just because of the way the question is posed; it can start something brand-new, coming as a surprise that goes beyond all expectation, as a discovery.

It is Luther himself — as recorded in the "Preface to the Complete Edition of Luther's Latin Writings" (1545) — who provided a perspective on his theological beginnings for his interpreters. An answer that brings freedom comes as the response to a question that struck terror; doors previously closed opened up.[2]

One generally identifies the breakthrough that is described in this preface as the reformational turning point in Luther's theology — which is supported by the language and specific detail, and which reinforces the point of what he says happened. What remains contested, however, concerns exactly *which* of those early perceptions can be identified as that specifically new way of thinking that he mentions in the preface. It has been common to examine the onset of what is really new in his thinking primarily by considering a variety of written texts that have some elements that provide enlightening insights but which in other aspects show him to be still in the dark, in the time period before the open confrontation with those who wanted to remain under the sway of the old ideas, at which time the content of the discussion changed, and thus before the controversy about indulgences. This so-called early dating stands in opposition to the "late dating" advocated most decisively by Ernst Bizer.[3] A point of agreement for both positions is that one must pay specific attention to Luther's personal testimony, mentioned already, as found in the preface of 1545. By being tied so closely to that statement, (a) insufficient attention has been paid to how much this personal testimony has been relativized by Luther's own reflections elsewhere and — in connection with that observation — (b) for the most part, the limits of what that statement can actually contribute to defining the reformational turning point are overlooked.

a. Some scholars — based chiefly on reflections contained in various table talk discussions — have sought to identify the reformational turning point as the discovery of what is meant by the righteousness of God, the *iustitita Dei,* when considered in conjunction with another of Luther's observations that points to the breakthrough of the fundamentally new awareness that was occasioned by discovering the difference between law and gospel. But that suggestion just compounds the problem since, unlike the issue of dealing with a criterion that one is still trying to ascertain, it is impossible to determine properly whether something like the understanding of "spirit and

---

2. *LW* 34:327-38 ("Preface to the Complete Edition of Luther's Latin Writings," 1545); cf. 337: "I beat importunately [Matt. 7:7-8] upon Paul at that place [Rom. 1:17], most ardently desiring to know what St. Paul wanted"; loc. cit., "here I felt that I was altogether born again and had entered paradise itself through open gates." Cf. *LW* 5:157-58 (on Gen. 27:38).

3. Ernst Bizer, *Fides ex auditu. Eine Untersuchung über die Entdeckung der Gerechtigkeit Gottes durch Martin Luther,* 3rd ed. (Neukirchen: Neukirchener Verlag, 1966).

letter," as discussed in the early lectures, corresponds even in a formal sense to the insights gained when he mentions them in the reflections.

A third set of reflective personal testimonies has not been taken into account in this discussion, identified by their use of the key term *promissio* (promise). The most important of such texts comes from the Genesis lectures, this one from 1545.[4] It uses the text that is being explained (Gen. 48:20-21) to provide a theological testament and concurrently a statement of certainty about the confession of faith.[5] It also talks about the reformational discovery and makes specific mention of what he considered to be new, which does not happen in the preface that was composed at almost the same time. The new discovery appears as what happened when the *promissio* of God could shine forth once again, though it "was obscure and unknown to all the theologians throughout the papacy."[6] Here the reformational discovery is linked specifically to the understanding of promise that Luther had articulated in 1520 in the *De captivitate* document. This same point is singled out now in the reflections Luther offers in his personal testimony, in connection with his theological testament, and states what he considered to be "reformational."

b. This observation clearly points out the limits of what one might expect from the "Preface to the Complete Edition" in regards to the definition of the reformational turning point: if one uses the new understanding of Romans 1:17 outlined in the preface by comparing earlier examples of his exposition of this verse, sufficient variation exists in the expositions to show that they do not complement one another, but actually contradict one another. The observations made concerning this phrase are so general that they do not even have value as a criterion to differentiate aspects of development in Luther texts, except to note that the formula has its roots in the Augustinian tradition and thus receives mention in the decrees of the Council of Trent,[7] showing that the formula of "righteousness of God" cannot define "reformational" precisely.[8]

4. *LW* 8:180-94 (*Lectures on Genesis*, chaps. 45–50). Cf. the introduction, n. 20.

5. *LW* 8:193-94; cf. 8:188.

6. "Formerly, under the papacy, when I was a monk, it was by no means customary to speak of a Word [= *verbum*] or promise [*promissio*]. And I give thanks to God that I may live at this time, when this word 'promise' resounds in my ears and in the ears of all the godly. For he who hears the Word easily understands the divine promise, which was obscure and unknown to all the theologians throughout the papacy [*quod in toto Papatu omnibus Theologis obscura et ignota erat*]" (*LW* 8:192).

7. *Decretum de iustificatione*, c. 7 (*Kompendium der Glaubensbekenntnisse und kirchlichen Lehrentscheidungen*, ed. Heinrich Denzinger and Peter Hünermann, 39th ed. [Freiburg: Herder, 2001], nos. 1528-1531, 506f.).

8. On the entire section, cf. also Gerhard Ebeling, "Luther II. Theologie," in *RGG*, 3rd ed.,

In light of what has been set forth so far, one can see that it is necessary to examine what is "reformational" on the basis of understanding what is meant by promise, so that one should understand the formulas that have been referred to in Luther's reflections within this framework, even when they do not specifically use the key term *promissio*.

In a first pass at defining what is "reformational," the concept of promise has come to the fore clearly enough and specifically enough to be used as the criterion; when looking for the real turning point in the history of Luther's theology, which is filled with turning points, it is necessary to find out when it appears for the first time. It has to be the main subject — under specific discussion — and must not just be mentioned in a fragmentary way; it needs to be presented in a discrete and clear textual context, so that in what it presents one need not refer back to what is already known — back to overarching concepts or basic structures — nor introduce later texts to interpret what is really meant.

The earliest text one encounters from this perspective is Luther's fifty theses in the disputation *Pro veritate inquirenda et timoratis conscientiis consolandis (For the Investigation of Truth and for the Comfort of Troubled Consciences)*, written in early summer 1518.[9] These theses, in their discussion of the sacrament of penance, anticipate what will be said concerning promise in *De captivitate* and provide at the same time an explication of Romans 1:17, since this biblical text is used to provide a "summa" at the end of the theses to draw the ideas together.

Since the key term "righteousness of God" (Rom. 1:17) presents a short formula that summarizes the theses about *promissio* and faith, though this concept is presented as being explicated by the theses that precede it, one can see once again the point of convergence in the reflections recorded in the preface (1545) and in the Genesis commentary. The theses set forth in *Pro veritate* — in the sense discussed thus far — are thus a reformational text, in

---

vol. 4 (Tübingen: Mohr, 1960), cols. 495-520, here 498: "The formalistic characterizations of the new understanding about the *iustitia Dei* in the late reminiscences are not enough to keep one from mixing this concept up with the Augustinian way of thinking, which one can find in the exegetical tradition of the Scholastics, along with others as well. That itself shows that the later reminiscences offer only minimal help in identifying the reformational turning point."

9. WA 1:629-33. The text is so slightly known that it does not appear in any modern compendium. With respect to the question about the reformational change, to my knowledge only Kurt Aland has referred to this text ("Der Weg zur Reformation. Zeitpunkt und Charakter des reformatorischen Erlebnisses Martin Luthers," *ThEx*, n.s., 123 [1965]: 108). On the one hand he emphasizes its significance; on the other hand he minimizes it ("the new understanding shines through here in several passages," 108).

fact: the *first* reformational text. For only when the *promissio* described in this text is understood in this way does one have an articulation of the *assurance of salvation;* this is the decisive point of contention between Luther and the representatives of the Roman Church — which reaches a high point in the hearing at Augsburg before Cardinal Cajetan in October 1518.

It is essential for understanding the reformational turning point in Luther's theology, and thus for understanding clearly what is "evangelical," to pay attention to the encounter with Cajetan, which Luther documents publicly. With a clarity that is unmatched elsewhere, Luther identifies the point at which being a Christian is distinguished from heresy. Luther's reformational discovery of the *promissio* and the assurance of salvation that comes with it, which by his own testimony first "makes one a Christian," is held by Cajetan to be "in error"; what Cajetan held to energetically is identified at this point by Luther as "heretical." "I do not wish to become a heretic in that I contradict that through which I have become a Christian; I would sooner die, be burned, be chased out, and be cursed."[10]

A misunderstanding is present here only in that deep sense in which a variety of approaches for assessing the same issue divide participants in a fundamental way.

3.2. *Promissio* as Speech Act That Frees and Gives Confidence

3.2.1. Statements That Establish and That Constitute

Luther's reformational rediscovery of the gospel takes hold of specific statements — such as "And remember, I am with you always, to the end of the age" (Matt. 28:20). Such statements are *promissiones,* promises, assurances. They can be characterized as what the English linguistic analyst Austin terms performative statements in the very sense found when he uses a "promise" as an example; he examines and explains this sense in *How to Do Things with Words.*[11] Though I essentially use Austin's idea, I differentiate the establishing function from the constituting function — which Austin identifies in another way.

A statement that establishes something is made with reference to a par-

10. WA BR 1:217.60-63 (to Karlstadt; October 14, 1518). Cf. WA 2:18.14-16, *Acta Augustana* (*Proceedings at Augsburg,* 1518). Cf. chap. 4.6.2 below, and chap. 12, n. 7. Further: Gerhard Hennig, *Cajetan und Luther* (Stuttgart: Calwer, 1966).

11. John L. Austin, *How to Do Things with Words,* William James Lectures (Cambridge: Harvard University Press, 1962); these were delivered at Harvard University, 1955.

ticular matter that is constituted already; its function is that of affirming something. A statement that establishes something thus allows something that exists already to be described. Something somewhat different happens when one uses a performative utterance, which Austin differentiates from the statement that establishes something. It actually constitutes a reality; it does not affirm something as if it exists already, but presents it for the first time. It is thus not by chance that Austin, when going into further detail about what a performative statement is, uses a judicial term, making reference to so-called "operative" statements.[12] Such a term is used for "the statements by means of which a juridical act is actually completed, in contrast to those — the so-called preamble — that provide with greater specificity the circumstances surrounding the judicial action."[13]

As the chief example of a performative statement, once again not by chance, Austin offers the promise. What am I doing when I say "I promise you . . ."? What happens when this is said or heard? I place myself under an obligation. An activity is described, but it is not what is asserted by an uninvolved observer who says, "He is making him a promise," but is rather an activity that actually constitutes a certain state of affairs. A relationship is created thereby that did not exist previously. This relationship will be destroyed if the promise is not kept but is broken instead. A further misuse of the promise takes place when the person who made the promise is not competent to keep it. The promise is worthless, empty, a trick, and a lie, if I enter into it without being authorized and empowered to make it.

Just the way this is described makes it clear already that a verbal utterance, a performative statement that takes the form of "I promise you . . . ," has a very different nature than a statement of assertion such as what is used in traditional logic, in that it has many more levels and is wider-ranging. In addition, it is "true" and "false" in a different way than is a statement of assertion. Because it deals with an activity that takes time and qualifies time, it cannot be falsified at any given moment by discounting the fact that time is needed, as one might analogously glance at the pointer on a measuring instrument to show that someone is late. (To cite one example, when can a marriage promise be verified or falsified?)

12. John L. Austin, "Performative und konstatierende Äußerung," in *Sprache und Analysis. Texte zur englischen Philosophie der Gegenwart,* edited, translated, and introduced by Rüdiger Bubner, KVR 275 (Göttingen: Vandenhoeck & Ruprecht, 1968), 140-53, see 140.

13. Austin, "Performative und konstatierende Äußerung," 140.

3.2.2. *"Ego Te Absolvo!"* (I Absolve You!)

It was a hard path that Luther trod on his way to coming to understand the gospel as the constituting speech act, as the Word that does what it says. That happened when he reflected deeply on the function of the sacrament of penance, which perforce led him to ponder the nature of indulgences. At first, Luther understood the priestly word of absolution *"Ego te absolvo!"* (I absolve you [of your sins]!) as a declarative act, an act that establishes something. The priest sees the remorse, takes it to be a sign of the divine act of justification that has successfully taken place already in the one to be absolved, though that person is not aware of it, and allows this state of affairs to be made visible out in the open; he verifies it, establishing that it is real already, in order to give assurance to the one who is being absolved. In this way the word of absolution, as a "judgment," is understood in the precise sense that classic logic understands an assertion.

Luther stayed at first completely within the framework of the way the ancients understood language, most especially as explained by the Stoics. That way of thinking was bequeathed to Augustine and its hermeneutics of signification. That concept is most generally employed still today as the way to understand language. According to this approach, language is a system of signs that refer to matters or circumstances, or else it uses signs that express an emotion. In both cases the sign — whether as an assertion or as an expression — does not equate with the matter itself.

That the *signum* itself is already the *res,* that *the linguistic sign is already the matter itself* — that was Luther's great hermeneutical discovery, his reformational discovery in the strictest sense. Luther sharpens this way to understand language in the following statement from a table talk: "Signum philosophicum est nota absentis rei, signum theologicum est nota praesentis rei" [The philosophical sign is the mark of something that is absent; the theological sign is the mark of something present].[14]

That which is decisively reformational is connected to the discovery of a meaning of the *iustitia Dei,* the righteousness of God. It cannot work apart from the mode and medium that God himself uses to distribute his righteousness by means of the trustworthy message of the promise of salvation: the *promissio* that constitutes the assurance of salvation.

Luther initially arrived at his reformational discovery in 1518 in his reflection about the sacrament of penance. Since the sign is itself already the thing it declares, this means, with reference to absolution, that the statement "I ab-

---

14. WA TR 4:666.8f. (no. 5106; 1540).

solve you of your sins!" is not a judgment, which merely establishes that something is true already. This would mean that someone could assume that absolution or justification has taken place already, in an inner, divine way for that individual. Instead, in this instance, a speech act actually constitutes a reality,[15] first initiating and creating a relationship — between the one in whose name something is spoken and the one who is addressed and who believes that promise. Luther calls this type of speech act *Verbum efficax,* that which establishes communication, which frees one and gives one confidence: an effective, accomplishing Word.

3.2.3. *Promissio* as the Center

Luther discovers the same type of performative Word in baptism and in the Lord's Supper — as also in the Christmas story (Luke 2:11: "To you is born this day a Savior!"), in the Easter story, and in the testimony of many other biblical passages. As has been mentioned, he calls all such statements *promissiones,* promises. They are the concrete way and manner in which Christ is present: definite and clear — clearly freeing one and giving one assurance. One cannot remember achieving such freedom and assurance in one's own private, inner monologue. It guarantees and constitutes itself only by the use of the medium of the promise made by another human being — not only when stated by the priest or preacher who holds office but when spoken by anyone who speaks it to me in the name of Jesus. I cannot say it to myself. It has to be spoken to me. For only in such a way does it demonstrate its truth, bringing thereby freedom and certainty.

In contrast to every metaphysical set of statements that teach about the deity, this assertion declares that God's truth and will are not abstract entities, but are directed verbally and publicly as a concrete promise to a particular hearer in a specific situation. "God" is apprehended as the one who makes a promise to a human being in such a way that the person who hears it can have full confidence in it. God's truth is grounded in his faithfulness, in which he

---

15. The same applies to blessing, identified precisely by Luther as "constitutive" use of speech. Blessing is a matter of promise and faith as a present gift; it is not just a wish, but is indicative and constitutive. It gives and actually conveys what the actual words articulate: "In scriptura sancta autem sunt reales benedictiones, non imprecativae tantum, sed indicativae et constitutivae, quae hoc ipsum, quod sonat re ipsa largiuntur et adferunt" [In Holy Scripture, however, there are real blessings. They are more than mere wishes. They state facts and are effective. They actually bestow and bring what the words say]. *LW* 5:140 (*Lectures on Genesis,* chaps. 26–30, 1542ff.). Cf. *LW* 4:154-55 (*Lectures on Genesis,* chaps. 21–25).

stands by the Word that has gone forth from him. God has obligated himself in such a way by the baptismal *promissio* that was spoken at a previous time. The one who is engaged in the agonizing struggle, empowered and encouraged by the message that comes from the spoken word of the sermon, can be touched, each time in a new way, when this one specific promise goes forth. In this way he can let himself be torn away both from his self-glorification and from despair.

A theology that reflects its most excellent subject matter, the gospel, using very specific, form-critical observations and making use of statements that describe the structure in a formal way, precludes in the first place a biblicism that treats every passage of Scripture as having equal importance. It is critical in that it pays careful attention, in a comprehensive way, to what is unique form-critically and in that it takes seriously the way the form of the language and its content are interrelated. Furthermore, it does not extract individual terms and "ideas" from the Bible, such as "love of the neighbor" and "freedom," or themes such as "justification by faith alone" and "a new heaven and a new earth, in which righteousness dwells." It is also not caught up in trying to discover what is meant, seeking to find the history that lies behind the text, or looking for a particular way to conceptualize human existence that is at the root of the text. Instead, this approach limits itself to being guided only by very specific statements, by very specific ways something is articulated, which one can certainly demonstrate are not being selected arbitrarily or are derived by applying some principle that is supposedly at work behind the text. The Bible itself is filled with promises and with statements that can easily be shown to imply promises without forcing the issue.

3.2.4. The Question concerning Competence

Let us delve more specifically into the problem of authority or legitimacy, or, to come at it from a different angle, let us examine the issue of verification, a question that is certainly not being posed to theology for the first time in the present age.

If the subject of theology is located in the promise, as it has been described, two negative rules must be articulated in regard to the problem of verification. First of all, one cannot take the promise, which is not a descriptive statement, and transform it into a descriptive statement. Secondly, one cannot take the promise, which is not in the form of a statement that shows how something ought to be done, and transform it into an imperative. If it were a statement that describes how something takes place, the criterion for whether it is true would be either that it is possible for it to happen or that it has happened already, whether the transaction can be fulfilled or has been fulfilled already, according to the way it was described in the statement. Then truth would be found in whether it happened. To transform the statement in this way, so that it fits within the framework of what can be verified as taking place, assumes a lack of coherence with the reality of what is stated in the promise.

By contrast, the truth of the promise — and no dialectic can get around this — is to be determined only at the very place where the promise was concluded; more accurately, where it was constituted. This means it is located within the relationship between the one who is speaking, who introduces himself for the first time when making the promise, and the one who hears, being linked to that person's situation, whose entire life history is lived out within world history. If it is correct that the one individual is in the position of hearer in the relationship that is constituted by this promise, and if that is verified, it excludes the possibility that he himself can verify the promise. Luther goes on the attack against those who "dream that faith is a quality that is latent in the soul," which one can claim and actualize. "What is really true," Luther continues, "is that at the time when the Word of God, which is truth, allows itself to be heard, and the heart hangs onto it in faith, the heart is saturated with this very truth of the Word and the Word of truth is proven thereby to be correct, is verified."[16]

To seek to verify this on one's own would be atheism; it would be no different for me to try to verify myself in my own subjective piety or if I would seek to verify myself by means of a defined atheism. In such instances the human being wants to speak his own truth about himself, but he makes God into a liar in the process.

3.2.5. Summary

1. What is meant by "God's righteousness" can be identified with specificity only through a new understanding of *promissio* and faith. This means: the reformational teaching about justification is simply a more general unfolding of the specific reformational teaching about *promissio* and the sacraments, understanding the faith in a distinctively literal way.

What does this mean for current theological work on controversial issues, intended as a means to achieve ecumenical understanding? Though the

---

16. WA 6:94.9-12 ("Explanation of the Twelfth Thesis of the Disputation *De fide infusa et acquisita,*" February 3, 1520).

viewpoint continues to gain in strength that the cause of division is not because of differences in understanding justification, but rather concerning different ways to understand the church,[17] it must be asserted once again that the real point of contention is thereby put under wraps but not really identified. If the theology that deals with controversies takes the original setting of the dispute seriously, then it needs to conceptualize the teaching about justification from the perspective of how *promissio* and the sacraments are presented. In Augsburg, Luther and Cajetan were deeply divided about the issues they each held most important in this dispute. It involved the power and scope of the Word of promise addressed to the sinner under the authority of Jesus Christ and therefore concerned the power and scope of faith. Starting with the disagreement about the Word and faith, differences in understanding followed concerning God and humanity, Scripture and tradition, priest and church.

2. That the entire wickerwork pattern of the traditional motifs tore apart only gradually, as time passed during the years 1518-1520, cannot be cited to discount the assertion that the breakthrough had already occurred at a decisive point in time. Instead, it illuminates the historical path that was taken as the new approach took hold and shows that it did not happen mechanistically. One can retrace the steps to see where traditional explanations were still in use as theology was undergoing this radical reconstruction, even though one might not see the new understanding of *promissio* as the starting point each time a particular topic was being reexamined. In addition to a new way to describe how the sacraments are to be understood and a new way to conceptualize the church (especially in regard to the priesthood and heresy), with significant contrast to the earlier theology of Luther, this new understanding gave sufficient impetus for a reexamination of how to conceptualize prayer, the person and work of Jesus Christ, the differentiation of law and gospel, and the relationship between faith and action — to note just the most important points.

3. If one reads Luther's theses in *Pro veritate* as the documentation of the

---

17. Thus even Joseph Lortz, "Martin Luther. Grundzüge seiner geistigen Struktur," in *Reformata Reformanda*, Festschrift for Hubert Jedin, ed. Erwin Iserloh and Konrad Repgen, vol. 1 (Münster: Aschendorff, 1965), 214-46, here 244: "One must recognize with all seriousness that (in contrast to the preceding 400 years) the article on justification no longer needs to be considered as one that has to divide the church. And rightly so." Correspondingly, most recently, Walter Kasper, "Situation und Zukunft der Ökumene," *Theologische Quartalschrift* 181 (2000): 175-90, here 186: "Now that the fundamental questions with respect to the doctrine of justification have been cleared up in dialogue with the Reformation churches, ecclesiological questions take priority now."

reformational turning point in Luther's theology, that also helps to clear up the problem about how answers given to *an individual,* in response to questions raised in the context of arguing specific historical views about church, theology, and piety, could come to be applied *to other individuals* as the foundation and confession of their faith. That such insights could be transferred to other situations can be understood if one does not err by pinpointing the reformational turning point as something that was never spoken out loud and that never could be: in some "deep level" that Luther "himself could only rarely [bring] up to conscious awareness";[18] it comes as a discovery that can be documented in a verbally articulated context. This solution means that his "life" is not contrasted to his "teaching"; instead, these purported alternatives coalesce. Looking for truth and comfort for the anguished soul, Luther had not come upon a monad from the original life-force that uttered nothing, nor did he chance upon a complex legal structure. As these theses demonstrate how comfort is really provided, he came upon something very simple, which could be spoken and heard using definite wording: the verbal statement of forgiveness and promise in the name of Jesus Christ, in a *promissio* that creates certain faith by the very power of its clear message. That which one encountered as "reformational" in this form could be transmitted in the words articulated in sermons and in catechesis and could be set forth and affirmed in written confessions.

4. *De captivitate,* which articulated the theses in *Pro veritate* in a more complete way, depicts the life of a Christian as the time of repentance, which involves being bound once upon a time to the baptismal promise given in the past,[19] which is preserved continually — by the *promissio* of the Lord's Supper.[20] The unique moment of the Word is thus created with the help that comes from both directions, from baptism and from the Lord's Supper. In this moment, the once-for-all-time nature of the promise carries with it the assumption that newly articulated promises are not able to surpass it. The unique nature of the first promise in baptism is reinforced every time one goes back to the baptism in the Lord's Supper.

The concept of what happens in connection with the spoken Word is applied when the concept of promise is used to interpret the Words of Institution, when they state that a gift is being given — "given for you" — which carries the same weight for Luther as the absolution formula: "your sins are

---

18. Hanns Rückert, "Die geistesgeschichtliche Einordung der Reformation," *ZThK* 52 (1955): 43-64, here 55: "a *punctum mathematicum* for his faith."

19. *LW* 36:60 (*The Babylonian Captivity of the Church,* 1520). For a brief definition, cf. 36:124: repentance is nothing but "a way and a return to baptism."

20. *LW* 36:60.

forgiven you!" This was the first place attention was directed when the reformational understanding of Word and faith was being applied. But at the same time, this new understanding can be detected in and was applied to the study of the entire Scripture and can be confirmed throughout as being at work.

The promise of the gift in the Words of Institution is thus not the only *promissio*. But it remains the embodiment of the unique formulation of the promise, which is identical to that of the gospel, as Luther makes use of it in contrast to the law. As a brief summary of the gospel, it establishes the basic text for every evangelical sermon, which has no other task than to articulate what that promise means.

According to a strict understanding of what is reformational, the "church" exists only where the *promissio* is the basic text of the sermon; for this reason, one needs to take careful note of the original circumstances in which systematic issues and issues of theological controversy were addressed, in the theses presented in *Pro veritate* and in the hearing at Augsburg, which reveal the reformational turn in Luther's theology.

3.3. The Distinction between Law and Gospel

Certainty assumes clarity. Clarity that produces certainty is visible only when a clear distinction is made between the gospel as *promissio,* as a categorical gift — "Take and eat!" — and the law, which makes demands and convicts one of sin, which of itself it is holy, just, and good, though it still cannot be fulfilled perfectly by us (Rom. 7:12; Gal. 3:10, 12; James 2:10; Gal. 5:3; Rom. 2:25). For Luther the gospel is the "other Word," the second and last, the definitive Word of God. When reflecting back on his reformational turning point, he reminisces in a table talk: "Previously I was not deficient in any way, except that I made no distinction between law and gospel, holding both to be the same and thinking that Christ was to be differentiated from Moses only in regard to when he lived and concerning the level of his perfection. But after I discovered the difference, that the law is one thing and the gospel is another, then I broke through."[21]

Correspondingly, Luther was able to describe this programmatically in his New Year's sermon of 1532, based on Galatians 3:23-29: "I wanted to demonstrate the two concepts without mixing them, . . . each one in its own

---

21. WA TR 5:210.12-16; cf. *LW* 54:442-43 ("Table Talk Recorded by Caspar Heydenreich" [no. 5518, winter of 1542-43]). On the gospel as the "other Word," cf. nn. 24 and 28 below.

proper place, according to its material sense: the law is for the old Adam; the gospel is for my despairing, terrified conscience."[22]

It is recorded in the same sermon that

> the opinion of Saint Paul is that a clear difference must be taught and learned in Christendom, both by preachers and also by hearers, namely, that between law and gospel, between works and faith. He also commands Timothy about this when he admonishes him to divide correctly the Word of truth [2 Tim. 2:15]. For this distinction between law and gospel is the highest art in Christendom, which all who boast of the name "Christian," or assume it as a name, can and ought to know. For wherever there is confusion about this matter, one cannot recognize how a Christian is different from a heathen or a Jew — this is how vitally important it is to make this distinction.[23]

According to Luther, if it is true to its task, theology must orient itself by means of the distinction between law and gospel in the way it discusses all its topics. It is to seek by such effort to reflect on the sequence of events whereby God confronts human beings verbally, so that they can believe and act freely. Not to distinguish between law and gospel — which in actuality is the predominant state of affairs — serves only the law that brings death. But, by contrast, to make the distinction serves to set forth what the gospel is in a clear manner. The classic passage where Luther explains this distinction is in the eighth and ninth sections of his tractate *On the Freedom of a Christian* (1520):

> But how can it be that faith alone can make one righteous and can provide such superabundant riches apart from all works, when it is obvious that so many laws, commands, works, estates, and instructions are prescribed for us in Scripture? One ought to note here with diligence and to consider with all seriousness that faith alone, apart from all works, makes one righteous, free, and joyful, about which we will hear more later; and one must know that the entire Holy Scripture is to be divided into two words: the commandments or the law of God and the assurances or the promises. The commandments teach and prescribe for us various good works; but the problem is that they do not thereby actually happen. They indeed do give

---

22. WA 36:41.30-32. The specific vocabulary concerning the sharp opposition between "law and gospel" is of course not biblical, but it is justified with respect to the matter as a whole, as 2 Cor. 3:6 makes clear. On this subject, see Otfried Hofius, "Gesetz und Evangelium nach 2. Korinther 3," in Hofius, *Paulusstudien*, WUNT 51 (Tübingen: Mohr, 1989), 75-120.

23. WA 36:25.17-26.

direction, but they do not help; they teach what a person ought to do, but furnish no power to make something occur. They are thus constructed to show that the human being will see his inability to do the good and will learn to distrust his own ability. . . . From this he learns to despair of his ability and to seek help elsewhere, so that he can live without evil desires, and thus he learns that the law was fulfilled by someone else, which he cannot do on his own. . . .

When the human being learns about and has discovered his own powerlessness on the basis of the commandments, that there will be only fear about how he is to do enough of what is asked in the commandment, because the commandment must either be fulfilled or he must be damned, then he is sufficiently humbled and turned into nothing in his own eyes. He does not find anything in himself by means of which he can be righteous. Following upon this comes the other Word, the divine assurance and promise [= *promissio*], which says: If you want to fulfill all the commandments, if you want to be free of your evil desires and sins, as the commandments pressure and demand, look here, believe in Christ, through whom I promise you all grace, righteousness, peace, and freedom. If you believe, you have it; if you do not believe, you do not have it: For what is impossible for you, by means of all the works of the commandments, which are many and which still cannot be of any value, is made simple and easy for you through faith. For God has made all things depend on faith, so that whoever has it shall have all things and be joyful; whoever does not have it shall have nothing. This is what the promises of God provide, what the commandments demand; they fulfill what the commandments demand, so that everything is from God himself, both commandment and fulfillment. He alone commands; he alone also fulfills.[24]

As has been pointed out already, when the subject matter of theology[25] is described in greater detail, special terms of theology such as "faith" and "justification" need to be defined more precisely. That is because the subject matter of theology is conceptualized as a dynamic event, which can be described only by making distinctions — which bring along their own tensions as well.[26] This observation applies most of all to distinguishing between law and gospel.

24. WA 7:23.24–24.20.
25. Cf. chap. 2.2 above.
26. Such distinctions resist being resolved so that they fit nicely into a larger unity; the lordly will of reason to construct a unity breaks apart because of them. Even a corresponding, theoretical construct of the unity of God shows itself to be impossible — even if one seeks to design such a unity from a trinitarian perspective (cf. chap. 15 below). In contrast to Luther, one

What one actually encounters at first is the law. In it God confronts me as one who is my opposite — with unavoidable, difficult questions: Adam! Eve! Where are you (Gen. 3:9)? Where is your brother (Gen. 4:9)? Such questions convict me; what I am not conscious of comes into the light. Yes, what happens first is that I am discovered: "You are the man!" — of death (2 Sam. 12:7, and 5). I cannot say that to myself; that must come to me from the outside, must be said by another. At the same time, I am so convicted at that point that, as David before Nathan, the prophet of God, I can speak my own judgment sentence to myself. The law that accosts me convicts me at the same time, from the inside out; just because it is outside of me does not mean that it is a law that has nothing to do with me, against which I would be nothing but a mechanistic echo; its externity is not a heteronomy.[27]

In a way that is quite different from the law, in which God speaks against me, in the gospel he speaks for me. The gospel is thus a "different Word,"[28] a second Word of God, which cannot be robbed of its force by being merged with the Word of the law to make it into a third Word — to describe something like a self-revelation of God. Neither of these two words can be derived from its opposite. For as long as we are under way in life (2 Cor. 5:7), the distinction between law and gospel cannot be removed by some cunning artistry that can elevate the two to the status of some unified concept that is higher or deeper.

The second, decisive, final Word of God, the gospel, speaks on my behalf. The "for me" *(pro me)* in the reformational theology of Luther is that the nature of Jesus Christ himself is that of one who communicates with me, in which the triune God promises to me and gives to me the Word made flesh, in baptism and the Lord's Supper, as well as in every sermon that proclaims what is consistent with what happens in baptism and the Lord's Supper. In

---

can see the problem of the dominant theoretical theological proposals of the last two hundred years. They have yielded to the insistent call of that lordly will of reason that one fit everything tightly into a system. In the process they have failed to note the harshness and sharpness of the three distinct settings noted already (see chap. 2.2 above), which simply cannot be further resolved.

27. If one seeks to avoid misunderstanding, the first ("political") use of the law, and with it the distinction between the grace that preserves creation and the grace of the new creation, which is that of the gospel, can only with difficulty be united with the second ("theological" or "convicting") use, so as to come up with a single overall function of the "law." It is important for clarity that the *usus politicus legis* (political use of the law) be described categorically in and of itself, and it needs to be shown to have its own unique function. Various terms are used to describe "two uses" *(duplex usus)* of the law, as for example, in *LW* 28:233 and 234 (*Lectures on the First Epistle to Timothy*, 1528); *LW* 26:308-13 (on Gal. 3:19 [*Large Galatians Commentary*, 1531]); *WA* 39I:441.2f. (*Second Disputation against the Antinomians*, 1538).

28. *WA* 7:24.9f.; cf. *LW* 31:358 (*On the Freedom of a Christian*, 1520).

this kind of encounter, with the promise of the forgiveness of sins, the sinner becomes a new creation and continues to have a lasting identity that comes from outside the self, from another being, from one who is a stranger: from the one who in a wonderful transfer and exchange of human sin and divine righteousness has taken each person's place.

Luther's way to distinguish between law and gospel needs to be considered in what follows under three aspects: first, in view of the sequence: first the law, then the gospel; second, in view of Luther's distinction between Christ as gift and Christ as example; and finally, in the third place, in view of the enduring systematic meaning of Luther's distinction between law and gospel — thus in view of its meaning for the present age.

3.3.1. The Sequence

Does the sequence of law and gospel that carried weight for Luther mean that the gospel is an accessory of the law, in every aspect assuming that the law is present, and making sense only in relation to the law?

When Luther emphasizes that the law, as it functions, is there already, already determining human existence — as sinful existence — he certainly acknowledges thereby that it in fact precedes the gospel, but not that it has ultimate priority over the gospel. The actual superiority of the gospel remains unaffected. That keeps one from thinking that the law provides the only setting within which it is possible to understand the gospel. For when the gospel comes on the scene and is interpreted in the context of what was experienced under the law, then it can be understood correctly. The person's earlier experience of God, which did nothing but delude the self, will now be replaced with what does not come from within the individual. It comes to the person with reference to the gospel, even though in actuality the gospel message was there beforehand. If the gospel is considered to be nothing other than the defeat of evil and sin, one runs a risk of minimizing the truth about creation. But Luther sees the work of God already in his creation, when he gives gifts without having to, coming solely by the grace of God, and in that sense already "evangelical."[29] As the means for dispensing the new creation, the gospel has a superabundance of positives, nothing like the way it is described when it is understood exclusively in the context of ways to deal with the negative.

In that the law brings an awareness of unbelief, it presumes the existence

29. Cf. chaps. 5.1.1 and 7.3 below.

of faith and the gospel, materially and logically. For unfaith, as a turning toward false gods, does not work death and destruction in and of itself; that happens in, with, and under the turning away from the true, only, good God. Unfaith is sin because of its rejection of the eternal fellowship promised by God. It is due to rebellion against such fellowship, and thus is rebellion against the gospel, if it is correct that the preamble of the Decalogue — God's self-introduction and self-communication — is pure gospel. In the same way, the threat of death (Gen. 2:17) can really be understood only in relation to the preceding promise of life and free provision of gifts (Gen. 2:16).

3.3.2. Christ as Gift and Example

According to Luther, the gospel was not to become law and the faith was not to become an action that tries to justify itself over against what it "ought" to do. The gospel turns into moralizing, just as the faith created by the gospel turns into moralizing, wherever Christ is made into an example of how to live one's life, as Luther observes and criticizes in the tractate *On the Freedom of a Christian.*[30] For this reason, in his *Brief Instruction on What to Look For and to Expect in the Gospels,* he impresses on the reader a distinction, which reiterates the way to distinguish between gospel and law in regard to Christology, and makes an application: how to distinguish between Christ as gift *(donum)* and Christ as example *(exemplum).*

This distinction between gift and example leads to a criticism of those who reduce the gospel and faith to moralizing, but at the same time, in a constructive way, it is instructive as it answers the question about the concrete form that good works take from within faith, as new obedience. Christ as gift creates the faith; Christ as example demonstrates works of love: "Christ as gift nourishes your faith and makes you a Christian. But Christ as example gives your works a workout. They do not make you a Christian, but they proceed from you, you who have already been made to be a Christian. As far as gift and example are to be distinguished, that is how far faith and works are to be distinguished. Faith has nothing of its own, but is only Christ's work and life. The works do have something that comes from you yourself, but are not to be seen thereby as your own, but are for the neighbor."[31] Right within the doc-

---

30. *LW* 31:357.

31. WA 10I/1:12.17–13.2 ("Ein kleiner Unterricht, was man in den Evangelien suchen und erwarten soll"; *Kirchenpostille,* 1522). Cf. Timothy F. Lull, ed., *Martin Luther's Basic Theological Writings* (Minneapolis: Fortress, 1989), 107.

trine of Jesus Christ, as recorded in the biblical witness, one can discern the distinction between law and gospel.

> For this reason you are to conceptualize Christ's Word, work, and suffering in two ways. One of these is as an example, which is placed before your eyes; you are to follow that and thus act in this way, as Saint Peter says in 1 Peter 4 [:1; cf. 2:21]: "Because Christ also suffered for us, leaving us an example." Just as you see him praying, fasting, helping people, and showing love, you ought to do the same, as regards you yourself and your neighbor. But that is the least important part of the gospel, according to which it is still not enough to be called gospel. For in that way Christ can help you no more than any other saint. His life remains with him and still does not help you and, to say it succinctly: This way of life does not make Christians, it only makes hypocrites; it has to go a lot further with you. For a very long time this has been the best (though still not practiced) way of preaching.
>
> The main point and the foundation of the gospel is that you first encounter and recognize Christ as a gift and present, which is given you by God and is now your own possession, long before you can think of him as an example. This is so that you, when you look to him or hear that he does anything or suffers anything, will not doubt that he himself, Christ, is your own in those actions and sufferings and that you can trust in those actions just as much as if you had done them yourself, yes, as if you were this very Christ. See now, this is the gospel as recognized correctly, that is, as the unsurpassing goodness of God, which no prophet, no apostle, no angel has ever been able to assert, concerning which no heart can ever be astonished sufficiently and can comprehend. That is the great fire of the love of God for us, about which the heart and conscience can rejoice, be confident, and be at peace; that is what it means to preach the Christian faith. That is why such preaching is called "gospel," which means what we would call a joyful, good, comforting message.[32]

This way to differentiate between Christ as *donum,* as gift, and Christ as *exemplum* is necessary to avoid the moralizing that is currently widely practiced, which can be so easily linked with a teaching that advocates "Christ alone" *(solus Christus).* The danger of such moralizing is much greater in the present, because of the influence of Kant's thesis that religion develops out of morality, than it was at the time of Luther, in which the dominant view was an Aristotelian-ethical understanding of reality, which was transferred in the teaching about sin and grace.

32. WA 10I/1:11.1–12.2.

3.3.3. Antinomianism and Nomism Today

According to Luther, what makes a theologian a theologian is being able to correctly distinguish law and gospel.[33] The issue addressed by this statement is not recognized with utter seriousness today or is even relegated "to the time-bound form of the Reformation and its theology."[34] But it continues to raise a ruckus in the midst of the problematic relationship between reason and faith, faith and politics, in the assessment of evil and its power — including the question about whether there is a chance that evil can be overcome — as well as in the question about the future of humanity. As in the past, and in the present as well, the issue deals with foundational questions of anthropology, ethics, and eschatology.

What raises a ruckus needs to be clarified. The following thesis seeks to give support to such clarification: *In its universalizing of the gospel, the modern age is antinomian, but at the same time it is increasingly nomistic.*

By its very name, which is crafted to characterize its self-understanding, the modern age distinguishes itself as having an "evangelical" character. It conceptualizes itself as a new age that cannot be outdone, standing under the banner of freedom. It is assumed thereby that the law has in principle been vanquished already: the human being is by nature free, good, and spontaneous. In this sense the modern age is *antinomian.*

But whatever the new human being of the modern age is, that is what he or she must first become.[35] The gospel of freedom, which is universally said to exist, puts the human being under the pressure to redeem himself at the very same time, and calls for him to achieve the potential that is by very nature his already. But if freedom is not promised and imparted, if instead it is characteristic of me from the outset, if I define myself in relation to it, then I am weighed down, in my individual and collective subjectivity, with having to fulfill the promise of what has been provided for me — not freed for freedom but at the same time "to freedom condemned" (Sartre).[36] It is not that I

---

33. "Therefore whoever knows well how to distinguish the Gospel from the Law should give thanks to God and know that he is a real theologian": *LW* 26:115 (*Lectures on Galatians*, chaps. 1–4, on Gal. 2:14 [1531]). Cf. *LW* 26:342 (on Gal. 3:23); WA TR 6:127-47, especially 142.8-12 (no. 6715).

34. Wolfhart Pannenberg, "Lebensraum der christlichen Freiheit. Die Einheit der Kirche ist die Vollendung der Reformation," *EK* 8 (1975): 587-93, here 590.

35. Cf. for example Hegel's thesis that "man must make himself to be what he is" (Georg Wilhelm Friedrich Hegel, *The Christian Religion*, trans. Peter C. Hodgson [Missoula, Mont.: Scholars, 1979], 160).

36. Cf. chap. 5, n. 5 below.

am able to be free, but that I *have to* free myself. Thus the reverse side of antinomianism is nomism.

When one tries to formulate a theological assessment in regard to the connections between morality and legalism, freedom and determinism, compulsion and insight, spontaneity and nomism, one can still not avoid coming to terms with the reformational distinction between law and gospel. This distinction should also provide help with respect to the postmodern reshaping of the modern age, as regards memory, diagnosis, and therapy if it is valid, to cite one example, to offer an assessment about the radical constraint to justify oneself, as well as the way the postmodern world seeks to compensate for this judgmental activity. This kind of compensation becomes visible in the flight from such excessive constraint to justify oneself into a hedonistic individualism and into the much-loved transformation of everything into aesthetics, as well as the attempt to cover our entire context in anonymity.[37]

3.4. Knowledge and Certainty

One needs to *know* how to distinguish between law and gospel. But one does not become *certain* about how one can distinguish them just by knowing that they are to be distinguished. This distinction between knowledge and certainty must also find expression in the manner and way in which dogmatic statements are constructed and presented.

> This art, namely, to divide law and gospel rightly, . . . is learned soon enough, as far as [it] concerns the words; but when it comes to the opportunity that one has to experience it and test it out in life and in the heart, then it becomes so out of reach and difficult for someone that he neither knows or understands anything about it at all.[38]

> There is no person on earth who rightly knows and understands how to distinguish between gospel and law. We indeed think that we have understood it when we hear preaching, but that widely misses the mark. Only the Holy Spirit can work with this skill. It was even lacking for Christ in his human nature on the Mount of Olives, so that an angel had to comfort him; he was in fact a doctor [that is, a learned professor] from heaven and the Holy Spirit had rested on him in the form of a dove; in spite of this he was

---

37. Not only the law becomes anonymous, but the gospel as well, insofar as God is described as source, power, etc.; the category of the personal loses its support.

38. WA TR 6:142.26-30 (no. 6716).

comforted by an angel. I would have thought with all certainty that I could do it, because I have written about it for such a long time and so often; but truly, when it comes to having it happen [that is, when it comes right down to it], then I see clearly that it is lacking in me by a wide, wide margin! Thus God alone ought to be and must be the most holy master and teacher.[39]

As mentioned already, Luther refers to the discovery of learning how to make this distinction as a breakthrough: "But after I discovered the difference, that the law is one thing and the gospel is another, then I broke through."[40] But such freeing does not have the character of an experience that one, as such, can leave behind and that one can keep at the ready as knowledge that can be used at will. It remains an art and a skill, a blessing that is experienced when one can distinguish properly in a very tough situation.

That is why it is difficult to come up with a written, teachable fixed definition — as was attempted when writing a confessional document such as the Formula of Concord, using authors rooted in a university culture who were familiar with disputations — to evaluate some proceeding with clarity because the liveliness of the way it happens cannot be captured by providing a description of the way it takes place. God himself is the Lord over distinguishing law and gospel, as well as Lord of the eschatological unity of law and gospel; we are not. But just so one does not let that be forgotten, one must also put forth the effort to teach about the subject theologically — admittedly to teach in such a way that this distinction is considered within its true "setting in life."

39. WA TR 2:4.7-16 (no. 1234; 1531); cf. *LW* 54:127 ("Table Talk Recorded by John Schlaginhaufen"); cf. chap. 1, n. 33 above. Cf. WA TR 468.24f. (no. 2457; 1532): "Miror autem me hanc scientiam non discere" [But I am amazed that what I know I do not learn].
40. Cf. n. 21 above.

Chapter 4 What Makes the Bible
Become Holy Scripture?

Holy Scripture is its own interpreter.

The question that deals with the authority of the Bible has assumed different aspects in the present age from what it had at the time of Luther. But Luther made important, basic hermeneutical decisions that have not lost their validity even today. As within this entire presentation of Luther's theology, questions from our own time need to be taken into account as well, most especially at this juncture.

4.1. The Priority of the Scripture
over the Hearers and Interpreters

Luther's foundational thesis reads: *Sacra scriptura "sui ipsius interpres"*[1] — the Holy Scripture "is its own interpreter." This thesis goes way beyond the methodology that involves work with a concordance, by means of which a particular scriptural passage is to be interpreted by other passages and must be brought into agreement with them. It refers specifically to the effect that the text has, with reference to the one who reads, hears, and interprets it. In this comprehensive sense the phrase *Sacra scriptura sui ipsius interpres* means: "The text itself causes one to pay attention."

Even with all the interpretive work, which can be carried out academically — by means of solid research that is clear and is subject to controls — the understanding of the biblical text is, in the final analysis, still unattain-

---

1. WA 7:97.23 (*Assertio omnium articulorum,* 1520); for the citation in its context, see 4.3 below (n. 17).

able. We have already noted this tension in Luther's characterization of theology: on the one hand, there is the foundational work — grammatical and philosophical training of the theologian and patient meditation and interpretation — but at the same time it involves the gift of the Spirit over which we have absolutely no control, as Luther himself received it as a gift with his reformational discovery, when "the doors of Paradise"[2] opened to him with the flash of insight concerning the righteousness of God. It is not the interpreter who makes sense of the text or makes the text understandable. The text itself needs to say what it has to say for itself. In that case, the distinction concerning Holy Scripture that is frequently made, which regards Holy Scripture as the formal principle of Protestantism and justification as its material principle,[3] finds easy resolution. The authority of Scripture is not formal but is highly material and is content driven. It is the voice of its author, who gives; who allows for astonishment, lament, and praise; who demands and fulfills. Scripture can in no wise be confirmed as having formal authority in advance, so that the content becomes important only as a second stage of the process. The text in its many different forms — particularly in the law's demand and the gospel's promise — uses this material way of doing business to validate its authority.

One must thus note that there is a priority of Scripture itself over its readers and hearers. The nature of this priority does not mean that they are somehow oppressed; instead, they are set free. For when I read and hear Scripture, then I note that these stories talk about me; they tell *my story*. I appear in them long before I obey them. In this way the text precedes me and this text addresses me. In that I myself am addressed, I am freed at the same time to listen, even if it means to listen critically, with all my powers, with my body and soul and all my thinking ability. One is not kept from interpreting just because he is being interpreted at the same time. Instead, it is only in this relationship that the doors are even opened to a playroom in which one can move about — and certainly not just as a marionette. The person who can confess "I believe that God has made me and all creatures" is much better prepared to make critical distinctions and to use the power of reason that is granted to him. By the authority of Scripture the hearer is placed into his proper relationship; the individual does not constitute himself, he is assigned a location: as creature.

---

2. *LW* 34:337 ("Preface to the Complete Edition of Luther's Latin Writings," 1545). Cf. chap. 3, n. 2, and chap. 1.1.

3. First proposed by August Twesten, *Vorlesungen über die Dogmatik der ev.-luth. Kirche*, vol. 1 (Hamburg: Friedrich Perthe, 1826), 258-60.

The fundamental, anthropological situation that is in force according to this perspective makes it possible to come at it with a different point of emphasis and with a slight adjustment in perspective in regard to the relationship between authority and criticism.[4] What is accentuated thereby is that there is a lack of symmetry in receiving and transmitting, in hearing and speaking, in reading and writing, which not only characterizes life itself as a process of translation, but also calls for something to happen even before that becomes possible; this can be seen paradigmatically in the way parents give guidance in physical and spiritual matters. When it comes to a critical — this means a discerning — apprehension of the world, I cannot empower myself. I must be empowered for it; I must be given the ability — from someone else who has the power to do it. According to the exact meaning of the word, "authority" (Lat. *augere*) is the power that multiplies, that allows for growth — the power that creates life. There is thus no critique without authority. If there is nothing that precedes the critical activity, it would go on emptily and would be sterile. Admittedly, when stated the other way, the only authority that can be treated as valid authority is that which is fruitful and empowers one to engage in critique, in a free apprehension of the world, which can make decisions and assessments and from its side can allow for still more growth. No true authority without critique.[5]

What contrasts present-day thinking from that of earlier epochs is its intention that one must in principle justify everything, starting out fresh at the same time from a point of nothingness, having to substantiate everything and — at a minimum, depending on the situation — constitute what is being stated without using presuppositions. Whatever does not appear to be reasonable, whatever cannot be justified on the basis of a reconstruction, be "explained," and thus be thought out in connection within the unity of self-consciousness, has lost its right to exist. "Religion, observation of nature, community, order within the state, everything has been subjected to most re-

---

4. For a more thorough treatment of the subject, cf. Oswald Bayer, *Autorität und Kritik. Zu Hermeneutik und Wissenschaftstheorie* (Tübingen: Mohr, 1991).

5. There are good reasons to use the term "biblical criticism." It is not to be applied in the customary sense of criticism *of* the Bible (objective genitive), whereby we intend "to master" the text; Luther cites 1 Tim. 1:7 to reject this approach. The appropriate criticism is that which is applied to me personally by the text (subjective genitive): "biblical criticism" is the capacity to criticize and the power to judge that free one from the fear of human beings because it is rooted in the fear of God. The fear of God is the beginning of wisdom: it comes when I recognize that I have not created myself and when I have insight that makes me aware of my own finite and dependent nature. There is a place for freedom within this dependent relationship: human freedom. But it is finite freedom.

lentless critique; everything must justify its existence before the judgment seat of reason or renounce its existence."[6]

It is plain that demanding and arriving at only such explanations as can be justified furnish one with an excellent means of emancipation. One can be exempted thereby from the burden of historical, traditional demands and claims. What is too close to a person is what one wants to get off one's neck or at least put at a distance. Then it will no longer pose a danger to me, no longer make demands of me and beckon me, no longer have expectations and impose obligations. When observing what was important in the Enlightenment, one notes that historical research received significant attention as well. The historical text was stretched out upon a Procrustean bed that made use of an a priori concept of truth, so that whatever was contingent and thus confining could be excised. What took place in historical time took a back seat; the aim was to distill the quintessential by recovering some timeless principle that could be detected behind the text, whether it was the "matter about Jesus," the "nature of Christianity," the "canon within a canon," etc.

Luther would speak against the subjectivity that is demanded in the present age, which seeks to interpret the text and which builds into such effort the principle of unity within one's own self-consciousness as this is assumed to exist. This way of thinking assumes that the person is actively involved in giving meaning. He would speak as well against the narcissistic claim that a type of reason exists that seeks to see only that which the self can extract according to its own proposals.[7] Luther considers the autonomy of the text that causes resistance: its authority to interpret the reader and hearer critically. "Note well," says Luther, "that the power of Scripture is this: it will not be altered by the one who studies it; instead, it transforms the one who loves it. It draws the individual in — into itself — and into its own powers."[8] The subjectivity and individuality that critiques itself, together with its individual style, which Luther takes into account as well, is not rooted here within the self; it also does not achieve self-awareness and self-authentication, as Descartes suggests. It is constituted outside the self. The Christian receives his subjectivity, which can evaluate itself critically, in the knowledge that something is written about him "in this book,"[9] that he himself is interpreted by the text of this book and thus by its author.

---

6. Friedrich Engels, "Anti-Dühring," in Karl Marx and Friedrich Engels, *Werke,* vol. 20 (Berlin: Dietz, 1962), 16. Cf. Karl Marx, "Brief an Arnold Ruge (1843)," in *Werke,* 1:344: "radical criticism of everything that exists."

7. Immanuel Kant, *Kritik der reinen Vernunft,* ed. Raymund Schmidt, 3rd ed., PhB 37a (Hamburg: Meiner, 1990), B XIII.

8. WA 3:397.9-11; cf. *LW* 10:332 (on Ps. 68:14 [*First Lectures on the Psalms,* 1513]).

9. Johann Georg Hamann, *Briefwechsel,* vol. 2, ed. Walther Ziesemer and Arthur Henkel

The substance of the text as given, which deserves careful attention by the "I" who reads and hears it, is not somehow absorbed by the individual. The text's power of resistance is too great for that. The text remains. But readers and hearers are changed by it. The interpreter does not interpret Scripture, but Scripture interprets the interpreter. Scripture thus takes care of its own interpretation; it is its own interpreter: *Sacra scriptura sui ipsius interpres.*

4.2. Church: Communion of Hearers

Hearers and readers of the biblical texts are interpreted within the church — within the communion of those who first hear and believe, and only then speak; "I believe, and so I speak" (2 Cor. 4:13). The hermeneutical questions and those of an intellectual and theoretical nature that are posed thereby essentially have a nature that is spiritual and ecclesiological; an appropriate concept of "theology" comes only within the framework of worship.

The community that gathers for worship is the true, universal, communicating communion, the communicating communion of the justified sinners that prays the psalms and uses the entire Bible in the same way it uses the Psalter, which Luther termed a "little Bible."[10] In his interaction with the Bible Luther knew he was positioned deep within the tradition of the one, holy, catholic, and apostolic church: "In summary, if you want to see the Holy Christian Church painted with lively colors and form, drawn in a little picture, then set the Psalter before yourself, for then you have a fine, clear, pure mirror that will show you what Christianity is. Indeed, you will see yourself there as well and you will find the correct *Gnothi seauton* [Know thyself] and, in addition, God himself and all creatures"[11] — in other words, the entire creation and history of the world.

Because at its deepest level it is the individualizing experience of myself as a sinner, who lives on the basis of the promise of the forgiveness of sins and by faith, the most individualized experience is at the same time the experience I can have only within the worldwide communion of the saints[12] — in a communion that spans all time and space. The Psalter, says Luther, brings you into the communion of saints, "since, no matter whether you have joy, fear,

(Wiesbaden: Insel Verlag, 1956), 9 (30-37) 33f. On the subject, see Bayer, *Autorität und Kritik*, 19-32.

10. Heinrich Bornkamm, ed., *Luthers Vorreden zur Bibel*, 3rd ed. (Göttingen: Vandenhoeck & Ruprecht, 1989), 65 (= *LW* 35:254 ["Second Preface to the Psalms," 1528]).

11. Bornkamm, *Luthers Vorreden zur Bibel*, 68; cf. *LW* 35:256-57.

12. Cf. chap. 12 below.

hope, or sadness, it teaches you to be of the same mind and to speak as did all the saints in their thinking and as they spoke."[13]

This *communio sanctorum* is wider and deeper, more concrete and realistic, than just the "community of researchers" who have been selected for their unique task from within the whole body.[14] We must give up on the notion that the question about the relationship between the authority of Scripture and reason must be framed on the basis of the model of a learned person at a writing desk, who has the Bible spread out before him. That assumes the fiction of an interpreting "I," who first establishes his relationship to the text when offering critique and when constructing his own interpretation.

This style of interpretive activity was still advocated by Johann Albrecht Bengel when he fashioned a phrase that encourages one to apply the text that is to be interpreted by turning its concerns to my own self: "Te totum applica ad textum: rem totam applica ad te!" [Turn your complete attention to the text; the matters (of the text) turn completely to yourself!]. This statement does indeed contain an aspect of truth, but it is true only in a relative sense when evaluated on the basis of the citation from Luther, according to which Scripture itself is that which changes its readers and interpreters, drawing the individual into itself.[15] Even this does not take place initially in the private activity of the individual scholar or for the one who reads the Bible all alone, but in the communicating communion of the justified sinners, most especially during the worship service.

To be sure, it is impossible to demonstrate the universal scope of this communicating communion in the abstract, as it is impossible to show the universal applicability of its biblical documents. As regards the Bible, just as in the worship service of the Christian communion that uses it, there is no pure a priori, no timeless axiom and principle, but rather a historically contingent and thus "impure" a priori.[16] One can hold certain observations to be

---

13. Bornkamm, *Luthers Vorreden zur Bibel*, 68; cf. *LW* 35:256.

14. Cf. Charles Sanders Peirce, *Schriften*, vol. 1, *Zur Entstehung des Pragmatismus*, ed. Karl-Otto Apel (Frankfurt, 1967), 260 ("catholic consent") and 261: the "all-encompassing unanimity that constitutes truth is in no way limited to human beings in this earthly life or to the human species as a whole, but extends to the community of all intelligent beings, to which we belong."

15. Cf. n. 8 above.

16. In his *Assertio omnium articulorum* of 1520, Luther calls Scripture the *principium primum* (first principle; cited in context below at n. 17). He is dealing metacritically with Aristotle's concept of scientific knowledge, according to which unlimited necessity is attributed to scientific knowledge; everything "which exists by unlimited necessity is eternal, and the eternal is without genesis and imperishable" (*Nichomachean Ethics* 6.1139b.22-24, trans. Franz Dirlmeier [Stuttgart: Reclam 8586-8590, 1969], 156). It is a huge affront when Luther calls the Bible the *principium primum*, since it is temporal, contingent, and historical. No one who refers to the

generally valid for interpreting Scripture, as well as for being interpreted by Scripture, as one comes to know about the self by means of Scripture; but one cannot set forth in advance some purely formal, hypothetical, and verifiable approach that can guarantee a result. An abstract, primal, and foundational rule of interpretation is impossible.

4.3. The Self-Disclosure of the Holy Scripture by Means of Law and Gospel

It is decisive for Luther's understanding of the Bible that he does not seek to establish its authority as Holy Scripture in advance as a *formal* "scriptural principle." Such a claim for authority, which is advocated by fundamentalists, is not possible because the conflict about the appropriate method of biblical interpretation is always at issue. This conflict can be resolved only in the *material* sense, using the substance of the actual texts to settle the argument.

In his conflict with the Roman papacy, Luther argues in a classic passage:

Say for once — if you can — according to which judge, according to which criterion, can a point of contention be decided when the opinions of two of the church fathers disagree with one another? In such a case, the decision has to be based on the judgment of Scripture, which cannot happen if we do not give Scripture pride of place. . . . Having said this, the Holy Scripture itself on its own, to the greatest extent possible, is easy to understand, clearly and plainly, being its own interpreter [*sui ipsius interpres*], in that it puts all statements of human beings to the test, judging and enlightening, as is written in Psalm 119[:130]: "The explanation," or according to its actual meaning in the Hebrew: the opening or the gate — "of your words enlightens and gives understanding to youngsters." The Spirit clearly points here to the enlightenment [of the Scripture] and teaches that insight is given only by means of the Word of God, as through an open door or (as those [scholastics] say) through a first principle [*principium primum*], from which one must start in order to come to the light and to insight.[17]

---

reformational "Scripture principle" should fail to take into account the paradox that lies therein. This Word makes sense only when understood as the description of a conflict — the conflict that academic theology presented at the time of Luther, still presents today, and will continue to present in time to come. Whoever speaks of the "scriptural principle" can do so only in radical criticism of a concept of academic study that assumes there is a timeless, pure a priori.

17. WA 7:97.19-29 (*Assertio omnium articulorum;* 1520).

But must not this affirmation also be categorized as the work of a single individual? Is it not Luther's private discovery? This *singularitas,* this type of viewpoint that is held by a single individual, was judged to be a deep form of evil for a monk; prereformational Luther was of the same opinion. Part of Luther's deepest struggle involved the question he posed as he critiqued himself time and again: Am I the only one who is right over against such a strong tradition?

And yet, Luther's thesis *sacra scriptura sui ipsius interpres,* which he claimed was correct in opposition to official Roman teaching, is not the bare affirmation of an individual; it is set forth in substantive detail when Luther identifies what he considers to be most essential in the "Preface to the Wittenberg Edition of Luther's German Writings" — with the three rules for theological study, *oratio, meditatio, tentatio*[18] — as well as in the "Preface to the Complete Edition of Luther's Latin Writings" — which discusses his discovery that the righteousness of God is provided for the sinner through the *promissio.*[19] To be sure, Luther describes this discovery when he looks back upon the way he himself traveled, but for him this involves much more than autobiographical information; for him it involves the paradigmatic description of all readers of the Bible who wrestle with the text with nothing less than the hope of salvation, who passionately knock on the door and hope thereby that a door of knowledge, that doorway to Paradise, to the true life, will open itself. Luther's description certainly sets the scene for the question about the authority of the Bible in dramatic fashion. According to it, one does not arrive at the solution to the question "in the passionless calm of a knowledge which is in the element of pure thought alone";[20] instead, it includes a change in the existence of the reader and interpreter. The Holy Scripture verifies itself, in that it awakens *faith.* As has been stated already,[21] it does not work for one to take the so-called scriptural principle and try to differentiate between a "Protestant formal principle" and a "Protestant material principle," which states the teaching about justification; one certainly ought not to treat them as separate. Both are one and the same: wrapped up in the event that takes place when the righteousness of God is actually given as a gift, at the moment the *promissio* is articulated, one encounters the authority of Scripture, its efficacy and clarity — its ability to enlighten — as well as its sufficiency: its power to bring one to salvation — if indeed Scripture is given "for

18. Cf. chap. 2.1.1-3 above.

19. Cf. n. 2 above.

20. Georg Wilhelm Friedrich Hegel, preface to the second edition of *Hegel's Science of Logic,* trans. A. V. Miller (London: George Allen and Unwin, 1969), 42.

21. Cf. n. 3 above.

the salvation" of human beings (2 Tim. 3:15). *The question about the signifi-cance of the reformational turning point in Luther's theology and the question about Luther's understanding of biblical authority are the same; they are one and the same question.*

It is not by chance that this authority to effect salvation came clear for Luther when he was engaged in the study of the Epistle to the Romans. Thus it is only at first glance that it seems arbitrary when he singles out Romans — along with the Epistle to the Galatians — as furnishing the criterion for the interpretation of the entire Holy Scripture in his 1522 preface: it is "a shining light" that is "fully sufficient for illuminating the entire Scripture."[22] Because it concerns the salvation of human beings, the "subject of theology" is "the guilty and lost human being and the justifying or saving God."[23] This is artic-ulated most clearly in Romans, which not only offers a short summary "of the whole Christian and evangelical teaching" but also offers the "point of entry . . . into the entire Old Testament."[24] Luther's identification of the subject of theology as "the sinning human being and the justifying God" corresponds exactly to what was noted earlier, that Luther had only one phrase of the en-tire German Bible typeset in capital letters: *SVNDE VERGJBT* (forgives sins) (Rom. 3:25), which he further identified in a marginal gloss as "the chief point" and the "center-point of this epistle and of the entire Scripture[25] — also of the Old Testament."[26] Luther's placement of Romans in the position of highest importance is determinative for his understanding and assessment of the individual biblical writings.

Both Roman Catholic and historical-critical camps have relegated Lu-ther's decision to elevate the importance of Romans to the status of nothing more than his personal decision, that of just a single individual. But if Scripture really is to be characterized as *sui ipsius interpres,* then this ability to interpret itself can take place only in a material fashion: in that the text itself creates faith or, to state it another way, in that the text itself distin-guishes between law and gospel for its hearers, readers, and interpreters. Only this material differentiation, which is the substance of Luther's refor-

---

22. Bornkamm, *Luthers Vorreden zur Bibel,* 177; cf. *LW* 35:366 ("Preface to the Epistle of St. Paul to the Romans"). Jörg Armbruster, *Luthers Bibelvorreden. Studien zu ihrer Theologie,* AGWB, vol. 5 (Stuttgart: Deutsche Bibelgesellschaft, 2005), indicates that a thorough orienta-tion to Romans or to Pauline theology as a whole yields the most important material presenta-tion of the rule *sacra scriptura sui ipsius interpres* (110-15, 140-42).

23. Cf. above, chap. 2.2.

24. Bornkamm, *Luthers Vorreden zur Bibel,* 196; cf. *LW* 35:380.

25. Cf. the introduction above, nn. 16 and 17.

26. Cf. 4.7 below.

mational discovery[27] but at the same time occurs afresh, ever and again, makes it possible to hear and to read Scripture on the basis of its center point, so that faith comes into existence. Scripture cannot claim to be normative in a formal sense. Rather, *its authority consists in that it works faith.* The Lutheran tradition has articulated this in such a way that its *auctoritas normativa* follows from its *auctoritas causativa* — because of the authority that it has to create faith.

Thus one must remain unconvinced by any of the three alternative models that have played a significant role in the history of the church and in spirituality. The first provides a formal teaching office, which exists in order to harmonize disputed passages. The second is to give formal affirmation to the notion that a preestablished harmony exists within Scripture, which is to be read in a flat way and which does not have a central message. The third is that there is a formal principle that lies behind the text and is to be extracted by critical reason.

"Scripture is clear and interprets itself. Indeed, this does not take place in such a way that it yields different meanings based on the understandings and perspectives of each interpreter, but it has one meaning, and this meaning is obvious; it itself makes the meaning clear; it is its own interpreter and does not need a human being — no matter who it is — to first help it along . . . by means of interpretive skills. . . . The normative function of Scripture demonstrates its claim to be normative by basing it on the way it is existentially verified when it interprets itself, in the way Scripture conveys its own intended meaning."[28] It is no secret that Luther got himself into a variety of conflicts as the Reformation progressed when he sought to use this self-interpreting ability in matters of theology and the church, and such conflicts continue even today for the church that calls itself by his name — in fact, in a way that is depicted in sharp relief by the challenge of pluralism.

4.4. Spirit and Letter

For a long time already scholars have emphasized that the biblical texts are really to be considered as God's Word — as the living voice, the *viva vox*[29] — only when they are preached, only when presented in oral fashion. To support this, words by Luther such as the following have been cited:

27. Cf. chap. 3.3 above.
28. Notger Slenczka, "Die Schrift als 'einzige Norm und Richtsschnur,'" in *Die Autorität der Heiligen Schrift für Lehre und Verkündigung der Kirche,* ed. Karl-Hermann Kandler (Neuendettelsau: Freimund Verlag, 2001), 61 and 65.
29. Cf., e.g., *LW* 3:306 (*Lectures on Genesis,* chaps. 15–20, on Gen. 19:29).

But that books even have to be written is already a great detriment and a weakness of the spirit, which has been forced by necessity, which is not the manner of the New Testament.[30]

One notes that Christ did not write; instead, he spoke everything; the apostles wrote little; mostly, they spoke.[31]

With such an exclusive emphasis on what is spoken, which follows Plato,[32] it has not been noticed that Luther placed high value on the written Word, as the source and deep foundational root of what was spoken aloud. Thus, in a sermon on 1 Corinthians 15:3-7, he emphasizes that Paul explained the death and resurrection of Jesus Christ initially by referring to human witnesses, but then gave primary emphasis to "Scripture"

in order to guard against the raving spirits who disdain Scripture and external preaching and seek some other heavenly revelation instead, since such spirits swarm everywhere at the present, being unsettled by the devil, who see Scripture as a dead letter and praise only the Spirit and yet stay true neither to the letter nor the Spirit. But you can hear at this point how Saint Paul presents Scripture as the strongest witness and shows that there is no enduring value in considering our teaching and faith as [nothing but] the physical or written word, composed of letters of the alphabet and preached verbally by him [that is, Paul] or by anyone else. For it is stated here in a clear way: Scripture, Scripture. But Scripture is not merely Spirit, as they slobber, that the Spirit alone must make things happen, since Scripture is a dead letter and cannot grant life on its own. Instead, it says: Even though the letters cannot of themselves give life, it [that is, the physical or written Word] has to be there anyway and must be heard or received and the Holy Spirit must work through these very words on the heart, and the heart can hold on by means of the Word and be strengthened in the Word in faith against the devil and all temptation.[33]

One can be sure that it was not only late in Luther's life that he rediscovered the meaning and the importance of what is scriptural. In the passage cited above from the 1522 sermon stating that books are needed because of "weakness of the spirit," he further declares:

30. WA 10I/1:627.1-3; cf. *LW* 52:206 ("The Gospel for the Festival of the Epiphany," 1521-22).
31. WA 5:537.11f. (10-22) (*Operationes in Psalmos* [on Ps. 18:45], 1520).
32. *Phaidros* 274b-278c. On the overall context of the problem in the history of theology, cf. Johannes von Lüpke, "Geist und Buchstabe," in *RGG*, 4th ed., vol. 3 (2000), cols. 578-82.
33. WA 36:500.23–501.8; cf. *LW* 28:76-77 (on 1 Cor. 15, 1532).

Christ has two witnesses to his birth and his rule. One is Scripture or the Word, which is written using letters of the alphabet. The other is the voice or the words that are spoken out loud through the mouth.[34]

And if it were helpful to express wishes, it would be best of all to wish that, to put it bluntly, all books would be destroyed and that throughout the world, especially for Christians, nothing else would remain but the plain, pure Scripture or Bible.[35]

The Bible as something that is in written form is thus identified as being more important than all other books. When it comes to understanding the gospel, the verbal proclamation is not given pride of place over against the written proclamation. Instead, faith enlightens both and unfaith darkens both — both the written Scripture and the words that are uttered verbally in the sermon.[36] Scripture aims to make the verbal happen; but the verbal does not set itself up as a rival or as an alternative to what is written. "We also see in the apostles that all their sermons were nothing other than explicating Scripture and basing their message thereon."[37] "There is no book that teaches the faith except Scripture."[38]

Thus, when it does come into being, faith begins in no other way than through the written words formed by letters of the alphabet, which have been transmitted in an impressive way in a form that one can trust, even though there are many inconsistencies in individual details, as has been determined on the basis of textual criticism. That which seeks to become new spirit and truth is ensconced in these alphabetic letters, empowered by the specific words to which God binds himself and lays aside his glory. But the new truth does not transcend the old. Instead, it returns to what is original to it and sets it in force again. God has given his oath, his word of honor, and that is not only transmitted *in* the letters of the alphabet but is also transmitted *to* the letters, entrusted to them. One could also say: God has given his oath, his word of honor — in a testament. This testament has both a verbal and a written aspect. The verbal announcement of the resurrection of the Crucified One, of victory over sin, death, and hell, is itself based on a definitive Scripture, happening indeed "according to Scripture," "in keeping with Scripture" (1 Cor. 15:3-4).

Setting it forth in written form is not setting it forth to develop a legal

---

34. WA 10I/1:625.14-16; cf. *LW* 52:205.
35. WA 10I/1:627.16-18; cf. *LW* 52:206.
36. Cf. *LW* 52:207.
37. WA 10I/1:626.5f.; cf. *LW* 52:205.
38. WA 10I/1:582.12f.; cf. *LW* 52:176 ("The Gospel for the Festival of the Epiphany").

codification of iron-clad, forced, tyrannical articulated rules; in this sense Christianity is no religion of the book, as is Islam with its Koran. For the texts of the Bible cannot be rounded out to become a system. It would be more fitting to say they create a space — indeed, by means of definitive outer bounds that cannot be probed more deeply, though there are many gaps and empty spaces that allow freedom for the readers and hearers;[39] but it does not establish an undefined freedom that would merely leave one frightened because no boundaries have been established. And yet one cannot come at it from the opposite side and maintain that one enters into a textual world in which everything matches up; one comes into a textual world where differences exist and where dissonant voices must be heard.

This is not pleasant. Time and again many have tried to smooth out what is rough, or at least to minimize such tensions. For example, the theologically well-trained and sharp-minded church father Gregory of Nyssa wanted to make "the hard, indigestible bread of Scripture digestible" with unfettered allegorical interpretation.[40] The hard bread of the literal text is made digestible in that Gregory is drawn back to a sense that was known already: what makes one feel strange gets domesticated.

By contrast, Luther remained solidly against all this allegorizing by staying with the simple meaning of the Word, the literal sense[41] — because of the clear meaning of the Word and because of the certainty of faith. If one lets the literal words stand as the "sure letter,"[42] as the sure prophetic Word (2 Pet. 1:19), then one gives recognition to the watchman who stands guard for a strangeness that serves to communicate, which forgoes resolving differences so as to remain open and thereby establishes a relationship. In this way the letter serves the spirit and faith.

What is thus of utmost importance — over against Bible fundamentalism on the one hand and the charismatic movement on the other hand, which elevates the importance of itself over that of the literal text — is that one take seriously that a *reciprocal relationship* exists between that which is fixed and that which is changeable, between the verbal and the written, between the living Spirit and the fixed literal text. Whoever does not take this to be true misses the

---

39. Freedom, above all, to apply the text to new contexts that are not in any way identical to the original situation.

40. Gregory of Nyssa, *In Canticum canticorum homilia 7* (MPG 44:925B/C).

41. On the way Luther used and abandoned the fourfold sense of Scripture: Gerhard Ebeling, *Evangelische Evangelienauslegung. Eine Untersuchung zu Luthers Hermeneutik*, 3rd ed. (Tübingen: Mohr, 1991; original 1942).

42. Friedrich Hölderlin, hymn "Patmos," in *Sämtliche Werke. Große Stuttgarter Ausgabe*, ed. Friedrich Beissner, vol. 2/1 (Stuttgart: Kohlhammer, 1951), 165-72, here 172, 225; cf. 2 Pet. 1:19.

point about the unique character of the authority of Holy Scripture, which is none other than the authority of the living God himself. Luther took into account that what is fixed and what is open-ended both exist concurrently.

4.5. "What Drives Christ Home"

In his "Preface to the New Testament" Luther speaks in an impressive way about the character of the gospel:

> *Evangelion* is a Greek word that means: good tidings; good story; good, new news; good announcement, about which one sings, speaks, and is joyful. When David defeated the gigantic Goliath, a good announcement and a comforting new message spread among the Jewish people that their detestable enemy was slain and that they were delivered, so that they were brought to joy and peace; of that they sang and leaped about and were joyful. In just that way this gospel of God and the New Testament is a good story and announcement, which resounded throughout the world through the apostles, about a true David who fought with sin, death, and the devil and who defeated them; thereby he made all who had been caught in sin, plagued with death, and overpowered by the devil into those who were righteous, living, and joyful, without any action on their part, gave them peace, and brought them back home to God once again. Of that you sing and give thanks, you praise God and are forever joyful, if you believe that steadfastly and remain firmly in faith. Such an announcement and comforting story, such an evangelical and divine new message, is also called "New Testament." Just as one speaks of a testament, in which a dying person gives instructions about how his possessions are to be divided among the heirs that are named, thus Christ also, before his death, commanded and directed that this gospel was to be proclaimed in all the world after his death, and made everything that he owned the possession of all who believe, namely: his life, by means of which he swallowed up death; his righteousness, by means of which he annihilates sin; and his salvation, by means of which he has overcome eternal damnation. Now, to be sure, the poor human being, dead in sins and ensnared in hell, cannot hear anything more comforting than such a precious, delightful message about Christ. His heart, from its very depth, must laugh and be joyful about that, insofar as he believes that it is true.[43]

43. Bornkamm, *Luthers Vorreden zur Bibel,* 168f.; cf. *LW* 35:358-59 ("Preface to the New Testament," 1546/1522).

If such an understanding of the gospel is accurate, then the question about the authoritative power of the verbal and also the written[44] Word can be answered only by pointing out that the Word — especially the preached Word — is Jesus Christ himself who is thereby present, as is the Spirit. The Word is "the voice . . . that says: Christ is now your own, with his life, teaching, works, death, resurrection and everything that he is, has, does, and can do."[45] The Word thus focuses on the sermon, since only in the midst of the community gathered for worship[46] can it unfold that for which it was given: life and deliverance are to be proclaimed and communicated.

In this way the measuring rod — the "canon" — is set up to establish what is absolute truth, what is truly new, which will never become old. That which is eternally new has a name: Jesus Christ.

> [In this way] all the correct holy books agree, in that every one of them preaches and drives Christ home. That is also the correct touchstone for evaluating all books: to see whether they drive Christ home or not, since all Scripture shows Christ, Rom. 3[:21], and Saint Paul desires to know nothing but Christ, 1 Cor. 2[:2]. Whatever does not teach Christ is not apostolic, even if Saint Peter or Saint Paul teaches it. Once again, whatever preaches Christ, that is apostolic, even if it were to be presented by Judas, Annas, Pilate, and Herod.[47]

With absolute clarity one can see where the dividing line falls that distinguishes Christian theology from a Bible fundamentalism. One cannot state it any more incisively than Luther does when he articulates the criterion that uses specific, material content — over against a claim for scriptural authority that is established on formal grounds.[48] The way and manner in which Scrip-

---

44. WA 7:97.1-3 *(Assertio omnium articulorum):* "nowhere can the Spirit be found more present and alive than in his holy books themselves, which he has written."

45. Bornkamm, *Luthers Vorreden zur Bibel,* 171; cf. *LW* 35:35.361 ("Preface to the New Testament").

46. Cf. 4.2 above.

47. Bornkamm, *Luthers Vorreden zur Bibel,* 216f.; cf. *LW* 35:396 ("Preface to the Epistles of St. James and St. Jude," 1546/1522).

48. Of course, one should note that precisely for the sake of material authority a certain "formal" room to move about freely is needed. Luther thus allows the writings that he regards as questionable, i.e., James, Jude, Hebrews, and Revelation, to remain in the canon in a "formal" sense, though they are not numbered. He does not exclude them from the canon, since others might find something canonical in them. Luther does not try to "master" Scripture; he approaches by anticipating that it is trustworthy, even at the point where he has great difficulty understanding it. A comparison of the first and second prefaces to the Revelation of John (1530) provides an example of how Luther's judgment turned positive toward it.

ture "drives Christ home" and what provides the "correct touchstone for evaluating all books," thus, the measuring rod for evaluation, is defined more specifically by the way law and gospel are to be distinguished:[49] "It has become a deplorable custom that the Gospels and the Epistles are treated like law books, in which one is to learn what we are to do, and in which the works of Christ are presented as nothing but an example held before one's eyes. Wherever this errant opinion remains within the heart, there neither gospel nor epistle can be read usefully and in a Christian way; such readers remain nothing but heathen, as before."[50] In short: the evangelical understanding of the center point of Scripture determines how to understand scriptural authority at all. The Word of Scripture that is preached and expressed verbally is nothing but Jesus Christ in his presence; he is present in the gospel as promise and gift and is to be differentiated from law.

Luther's ingenious distinction and the relationship he describes concerning the inner and external clarity of Scripture correspond to this very specific and reflective use of Scripture — to one's interaction with Scripture when applying it to the practical issues of life, which defines its "knowledge" as that by which one becomes known.

4.6. The Three Fronts for Luther's Understanding of Scripture

4.6.1. Against the Skeptical Humanism of Erasmus of Rotterdam

The clarity of Scripture is twofold, just as its darkness has a twofold character: The one, the external, is placed in service of the spoken word; the other is located in the knowledge of the heart. If you speak about an inner clarity, no human being can consider even an *iota* of Scripture to be true, unless he has the Spirit of God. Everyone has a darkened heart, so that even when they can speak about and know how to set forth everything that is written in Scripture, they are still unable to consider anything true or to recognize it truly, nor do they believe God, neither that they are creatures of God nor anything else, which corresponds to the statement in that psalm: "The fool says in his heart: God is nothing [Ps. 14:1]." The [Holy] Spirit is namely necessary for understanding the entire Scripture and every single one of its beloved parts. If you speak of the *external* [clarity], nothing remains that is dark or that can have two meanings; instead,

49. Cf. 4.3 above, and chap. 3.2.
50. WA 10I/1:8.14–9.5 ("Ein kleiner Unterricht, was man in den Evangelien suchen und erwarten soll"; *Kirchenpostille*, 1522). Cf. chap. 3.3.2 above.

everything is placed into the light through the Word and what is in Scripture is announced to the entire world.[51]

What distinguishes Erasmus from Luther is that Luther holds fast to the principle that the Holy Scripture is clear and has one meaning in those statements that are decisively important, even though some dark passages remain.[52] This principle can be formulated because Christ is its center point. In a passage that runs parallel to the closing sentence of the passage just cited, one reads:

> What can remain hidden in Scripture as regards what is exalted after the seal has been broken, the stone has been rolled away from the door of the grave, and thereby the greatest secret has been revealed: Christ, the Son of God, has become a human being, God is both triune and one, Christ has suffered for us and will rule eternally? Is that not taught even in elementary schools and sung about there as well? If you take Christ from Scripture, what else will you find in it? What is contained in Scripture is brought there to make it publicly known, even if there are a few passages that have remained dark because the meaning of the words is not known.[53]

The entire Scripture must thus be read and interpreted on the basis of Jesus Christ and in regard to what deals with him: based on what drives Christ home!

Luther differentiates between the external and the internal clarity of Scripture, without allowing the two to be separated. Whereas Erasmus argued that what does not make sense on the basis of its external wording was simply to be left to its own devices and honored "in mystical silence,"[54] Luther accentuated the relationship between the external and the internal: the external clarity of Scripture *(claritas externa scripturae)* is sufficient, in spite of the dark passages, for one to recognize Christ as its center point. The inner clarity of Scripture is the light provided by the Holy Spirit, and thus the power of God himself, which enlightens the darkened heart of the human being who is caught up in himself and is thus blind. It is the true light of enlightenment,

---

51. WA 18:609.1-14; cf. *LW* 33:28 (*Bondage of the Will*, 1526).

52. *LW* 33:26.

53. WA 18:606.24-31; cf. *LW* 33:26.

54. Erasmus, *De libero arbitrio* 1a.9. Luther is harshly critical of Erasmus's indifference, expressed in his silence on this point ("Quae supra nos, nihil ad nos" [Things that are above us, you would say, are no concern of ours]; *LW* 33:23). He is also displeased with the way Erasmus discusses this from a distance and orients himself with a view to compromise (*LW* 33:23). On the subject: Thomas Reinhuber, *Kämpfender Glaube. Studien zu Luthers Bekenntnis am Ende von De servo arbitrio*, TBT 104 (Berlin and New York: De Gruyter, 2000), 6-8.

the Holy Spirit, who justifies the godless person — the one who denies God. This light creates the human being anew, so that he confesses and recognizes himself to be a sinner and confesses and recognizes God as the one who justifies the sinner. His "knowledge" is constituted in that he is known by God and thus knows — not about himself but about the fact that God knows him.

And yet this inner clarity of the Spirit does not come except by means of the external Word.[55] Only by placing trust in the external Word and the authority of Jesus Christ that is operative therein, by the power of the Holy Spirit, can one read the Bible as Holy Scripture. By contrast, Erasmus dealt with Scripture, to state it as succinctly as possible, as a text like any other, in that he linked the question about salvation to it only indirectly.

4.6.2. Against the Formalism Advocated by Rome

From within its material center point and based on Scripture as read in this way, Luther hears the clear Word that creates assurance (of salvation). This certainty is located in the *fides specialis*[56] "by means of which I have become a Christian."[57] Cardinal Cajetan, making specific reference to just this understanding of the Word and faith as he interrogated Luther in 1518 in Augsburg, stated clairvoyantly: "This means that a new church is established."[58] In reality, even in the present there is evidence for the serious nature of opposing viewpoints between Roman Catholicism and the evangelical church in regard to understanding the Bible — not so much as this involves understanding individual texts as with reference to defining the relationship between Bible, church, and faith. The most contentious issue is to determine to which group the reproach about being a "new church" applies. Whereas from the Roman viewpoint Protestantism is a new phenomenon that presents itself in opposition to fifteen hundred years of church history, the Reformers claimed that their understanding of the Word and Scripture meant that they were returning to what was the true church, whereas the papacy was to be seen as a new phenomenon that had appeared in the meantime.[59]

These contrasting views are stated with particular clarity in the way Lu-

---

55. Cf. 4.4 above, and chap. 11.2-3 below.

56. That special and specific faith that is directed to the concrete *promissio* (cf. chap. 3.1 above, and chap. 12, n. 7 below).

57. Cf. chap. 3, n. 10 above.

58. "Hoc est novam ecclesiam construere" (Opuscula, Lyon, 1575, 111a, 7f.). Cf. chap. 12.1 below.

59. Cf. most especially *LW* 41:193-211 (*Against Hans Wurst*, 1541).

ther states his understanding of Scripture in his *Renewed Call for a Christian, Free Council* (1520): Only within such a council can it be guaranteed that "the papal power will not be over or against, but for and under Scripture and divine truth."[60] Otherwise it will come to the point "that from now on no one will be permitted to confess Christ or to read the Holy Scripture openly and will thus be forced to fall away from the correct, true, Christian faith and from the assertions of Scripture and fall into plainly false, human conceptualizations and opinions, and be driven to misleading fables."[61] The authority of Scripture clearly must be returned to have pride of place over against canon law: "I . . . yearn, first of all, second of all, third of all, that the apostles will be given to me . . . , especially by you, notaries and testamentaries."[62] Correspondingly, in the reason given in *Why the Books of the Pope and His Disciples Have Been Burned by Martin Luther* (1520), it is stated "that the pope has the power to interpret and explicate Holy Scripture according to his own will, and no one is permitted to furnish it with another meaning other than what he wants. In this way he places himself above the Word of God [cf. 2 Thess. 2:4] and rips to shreds and destroys the same."[63]

The current picture of the Roman Catholic Church and its understanding of the Scripture is presented in a more refined way. But it cannot be said that Luther's concerns have been overcome by the passage of time. According to its own declaration, Roman Catholic theology, in the present as well as in the past, sees itself bound to several "sources that furnish testimony," which to be sure are supposed to involve various levels of importance but are primarily to function together to set forth the Word of God, which remains valid and in effect today: Holy Scripture, tradition, the understanding of the faith by the people of God *(sensus fidelium)*, the church's teaching office, and finally academic theology.[64] A response offered by the Tübingen evangelical-

60. WA 7:87.23f. Cf. once again WA 7:95.10-14; 96.9-19 (*Assertio omnium articulosum;* 1520).

61. WA 7:88.1-5.

62. WA 7:88.13-15. Kurt-Victor Selge considers this in a larger context in "Das Autoritätengefüge der westlichen Christenheit im Lutherkonflikt 1517 bis 1521," *HZ* 223 (1976): 591-617.

63. *Loc. cit.*, 175.8-12 (no. 29). Cf. *LW* 31:394-95 (*Why the Books of the Pope and His Disciples Have Been Burned by Martin Luther,* 1520): "I am willing to let everyone have his own opinion. I am moved most by the fact that the pope has never once refuted with Scripture or reason anyone who has spoken, written, or acted against him, but has at all times suppressed, exiled, burned, or otherwise strangled him with force and bans, through kings, and other partisans."

64. *Communio Sanctorum. Die Kirche als Gemeinschaft der Heiligen* (Paderborn and Frankfurt am Main: Otto Lembeck, 2000), no. 44-73 (in what follows, cited as *CS*). The document was published at the end of 2000 by a bilateral working group of the Conference of German Bishops and the United Evangelical-Lutheran Church of Germany (VELKD). It attempts to formulate a

theological faculty[65] reads: the evangelical phraseology about Scripture as the norming norm *(norma normans)* is in fact accepted,[66] but the following sections that deal with the teaching office show that the "normative nature of Scripture for the Roman Catholic side [is] one factor, but not the critically determinative one, by which all other claims achieve their validity."[67] If tradition is identified as what "cannot be dispensed with for understanding Scripture,"[68] then "both elements, Scripture and church tradition, are regarded as having the same level of authority."[69] According to the viewpoint advocated in the Tübingen statement, participation of all believers in passing on the faith itself[70] ought not to be understood in the sense that one is participating in the process of revelation. It would be more appropriate, in a reformational sense, to say that the proper task of believers is "to pass on the external Word of the gospel that has been transmitted to them, along with their own confession of faith in this Word."[71]

Particularly in dispute, in the past as well as the present, is the question about the church's teaching office.[72] The following interpretation was offered to the Lutheran side: the "teaching office that is infallible under specific circumstances" — under which theology is to be subsumed[73] — should be considered to have been established by the self-interpreting nature of the Word of God, as "an instrument of God," "which serves to set forth the Holy Spirit's truth in the church and which thus does not stand in opposition to the self-interpreting power of Holy Scripture."[74] The Tübingen statement speaks against such implicit harmonizing: its opinion is that such a view maintains

---

common understanding of the church; an addendum seeks to explain elements that are specific to the Roman Catholic Church (the office of the papacy, prayers for the dead, veneration of the saints and Mary), which evangelical Christians should understand as well. The fact that evangelical conversation partners shared in the editing of the document does not mean that the principal point of the evangelical confession came to be acknowledged.

65. *Opinion on the "Communio Sanctorum,"* epd-Dokumentation no. 11 (March 11, 2002).

66. *CS*, no. 48 and 72f.

67. *Opinion on the "Communio Sanctorum,"* 14.

68. *CS*, no. 54.

69. *Opinion on the "Communio Sanctorum,"* 15.

70. *CS*, no. 57.

71. *Opinion on the "Communio Sanctorum,"* 16.

72. For a critical Roman Catholic opinion on the subject, cf. Bernd Jochen Hilberath, "Die Wahrheit des Glaubens. Anmerkungen zum Prozess der Glaubenskommunikation," in *Dimensionen der Wahrheit. Hans Küngs Anfrage im Disput,* ed. Hilberath (Tübingen and Basel: Francke, 1999), 51-80.

73. *CS*, no. 70.

74. *CS*, no. 68.

"that the 'Word of God' in actuality is taken to refer to the interplay between Scripture, tradition, and the teaching office, so that the self-interpreting power of the Word of God is thus merely the self-interpreting power that comes from the interplay of these three. But that would mean there could never be a confrontation between Scripture and the teaching office, since Scripture can have its correct sense uncovered only . . . *within* this interplay."[75]

Thus, now as in the past, the critique must be offered that the Roman Catholic viewpoint maintains that "the incarnation directly causes the church to be established as a social organization that has specific structures, to which the revealed Word of God is entrusted by the incarnate Son of God in such a way that faith can come into existence only *within* it (within the social organization of the church) — in fact in the interplay between various authorities, as sketched out, factoring in various sources that furnish testimony."[76] The five components that are identified, to use an illustration, are said to be held together by a rubber band; no one of them can speak independently — and potentially against the others — not even Scripture. When these components are discussed as an aggregate, one is left with the initial impression that something harmonious has been constructed. And yet, in light of admitted tensions and different interpretations, decisions are made in the end by the Roman teaching office.

4.6.3. Against the Spiritualizing Enthusiasts

And in these sections that deal with the verbal, external Word, one can continue to be sure that God gives no one his Spirit or his grace except through the Word or by means of the external Word that has been set in motion beforehand. This is how we protect ourselves from the Enthusiasts, that is, from those Spiritualists who boast that they have the Spirit apart from and prior to hearing the Word, and who thus judge, interpret, and reshape Scripture or the spoken word in whatever way they please. That is what Müntzer did, and many still do the same today, seeking to be a perceptive judge who can distinguish between the spirit and the letter and who know not what they are saying or advocating.[77]

---

75. *Opinion on the "Communio Sanctorum,"* 18.

76. *Opinion on the "Communio Sanctorum,"* 19.

77. *BSLK* 453.16–454.7; cf. SA III, 8, 3, in *BC,* 321. Münzer had described the Wittenbergers as "scribes of Scripture" but himself as "a scribe of the Holy Spirit." Smalkaldische Artikel, in *BSLK*, 10th ed., 454 n. 2; cf. *LW* 41:170 *(On the Councils and the Church);* WA 54:173.5-7 ("Sermon on Titus 3:5," October 12, 1537).

Where reference to the clear, lively, and external Scripture is lacking, the doorway and gateway are opened to capricious interpretation. Luther saw a threat to order in the church, but most of all to the assurance of salvation for the believers, if every theologian and preacher could step forth claiming to possess the Spirit immediately, without any way to prove that his claim was right or wrong.[78]

"That is just what the old devil and the ancient serpent did, who also made Adam and Eve into Enthusiasts, leading them away from the external Word of God to spiritualizing and to what comes from one's own imagination."[79] Whoever positions himself in this way above Scripture attributes to human interpretive skill and interpretive authority what only Christ can actually accomplish, as the center of Scripture and as the one who can interpret Scripture only by the power of the Spirit, namely, that he can put the living gospel into words and set its work in motion: to create assurance of salvation. "Therefore we ought to and must persevere in this, that God does not seek to deal with us human beings apart from his external Word and Sacrament. Everything that is praised concerning the Spirit, apart from Word and Sacrament, such is of the devil."[80] What remained latent in the humanism of Erasmus[81] came into clear view with the Enthusiasts: the inner and external clarity of Scripture are torn asunder.

Against this viewpoint Luther emphasized that the external clarity of Scripture is located within the office of the Word; "it is established in the service of the spoken Word";[82] it is a matter of establishing, of "instituting." The external clarity of Scripture involves grammatical study and includes philological criticism and hermeneutics. But it must be just as clearly noted that though such work is certainly a most important aspect, it does not explain what is meant by the external clarity of Scripture in the comprehensive sense, especially not when it comes to what is articulated most uniquely. This activity is done in service that is appropriate to the external spoken Word, in the

78. If the "enthusiasm" of this group is examined in light of the structure of thinking that is at its roots, then — in spite of the sharp contrast that seems apparent between Rome and the spiritualistic groups that were so against institutions — one can detect a way of thinking on their side about how to understand Scripture that corresponds to the Roman Catholic viewpoint. Concerning what seems at first glance to be such an astounding thesis — in light of the great differences that the two groups have concerning their understanding of the church — cf. chap. 11.2.2 below.

79. *BSLK* 454.12-15; cf. SA III, 8, 5, in *BC*, 322.

80. *BSLK* 455.31–456.5; cf. SA III, 8, 10, in *BC*, 323.

81. Cf. 4.6.1 above.

82. WA 18:609.5; cf. *LW* 33:28.

"instituting" of the "lively external Word," about which the Augsburg Confession speaks in article 5. Corresponding to this, when Luther describes the "external" clarity of Scripture, he says: "instead, everything is placed into a light that is completely clear by means of the Word, and what is in Scripture is *proclaimed* to the entire world."[83]

4.7. The Relationship between the Old and New Testaments

Law and gospel define more specifically in what sense and in what way the biblical writings of the New and Old Testament "drive Christ home" and what is "the correct touchstone for evaluating all books,"[84] thus, what measuring rod is used for critique — as discussed already. More than anywhere else, Luther's prefaces to the Bible demonstrate how he used the distinction between law and gospel as the key for understanding and for interpreting the entire Bible.

It thus states in the "Preface to the Old Testament": "here you will find the swaddling clothes and the manger in which Christ lies, to which the angels also point the shepherds. They are homely and insignificant swaddling clothes, but the treasure that lies therein is dear, Christ."[85] Luther finds both law and gospel in *both* Testaments; he finds both the sharp demand, which convicts one of sin, and also the freeing promise and gift, which saves.[86] The Old and New Testaments are obviously different only in their emphases: "As the main teaching of the New Testament is to proclaim grace and peace through the forgiveness of sins in Christ, the main teaching of the Old Testament is to teach the laws and to point out sins and to demand good actions."[87] But in principle there ought not be a division that assigns the law to the Old Testament and the gospel to the New Testament.[88] The Torah does in

83. WA 18:609.1-14; cf. *LW* 33:28.

84. Cf. n. 47 above.

85. Bornkamm, *Luthers Vorreden zur Bibel,* 42; cf. *LW* 35:236 ("Prefaces to the Old Testament," 1545/1523).

86. *LW* 35:236-37.

87. WA DB 8:12.18-21; cf. *LW* 35:237.

88. *On the Freedom of a Christian* states directly: "therefore the promises are God's Word of the New Testament and belong in the New Testament" (WA 7:24.20f.; cf. *LW* 31:349). In addition, the "Preface to the New Testament" of 1522 (Bornkamm, *Luthers Vorreden zur Bibel,* 167f. [= *LW* 35:358]) in some sense gives the appearance of such a division. Despite this, the position of the opponents must be noted here: Luther is writing against Karlstadt's division of the New Testament into legal, historical, prophetic, and wisdom books, and so he is emphasizing that the *one* gospel is the essential content of the entire New Testament. On this subject, cf. Armbruster, *Luthers Bibelvorreden* (cf. n. 22 above).

fact teach much "law";[89] but the Proto-evangelion precedes it in Genesis 3:15: "I will put enmity between you — the serpent, the devil — and the woman, and between your associates and her descendant. That one will tread on your head." That help comes through Christ, the "seed of the woman, who has trodden on the head of the devil, that is, on sin, death, hell, and all his powers."[90] For Luther, the gospel in the Old Testament is present not only in this direct way, but also indirectly — namely, insofar as the law is understood "rightly," that is, as that which leads one to the gospel:

> What then are these other books of the prophets and of history? Answer: Nothing other than what Moses is. For they all make Moses' office manifest and hinder the false prophets, so that such prophets do not lead the people to perform works, but that the people are kept within the correct office of Moses and within the knowledge of the law and hold fast to it, so that, by means of a correct understanding of the law, the people are made aware of their own incapacity and are driven to Christ [Gal. 3:24], which is what Moses does.[91]

Luther's systematic interpretation kept his sights on the entirety of Scripture because of its importance for salvation. Not every one of his observations stands up when assessed in a historical-critical way. But some of the methodologies of historical-critical exegesis admittedly have to be examined in their own right; one must ask whether and to what extent they still can or want to realize that there is a valid relationship between the various biblical writings and thus whether there is coherence within the biblical canon.

4.8. "My Katie von Bora"

A lifelong relationship develops, in fact a love relationship is formed, between the biblical text that is at hand for study, with its freeing authority, and those who interpret it, within the freedom that is granted them; it is also within certain confines that they examine this text critically, this very text that interprets them and gives them understanding: "The Letter to the Galatians is my little epistle, to which I have pledged my love [that is, to which I am married];

---

89. Bornkamm, *Luthers Vorreden zur Bibel*, 167; cf. *LW* 35:358.

90. Bornkamm, *Luthers Vorreden zur Bibel*, 169; cf. *LW* 35:359. For further evidence of the gospel in the Old Testament, Luther cites the promises in Gen. 22:18; 2 Sam. 7:12ff.; Mic. 5:1; and Hos. 13:14 (*LW* 35:359-60).

91. Bornkamm, *Luthers Vorreden zur Bibel*, 55; cf. *LW* 35:246-47.

it is my Katie von Bora."[92] It hardly needs mentioning that this love relationship cannot last for a short time only; it describes a faithful relationship that lasts a lifetime.[93]

Whoever allows himself to be interpreted and understood by means of the biblical text as "the proper way to *Gnothi seauton* [*Know thyself*]"[94] encounters therein none other than its divine author.

92. WA TR 1:69.18-20; *LW* 54:20 ("Table Talk Recorded by Veit Dietrich" [no. 146, between December 14, 1531, and January 22, 1532]). Cf. Oswald Bayer, "Lust am Wort," in *Gott als Autor. Zu einer poietologischen Theologie* (Tübingen: Mohr, 1999) 221-29; here 226f.

93. Luther's second rule of theological study speaks of this: *LW* 34:286 ("Preface to the Wittenberg Edition of Luther's German Writings," 1539). Cf. 2.1.2 above *(Meditatio)*.

94. Cf. n. 11 above.

B. INDIVIDUAL THEMES (SPECIFIC ELEMENTS OF DOGMATICS AND ETHICS)

Chapter 5   Creation: Establishment and Preservation of Community

I believe that God has created me together with all creatures, without any of my merit and worthiness.

That the teaching about justification is not an isolated topic, but that it affects the whole of theology and has importance not least of all for a theology of creation, could have been known by every Lutheran child since 1529 — namely, from the Small Catechism.

5.1. Without Word, No World

5.1.1. Justification as Creation; Creation as Justification

Luther's Small Catechism does not begin to use the explicit terminology of justification only when it arrives at the explanation of the second or the third article of the Apostles' Creed, which is what one would expect to be the case; it surprisingly appears already in the explanation to the first article, the article that deals with creation:

> I believe that God has created me together with all creatures, has given me body and soul, eyes, ears, and all body parts, reason and all senses and still preserves [them]; in addition, clothing and shoes, food and drink, house and home, wife and child, fields, cattle and all goods, provides me richly and daily with all necessities and sustenance for this body and life, protects me against all danger and guards and protects from all evil — and all that purely because of fatherly, divine goodness and mercy without any of my merit and worthiness. . . .[1]

1. *BSLK* 510.33–511.8; cf. SC II, 2, in *BC*, 354.

The word "merit" has its roots in the dispute that dealt with the teaching concerning justification; the word "worthiness" comes from the dispute concerning the teaching about the sacraments. One can detect decisive significance for the understanding of justification when justification vocabulary is brought up for discussion in the article on creation. To come at it from the other side, it is decisive for an understanding of creation that justification terminology is specifically used in its articulation. It is worth the effort to follow this pointer. Then, with Luther, we will arrive at a suitable way to define the parameters for teaching about justification, by means of which it will be possible to correct and avoid the usual constrictions that are imposed, and at the same time be able to articulate an ontology that is theologically responsible and that can be discussed philosophically.

When it was used in ecclesiastical tradition, the vocabulary used to describe justification, to which the question about "merit" belongs, was directed toward the future, dealing with balancing the books and wages, accomplishment, and completing a task, with a view cast toward the end of an individual person's life story and that of the whole world — with respect to what we have coming to us, what we deserve because of what we have done or have failed to do as individuals, as a community, and as a society that spans the whole world. Since Luther applies the concept and specific terminology about justification to the article about *creation*, it declares: it is more than simply that God no longer needs to offer a reward when he acts as judge. Instead, not owing a debt, for no reason, that is my origin and present life already.

This is made clear in the following anecdote: "Once, when Luther was traveling to Jessen [a little town on the Black Elster River] to recuperate, along with Dr. Jonas, Veit Dietrich, and other table companions, though he himself did not have all that much, he gave alms to the poor there. Dr. Jonas followed his example, with the explanation: Who knows where God will provide the same for me another time! To which Luther replied with a laugh: As if your God has not provided it for you already."[2]

The world was called into existence (Rom. 4:17) without having done anything to make it happen, purely out of freedom and purely out of goodness. "Creation out of nothing" means that everything that is made comes out of pure goodness — not because of any obligation: "and all that purely because of fatherly, divine goodness and mercy without any of my merit and worthiness."

Creatio ex nihilo, creation out of nothing, the formula that serves as the

---

2. *Reisen zu Luther. Erinnerungsstätten in der DDR,* ed. Udo Rössling and Paul Ambros (Berlin and Leipzig: Tourist Verlag, 1983; 2nd ed., 1988), 190.

basis for Jewish and Christian teaching about creation, is to be understood in the sense that Luther uses it, as a term for the doctrine of justification. Every calculating *do ut des* (I give to you, so that you give to me) is annihilated — which corresponds to the rhetorical question that Paul poses in Romans 11:35, citing Job 41:3: "Or who has given a gift to him, to receive a gift in return?" Just as all other creatures, I have, in fact I am, what was given to me. What are you, that was not given to you (cf. 1 Cor. 4:7)?

The creative Word of God that justifies, which causes one to reflect not only on its existential depth but also on its cosmological and ontological breadth, contradicts in the sharpest way possible the universal human desire for creating oneself, for self-realization, which has come into particular prominence in the present age. Fichte, Marx, and Sartre all maintain that a human being demonstrates what he is, in a much more radical sense than was the case for the human being of the Middle Ages with whom Luther had to deal, from first to last by being a doer and producer — according to Marx: in a "procreation of self" through "work."[3]

The human being who wishes to procreate himself and his world by work fails to recognize the Sabbath and Sunday; such a person fails to recognize justification by faith alone, which is effective in distinguishing between Sunday and the workday, and which can be seen in the way they are differentiated. Fichte thinks acting defines what it means to be human: "you are there for action; your action, and your action alone, determines your worth,"[4] which Sartre then articulates in the thesis that it is not one's existence that comes out of one's essence, but the reverse: the essence of the human being is the result of his existence. The human being is exactly that which he makes of himself — no more and no less; he is that which he does, condemned to his freedom.[5] "I become for myself," says Fichte, "the only source for all my being and all my outward appearance; and from now on, undetermined by anything outside myself, I have life within my own self."[6] According to the way Fichte understands it, "in the beginning" stands the action; if that is the case,

---

3. Karl Marx, *Nationalökonomie und Philosophie,* in *Die Frühschriften,* ed. Siegfried Landshut (Stuttgart: A. Kröner, 1968), 225-316, here 269. At issue is that one understands that the "true human being, because it is the actual human being, is the result of his *own* work."

4. Johann Gottlieb Fichte, *Die Bestimmung des Menschen* (1800), in Fichte, *Gesamtausgabe der Bayerischen Akademie der Wissenschaften,* ed. Reinhard Lauth, vol. 1.6 (1981), 253.

5. Jean-Paul Sartre, *Existentialism and Humanism,* trans. Philip Mairet (London: Methuen, 1949): "existence comes before essence" (26, 28); "man is nothing else but that which he makes of himself" (28); "man is condemned to be free" (34); "he is responsible for everything he does" (34).

6. Fichte, *Die Bestimmung des Menschen,* 285.

the first sentence of the Gospel of John would have to be rewritten to read: "In the beginning was the action" — my action. It is thus not surprising that Fichte said that the "assumption of a creation" is "the absolutely fundamental error of all false metaphysics and false religious teaching; one cannot follow an orderly way of thinking to arrive at the idea of a creation."[7] There is no way to get around it; this says: justification by faith alone is nonsense.

So it is clear to see: justification is not simply an isolated topic, next to which other topics can exist; it has essential importance and is connected with every topic. Justification does not affect just my individual life, not even just the history of the world, but impacts the history of nature as well; it affects all things. It is thus not sufficient to speak of the article on justification solely as the *articulus stantis et cadentis ecclesiae*[8] — as the article on which the *church* stands and falls. Instead, the meaning of justification must be taken seriously in its breadth, with ramifications that have application for a theology of creation and for ontology. In a prominent position in the Smalcald Articles Luther says: "One cannot go soft or give way on this article, for then heaven and earth would fall."[9] "Without the article on justification the world is nothing but death and darkness."[10]

The biblical and reformational understanding of a generous God, who is continuously giving, sharply contradicts the activism that is advocated in the present age, which wants nothing to be given as a gift. But God is categorically the one who gives. His giving nature defines the form that his actions take, as the one "who justifies the ungodly" (Rom. 4:5) and who in the same way "gives life to the dead and calls into existence the things that do not exist" (Rom. 4:17). Creation and new creation are both *categorical gift*. The first Word to the human being is a gifting Word: "You may freely eat of every tree!" (Gen. 2:16) — renewed in the gifting Word of the Lord's Supper: "Take and

7. Johann Gottlieb Fichte, *Die Anweisung zum seligen Leben oder auch die Religionslehre. In Vorlesungen gehalten zu Berlin, im Jahre 1806,* in *Johann Gottlieb Fichte's Sämmtliche Werke,* ed. Immanuel Hermann Fichte, vol. 5 (1845-46), 479 (sixth lecture).

8. Theodor Mahlmann, "Zur Geschichte der Formel 'Articulus stantis et cadentis ecclesiae,'" *Lutherische Theologie und Kirche* 17 (1993): 187-94, refutes the common assumption that the formula appears first in Valentin Ernst Löscher (*Vollständiger Timotheus Verinus,* vol. 1 [1718], 342f.). Cf. Friedrich Loofs, "Der articulus stantis et cadentis ecclesiae," *ThStKr* 90 (1917): 323-420, here 345. To be sure, as early as in the interpretation of Ps. 130:4, Luther states: "If this article stands, the church stands; if it falls, the church falls" [isto articulo stante stat Ecclesia, ruente ruit Ecclesia] (WA 40III:352.2f.), but he intends thus to accent the overall significance of this teaching and in no way seeks to limit the sphere of its effect to the church (cf. the passages cited in Loofs, 324-33).

9. *BSLK* 415.21f.; cf. SA II, 1, 5, in *BC,* 301.

10. WA 39I:205.5 ("Promotionsdisputation von Palladius und Tilemann," 1537).

eat. This is my body, given for you!" According to Luther, God's entire trinitarian being, within his own being as well as for us — though it is not usually emphasized in the theological tradition — is to be apprehended as giving and giving as a sacrifice.

Taking this emphasis seriously means that the first article of the confession of faith, concerning which one must pay careful attention because of the comprehensive and penetrating way it conveys the meaning of justification, is not a Court of the Gentiles. It cannot be understood without faith in the triune God; instead, it articulates the entire trinitarian faith. With love and mercy that come without any reason, God as the Father through the Son in the Holy Spirit promises to bind himself to human beings, sacrifices himself completely, shares his nature, holds nothing back for himself, hands out everything. This is how Luther summarizes the three articles of the Apostles' Creed in his *Confession* of 1528:

> This is the three persons and one God, who has given himself to us absolutely and completely, along with all that he is and has. The Father gives himself to us with heaven and earth and all creatures, so that they can serve us and be useful. But this gift has been darkened and has become useless through the fall of Adam. For this reason, at a later time, the Son gave himself to us as well, gifted us with all his works, suffering, wisdom and righteousness, and has reconciled us with the Father, so that we, once again alive and righteous, can also recognize and can have the Father with his gifts. But because this grace could not benefit anyone if it would stay hidden away very secretly and could not come to us, therefore the Holy Spirit comes and gives himself completely to us as well. He teaches us how to recognize such a wonderful blessing of Christ, which is shown to us, helps us to receive it and to hold onto it, shows how to use it profitably and how to give it to others, to multiply it and to advance it. He does this for us both inwardly and outwardly: inwardly through faith and other spiritual gifts, but outwardly through the gospel, through baptism and the Sacrament of the Altar, by means of which he comes to us as if through three means or manners, and works the suffering of Christ in us and lets it serve to give everlasting bliss.[11]

That God gives himself to us completely "with heaven and earth and all creatures" is emphasized by Luther in the Small Catechism to point out what is most elementary and thus to make clear, in its full ontological breadth, what it means to be justified only by faith in God's Word. It is not something *in ad-*

---

11. WA 26:505.38–506.12; cf. *LW* 37:366 (*Confession concerning Christ's Supper*, 1528).

dition to the human being, but in its own being, in the most fundamental, broad sense of what faith is: to have it pointed out that life and what is necessary for life has been given to me. Waiting for it, reaching out for it, that is faith; at the same time it describes my own existence, if it is true that this comes out of pure goodness and is guaranteed ever anew against any danger, purely because of mercy.

Corresponding to this, the central thesis of Luther's famous *Disputatio de homine (The Disputation concerning Man)* of 1536 articulates his theological definition of the human being: *hominem iustificari fide*.[12] The "human being" *is that being that is justified by faith alone* (sola fide), *that is, by God alone*.[13] This definition does not simply mean that justification can take place only by faith for a human being who is already alive and who has fallen into sin. It is more accurate to observe that this thesis concurrently carries with it a meaning that goes to what is fundamental anthropologically and ontologically, since it states that the essence of a human, his actual *being*, is that he can be justified only by faith.

That this ontological breadth does not imply some type of automatic soteriology — as if one could say that each human being believes in Jesus Christ already — is made clear by Luther in thesis 33: "Whoever says about a human being that he needs to be justified [*qui iustificandum dicit*] states with certainty that he is a sinner and is unrighteous and is therefore guilty before God, but that he can be saved by grace [*per gratiam salvandum*]."[14] Luther comes at it from the other side in thesis 32, where he does not deny status as a human being to anyone who does not believe in Jesus Christ. More to the point, it is also appropriate to speak fundamentally about the *nature* of a human being as a creature, even though he is corrupted by means of the *unnaturalness* of sin.[15]

In fact, in the broadest sense, it is not only in the anthropological sense but also in the comprehensive, ontological sense that one can say about creation: *mundum iustificari fidei*. Not only the human being, but the entire world is justified by faith.

But if every human being and, at the same time, the entire world have been created by God's Word and by faith, then "faith" — in the sense of the Hebrew word *emeth* or *emunah* — can be understood only as the trustworthy nature of what is given and what reaches all creatures by God's Word of ad-

---

12. WA 39I:176.34f.; cf. *LW* 34:139 (*The Disputation concerning Man*, 1536, thesis 32).
13. Cf. chap. 7.1 below.
14. WA 39I:176.36f.; trans. Gerhard Ebeling, II.Bd. 2, 297. Cf. *LW* 34:139.
15. Cf. chap. 8.1 below.

dress and promise, and faith is thus the work *of God.* Thus when Luther translated the Psalter during the years 1524-1528, he did not demonstrate the same consistency that he showed later when translating *emeth* or *emunah* as "faithfulness" or "truth" whenever God was the subject; in many passages he used the word "faith" — because the Creator gives the creature who is addressed a trustworthy foundation through and with his Word, so that this person, out of God's faithfulness and faith, exists "in faithfulness and faith." "[It] is often said to God in the Psalter: your faith, or: in your faith, because it is he who gives such faith and builds on the basis of his faithfulness; this means that the two words 'truth' and 'faith' are almost the same in Hebrew and, simply put, one can use one for the other. As we also say in German: he who is true and faithful 'keeps faith.' And it is also true that the one who 'breaks faith' is considered false and untrustworthy."[16] Luther thus advocates a three-dimensional concept of the faith: the *fides specialis,*[17] which is the saving faith of the human being in the special sense that accepts as true about himself that he is a "new creature" (2 Cor. 5:17); that which is pointed out to human beings and to all creatures that God graciously provides for all their needs; and finally, the faithfulness of God, in that he in fact has guaranteed and still guarantees such existence. Based on this guarantee and assurance — in a way that is not customary for us today — Luther can speak about a faith *of God,* as is illuminated by his translation of Psalm 146:6: "Who made heaven, earth, the sea, and all that is in them; who keeps faith forever."[18]

This broad concept of faith thus impacts the theology of creation, in the sense that creation takes on the character of a communication: *Creation is the establishment and preservation of community.*

5.1.2. Creation as Speech Act

Since creation establishes and preserves community, it is a dialogue between the God who speaks and the creatures who answer him freely, who not only answer him back but are also moved to engage one another in verbal exchanges that cause communication to happen: "Day to day pours forth speech, and night to night declares knowledge" (Ps. 19:2).

For Luther, God's address that is trustworthy, creates faith, and can be be-

---

16. WA DB 10I:96.4-9 ("First Preface to the Psalter," 1524). Cf. Rom. 3:3.

17. Cf. chap. 4, n. 56 above.

18. Thus the Luther translation from 1545 to 1912; today: "der Treue hält" (who remains faithful).

lieved, his *promissio,* is fundamental not only in the realm of sacrament and preaching, but also in the realm of the teaching about creation — which has not been noted until recently in Luther studies. This transfer of the category of *promissio* to the arena of teaching about creation admittedly causes problems: Can one describe both the activity of salvation and the activity of God in the world at large with one single category?

Support for the thesis that Luther himself understands creation fundamentally as a speech act, and that this is not just the construct of an interpreter, can be seen in Luther's translation of Psalm 33:4, a creation psalm: "For the word of the Lord is true; and what he promises, he certainly holds to it." This translation is most instructive for Luther's understanding of creation. Whereas the Hebrew text speaks of God's "work" in a noun clause, which takes place "in faithfulness," Luther, with his bold translating, testifies that God's work of creation is certainly a work, but it is concurrently a speaking work. God's work speaks on its own behalf, it is *sui ipsius interpres:* it makes itself understood. It is the working Word of address — a work by which God's faithfulness speaks: a promise.

With his trustworthy and loving Word God rules the world. Whoever responds to the Word and lives thereby, that person believes. Whoever closes himself to this Word, that person's heart, mouth, and hand shut themselves up; the entire world is too confining for him. He becomes fearful and experiences God's wrath. Then the world is no longer the medium that delivers on the promise to me, by which, having been addressed by God, I am installed into a place to live that is bestowed, with the bestowed rhythm of day and night, summer and winter, youth and age, and by which I am able to enjoy life and to relish it. If the world is not believed in as that which is promised, then it will be experienced as a "fearful natural realm,"[19] as a relentlessly necessary, oppressive law, which says: you must squeeze some sense out of this chaos, this fearful natural realm in all its uncertainty; you have to be in charge of making sense in this and out of this chaotic world; you yourself have to establish its order! If the world is not believed to be that which is promised, then it becomes, as Nietzsche aptly observed, "a thousand deserts, mute and cold."[20] In such muteness and such coldness I experience God's wrath — admittedly so anonymously that I simply cannot even identify it as *God's* wrath. All creatures around me — and it could be nothing more than a rustling leaf that

---

19. Arnold Gehlen, *Anthropologische Forschung. Zur Selbstbegegnung und Selbstentdeckung des Menschen* (Reinbek b. Hamburg, 1961), 68.

20. Friedrich Nietzsche, "Der Freigeist, 1. Teil: Abschied, 3. Strophe" (*Werke,* Kritische Gesamt-Ausgabe, ed. Giorgio Colli and Mazzino Montinari, VII-3 [Berlin and New York, 1974], 37 [from the posthumous fragments, fall 1884]).

scares me[21] — announce and speak this wrath, but most of all it comes within my own heart in its obstinacy and in its despair. Luther knows of no neutral territory beyond wrath and grace. That view frames his opinion that the world is made up of two fundamentally opposite positions; it shapes his speech and his understanding of history; it explains the reason why the battle must be waged. And it guided Luther his whole life long.

Luther was not laid so low by temptation that he sought another solution for clarifying his ideas than what is offered by the trustworthy Word of promise. That explains why the world is not transparent for him, not something that one can continuously figure out and have under one's control; his theology is obstinately opposed to any type of speculation that seeks a unified picture that could be constructed by a philosophy of history. To the degree that his theology speaks against such speculating — as for example against the illusory notion that world history is making continuous progress — it is sober, realistic, and shaped by actual experience of the world.

The "worldliness of Luther" that is brought up for discussion and is so often misunderstood is thus shaped theologically, through and through. The theological frame of reference shows that one can apprehend the world as having been created by the trustworthy Word of God and is being continually preserved, even though assailed by continuous dangers; one comprehends it on the basis of judgment and grace.

Creation is speech act. Such a view brings wide-ranging consequences in the present as well, with respect to academic theory. In the situation presented by the ecological crisis, it becomes increasingly necessary to speak theologically about the *immanence* of God *in the world*. Such a call is all the more necessary when one understands that theology has been caught up for a long time in an individualistic view of God that has sought to be distanced from the world, advocating that one is to seek direct dialogue with God without seeming to be bound by space and time. But the danger today is that the character of the creative activity of God as *address* is no longer adequately appreciated when one adopts the model of process philosophy or a theoretical model shaped by cybernetics. The history of the emancipation of the natural sciences, which has concurrently resulted in their growing isolation from any connection with the living world and with wisdom, can be described in large measure almost as a history of *removing the role of speaking from one's view of the world*. Assuming a schema of causality has left the Cre-

---

21. Luther often cites Lev. 26:36. Cf., e.g., *LW* 45:58 (*A Sincere Admonition by Martin Luther to All Christians to Guard against Insurrection and Rebellion*, 1522): "The sound of a rustling leaf shall terrify them."

ator with nothing much but to play the role of "first cause," and the creation is the "effect." The implications of the history of this schema, which started with the Platonic and Stoic *Logos* concept and achieved a more important role when the Scholastics made use of Aristotle, were not so apparent to Luther as to us today. In spite of that, Luther identified the crucial issue when he understood creation as a gift and promise — creation as establishment and preservation of community — and thereby opened up perspectives that can be particularly instructive and fruitful for discussion and for an exchange of ideas in this day and age, as we interact with the natural sciences and natural philosophy.

To achieve a clearer picture of Luther's understanding, it is helpful to make a brief comparison with the Calvinist-Reformed tradition, in which God is considered much more to be the transcendent one who operates in a vertical sense from above and has a propensity to be mute about what he causes. In light of this view, "the reality of being a creature is primarily characterized in the way it describes reliance on God";[22] Schleiermacher's "feeling of absolute dependence" and his understanding of God as absolute causality stand in this Reformed tradition. As much as "the world of creation is dependent upon the ongoing action of God and reflects his omnipotence," just that little, according to this Reformed viewpoint, "is it thinkable that the power of the Creator is the kind of power that can enter into what is created. By contrast, without restricting God's freedom, Lutheran theology interprets the reality of creation above all as the context for communication."[23] God did not reveal himself for the first time in the redemption of the world, but already at its creation and in its preservation; he poured himself out; he gave of himself completely; his almighty nature is one that humbles itself. Creation thus understood is gift and promise — both as establishment and as preservation of community, and in this sense it is speech act!

One can also track this understanding of creation — as one that involves communicating — in our own time, wherever the world is comprehended as a text to be read.[24] This admittedly takes place with less obvious intensity and by means of metaphors — such as when one speaks about the "genetic code" or when using the word "information," which cannot be completely abstracted from its verbal connection and linguistic connotations.

Responsible discussion that deals with the theology of creation must be

---

22. Johannes v. Lüpke, "Schöpfer/Schöpfung VII. Reformation bis Neuzeit," in *TRE* 30 (1999), 305-26, see 312.

23. Lüpke, "Schöpfer/Schöpfung VII," 312.

24. Cf. Hans Blumenberg, *Die Lesbarkeit der Welt* (Frankfurt am Main: Suhrkamp, 1981).

articulated in the present time by critically assessing two extremes. It must chart a course between a personalism that is *distanced* from the world, represented by approaches such as dialectical theology, and an *immanent* way of thinking that finds complete happiness in this world, connected most of all in the modern era with the name Baruch Spinoza. In light of the task to avoid both extremes — that of personalism and that of Spinoza's way of thinking — one can learn what is decisive from the Old Testament scholar Luther. He continues to hold fast to God's primordial promise: "I am the Lord, your God,"[25] thus holding to the character of the creation as address. But at the same time, he accentuates the presence of the Creator within his creation as a freely willed immanence and as a penetrating presence: God is "in a manure bug or even in the cesspool . . . no less than in heaven."[26] Both aspects — that which involves immanence and God's address — belong inextricably together.

5.1.3. God's Nature as the One Who Comes Beforehand

This connectedness can be articulated in the following thesis: God *comes* in the Word to me, together with all creatures, as the one who has *always already come beforehand* in the Word, who is with me and in me.

Talk about God coming to the world says that his presence in the world is not self-evident and is not deserved. But God comes to the world only as the one who is always already present in the world: *among* all creatures and *in* all of them — "deeper, more within, more present than the creature himself," as Luther stated it when he reformulated Augustine's famous statement that God is closer to me than I am to myself.[27] In this deepest presence he is the *Deus actuosissimus,*[28] the most active God, as Luther demonstrated in *De servo arbitrio* by contrasting that with the *Deus otiosus*, the idle, inactive god who keeps his hands on his lap, which is what the Epicurean gods do.

But only when one speaks about the God who is already present and who has come beforehand, concentrating on the fact of his coming, is it clear that

---

25. Exod. 20:2; LC II, 8.

26. WA 18:621.16-18; cf. *LW* 33:45 (*The Bondage of the Will,* 1526). Luther takes up a challenge from Erasmus (*De libero arbitrio* 1.a9) and states it even more strongly.

27. WA 23:137.33; cf. *LW* 37:60 (*That These Words of Christ "This Is My Body," Etc., Still Stand Firm against the Fanatics,* 1527). Cf. Augustine, *Confessiones* 3.6.11. On the subject: Joachim Ringleben, *Interior intimo meo. Die Nähe Gottes nach den Konfessionen Augustins,* ThSt 135 (Zürich: Theologischer Verlag, 1988).

28. WA 18:747.25; 711.1; cf. *LW* 33:233; 33:178.

God's presence is certainly not self-evident, particular in regard to *how* he is there. For in his presence and in his nearness in the innermost being he can affect me just as much in an oppressive way, burning like a consuming fire, as he can be near me in a freeing and enlightening way. For liberation and enlightenment to take place, the coming must take place in the Word that addresses one with an offer of assurance, in which Word God allows himself to be found. It is somewhat different, Luther emphasizes, "when God is there and when he is there *for you*. But he is there *for you* when he applies his *Word* and binds himself to it and promises: you are to find me here."[29]

In the congruence of the coming and the fact that God has always come beforehand already, the creation takes place as a community of the Creator and the creature, as well as the creatures being in a community with one another. Both settings and factors belong together in an inseparable way; neither can be disengaged from the other. If God were always very obvious among and in his creatures already, he would not need to come to them. If God would remain as the absolutely transcendent one, no dialogue could take place. In any case, petition and lament would be inappropriate; resignation would be all that would be left. But the non-Priestly creation narrative speaks about a God who communicates, who deals in such an earthly and creaturely way that "the dust of the ground" (Gen. 2:7) is not too dirty for him to come to human beings through it; the new creation takes place in this way as well (Mark 7:33; John 9:6).

5.2. "Be Opened!"

In a most remarkable way, Luther preached on September 8, 1538, on the story of the healing in Mark 7:31-37, the Gospel text for the day (Twelfth Sunday after Trinity). This sermon[30] is most remarkable in the way it addresses the question about "natural theology" as that relates to the teaching about creation.

5.2.1. Unable to Communicate

Luther's sermon is marked from beginning to end by the dualism of faith and unbelief, being closed to communication by one's own self or being open for it, deafness and hearing, blindness and seeing; it preaches about the power of unbelief and the still stronger power of faith.

---

29. WA 23:150.13-17; cf. *LW* 37:68.
30. WA 46:493-95.

On the one hand it says: "The entire world is deaf . . . !" "They have ears but do not hear";[31] "they have eyes but do not see."[32] On the other hand it says: "The whole earth is filled with speaking." If we would give ear, we would hear wonderful things. "Pythagoras, the heathen philosopher, says that the movement of the constellations provides a very lovely consonance and harmony, being in accord with one another in a fine way; but human beings are now satiated and bored because of persistent habit. So it is with us; we have such beautiful creatures, but no one notices them because they seem so common."[33] The whole world is filled with speaking — the whole world is deaf! Corresponding to these observations, two series of formulas that characterize opposites are presented in one and the same sermon; they are appropriately based on the Pauline formulas that set forth complete opposites, according to which God consigned all to disobedience so that he might have mercy on all (Gal. 3:22; Rom. 11:32) and that faith came to them in this way.

But the dualism of faith and unbelief is not static, not fixed. It is more correct to say that it involves a conversion from unbelief to faith that results in the abrogation of the dualism. It involves a change of orientation from unbelief to faith a decisive turn to faith, which does not consider the dialectic to be permanent in principle, to be an oscillating back and forth. Nevertheless, this change of orientation from unbelief to faith is not to be thought of as a chronological progression, as was often taught within Pietism — as if a person changed direction once, at a particular moment in the past, and then made linear progress, both in going forward and in going upward — as if we could ever leave far behind us this change of direction from unbelief to faith, while we are still on our journey through life; we realize instead that it is more correctly always still in front of us, so that we believe and thus "wait" for it with eager longing (Ps. 104:27; Rom. 8:19).

The transitional point, the change in orientation from unbelief to faith, involves a conversion to the world, a turning toward the creature. It involves a conversion toward the world as conversion toward the Creator when one hears his "voice,"[34] which he allows to be heard through all his creatures, in which he addresses us through the creatures.

Luther's understanding is expressed in exactly the same way by Johann Georg Hamann, who crafts the following formula in his *Aesthetica in nuce:*

31. WA 46:495.1.
32. WA 46:495.32.
33. WA TR 5:225.11-14 (no. 5539; 1542-43).
34. WA 46:495.24.

"Creation" is "address to the creature through the creature."[35] Rörer's sermon transcript preserves this understanding in the six different ways it is depicted[36] — with the most stimulating being the following phraseology: "Sheep, cows, trees when they bloom, say: 'Ephphatha.'"[37]

"Be opened!" (Mark 7:34). Is not this the Word of Jesus Christ himself? His own Word that he spoke? Must one disagree with Luther when he seems to slip such words without much fanfare into the mouths of sheep, cows, and blossoming trees? Is Luther not falling into the heresy of natural theology? Or, to judge less harshly, does he try out some ingenious game, for which a poet might be given license but not a preacher and a theologian?

What is represented in this sermon is designed to bring together what for us is commonly distinguished, what would normally be assigned to separate categories and treated as opposites, such as Christology and natural theology; salvation and healing; Word and nature; creation, reconciliation, and final consummation. What we separate carefully, as if under a strict taboo, seems to be all mixed together here.

It can help to sharpen the point being made in this sermon and the peculiar way in which the ages are intertwined, as they are here, if we listen to what comes in a table talk from roughly the same time period:

[We] are presently in the dawn of the age to come, for we are beginning to acquire once again the knowledge of the creatures that we lost through Adam's fall. Now we can look at the creatures much more correctly, more than at any time under the papacy. But Erasmus is not interested in and is hardly concerned about how the fruit forms in the womb of the mother, how it is given shape and is made; he is also hardly concerned about the marriage relationship, as majestic as that is. But we begin, by the grace of God, to recognize his majestic works and wonders even within the little blossoms, when we reflect about how almighty and good God is. Therefore we praise and glorify him and thank him. We recognize the might of his Word in his creatures, how powerful it is. For he spoke and it came to be [Ps. 33:9] — even through a peach stone. Even though its outer shell is very hard, in its own proper time it must open up because of its soft center, which is inside. Erasmus passes over this artfully and looks at creatures the way the cow looks at a new [barn] door.[38]

---

35. Johann Georg Hamann, *Sämtliche Werke*, ed. Josef Nadler, vol. 2 (Vienna: Thomas-Morus-Presse im Verlag Herder, 1950), 198, 28f.

36. WA 46:494.4f., 21; 495.2, 6, 21f., 23f.

37. WA 46:495.21f.

38. WA TR 1:574.8-19 (no. 1160).

The first sentence in this table talk, which serves as a kind of summary, makes clear that this describes no idyllic scene. Nor does it give evidence of some arrogant awareness that one belongs to a new era that has just now broken in; it does not go so far as to say that one can call such a world into existence by one's own reason and strength. The "dawn of the age to come" seems to have much more to do "with the grace of God." God's grace allows itself to be heard afresh "now" (cf. 2 Cor. 6:2) and opens ears, eyes, heart, mouth, and hands to apprehend the world as creation: "We are beginning to acquire once again the knowledge of the creatures that we lost through Adam's fall."

This astonishment is something quite different from a piety about the cosmos of a type that has never detected any disruption, as is called for at present — in the ecological crisis — by more than a few as a means of restoration, for which many yearn with eager longing in any case. The new astonishment, the second naïveté, comes rather because of the defeat of a world of death, into which the human being has allowed himself to be dragged and into which he has dragged his fellow creatures — because of his own fault, stubbornly.[39] Everyone who hears must view himself being addressed within the context of sin that universally connects everyone, and no one can somehow relieve himself of the burden by pointing to the common history shared by all human beings.

The plot, according to which this sermon will consign each person who is caught up in his deafness and dumbness to a sickness unto death, is provided for Luther by Paul (Rom. 1:18–3:20): each person — because God makes it happen — can hear God through his fellow creatures and can respond to him with praise and thank him; but none does it, not even one.

The ungrateful nature of the human being is depicted in a multifaceted repetition — drastically, distinctly, concretely: if we had our eyes and ears open, then the flowers would speak to us, as would our possessions and money; "even the grain would talk to us: 'Be joyful in God, eat, drink, use me and serve your neighbor with me.'"[40] But what comes instead of this: ingratitude and covetousness. "Thus we ruin the joy for ourselves with cares and coveting, so that we shame our Lord, God."[41] "Your cares and coveting" do not run their full course because of God's long-suffering nature and patience,

---

39. Luther accentuates the way guilt and hardening are intertwined through his noteworthy use of Ps. 135:15-18 (WA 46:494.35ff.): he interprets having ears yet not hearing in the sense it is used in Isa. 6:9-10. Cf. Rom. 1:18-23 and 1 Cor. 1:21.

40. WA 46:494.15ff.; cf. Eccles. 9:7. Luther is always concerned with the move toward service to the neighbor — as a move away from covetousness (lines 9, 12, 14, 17, and elsewhere).

41. WA 46:494.24f.

because of "his profound goodness,"[42] not because of us. "We are not worthy [that even] a bird should sing and that we should hear a sow grunt."[43]

The ingratitude is reinforced by the cares and the coveting that come when the human being turns away from his Creator, closes himself in on himself and at the same time closes his ear, his heart, and his hand to his neighbor. The great emphasis that Luther places on coveting calls for special attention; each time the list ends with coveting and with greed.[44] Luther sees coveting as the action of a person who closes in on himself, the *incurvatio in se ipsum,* which has come to its concluding point — to an end that has demonic depth. Turning in on oneself is idol worship (cf. Col. 3:5).[45]

Being possessed in this way, being possessed by the self, shows that I have misconstrued and dislodged my creaturely nature and my function within creation as a whole, as Luther notes when he refers to the Old Testament criticism of the worship of idolatrous images.[46] "The idols of the nations are silver and gold, the work of human hands. They have mouths, but they do not speak; they have eyes, but they do not see; they have ears, but they do not hear, and there is no breath in their mouths. Those who make them and all who trust in them shall become like them" (Ps. 135:15-18). But in a way that differs from the Old Testament text, Luther does not speak about other people but about us ourselves. "We" are like the idols, about which Psalm 135 speaks; no one can extract himself from that condition. Luther cites these verses because of the conclusion that is drawn, according to which not only do the images look like the image makers, but the image makers look like their images. According to Luther — though it is not stated this way in the psalm — this has universal application. Each person is affected by this assessment in his relationship to the world and to himself. "This is now the citizen, the farmer. They do not serve God but each himself. But they cannot see that the gold, silver, and grain, which they have and which they hold tightly, those things cannot see and hear; such is a dead god. . . . Briefly: As

---

42. WA 46:494.31

43. WA 46:494.35.

44. In addition to the passages named in n. 40, cf. WA 46:494.23, 25, 31f.; 495.9, 34f. ("withhold the grain"), and 39.

45. Cf. especially the context in WA 46:494.35–495.4, 9: "They were greedy and worshiped their idols." Cf. *On the Freedom of a Christian:* "Does not a man who does this deny God and set himself up as an idol in his heart?" (in *Three Treatises* [Philadelphia: Fortress, 1960], 285). The German version reads that man "denies him with such unbelief and sets up an idol that he himself invents, against God, that he himself conceives" (WA 7:25.16-18). See chap. 8 below.

46. WA 46:494.35ff.

their gods are blind, so are they, for they have ears and cannot hear what God calls out through his creatures."[47]

Luther's analysis and portrayal of fallen human nature have not become less of an issue in the present age; instead, to a shocking extent, such a view has won the day. God can no longer address us and call us through the natural world. He cannot do so any longer, since such dealing with nature cannot only be partial — which is right and necessary — as possessing, owning, and using. Instead, everything takes place now as an insatiable grabbing for all that one can get. Such behavior needs to be evaluated in terms of its meaning, on the basis of what Luther says in a sermon: they do not serve God; thus they do not serve one another either, but they serve the gold, silver, and grain that they possess and that they want to clench tightly — in coveting and by being in love with what is dead. They cannot hear the Creator any longer from within the things of the world, because they no longer use them in a communicative way that involves thanking, receiving, and distributing to others.

"We do not hear, even if the entire world and [all] creatures call out and [through this medium] God [himself] makes promises [to us]"[48] — but it is still this same God who, as we have heard already in Luther's *Confession* of 1528, "has given himself to all of us, fully and completely, along with all that he is and has. The Father gives himself to us with heaven and earth and all the creatures, so that they can serve us and are to be used."[49] *The central point of Luther's understanding of creation is that the whole world and all creatures call upon him and that God uses this medium to promise and to give himself completely to us.* The creation is "our Bible in the fullest sense, this our house, home, field, garden and all things, where God does not only preach by using his wonderful works, but also taps on our eyes, stirs up our senses, and enlightens our heart at the same time."[50] This "Bible in the fullest sense" can admittedly be recognized only by faith, "which we have already established previously on the basis of Scripture. . . . Chris-

---

47. WA 46:494.37–495.2.

48. WA 46:495.4f.

49. WA 26:505.38-41; cf. *LW* 37:366. The entire trinitarian-theological context must be kept in mind when one seeks to understand this text completely: *LW* 37:366. Cf. the conclusion of the exposition of the creed in the Large Catechism (1529): "how God gives himself completely to us, with all his gifts and power" (LC II, 69, in *BC*, 440).

50. Sermon of May 25, 1544, on 1 Cor. 15:36ff.; WA 49:434.16-18; see pp. 422-41. The goal of this sermon: we should "learn to strengthen our belief in the resurrection of the dead by means of the work that God exercises daily toward his creatures through his omnipotence" (WA 49:423.10-12).

tians can thus talk with the trees and everything that grows on the earth, and those plants can answer back."[51]

For Luther the world is the world that God promises. *Creation is the promised world.* But whoever closes himself off from the promised world, as has been mentioned already, the heart, mind, and hand close themselves off for that person; the whole world is too constricting for him. He gets afraid and suffers the wrath of God thereby. All creatures around me announce and articulate this wrath, but my own heart is the worst culprit in its stubbornness and in its despair, alone with itself and with those who are like it, squatting down on its own haunches. That is the original sin. That is the sickness unto death: the human being sits down on himself, is possessed by his own self, and thus binds himself off from life.

What this has to say with specific reference to the problems of the modern way of designing the world and controlling the world — with very specific reference to the claim of instrumental reason for dominion — was formulated for the first time for the philosophical consciousness by Blaise Pascal and is noted even today as a benchmark in its history. He talked about nature as that which speaks, but which merely gives hints that there is a "lost" and "hidden" God: "Nature is such that it [can do no more than] point out the loss of God everywhere — both within the human being and outside the human being — and it points to a corrupted nature."[52] Hegel took up this fragment from the *Pensées* and the diagnosis that was attached to it, expanded upon it, and spoke about the "death" of God.[53] Others, not the least of which was Nietzsche, have also spoken about the death of God when they articulated their own historical location.[54]

5.2.2. Word of Power in Sighing

Only a word of power can conquer death. Two passages from the sermon speak directly and openly about the Word of power uttered by Jesus Christ,

---

51. WA 36:646.15-20; cf. *LW* 28:180 (sermon of December 22, 1532, on 1 Cor. 15:36ff.).

52. *Pascal's Pensees,* introduction by T. S. Eliot (New York: Dutton, 1958), 124.

53. Georg Wilhelm Friedrich Hegel, *Faith and Knowledge,* trans. Walter Cerf and H. S. Harris (Albany: State University of New York Press, 1977), 190. On the subject, Edgar Thaidigsmann, *Identitätsverlangen und Widerspruch. Kreuzestheologie bei Luther, Hegel und Barth* (Munich: Chr. Kaiser Verlag, 1983), chap. 2.

54. Dieter Henke, *Gott und Grammatik. Nietzsches Kritik der Religion* (Pfullingen: Neske, 1981), has shown that Nietzsche's cry "God is dead!" is not a statement of fact, but a prophetic pronouncement about the age.

which turns death into life, sickness into wholeness, driven to being possessed by oneself into openness, being closed in on the self into participating in community.

The first reads: Because the devil "hinders, even turns [praise and thanksgiving] in the opposite direction, so that we misuse [our tongues] by blaspheming God and wronging the neighbor — to our own damnation — for this reason he [Jesus Christ] sings out: 'Ephphatha!'"[55] More important even than this first passage is the second, which discloses the background and the way the Word of power uttered by Jesus Christ against the devil functions; in its context it reads: "You can thereby [because of the fatherly concern of the Creator] be happy and you can see and comprehend this [the goodness of God]; but even though we have eyes, we do not see. For this reason the Lord sighs on account of us."[56]

Whoever sighs is pressed hard. He is driven into narrow straits and fear; for this reason he laments and calls out. Only when Jesus sighs does the uniqueness of his Word of power become apparent. Taken by itself, this utterance could be understood as a simple word of command from above. But since this Word of power comes from below as well, out of the depths, it points to the sighing. It is God's Son, the Lord, our brother, who sighs. In this way he takes part in the fallen world and lets himself be pressed hard by obsessions. Sighing is the way and means whereby Jesus, as the true human being and as our brother, expresses solidarity with the fallen creation.

Jesus' Word of power thus does not come separately from sighing and suffering, not apart from his death. This undoubtedly active moment — the anger, the aggression against the power of perdition, against sickness, against dumbness, against closedness, against that which contradicts God's original creative will, against the demonic and devilish, against what is perverse — this undoubtedly active moment is connected integrally with a passive moment: when he joins in the suffering, when he takes part in the fallen creation and its misery. Jesus Christ is not only the Lord in his Word of power that brings freedom, but he is also brother; he is not only true God but also true man.

He sighs as man and God, as one who suffers with others and as one who overcomes suffering, because of love in the form of a wrath that acts in mercy.[57] This active mercy is most creaturely, worldly, and human in its divine power, using what is material in an offensive sort of way; in the address it

---

55. WA 46:494.13-15.

56. WA 46:495.31f.: "Dominus propter nos gemit" [The Lord sighs because of us].

57. So there is no alternative between Jesus' mercy and his wrath (cf. Mark 1:41; contra Eduard Schweizer on the passage [NTD 1, 11th ed. (1967), 31]: "not Jesus' mercy . . . , but . . .").

makes use of utterly material means. As the Creator, in his humility and condescendence, got his hands dirty and took hold of the soil, in order to create human beings (Gen. 2:7),[58] in the same way Jesus Christ, in order to re-create this fallen, possessed, sick man who lived in the world of death, put "his fingers into his ears, and he spat and touched his tongue" (Mark 7:33).

Not separated from this address by creaturely means, right in the middle of this healing process that is effected thereby, there comes the decisive Word: "Open up!" The turning point from the old to the new world, from the fallen to the redeemed world, from unfaith to belief is concentrated in this Word. "Open up!" That is the Word of Jesus Christ the Crucified, who lives. His Word — his self-revelation — is *verbum efficax;* it is "promise" in the categorical sense, *promissio.* It does not make a promise in the sense that it sets something forth as an expectation and thereby puts you off until later. *This promise is much more; it is its own fulfillment; it fulfills itself, and this actually does not take place at a later time, but at the very moment it is uttered; it is* promissio *as a valid promise that takes effect immediately.* The ear and the mouth open up right when Jesus Christ speaks; locked doors open up; chains release their hold. In this way the Word is an active, efficacious Word.

5.2.3. "Natural Theology"?

Without question, Luther assumes that the miracle story does not report an isolated miracle. The Word of Jesus Christ that re-creates, "Open up!" takes place instead in such a way that *all* creatures begin to speak at the same time; the world that has been closed to me up to this point becomes in a new way an address from God. "It is preached here, so that we are enabled to hear. Sheep, cows, trees when they blossom, say: 'Ephphatha!' . . . All creatures call to you! Therefore: Go ahead, open your ears!"[59] One ought not miss the point that a petition is integrated into the powerful Word. The Word of creation and of the new creation does not suppress the petition, but gives it proper place.

The most surprising point in the entire sermon is that Luther, without digressing and in a theologically bold way that is most strange to our ears, takes

58. Luther stresses this in the *Disputation concerning Man* (1536), in opposition to the god of metaphysics, especially the god of Aristotle, who is sunken in himself and is not turned toward man in any emotional and physical way: *LW* 34:143 (cf. 1:84 [*Lectures on Genesis,* chaps. 1–5, 1535-36, on Gen. 2:7, 1535]): "In short, philosophers know nothing about God the creator or about man made of a lump of earth" (*LW* 1:84 translates "reason . . . knows practically nothing about God, etc."). Cf. 33:291; WA TR 1:57 (no. 135; 1531); 73 (no. 155; 1531-32).

59. WA 46:495.20-24.

the Word that Jesus Christ himself speaks in the miracle story and claims it as a Word that every creature speaks to us. For Luther, this means that Jesus Christ is so powerful when he speaks his Word that he discloses the entire world to us. The speaker is powerful in his speaking because of his sighing, his passion. It is established in his passion that the world opens itself; no longer does it have to be mistaken due to unbelief, but it can be correctly apprehended by faith. As has been noted already, this presents a very unique point of access to nature, and it is in no sense naive. An aesthetically direct relationship to nature is no longer possible, after "the sun's light failed" and "darkness came over the whole land" (Luke 23:44-45). At the same time, when Jesus cried out on the cross, he tore asunder the difference between an aesthetic view of creation that is pious about natural things and that second naïveté, by means of which he allows the lilies of the field and the birds under heaven to communicate the care and goodness of the heavenly Father — he, the Crucified One, who lives. Only through the mediation of the One, through his Word, can nature speak as creation; he is the mediator of creation.

Luther answers the decisive question about whether the swallow of a single healing miracle makes the entire summer of the reign of God, and what this one healing miracle — experienced at that time and place by one single human being — can mean for the restoration of the whole world by using the figure of speech: *per minora ad maxima*: "By means of that [single] little miracle he awakens us, so that we can understand the larger issue, that the entire world is deaf because it does not understand."[60] In this way Luther presses on energetically and quickly beyond the one, individual miracle — which he observes: it is not all that significant when compared to others — to speak of everything as a miracle, of the world as a miracle, of the entire creation.[61] A new understanding

---

60. "Per minora illa miracula excitat, ut intelligamus maxima, quia totus mundus est surdus, quia non intelligit" (WA 46:493.26f.).

61. The same thought is present in the sermon on Mark 8:1-9 from Cruciger's *Sommerpostille* (1544): "For one sees him doing this every day throughout the whole world. All that the world has takes place purely by means of such miracles that are not any punier or less significant or smaller than this (as also the holy Augustine [MPL 35, 1593] says). Of course, we are so used to the grain growing out of the earth each year, and through such habit we are so blinded that we pay no attention to such activity. For what we see and hear daily we do not regard as miraculous, and yet it is in fact just as great a miracle — indeed, if we should rightly speak of it, an even greater miracle — that he gives grain from sand and stone than that he feeds the crowd here with seven loaves. . . . These are the very miracles that were established from the beginning of the world and that come forth within it daily, so that we are quite overloaded by them, yet — since they are so common — our eyes and senses do not take it in. At times, then (as he does here), God must perform not some greater miracle, but some special one that does not happen according to the usual course of nature, in order to wake us up. Through these particular and

of what is "natural" and temporal is stated thereby; God's activity as Creator can be comprehended in the penetrating way it plays out in the here and now.

If one considers the sermon as a whole, it is surprising how Luther preaches the text as a *concretum universale:* universal — but not speculative; personal — but not individualistic; existential — but not as a demand to pull back from the world, as an abstraction from the world, but in the interplay of consciousness of the world and of the self. Existence and the world are held together in the same way as are salvation and restoration. But Luther does not veer off into pure contemplation. As long as we are still on the pilgrimage, it is always about unbelief, which the law discovers, and faith, which the gospel creates by its promise. "You will never acquire what you strive for in your greed. [But] you, whose eyes have been opened, remain in your joy. . . . You will have enough!"[62] "As you believe, so you have!"[63]

It is clear in this sermon that the world in Luther's view does not allow one to perceive it as creation in a pristine way; the article on creation is an article *of faith.* Creation faith is faith in the triune God. I recognize the Father once again only through the Holy Spirit — empowered by the work of Jesus Christ. The teaching about creation cannot reflect the world as creation in an immediate way; one must remember there is brokenness: the breakdown and the new creation. Sin has distorted communication between God and the human being, between God and the world; it has in fact corrupted it. Thus one ought not to fear that Luther's teaching about creation will transfigure the world as it now stands. It is marked by courage for living that destroys and overpowers the alternatives of optimism and pessimism, passion for the world and fleeing from the world.

5.3. Consummation of the World as Reestablishment of the Creation

The most important temporal mode in the Bible is the present. The future of the world comes from within God's present. The salvation being distributed in the present comes with the guarantee that the world will reach its consummation and permits the contradiction between the suffering and sighing creature of the old world and the experience of the promised creation, the

---

special miracles he must direct and lead us into the daily miracles that happen in the whole wide world" (WA 22:121.1-22).

62. WA 46:495.39f.

63. WA 7:24.13; cf. *LW* 31:348-49.

original world, to be experienced through pain. God's new creation makes the old world into the old one and restores the original one once again.

This unique way that Luther intertwines the tenses is characteristic of his understanding of creation. In his interpretation of the biblical story of creation, he provides the following hermeneutical key for teaching about creation:

> We speak about these goods as if they are a treasure that we have lost, and we are right to hope, even while sighing, for that day on which everything will be reestablished once again. Of course it is useful both to remember the goods that we have lost, as well as the evil that we endure and in which we live most miserably, in order to be spurred on to that hope of the redemption of our bodies, about which the apostle speaks in the eighth chapter of Romans. Concerning what relates to the soul, we are freed through Christ, and we hold firmly to this deliverance in faith, until it becomes visible.[64]

When he offers this aid for reading, what Luther advocates for learning the story about creation is neither simple remembrance nor simple hope; instead, it is grounded in present experience as it affected him and his theology when he experienced the reformational turning point. The hope for the creation, which involves remembering its glory that was lost, is grounded in faith in the promise of the forgiveness of sins, as it can be heard in the words of absolution, in baptism, and in the gifting words in the Lord's Supper — as well as in every correct sermon.

God reigns by this verbal, physical, and creaturely promise and the faith that is created thereby. Just as the Word of the promise of salvation also works when it is not believed, namely, in unfaith as judgment, so also the Word of promise for the world functions apart from the faith of human beings — even against one's unbelief and against one's sins, in actuality even through them, in that "God punishes one scoundrel by means of another."[65] God's promised world continues to exist because of his faithfulness. With his long-suffering nature and patience, God preserves the world from the chaos that we human beings have caused, and he preserves it for his own future time.

---

64. WA 42:80.35-40; cf. *LW* 1:106. The distinction and also the connection between "soul" and "body" are used here in the same specific sense as in *On the Freedom of a Christian* (1520). The tractate provides evidence that Luther is referring to the unique overlapping of the ages mentioned above when he uses this distinction — as well as when he speaks of the "internal" and "external" human. The temporal concept of the "new" and "old" man helps one understand how Luther uses the distinction between "soul" and "body," and "inner" and "outer" human. Cf. especially *LW* 31:344, 358.

65. *BSLK* 600.16; cf. LC I, 154, in *BC*, 407.

Because of a hardheaded misunderstanding — rooted in prejudices of the modern age — it seems that talking about how God as creator acts to preserve things now is hard to square with talking about a future that one expects yet to come from God — it sometimes seems that one directly contradicts the other. This misunderstanding can be cleared up. It arises because it seems that one looks back to an absolute beginning when one uses the word "creation," whereas what really matters when looking toward the future seems to be that it is directed toward an absolute goal of pure future, with tendencies toward progress, which is the opposite of having restorative tendencies. This orientation, which has held sway since the French Revolution, is at odds with the understanding of creation that is taught by Luther from the Bible; it is thus our task to get past the unfortunate way that progress and restoration have been juxtaposed as an alternative, and certainly not just acquiesce.

Right within its name, which summarizes the way it understands itself, the "modern age" makes a salvation claim — the claim that it will bring forth what is completely new, that the good it brings is unsurpassable newness. But it has brought terror as well. This occurs not least because of the constant desire to go still further yet, beyond what is new, demanding that salvation will come through permanent revolution.[66] What this modern age wants to set in motion as unsurpassable newness is what an uncritical theology sees as the newness of the new creation of God.

This consciousness of time in the modern age and in a theology that tries to accommodate itself to such a view fails to recognize the way the times are interwoven, which is determinative for Pauline theology and for Luther's theology. From within what is already new in God's present comes the future of the world; the new creation that opens itself up in the present time in baptism and in the Lord's Supper makes the old, perverted world into the old, past world and presents once again the original world as creation.

It is not only hard to conceptualize how the ages are connected to one another since these times are not all happening at the same time and yet they are uniquely interwoven; it is even more difficult to live it. It is understandable that one would rather retreat to a universal chronology and a conceptual

---

66. With all the factually unavoidable, and essentially necessary, conflict over the articulation of self-understanding in the modern age, no one can overlook the theological elements. On the subject cf. Günther Bornkamm, "Die Zeit des Geistes. Ein johanneisches Wort und seine Geschichte," in *Geschichte und Glaube* I [*Gesammelte Aufsätze*, vol. 3] (Munich: Kaiser, 1968), 90-103; Ernst Wolf, "'Erneuerung der Kirche' im Licht der Reformation. Zum Problem von 'Alt' und 'Neu' in der Kirchengeschichte," in *Peregrinatio,* vol. 2 (Munich: Kaiser, 1965), 139-60; Gerhard Ebeling, "Erneuerung aus der Bibel," in *Erneuerung aus der Bibel,* ed. Siegfried Meurer (Stuttgart: Deutsche Bibelgesellschaft, 1982), 14-26.

framework for history as was done by Johann Albrecht Bengel,[67] or instead, that one would choose to go the opposite way, to isolate the "here and now" in "the moment," as was done by Bultmann and Kierkegaard, with making a leap through by means of one's "decision." Luther does not focus on such a momentary moment, nor does history become transparent in his view by discovering a chronological ordering of time;[68] for him the key to understanding the world is not in the number, but in God's promise.

Insofar as Luther's theology, along with his understanding of creation, contradicts all historical speculation — such as the illusion of continuous progress as world history unfolds — it is sensible, realistic, and full of concrete experience of the world. By contrast, the hope of faith — the hope "that God alone is just"[69] — does not come about by experiencing the world. Just as in the book of Job and for Paul (Rom. 11:33-36), such hope for Luther is rooted instead in faith in God the Creator, for which the passive righteousness of faith frees a person. Hope in God's future for the whole world, yearning for the "light of glory,"[70] turns itself toward creation. It trusts the efficacious Word, which creates life, which protects and preserves community. Justification of the ungodly, resurrection of the dead, and creation out of nothing[71] take place only through this promise.

67. Johann Albrecht Bengel, *Ordo temporum* (1741). For a comprehensive treatment: Gerhard Sauter, "Die Zahl als Schlüssel zur Welt. Johann Albrecht Bengels 'prophetische Zeitrechnung' im Zusammenhang seiner Theologie," *EvTh* 26 (1966): 1-36.

68. Luther's ideas on chronology and his calculations — cf., above all, the appended charts for the whole of history in the *Supputatio annorum mundi* (WA 53:1-184; 1541/1545) — are not decisive for his understanding of history. This understanding lies rather in the fact that "the human being is determined by his affective states, both in his passive and his active relationship with history" (Reinhard Schwarz, "Die Wahrheit der Geschichte im Verständnis der Wittenberger Reformation," *ZThK* 76 [1979]: 159-90, 182 n. 62). One should note when comparing Luther with Bengel that the wisdom element is no more lacking in Luther than is the existential in Bengel.

69. Heinrich Bornkamm, ed., *Luthers Vorreden zur Bibel*, 3rd ed. (Göttingen: Vandenhoeck & Ruprecht, 1989), 59-61, here 60 ("Preface to the Book of Job").

70. *LW* 33:292 (in the context of pp. 288-92, *The Bondage of the Will*).

71. Particularly in his *Large Commentary on Genesis*, Luther set forth his understanding of creation out of nothing. For current discussion of the subject, cf. Johannes Schwanke, *Creatio ex nihilo. Luthers Lehre von der Schöpfung aus dem Nichts in der Großen Genesisvorlesung (1535-1545)*, TBT 126 (Berlin and New York, 2004).

Chapter 6

The Order of the World:
Church, Household, State

Here is the institution of the church;
it is before household and state.

In his overflowing goodness, the Creator creates for his creatures the space that is necessary for life — but he does not retreat afterward so as not to get in the way of his creatures as they act independently. Instead, he uses his communicating Word, by which he provides regulations and guidelines to establish relationships that make communication, exchange, and community possible; he fills everything everywhere and, without begrudging it, exercises the virtue of giving freely.

The freedom that is promised to the human being is to be used to take note of the world around him, to give it order — by assigning names (Gen. 2:19-20) — and to organize it.[1] This activity takes place within a framework of responsibility, which Luther teaches in a principled and yet elementary, catechetical fashion when he teaches about the three estates.

To our way of thinking today, "standing" (being stationary) is used opposite "mobility" (being on the move), which is the way modern society is characterized. The older concept of estate lost its meaning at the latest in the middle of the nineteenth century. In modern German it merges [Trans.: and has dropped completely from current English usage in this sense], as a historical and sociological term, with terms like the "state of estates" and the "society of estates" and is used in everyday speech to describe little more than "interests of a group," special interests. Only in the words that describe one's "ethical stance" and "standing of the family," along with the "registry office" that keeps track of one's legal "standing," is the earlier meaning still present. When sociology speaks of one's "status" or "standing," it refers to the station or standing "acquired" by the

1. Cf. chap. 7.2 below.

self as one rises and falls socially; it distinguishes this from what was considered in an earlier age to be "assigned," when one's standing came to a person by birth; one's social location today, in which one lives one's life, is no longer a matter of inheritance; it comes by one's own effort.

"Rapid social change" has become the chief identifying marker and the term that is used to describe being orientated toward continuing to make things change. What remains is change; the constant is that nothing is constant. Nevertheless, it is not merely that the only constant is that there are no constants; constants still exist. There are basic needs, such as hunger, thirst, and sexual drives, which seek to be satisfied but cannot be satisfied in a completely satisfactory manner because such needs never go away.

Language is decisive when it comes to characterizing the changeable nature of human beings, furnishing us with a wide-ranging first step in the process of developing symbols. Language provides a way to give nature a conceptual framework, identifies categories, arranges the steps to be taken as something is dealt with; it is only through the use of language that human life is possible from the perspective of what is remembered and what is hoped for. Luther reflects on the concepts that are at issue here in his teaching about the three stations or estates. The main point here is to unfold what is meant by "the element itself" and "the way it is applied," which cannot be further refined to unify the two aspects. If one were to seek a way to apply what Luther says concerning questions posed at present by anthropologists and sociologists, the comparable terms would be "nature and institution."

In what follows, Luther's teaching about the three estates will first be presented in light of the main features of each (1), guided by his theological testament, the *Confession* of 1528.[2] After this will come an extensive treatment of the first of the three estates, the church, as an order of creation (2); the problem of natural theology discussed in chapter 5 will be elucidated from this perspective.[3] A third section will examine the other two estates, the household and the state, in greater detail (3), before we come to the concluding section (4), which will show how love establishes the criterion for proper teaching about the three estates.

---

2. WA 26:503.35–505.28; cf. *LW* 37:363-65 (*Confession concerning Christ's Supper,* 1528). Of course, this text is so short that it takes on the character of a formula or thesis statement. One needs to consult more detailed parallel texts to illumine its meaning with respect to individual motifs.

3. Chapter 5.2 was arranged *christologically.* From that vantage point, the *extent* of creation that was affected by the healing miracle was at issue. In this chapter we will come at it from the opposite direction. The *extent* of the concept of creation and religion will be discussed with respect to the *specifically Christian* understanding of God.

6.1. Main Features of the Teaching about the Three Estates

Luther's teaching about the three estates refers to the way he interprets for his contemporaries the primeval biblical history in terms of a theology of creation, a theology of sin, and ethics for society, and how he applies such insights: "these estates of God are to be found in and remain in every kingdom, as far as the world extends, and will last until the world comes to an end."[4] The teaching about the three estates in life has such a primeval and fundamental meaning for Luther that he uses it to articulate the first rule of scriptural interpretation: "In the first place, the Bible speaks and teaches about the works of God; about that there is no doubt; but these are divided into three hierarchies: household, state, and church. If there is a statement that does not fit for the church, then we allow it to stay in the realm of the state or the household, wherever it best fits."[5]

The most pregnant summary of his mature understanding is to be found in his interpretation of Genesis 2:16-17, from 1535:

This is the establishment [*institutio*] of the church, before the household and the state existed. . . . A church is thus established [here] that has no walls or any kind of external features, set in the broadest and most pleasant space. After the church was instituted, then the household was established as well. . . . So the temple comes before the house, just as it is also placed on a higher level. There was no state before there was sin, since it was not yet necessary. The state is the necessary means for dealing with the depraved condition of nature.[6]

Luther speaks here about three fundamental forms of life, in which God's promise organized human existence and organizes it still; following tradition, Luther calls these "estates." They can be described briefly as follows:

a. The fundamental estate is that of the human being who is addressed by God, who is furnished with the ability to respond freely in thankfulness. For the human being to be human means that he is addressed and he can thus hear, and he himself can speak in response, but he also must respond. The divine address and the expectation that the human being will respond set the basic framework for what happens in the religious realm — for honoring God, for the basic way

---

4. WA 31I:410.16f.; cf. *LW* 13:369 (on Ps. 111:3, 1530).

5. WA TR 5:218.14-18; cf. *LW* 54:446 ("Table Talk recorded by Caspar Heydenreich" [no. 5533, winter of 1542-43]). As an example, WA TR 2:642.27f. (no. 2762; 1532).

6. WA 42:79.3-14; cf. *LW* 1:103-4 (*Lectures on Genesis*, chaps. 1–5, 1535-36). Cf. 1:115 (on Gen. 2:18) and 131 (on Gen. 2:21), as well as pattern: WA 42:22.17-32.

church and religion operate — which is understood here as an order of creation;[7] all human beings and all religions belong to it. Every human being belongs as a human being — which is what defines one as human — to the church, because it is an order of creation. It no longer actually exists as the church because it has been corrupted by human ingratitude, because of sin.

b. Inserted within the fundamental estate of the church, within this fundamental estate of Word and faith or else Word and unfaith, permeated and enveloped by it, one sees another estate, also an order of creation, the household, which is at times also referred to by the term "economy." Luther articulates what is meant by this estate as the relationship between parents and children, between a husband and a wife, between human being and field, thus, as work: the interrelationship of the human being with nature, the acquisition of his means of sustenance, his daily bread.

c. Luther would not recognize the third estate, the political or what is often referred to today by the word "state," as an order of creation; it is an order made necessary at the time of the fall into sin — even though he certainly knew that the state is established within the household,[8] which must have been included from the outset if one would consider the ramifications of the household estate.

These three basic establishments[9] are "three institutions or orders"; Luther identifies them elsewhere as "estates" or "hierarchies," "comprehended in God's Word and by his command." "But what is established in God's Word must be a holy thing, since God's Word is holy and sanctifies everything about it and in it."[10]

But the state came into being because of the fall into sin, with its ability to force compliance to maintain just order, but that is not all; sin corrupted the two orders that clearly belong to the orders of creation: the foundational estate (the church) and the household estate (the economy). But in spite of their depravity, they are not destroyed; even though they are corrupted, they are still held fast by God's promise and are thereby sanctified. Even through their depravity one can still recognize and believe in the power of the Word of God that creates and forgives.

---

7. Cf. especially *LW* 1:103 and 106 (on Gen. 2:21).

8. Cf. nn. 97-99 below.

9. Though each individual can design the specific way in which these three basic estates can take specific shape in one's own life, this in no way gives them "the character of a tempting offer" (versus Ernst Wolf, *Sozialethik. Theologische Grundfragen*, ed. Theodor Strohm [Göttingen: Vandenhoeck & Ruprecht, 1975], 171), which could also possibly be refused and rejected. No one can escape from these basic estates as such.

10. WA 26:505.8-10; cf. *LW* 37:365.

In his preface to the Smalcald Articles, Luther articulates in the briefest fashion the reformational self-understanding: "Our churches are now enlightened and equipped by God's grace with the pure Word and the correct use of the sacraments, with a recognition of all estates and right actions, so that we from our side no longer ask for a council, and concerning these issues we know that we could not hope for or expect anything better from a council."[11] The correct apprehension of the Word as sacrament and the sacrament as Word, on the one hand, and the estates, on the other hand, is described, in the same concise way as in the Smalcald Articles, also in various table talks,[12] with attention given to these two topics as the two chief points. Luther can boast that they are the embodiment of his "Reformation."[13] Luther's *Confession* of 1528 concentrates on these two main points,[14] as does the Augsburg Confession in its overall arrangement.[15] They identify the two major emphases of the catechism as well; *On the Councils and the Church* concludes in a noteworthy way with two special emphases, which correspond to the first and second tables of the law.[16]

Such a preponderance of evidence leads one to conclude: Luther's own testimony shows that the teaching about the three estates carries much greater weight for him than the teaching about the two realms of God.[17] The

11. *BSLK* 411.20-26; cf. SA, preface, 10, in *BC,* 299; cf. SA, preface, 14, in *BC,* 300.

12. Cf. especially WA TR 1:573.14-23 (no. 1158); 3:689.18-34 (no. 3889; 1538); 4:179.10-12 (no. 4172; 1538). Cf. also *LW* 54:42-43 ("Table Talk Recorded by Veit Dietrich" [no. 312; 1532]); *LW* 54:43-44 (no. 315; 1532) and n. 4 above.

13. "Yes, I think I have held a council and created a reformation. . . . For it is true that the correct catechism is on its proper course with our little band, that is, the Lord's Prayer, the confession of the faith, the Ten Commandments, and also what is involved in repentance, baptism, prayer, the cross [i.e., suffering], life, death, and the Sacrament of the Altar. In addition, it deals with what is involved with marriage, temporal authority, father and mother, wife and child, a man and his son, servant and maid. In brief, I have brought to proper awareness and order all the earthly estates, so that each knows how to live and how to serve God in his estate" (WA 26:530.7f., 28-34; cf. 26:531.26-34 [Luther's preface to *Concerning the Marriage as Priest of the Honorable Licentiate Mr. Stephan Klingebeil,* 1528]). Cf. *LW* 43:11-12 (*Personal Prayer Book,* 1522).

14. The bulk of the material in the *Confession* consists of passages that teach about the estates and that discuss ecclesiology, which is based on an explication of the Word itself. The large amount of material dedicated to this topic is not here just by chance; this text was presented with utter seriousness before both God and the world, consciously and on purpose. (On the relation of the *Confession* of 1528 to SA III, see *BC,* 298.)

15. Cf. Wilhelm Maurer, *Historischer Kommentar zur Confessio Augustana,* 2 vols. (Gütersloh: Gütersloher Verlagshaus, 1976/1978); Oswald Bayer, *Leibliches Wort. Reformation und Neuzeit im Konflikt* (Tübingen: Mohr, 1992), 57-72 (with the two main points: the "public character of faith" and the "freedom of life").

16. Cf. *LW* 41:9-178, here 148-66 (especially 165-66) on the one hand, and 166-67 on the other.

17. Cf. chap. 14 below.

teaching about the two realms does not appear in those texts that offer summaries and testaments.

If greater weight were given to Luther's teaching about the three estates when his writings are appropriated for today, many futile discussions could be avoided. There is danger when it comes to Luther's teaching about the two realms that one can single out sexuality, marriage, family, rearing, education, and business and assign such topics to the political sphere as "temporal" rule, playing these off against "spiritual" rule. One might even go so far as to summarize the contrast of the two realms by reducing it to a simplistic contrast between state and church. Taking it further yet, it is usually not noticed, when spiritual and temporal rule are distinguished, that the spiritual aspect is not only an inward concept but is also externally involved in temporal matters and that temporal matters, in just the same way, are spiritual — insofar as they deal with the temporal rule *of God*. The teaching about the three estates thus prevents the various settings just mentioned from being played off abstractly against one another or from being treated as altogether separate issues.

In light of the strict differentiation that he makes between the spiritual and the temporal in his teaching about the two realms, it is most astounding that Luther, when he teaches about the three estates, lines up the spiritual estate with the other two estates, treating it together with what he otherwise distinguishes sharply as the "temporal" over against the "spiritual." He makes it possible and urgent — which materially goes against the rigid opposites assumed by dialectical theology — that one reflect on Christianity as religion, institution, and a world phenomenon, as well as to provide a theologically responsible way to deal with the unavoidable problem of civil religion.

To start with, the fundamental estate, the church, must be distinguished from the other two estates — which admittedly should not be treated on the same level either; the *oeconomia* is more fundamental than the *politia*. The fundamental estate deals with the relationship to God, with faith and unbelief. At the same time, the *status ecclesiasticus* is not to be equated with God's spiritual rule. After the fall into sin and before the eschaton, the Christian church is not the pure kingdom of God, as is the invisible church; instead, visible and invisible elements permeate it. In this world and in this age the *status ecclesiasticus* is also an estate of government: pastors are paid; they can be removed after a process wherein objections are brought concerning their teaching or for disciplinary reasons, etc.[18] In that sense spiritual rule is also temporal, and as such the ambiguity of the actions that stand under judgment cannot be eliminated.

18. Cf. chap. 12 and chap. 14.6 below.

Neither the teaching about the two realms of God nor the teaching about the three estates ought to lay claim to greater importance at the expense of the other. When one cites a passage from Luther, one must at a minimum take into account the astonishing versatility of the way Luther uses specific accents drawn from his interpretation of Scripture to inform the conscience in a specific situation. Then he shifts once again — a versatility that corresponds to the overall approach he uses when he is moved to say something at one point and uses the schema of how to distinguish the two authorities. Then he jumps to distinguishing among the three estates, even though the distinguishing elements are often interrelated. In any case, Luther's versatility precludes a simple and schematic articulation of his ethics by evaluating something such as his teaching about the two realms. On the other hand, one ought not err by advocating that the teaching about the two realms can be easily integrated with the teaching about the estates.

6.2. Church as Order of Creation

When one speaks of the foundational estate of the human being, the church, as an order of creation *(status ecclesiasticus)*, the question is posed once again about natural theology, which we examined earlier with reference to Luther's preaching on the healing miracle in Mark 7.[19]

The first Word of God to the human being, according to the non-Priestly creation story, is the promise of life (Gen. 2:16): "You may freely eat . . . !" This promise of life is protected by a threat of death (Gen. 2:17): "But of the tree of the knowledge of good and evil you shall not eat, for in the day that you eat of it you shall die." About this promise and threat Luther observes concisely in his 1535 Genesis lecture: "This is the establishment of the church, before the household and the state existed";[20] no special church, but a general one: "without walls."[21] It exists in Word and in faith — in that God calls the human being to life, "preaches" to him in this way, "sets his Word before him,"[22] and thus "desires only that he praises God, offers him thanks, so that he will rejoice in the Lord."[23]

It seems astonishing at first glance that worship of God, that the church,

---

19. Cf. chap. 5.2 above.
20. "Haec est institutio Ecclesiae, antequam esset Oeconomia et Politia" (WA 42:79.3; cf. *LW* 1:103); cf. n. 6 above.
21. WA 42:79.4; cf. *LW* 1:103.
22. WA 42:80.2; cf. *LW* 1:105.
23. WA 42:81.3f.; cf. *LW* 1:106.

is located already in an "order of creation" and is not a uniquely Christian institution. The benefit of the knowledge that is gained through this thesis will be demonstrated in what follows.

From the primeval promise of life that is valid for every person (Gen. 2:16), together with the self-revelation of God: "I am the Lord, your God!" (Exod. 20:2), and from the first commandment, to have no other gods beside him (Exod. 20:3), which uses the threat of death to protect the promise of life (Gen. 2:17), an appropriate "natural theology" comes forth, and concurrently, a religious phenomenology. In the sense that it is used in Romans 1:18–3:20, it assumes that there is a relationship with God that is lived out by every human being, but which is actually and in practice always a failure; it is a broken relationship. Reason — not primarily the theoretical, but rather the practical variety that is guided by the power of the imagination — is grasping for God already, but always misses the mark, so that Luther (concerning Jon. 1:5: "Then the mariners were afraid, and each cried to his god") can formulate the concise statement "that these people in the ship all knew about God" "but had no certainty of God."[24] To make God the true and certain God is the office of Jesus Christ.

6.2.1. Reasonable Knowledge of God

Jonah 1:5 calls for reflection about the relationship to God for those who are not Christian, over against the relationship that Christians have to God; Luther, in fact, interprets the book of Jonah as Christian theology. Decisive here is what is brought into the discussion by Romans 1:18-21: "For the wrath of God is revealed from heaven against all ungodliness and wickedness of those who by their wickedness suppress the truth. For what can be known about God is plain to them, because God has shown it to them. Ever since the creation of the world his eternal power and divine nature, invisible though they are, have been understood and seen through the things he has made. So they are without excuse; for though they knew God, they did not honor him as God or give thanks to him, but they became futile in their thinking, and their senseless minds were darkened." Some would like to see this passage stricken from the Bible. But it not only exists there; it is also true: "Here you see that it is true, what Saint Paul says in Romans 1, how God is known to all the heathen, that is: the whole world knows how to speak about the deity, and natural reason recognizes that the deity is something great — above all other

---

24. WA 19:208.21f.; cf. *LW* 19:56 (*Lectures on Jonah*, 1526).

things."[25] Just as Paul makes use of Stoic thinking in his argumentation that this means that no human being can be excused, thus Luther also makes his argument — note carefully: not unsubstantiated, but by using the text from Paul — by using a type of evidence for God that is affirmed by common human consensus *(e consensu gentium),* as it is known to him from Cicero's *De natura deorum:*[26] by pointing to evidence for God that is held in agreement by all peoples. On this point Luther considers himself to be one with Paul, with the Stoics, in fact with "the whole world": "The whole world knows to speak about the deity."[27] Correspondingly, his explanation of the first commandment in the Large Catechism reads as follows: "For there has never been a people that has been so sacrilegious that it has not arranged for and held a worship service."[28] Luther certainly takes into account that the *consensus gentium* concerning the existence of God or concerning the existence of a variety of gods that are to be honored is not without its detractors. Certainly, he writes, there were "some like the Epicureans, Pliny, and the like who denied it with their mouths, but forcibly and powerfully they try to deny the light that is in their heart." They "do it as do those who forcibly stop up their ears or shut their eyes, so that they do not see and do not hear. But it does not help them at all; their conscience tells them something different."[29] It is noteworthy that not only when the argumentation begins but also here, after Scripture has been cited, it says: "Paul does not lie."[30] The biblical text is not accorded a purely formal rule. It convinces, it enlightens; its truth cannot be denied. It can also be demonstrated in the sense used in the phenomenology of religion: "That is shown when these individuals . . . called upon God, even though they were heathen. For if they had known nothing of God or of the deity, how would they have desired to call upon him or to cry out to him?"[31]

When Luther wants "to learn from nature and reason,"[32] as he interprets Jonah 1:5, it shows that what he thinks can be learned from nature and reason

---

25. WA 19:205.27-30; cf. *LW* 19:53.

26. Just as was common throughout Western tradition, Luther also used this text as a fundamental reference point when he discussed the problem of natural theology. It was first removed from the discussion, as such, by David Hume in his *Dialogues concerning Natural Religion* (appearing posthumously in 1779).

27. Cf. n. 25 above.

28. *BSLK* 563.37-40; cf. LC I, 17, in *BC,* 388.

29. WA 19:206.1-5; cf. *LW* 19:53-54. Cf. John Calvin, *Christliche Unterweisung. Der Genfer Katechismus von 1537* (Christian instruction: The Geneva Catechism of 1537) (Gütersloh, 1978), first part, especially 7-11.

30. WA 19:206.5f.; cf. *LW* 19:53-54.

31. WA 19:205.30-32; cf. *LW* 19:53-54.

32. WA 19:206.7; cf. *LW* 19:53-54.

is to be found in the Scripture.[33] It will not take long for us to come to the point in his interpretation where Scripture and reason will be juxtaposed irreconcilably at opposite extremes, and the essence of the matter will cause reason to be described as the "whore":[34] "Faith kills reason."[35] But here at this point Scripture and reason are in agreement. One must thus differentiate and consider carefully the point of reference, noting at which time an irreconcilable antithesis exists that cannot be overcome by thinking it away — and contrast this with what is discussed in a different context in which the two are in agreement.

Simply put: Where exactly is the point of agreement? It refers to a specific act and inseparably, almost indistinguishably, to a specific content.[36]

As far as the specific act, it is expressed when one "cries out to God" in a petition that comes ecstatically — from within deepest need. Prayer even from one who is not a Christian shows that "natural reason"[37] has some type of knowledge that some sort of god exists.

The act of prayer, of calling out to God, is tied to a specific expectation. Even though the heathen who fear they are going to lose their lives "do not believe in God in the right way, they still have such a sense and opinion that God is such a being who can help them there in the sea and in all times of need."[38] "Such people view God as a being that can help them out of all evil. It follows thereupon that natural reason must acknowledge that all good things come from God. For the one who can help a person out of all evil and misfortune is one who can also give them all good things and happiness."[39] Luther's treatment of the first commandment in the Large Catechism also states that all human beings expect from God good things, happiness, and at the same time deliverance from all misfortune, rescue when in need:

33. This insight also guides the discussion of the problem of natural theology in old Protestant orthodoxy. What nature and reason have to say for themselves they say according to the witness of *Scripture*. Scripture itself says that nature speaks and that God reveals himself through nature — "day to day pours forth speech" (Ps. 19:2).

34. Cf. chap. 7, n. 17 below.

35. *Fides occidit rationem* (WA 40I:363.6; cf. *LW* 26:228 [on Gal. 3:6]). Cf. Gerhard Ebeling, *Fides occidit rationem, Luther-Studien*, vol. 3 (Tübingen: Mohr, 1985), 181-222.

36. In reference to a specific act by which and in which one believes, hopes, and trusts; an expectation directed toward something (*fides qua creditur*), and in reference to a specific content, the *fides quae creditur*, that which is believed — a distinction used in this formulation since Augustine (*De Trinitate* 14.8.11).

37. WA 19.205.29; cf. *LW* 19:54.

38. WA 19.205.33f.; cf. *LW* 19:54.

39. WA 19.206.8-11; cf. *LW* 19:54.

A god is that from which a person expects all good things and that to which a person will flee for protection in every time of need. Thus, to "have a god" is nothing other than to trust and believe in him with all one's heart. As I have often said, it is trust and belief in the heart alone that makes both God and an idol. If the faith and trust are rightly placed, then your God is true as well and, by contrast, if the trust is false and not genuine, then the true God is not there.[40]

Thus what is essential, according to the opinion of all the heathen as well, states that to "have a god" means trusting and believing, but the problem is that their trust is false and not genuine; for it is not oriented toward the one God, apart from whom there is truly no God in heaven or on earth. For this reason the heathen actually make their self-conceived darkness and their dream about God into an idol and place their trust in mere nothingness.[41]

Luther maintains that such false faith does not know any differently about God than does the true faith; those "who do not believe in God in the right way"[42] know the same things about God as do those who believe in him in the right way. For both expect God's goodness that gives gifts and mercy that delivers. Astounding! Luther insists: "Such light and reason is in every human heart and does not allow itself . . . to be extinguished."[43] "This is how far the natural light of reason extends, that it considers God to be one who is good, gracious, merciful, mild; that is a great light."[44] Luther speaks this magnificently and boldly about reason, which he calls a "whore" at other times — which means: such reason wrongly uses what is good.

6.2.2. True Belief in the Creator

In what way does reason wrongly use its proper knowledge about God, namely, concerning his goodness and mercy? Natural reason "is deficient in

---

40. *BSLK* 560.10-21; cf. LC I, 2-3, in *BC*, 386. On the existential aspect, cf. LC I, 5-6, in *BC*, 387: "There are some who think that they have God and everything they need when they have money and property; they trust in them and boast in them so stubbornly and securely that they care for no one else. They, too, have a god — mammon by name, that is, money and property — on which they set their whole heart. This is the most common idol on earth."

41. *BSLK* 564.9-19; cf. LC I, 18-20, in *BC*, 388.

42. Cf. n. 38 above.

43. WA 19:205.35–206.1; cf. *LW* 19:53.

44. WA 19:206.12; cf. *LW* 19:54.

two major aspects,"[45] in that the knowledge about God has a direct impact on (a) one's own existence and (b) in the precise way that the encounter with God takes place.

The phraseology "is deficient in two major aspects" seems to suggest that "natural knowledge"[46] simply needs to have something "still more" added to it because something is missing — maybe so that some grace could be added to bring it higher, which would not counteract what is there by nature but would only bring it to completion. But such appearances are deceiving. If one examines the matter more carefully, one can see that the issue is not that two extra aspects are needed, it is not about quantifiable modifications, but is rather about what is qualitatively different.[47] True faith does not have something added to it, so that it simply has more of something than what false faith has, but it is something totally different — this same knowledge but undamaged; and yet false faith knows just as much about the goodness and mercy of God as does true faith.

a. What is that line from *The Threepenny Opera*? "And one remains totally ordinary!" True love, by contrast, does not remain "totally ordinary." The same holds true for true faith. True faith "has no doubt that God wants to be merciful not just to others but to me as well. That is a proper, living faith and a great, rich, rare gift of the Holy Spirit."[48]

Is such talk not scandalous for every system of logic? Is it not true that whatever I know to be true in general is what, in particular, I am able to apply to myself as well — and according to logic must apply to myself? Mentally, in a certain intellectual sense, I can indeed do it — but not with a true, that is to say, certain, faith. I know, for example, that I must die. But do I believe it as well? We encounter here — with Luther's identification of the first of the two "major aspects," which is missing in natural reason — the famous reformational *pro me* (for me), which is most often misunderstood: true, living faith, which is a great, rich, rare gift of the Holy Spirit, is that "which has no doubt that God wants to be gracious, not only to others but to me as well."

In neo-Protestantism of the Kantian variety, this *pro me* has been and continues to be misused as a methodological principle, in order to eliminate anything that is objective concerning what faith believes, and to characterize faith

---

45. WA 19:206.14; cf. *LW* 19:54.

46. WA 19:205.29; cf. *LW* 19:54.

47. If *noch* (besides) is to be construed as *doch* (yet) — a possibility according to sixteenth-century usage — the word would be used adversatively. It would not be correct to assume something that is complementary or quantitative.

48. WA 19:206.28-30; cf. *LW* 19:54.

as that which happens to each one individually.[49] If true faith, which does not doubt that God wants to be merciful "to me," is not to be understood in the sense of a certainty that is formal and existential — then how is this meant?

b. We grasp what is decisive when we do not simply consider the second of the two "major aspects" that natural reason is missing to be something that has to be added to the first. The two elements that Luther mentions are related much more integrally — indeed, in such a way that the second interprets the first, and this provides a specific answer to the question about the sense in which *pro me* is to be understood.

To proceed cautiously at first with the description, we note that the second aspect is a damaged ability to make judgments:

> that reason cannot discern the deity [understood as a general term] correctly, nor can it attribute to him what is proper to him alone. It knows that God is. But who or which one it might be who is to be called the true God, that it does not know. And so it happens to reason exactly as it happened to the Jews, when Christ was going about on the earth and when John the Baptist gave testimony that he was at hand. Their heart at that time was such that they knew Christ was in their midst and was going about among the people. But who this person might be, that they did not know; no one could comprehend that Jesus of Nazareth was the Christ. Reason plays "blindman's bluff" with God and makes purely errant grabs and always misses the mark, so that it names as god what is not God, and on the other hand does not name as God what really is God; it could do neither of these if it did not know *that* God exists or even know *which one or what*[50] God might be. So it gropes around clumsily and gives the name and the divine honor to "god" and calls "god" that which it thinks it means to be god and thus it never really hits upon the true God but instead continually ends up with the devil or else with its own invention, which the devil controls. Therefore it is radically different to know *that* there is a god and to know *what or who* God is. Nature knows the first, and it is written in every heart. Only the Holy Spirit teaches the second.[51]

Looking back to the first aspect, it is clear that true faith, which does not doubt that God is merciful *to me,* cannot be framed within some epistemo-

---

49. On this subject cf. Hans Joachim Iwand, "Wider den Missbrauch des pro me als methodisches Prinzip in der Theologie," *EvTh* 14 (1954): 120-24 (= *ThLZ* 79 [1954], cols. 453-58).

50. More precisely: "which one (masculine) or who" (according to WA 19:206.33; cf. *LW* 19:54).

51. WA 19:206.31–207.13; cf. *LW* 19:54-55, italics added.

logical theory that sees the christological nature of faith, identified by Luther as that second aspect, to be something that can be considered apart from faith, or that it can interpret this element and thereby make this second element of faith into something that can be acquired by natural reason: "Free will can do no more here";[52] natural reason can do no more here. It simply does not have the ability to turn itself toward grace, as Luther demonstrated adequately against Erasmus.[53]

The interpretation of Jonah 1:5 was published in 1526. *De servo arbitrio* appeared a year earlier, in which Luther disputed with Erasmus, who advocated that there must be at least enough free will to be able to say yes to the offer of salvation.[54] Luther persevered in saying that only Christ, through the Holy Spirit, unlocks Scripture and thereby gives salvation as a gift.

That God is gracious to me is thus identical with the fact that he has bound himself for all time to the human being, Jesus of Nazareth, to his life, suffering, and death. That Luther ties the *pro me* in the closest possible way to Christology, going so far as to explain the phrase in a completely christological sense, means that he contradicts Erasmus and "healthy human reason." Precisely this, that natural reason does not know that God's goodness and mercy that is valid for me is identical with Jesus Christ. At this decisive point it wastes its time, as Luther says with precise clarity: "Reason plays 'blindman's bluff' with God in the same way and makes purely errant grabs and always misses the mark, so that it names as god what is not God, and on the other hand does not name as God what really is God."[55] Christology for Luther is thus not simply a mental construct; it comes up for discussion only within a very specific context; it involves the certainty of faith that is effected by Jesus Christ taking our place.[56]

It is thus clear: there can be no talk of a smooth transition from the activity of prayer and knowledge that both proceed from natural reason, from its act of faith and its faith content, to the faith taught by the Holy Spirit, that this man Jesus is God himself for me. Between natural reason and faith is a deep crevice that cannot be negotiated by natural reason itself; this crevice points to a qualitative difference. "Therefore it is radically different to know *that* there is a god and to know *what* or *who* God is. Nature knows the first, and it is written in every heart. Only the Holy Spirit

---

52. WA 19:206.22; cf. *LW* 19:54-55.

53. Cf. *LW* 33:112-13 (*The Bondage of the Will*, 1526). Cf. chap. 8, nn. 30ff. below

54. *Erasmus-Luther Discourse on Free Will*, trans. Ernst F. Winter (New York: Frederick Ungar, 1961) (cf. chap. 8, n. 29), 2a, 11, pp. 28-29; 1b, 10, p. 20. Cf. chap. 8.2 below.

55. WA 19:207.4-6; cf. *LW* 19:55; cf. n. 51 above.

56. Cf. chap. 10 below.

teaches the second."[57] "No one can say 'Jesus is Lord' except by the Holy Spirit." Luther applies the depth of what is articulated in this statement by Paul (1 Cor. 12:3). "Lord" ("Kyrios") is the word that the Septuagint[58] uses for God himself. Natural knowledge gropes in vain to comprehend how one can identify God with the human being Jesus — as Luther identifies him with harsh clarity in a way that continues to sound shocking, in his hymn "A Mighty Fortress Is Our God":

> Jesus Christ it is, of Sabaoth Lord,
> And there's none other God.

> (*LSB*, #656, v. 2; cf. *LBW*, #229)

But that is just it: "no one can conceptualize that Jesus of Nazareth could be the Christ";[59] no one has ever thought this thought. Whoever, like Kant, wants to think about God "within the boundaries of pure reason" cannot identify Christ with Jesus of Nazareth. This identification is paradoxical; it goes against the opinion that everyone has about God and his goodness and mercy.

And yet this paradox that plays theology off against Christology is not incomprehensible in every respect. The point is that the blindman's bluff game with God would not have to be played if natural reason (a) "did not know *that* God exists" or (b) "already knew *who* he is."[60] That is a biblical argumentation. Thus the "I Am" words of the Johannine Christ — for example, "I am the bread of life" — assume a hunger for life, the search for happiness, which every human being knows, and it knows about the goodness of God at least in that way. But it is paradoxical that Jesus Christ, as the bread of life, calms this hunger and answers thereby the question about God. "That Jesus of Nazareth could be the Christ, no one can think that way." This paradox is quite close to what Pascal says: "I see too much (of God, the creator) to deny (him), and too little to be certain."[61]

Concerning his thesis on the relationship, or more properly, on the disproportion of nature and grace, of faith rooted in reason and faith rooted in Christ, Luther offers a "for instance"[62] — and not an arbitrary one: it is articulated in regard to works righteousness and the central aspect of that issue,

---

57. WA 19:207.11-13; cf. *LW* 19:55, italics added.

58. The Greek translation of the Old Testament from the third and second centuries B.C.

59. WA 19:207.3; cf. *LW* 19:55. Cf. n. 51 above.

60. WA 19:207.6f.; cf. *LW* 19:55, italics added.

61. *Pascal's Pensees*, introduction by T. S. Eliot (New York: Dutton, 1958), 64.

62. WA 19:207.14; cf. *LW* 19:55. Cf. the parallels in 19:98-99.

wherein one seeks to justify oneself. The human being justifiably expects from God all good things and all manner of help. But he wants this help to come in another way. Apart from the Holy Spirit, "by means of one's own reason and strength,"[63] he fails to arrive at the goal of his faith act; he "makes purely errant stabs," and he certainly seeks what is right, but he gropes around instead and always misses the mark in his delusion.[64]

Sin as one's own failure is thus not a quantitative determination — as it is for Schleiermacher, for whom sin is a deficient, dull, weak awareness of God, which is strengthened, reinforced, and purified by Christ. As the Greek term and its Hebrew equivalent both demonstrate, sin is failure in the sense of missing the mark. Luther impressively depicts the scenario with clarity when he uses this etymology to describe natural reason by using the analogy of the blindman's bluff game.

6.2.3. God and Idol

This missing of the mark, this hitting something off to the side, which does not just mean getting close but means hitting precisely what is next to what one aims for, is caused by striving for self-justification: in my attempt to convince myself that the basis for my existence, my right to exist, is located within me myself, or even that I myself am in charge of reaching my potential. That is the *peccatum originale,* the original sin, which is the source of the thousand different forms it takes: the original sin that one tries to be like God. Luther speaks in this entire section about this inherited sin — which cannot be relegated to the distant past in a historical or biological sense but is always at the same time my own sin in the present moment[65] — as he interprets Jonah.[66] He states his main point in the following thesis: "Thus, here you see," "that all these people in the ship know about God; but they do not have any true God."[67] They do not have, which is the same thing, any "faith in Christ."[68]

Luther's long description of the root error can be summarized briefly as follows: whoever does not have a true and certain God, whoever does not believe "in Christ," does not succeed sufficiently with his many gods by going

63. *BSLK* 511.46f.; cf. SC II, 6, in *BC,* 355; cf. chap. 11 below.
64. WA 19:207.4f.; cf. *LW* 19:55.
65. Cf. chap. 8.3 below.
66. WA 19:207.14–209.14; cf. *LW* 19:55-57.
67. WA 19:208.21f.; cf. *LW* 19:56.
68. WA 19:208.18; cf. *LW* 19:56.

about seeking other, foreign gods; instead, it happens when he ends up seeking the one true God in places other than where God allows himself to be found: in Jesus Christ. It is not that other foreign gods are worshiped in sinfulness and in unbelief; more accurately, it is that the one true God is worshiped in a false way. That is the source of polytheism.

The idol that is always at hand is that power that "leads us astray from God and turns us away from correct worship of God."[69] "They have forsaken me, the fountain of living water, and dug out cisterns for themselves, cracked cisterns that can hold no water" (Jer. 2:13). Such turning away from God, as the original sin, is identical with turning inward into myself, *incurvatio in me ipsum,* being closed in upon myself. That is how I lose God as subject, as object, as one separate from me, and I find myself alone by myself and with those who are like me.

To summarize: Luther's understanding of the church as an order of creation states that faith comes from God to each person, but nevertheless, because of a false perception of the Creator due to sin, "not all have faith" (2 Thess. 3:2).

6.2.4. Certainty Is Concrete

Luther's understanding of the church as an order of creation, which offers at the same time his way of dealing with the problem of natural theology, sets certain parameters. It establishes that theology cannot deal with its subject matter concurrently from the outside and from the inside; nor can it confront the issues it addresses with an air of neutrality. It cannot assume that everyone has a feeling of absolute dependence, and thus it cannot function as if the thoughts and actions of each person are grounded in some absolute certainty, to which one can appeal in each person, because such certainty is purportedly provided directly when that person comes into existence. One cannot discover a way for the uncertainty that is dominant in actuality and the certainty that is concrete, when delivered by a promise in the specific Word of Christ, to be made to converge when one gets down to the ontological level; nor can one formalize the two to become one ontological certainty that assumes that an ontic uncertainty and an ontic certainty both existed all along and were both meant to go on existing. Whoever follows Schleiermacher and argues this way plays a philosophical game

---

69. WA 19:207.33; cf. *LW* 19:56. The syllable *ab* corresponds to the Latin *a* and the Greek ἀπό: "away from." Sin is *aversio a Deo,* turning away from God. See chap. 8.1.3 below.

that is designed from the perspective of actual uncertainty, in which the individual who himself wants to be God is caught, caught in sin. He fails to see that the person who is caught up in himself, along with those who are like him, can hardly recognize his actual uncertainty for what it is, and thus does not consider himself responsible for the certainty that he needs above and beyond his uncertainty.[70]

Instead, certainty comes to exist in a concrete way. It takes place through the use of certain performative statements of Christian proclamation of the type used in the promise of the forgiveness of sins. Nothing can be abstracted from this concrete activity to concoct a statement that supposedly has general applicability, that would provide a place of refuge in a phenomenological, religious sense, that would have some overarching validity wherein all religions could find commonality. For Luther it follows that atheism is the high point among religions, which is most clearly seen in the religion of self-actualization, in which the human being seeks to make himself reliant simply on himself.[71]

But does Luther not reduce the ontological opposition between faith and unbelief, "the opposition of one side and the other" (Schleiermacher), to a common ontological denominator as well? Does he not speak about "trust of the heart, which makes both: God and idol"?[72] One could be tempted to think that the same basic drive is assumed or that the same basic nature of humanity is claimed when this formal integer of "trust" is used, which matches Schleiermacher's "feeling of absolute dependence." But the material difference between the two is stronger than the formal terminology that is used in common. For Luther, "false trust" is in such harsh opposition ontically to "true trust" that it would be senseless to come up with a common, overarching term, such as "trust" that is neutral or "certainty" that is neutral.

Correspondingly, theology cannot begin with formal principles, with

---

70. Every transcendental-philosophical and transcendental-theological way of thinking proceeds from a unified — at any rate, formally unified — universal openness, in which the universal aspect of sin as something directed inward has been overcome already. Accordingly, the nature of the human being consists in his openness to the world and to the self-disclosure of God, which in turn assumes that the human being is open and receptive. Such thinking harbors an illusion. By contrast, the only thinking that is without illusion is the kind that neither glosses over the contrast between sin and grace nor seeks to find or form an a priori — even a logical a priori — before or behind, in or beneath this contrast.

71. Luther emphasizes this in a clearly blunt manner when he puts the Muslims on the same level with the papacy and the Enthusiasts. He does not distinguish between religions and confessions, but only between true and false faith. Everyone who attempts to justify himself apart from Christ is caught up in unbelief, no matter what form it takes.

72. *BSLK* 560.16f.; cf. LC I, 2, in *BC*, 386.

eyes looking through the narrow slit of the helmet, but must start by examining its own material subject matter, with the visor up. In a way that differs from Schleiermacher, Luther does not seek to articulate some general principle, so that he can use it when he tries to explain the first commandment. Just the opposite: he analyzes "religion" on the basis of the first commandment; it is: "trust of the heart" (cf. how it is articulated in Deut. 6:5). This "trust" is not transcendent but is what is created specifically by God's self-revelation and by what is demanded in the first commandment; it does not allow itself to be comprehended in a formal/ontological sense, but only in a material/ontic sense. Opposition to God's self-revelation and to the first commandment is described in the same concrete way, namely, as "false trust." It is so concrete that it does not permit itself to be relativized by some overarching transcendental term, to describe something it has in common with "true trust." Concerning the relationship between the two actions of "trust," it means that only from within true trust, from within faith, will it be clear what false trust is, what unbelief is — and not vice versa. But the very fact that the relationship is defined in this way, and that it cannot be stated the other way around, leads to the expansive way, otherwise unheard of, that Luther uses to flesh out his concept of religion when he interprets the first commandment.

What Schleiermacher sought to achieve when he tried to formulate a formal, transcendental/philosophical definition from the outset, when he designed a logical definition that could be all-inclusive for describing the Christian faith, was based on an academic understanding of how to explain all of what is included in the concept "religion." Luther, by contrast, does not subsume the first commandment under some overarching principle to describe religion; instead, he derives his comprehensive definition of the concept of religion — which is intentionally polemical as well — by interpreting this concrete biblical text.[73] This can be seen in Luther's explanation of the first commandment, which Schleiermacher, precisely in his attempt to arrive at the widest possible view, actually narrows down when, *per definitionem*, by orienting his overall frame of reference toward self-actualization, he excludes anything that suggests that a "way to believe" is involved. But that is exactly what he advocated, in contradiction to true faith.

Thus, already within the teaching about creation, the question about justification is at issue. To say it clearly: The question about justification is more

---

73. Thus, no universal science of religion can be assumed in terms of forming "the appropriate framework for the practice of Christian theology and all its disciplines" (versus Wolfhart Pannenberg, *Theology and the Philosophy of Science*, trans. Francis McDonagh [Philadelphia: Westminster, 1976], 361; German: *Wissenschaftstheorie und Theologie* [Frankfurt, 1973], 364. But cf. the important relativizing statement on pp. 421f.).

important than the question about the existence of God.[74] And yet, when one acknowledges a feeling of utter dependence — as a formal abstraction — it is already recognized that "God made me together with all creatures." But what is not taken into account in this formal statement is that the human being does not recognize this dependence; he recognizes he will pass away, but does not believe it. Schleiermacher minimized this rebellion from the outset, in that he characterized "consciousness of sin" as nothing more than a restriction and thus permitted the concept to become too weak and vapid to carry any significance.

Luther's understanding of the church as an order of creation has significant meaning for discussion and dialogue with the world religions. In that regard the theological dimension of sin stands in the foreground, since the community that exists because of the self-revelation of God in his creation is always distorted from the outset and the church as an order of creation is corrupted as well; the entire creation is drawn into this corruption and "sighs" (Rom. 8:18-23).

We are drawn into an issue that is important for the academic study of religion when we begin with how Luther's theology portrays the general worship of God that is offered by all people, instead of starting with specifically Christian worship of God,[75] and as we take note of its radical corruption. The perspective that is necessary for examining the world history of religions is presented only by what is in the "center" of such worship (Gen. 2:9), which is established in primeval times by the promise of life that holds true for all people — along with all creatures — and which is heard nowhere else in a more critical and comforting sense than in the preamble to the Decalogue and in the first commandment: "I am the LORD, your God. . . . You shall have no other gods apart from me!" (Exod. 20:2-3).

Luther's explanation of the first commandment in the Large Catechism announces in an impressive way that the concept of religion is wide-ranging, with a breadth that is unheard of elsewhere, as can be apprehended by observing how the first commandment is interpreted. This religious concept makes the theological dimension of creation explicit and — as the teaching about the three estates demonstrates — shows thereby how to take seriously the interrelationships that take place within society as well as in one's individual manner of life because of an elementary way in which the world is experienced.

---

74. This is to be maintained against the main point emphasized in the concluding statement of the general assembly of the Lutheran World Federation at Helsinki, 1963.

75. Cf. chap. 12 below.

6.3. Household and State

6.3.1. The Spiritual Importance of the Temporal

Luther's teaching about the three estates cannot be disconnected from its polemical aspects. One text that is typical of this observation is found in the theses of the Circular Disputation on Matthew 19:21, dated May 9, 1539, titled *Concerning the Three Hierarchies: The Ecclesiastical, Political, Economic, and That the Pope Is Not to Be Located within Any One of Them, but Is Rather the Public Enemy of All of Them.*[76] The teaching about the three estates does not in fact arise primarily from the negative assessment offered by Luther when he criticizes the monastic understanding of discipleship, along with its denigration of the spiritual worldliness of the *status oeconomicus* and *politicus*. At the same time, Luther's position is inextricably bound up with this negative assessment — just as he reacted negatively to those who followed the pattern of monasticism and "deserted" the world by following the "Enthusiasts" and "Anabaptists." But Luther's theology, and his ethical teachings as well, cannot be understood without noticing the polemical stance he takes against both sides; he thinks that each matches up perfectly with the other and considers his own way as a "middle path"; he wants to plunge headlong "neither to the right nor to the left."[77]

There is no question that the life and the theology of the Augustinian monk Martin Luther were characterized by strictest asceticism up to the time of his reformational turning point. He viewed everything connected with the world and nature to be under the demand to deny the world: he was to deny himself with respect to place, time, and means, and was to withdraw from all sinning, from every urge to seek to take care of himself and what was his. The radical demand, concentrated in the vows of the monks, to forgo marriage, to be poor, and to be obedient considers everything in the realm of the world and nature solely as necessary material and means for earthly existence; in daily confession one was to reflect back negatively on the self and was to allow the self to be drawn back into its nothingness. One's own worth or any positive, spiritual importance is never attached to what is of the world and nature in the prereformational Luther.

It is most surprising that Luther studies to this point have not pursued

76. WA 39II:44.8-13 and 52.6–53.14; cf. the introduction, n. 8.

77. WA 18:112.33f.; cf. *LW* 40:130 (*Against the Heavenly Prophets in the Matter of Images and Sacraments — Part One*, 1525). On "desertion": *deserere oeconomiam, politiam* = "to forsake the household, the political order," *LW* 15:4 ("Notes on Ecclesiastes," preface, 1532), and Augsburg Confession, article 16 (CA 16) (*BSLK* 71.6: "deserere").

the question about how this turn from a radical denial of the world to an impressive affirmation of everything that is of the world and nature took place, which shines forth more brightly in Luther's writings from 1520 on, with ever increasing emphasis. When compared with his later writings — and not only the catechisms — the following assumption takes shape in retrospect: *After Luther was thoroughly convinced, because of his new understanding of Word and sacrament, that the spiritual is constituted in the form of what was earthly — not only negatively but also positively — the spiritual importance of all things earthly was opened to him in a positive sense as well.* Most importantly, this had application in the realm of marriage and parenthood, but it also impacted the wider realm of the household, as well as in matters of justice in its connection with temporal rule.

Because of the one faith that came by the power of the one baptism for all Christians, Luther saw that the earthly estates had a worth that they certainly did not have previously in any "ideological" sense and therefore in actuality had only in a restricted sense. Now also the "judges, office holders, government officials, scribes"[78] who had become important during the late Middle Ages, during an era that witnessed the development of culture in cities and palaces, when "callings" became specialized, as well as the estate of "servants and maids,"[79] which was considered the lowest and most scorned of occupations, had become a "holy" order.[80] "I seek to place, as more important, the faithful and just work of a jurist and a scribe above that of the holiness of all the clerics, monks, and nuns, when the latter are at their best."[81] "From this it comes that a pious maid, as she goes to her assigned tasks and because of her office, who has to sweep the yard or has to carry out the manure or as a like-minded servant who plows and drives, goes straight to heaven, on the right path, whereas another, who goes to Saint James or to the church, letting his office and work go, goes straight to hell."[82]

78. WA 26:505.5f.; cf. *LW* 37:365.

79. WA 26:505.6; cf. *LW* 37:365. Luther can use the word "estate" even with reference to social organization and structure. At the same time, though it scarcely needs to be mentioned, it has a quite different meaning than when one teaches about the three estates; Luther's understanding of the three estates is not intended as a social ranking or as a scale of prestige.

80. WA 26:504.30; cf. *LW* 37:364.

81. WA 30II:561.11-13; cf. *LW* 46:241 ("Sermon on Keeping Children in School," 1530).

82. WA 10I/1:310.9-13 ("On John 21:19-24"; *Kirchenpostille*, 1522).

6.3.2. Family and Marriage

Oeconomia encompasses for Luther everything that we today, in our economically differentiated situation, place into three different categories: marriage and family, business, and education and academic study; he is rooted in the Aristotelian tradition, which understands economy (οἰκονομία) as coming from the house (οἶκος), from the way a household operates. The available parameters do not make it possible to present the wide variety of observations that Luther makes concerning these three dimensions of *oeconomia*.[83] Paradigmatic in what follows is his understanding of family and marriage, with the main point of emphasis being that of marriage.

Whoever wants to comprehend Luther's understanding of marriage must first look at the family. This perspective, which is uncommon for today's way of thinking, comes from the fact that for Luther the fourth commandment ("You shall honor your father and your mother!"), among those that are concerned with matters of earthly life, is seen as "the first and highest":[84] "God has especially given the prize, above all the other estates, to the estate of being father and mother."[85] With reference to the ingratitude, in which the human being forgets to whom he owes thanks for his life, Luther says in the Large Catechism: "God knows such bad manners in the world only too well. For this reason he reminds them and presses upon them with commandments, so that each one can think about what his parents have done for him, so that he discovers that he has gotten his body and life from them, and in addition that he was fed and raised; otherwise he would have been stuck in his filth a hundred times."[86] Only through my parents is life given to me. This sentence sounds trite. But in a time of individualism and of the generation gap, it is hardly that; it is appropriate that one learn anew that the world and our own life, our own life history, do not begin with us ourselves. More properly we

83. For descriptions of specific economic aspects, cf. Hans-Jürgen Prien, *Luthers Wirtschafts-ethik* (Göttingen: Vandenhoeck & Ruprecht, 1992); Andreas Pawlas, *Die lutherische Berufs- und Wirtschaftsethik. Eine Einführung* (Neukirchen-Vluyn: Neukirchener Verlag, 2000). On education and academic matters, cf. Werner Reininghaus, *Elternstand, Obrigkeit und Schule bei Luther*, PF 38 (Heidelberg, 1969). For Luther, the school is an extension of the parental home and task and is not primarily a concern of the state (cf. *LW* 41:176-77 [*On the Councils and the Church*]).

84. *BSLK* 586.48f.; cf. LC I, 103, in *BC*, 399.

85. *BSLK* 587.7-9; cf. LC I, 105, in *BC*, 399; cf. LC I, 125, in *BC*, 403. "For it is certain that for their children father and mother are apostles, bishops, pastors, since they make known to them the gospel. Briefly: there is no greater, nobler power on earth than that of parents over their children, since they have spiritual and temporal power over them" (*LW* 45:46 [*The Estate of Marriage*, 1522]).

86. *BSLK* 593.21-28; cf. LC I, 129, in *BC*, 404.

ourselves are indebted to a word, to a will, to an affirmation that preceded our life, that anticipated it. Only within this protected and opened space can I also enter into a marriage.

As at Luther's time, questions such as the following are posed today: How can I be certain that marriage is the right way to live life? Do I not have more freedom if I stay single? How can I be sure that this one and no other is to be my wife, this one and no other is to be my husband, and that it will last even when my spouse no longer pleases me? How am I to handle myself in crises and conflicts? Should I play with the thought that another would possibly please me more? Can I find a solid "estate" — a solid standing — and take measured steps on solid ground, in the midst of such teetering and tottering?

It is from this vantage point that we understand how Luther could speak so explicitly about the "estate" of marriage. For Luther, the steadfastness of the estate was endowed with the highest level of liveliness.

The steadfast nature of the marriage estate takes on its character for him because of a trustworthy Word, which guarantees the permanence and cohesiveness of the life to be lived together. It is the binding twine that holds everything together at every moment of the lifetime that is ever on the move, in its beauty and joy, in its crises and conflicts. It is what makes the estate an estate. God's Word creates the union of a particular man and a particular woman in a way that is unconditional and is not given time limits.

As God's Word about marriage, Luther pays attention to the Word of Jesus that discussed the relationship between man and woman, which is not to be divided, known to us in the evangelical marriage service: "What God has joined together, let not man put asunder" (Mark 10:9). Jesus makes reference thereby to the two narratives of creation (Gen. 1–2) to explain that the original creative will of God can finally become reality: "It is not good that the man should be alone!" (Gen. 2:18).

With this creative Word God listened to the lament of human loneliness; it had already been in his mind beforehand. With this creative Word he protects against loneliness, as he brings man and wife together: "gives together," "speaks together" makes "being together" possible for humans, in which one — surprisingly — knows and recognizes the other; sameness and uniqueness do not exclude; they include.

Luther's understanding of the Word of God concerning marriage comes forth most clearly and impressively in his marriage sermon from January 8 [?], 1531.[87] "Who does not know that the estate of marriage has been consti-

---

87. WA 34I:50-75 ("Sermon on Heb. 13,4"); in a "translation" into New High German by Frieder Walker and Alfred Holbein under the title *Ehe-Gabe* (Fürth: Flacius Verlag, 1984).

tuted and instituted by God, created in Paradise, and established and blessed even outside of Paradise? That is what Moses pointed out: Genesis 1; 2; 9. Everyone knows that. And I have even learned to recite these words." But to really hear and learn them, "that is a type of skill that I do not yet possess; I continue to learn more about them."[88] Why must one go on to really learn these words and have actual experience with them? Because they describe and give shape to our life and eliminate ambiguities and aim to make things clear. It is most important for Luther to emphasize that God's Word offers clarity of purpose to the chaotic natural forces that drive human life and that it gives a person specific guidance concerning a different way to live.

Without the Word the estate of marriage would be no marriage estate. If a husband and wife do not see the Word of God as part of their marriage, if they do not take their mutual participation in faith in this Word seriously, then their reason will be blind.

In his writing titled *The Estate of Marriage,* Luther distinguishes sharply between the view of blind reason and reason that is enlightened by faith in God's Word.

> If natural reason looks thus at married life, which is what the heathen follow, at the point where they want to be the smartest, then it turns up the nose and says: Ah, do I have to rock the baby, wash the diapers, make beds, smell stink, stay awake during the night, care for it when it cries, treat its rashes and sores, afterward take care of the wife, support her, work, have cares here, cares there, do that, do this, suffer that, suffer this, and all of what else the marriage estate teaches about what is disgusting and wearying. Oh, should I get caught like that? Oh, you miserable, poor man, if you have taken a wife, phooey, phooey, with the misery and messiness. It is better to remain unattached and, without troubles, to lead a peaceable life. . . .
>
> But what does the Christian faith have to say about this? It opens his eyes and sees all these small, insignificant, and despised works through the Spirit and is most sure that they are all decorated with godly pleasure as with costly gold and precious stones and says: Ah, oh God, since I am sure that you have created me as a human being and have produced this child through my body, I thus know for sure, as well, that it pleases you best of all, and I confess to you that I am not worthy to rock the little one, to wash his diapers, and to care for his mother. How have I come to be worthy of this without merit, that I have become sure of how I can serve your creature and your loving will? Oh, how gladly I will do such things, even such things as could be less important yet and more despised. Therefore, neither

88. WA 34I:52.22-27. Cf. chap. 3, n. 39 above.

frost nor heat, no amount of effort or work will grieve me, since I am sure that such work is so pleasing to you.[89]

Such confidence of faith comes from the certainty of the Word, as it applies to marriage. Looking at this from the outside, which views it apart from this Word, it cannot discover the difference between reason that is blind and reason that can see. It cannot distinguish between living together within marriage and living together without the benefit of marriage.

Even the present legal form of civil marriage points out, concerning the relationship between husband and wife, that it is to be understood on the basis of the Word of God. It is both necessary and good to recognize God's Word and will during the entire story of how it starts with mutual attraction, then the relationship is tested, and finally comes the decision to be firmly bound together, right up to the official sealing of the marriage before the registrar of marriage, and to confess to believing in the same: he has drawn me together with this woman, with this man, given us to each other and spoken us together. We cannot understand our marriage solely as the result of our own will by seeing it as nothing more than a contract, which either one can dissolve by mutual consent.

Since Christians cannot understand their marriage primarily as the result of their own wills, the very middle of the evangelical marriage service calls for a confession to God that he has created this new communal relationship. He is thanked for this partnership. Its continual existence is entrusted to him. Based on his promise of forgiveness, its unbreakable permanence is expected and implored. "What do you have that you did not receive?" (1 Cor. 4:7). The path to the altar takes this into account when it becomes a confession of one's own poverty, a witness of one's own poverty.[90]

Evil is at work to endanger and to destroy that which was created good; yes: the evil one. God's good creation is the communion between man and woman, their harmony; but the devil sows disharmony. "It is God's estate and order that whoever enters the estate of marriage goes into a real cloister, which is full of temptation." To preserve love

is not under your own control. You have a powerful foe, whose name is: the devil, who is pleased from the depths of his heart to see that someone in a house grumbles and gripes, upends chairs, benches, and tables, bats his wife around the room or slaps her on the face. That is music for the devil; he laughs up his sleeve about that, since that is exactly what he has in mind.

89. WA 10II:295.16–296.11; cf. *LW* 45:39-40.
90. Cf. *BSLK* 530.15-26; SC, "A Marriage Booklet for Simple Pastors," IX, 4, in *BC,* 368.

He rejoices when that happens, so that no man would stay with his wife and that no wife loves her husband. Therefore you ought not look at the married life from the outside, for when you see it that way you will see that it is filled with temptation and sadness. Instead, you must look at this estate on the basis of the Word, be adorned with it, and in the way that it is instituted. This Word will surely make honey for you out of the bitterest wormwood and will certainly change the sorrows into joy once again.[91]

In God's Word there is an authority that does not seek to strike the human being down, but seeks to free him instead; it is a power for togetherness that does not come from within the human being, based on his state of mind and his sensitivities — not even based on his own decisions — it is an authority that brings one through crises and conflicts. The Word of God concerning marriage does not discuss the realities of married life beyond the actual situation and over one's head; it protects against temptation and trial. It is not positivistic and cannot isolate from temptation and trial. It is not valid in and of itself; it is a Word that cares for the soul.

When one is tempted, decisions that are made when things are stable do not bring comfort; temptation can break a person, particularly when it is severe. Feelings of affection do not bring comfort when one is tempted; temptation can extinguish them. In a time of temptation the external law does not bring comfort either; it does not free someone — even though it can serve the purpose of applying external pressures to preserve a relationship so that it can spring to life again and can once again be affirmed freely. The only thing that can bring comfort is the Word, which guarantees the communal relationship.

The main accent in Luther's concept of this estate, which is still important today, is rooted in the personhood of fellow human beings, which is constituted by words. For Luther, there is no theological sense in which the word "person" is to be understood individualistically; the word is always characterized in a way that involves being in conversation: "Who am I?" is determined by the fact that I am addressed and that I myself can and thus must give a response. Corresponding to Luther's intention, the way one reflects a theological understanding of how this is instituted must remain personal, which means to keep it as word-centered as possible,[92] whereby it

91. WA 34I:64.1-14 ("Sermon on Marriage," 1531).

92. The reliability of the Word of God provides the sure basis for whatever is properly established as an institution. But those who "recognize" the institution of marriage "are those who firmly believe that God himself instituted it, brought husband and wife together, and ordained that they should beget children and care for them. For this they have God's word, Genesis 1[:28], and they can be certain that he does not lie" (*LW* 45:38).

must remain obvious, or needs to be made obvious, that what is truly personal is located distinctively within what is instituted as community, in the way it is formed together as such, and that without it any personal quality would be empty personhood — it would be no personhood at all, but merely mood or pure duty.

The question about how I can be sure of my station in life or my calling,[93] my vocation and thus the path my life should take, unlocks the breadth and depth of how Luther's understanding of the Word provides practical life applications.

6.3.3. State

Discussions concerning the third estate, the state, will show in a special way how this presentation of Luther's theology succeeds in what it aims to do systematically, which means in the way it is vindicated in the manner it has application for today. New perspectives and questions, other than those Luther confronted, must be taken seriously and evaluated carefully. Most especially when we come to this particular topic, I think Luther's views are to be evaluated critically. At the same time, in what follows — particularly concerning how one distinguishes between "power," "force," and "dominion" — I would not have discovered a positive view of the state without Luther's conceptualization of matters connecting with the political estate.

At the time of Luther, and today as well, two clearly different orientations guide views about the state. The first bases its ethic for political matters, for order in the state, in the theological concept of sin, which considers the state to be "a necessary antidote against the ruined natural world."[94] The second orientation is rooted in an optimistic view of the human being: the assumption that it was originally possible for the human being to live in freedom. As I evaluate both orientations critically, I present a third option, which makes use of and applies an element of truth that is to be found in each.

The first orientation results from the justification for a political ethic that has been connected in modern times with the conception of a primitive state

---

93. If one spoke of a "calling" instead of an "estate," it would be clearer that getting married is not something that just happens of itself. The one who stays single requires a special calling; and yet, only those who know they are called to it should marry. The meaning of "calling" has been particularly articulated by Gustav Wingren, *Luthers Lehre vom Beruf* (1952); in English, *Luther on Vocation* (Eugene, Oreg.: Wipf and Stock, 2004).

94. WA 42:79.8f.; cf. *LW* 1:3-359 (*Lectures on Genesis*, chaps. 1–5, 1535-36, on Gen. 2:16-17: "Remedium necessarium naturae corruptae"). Cf. n. 6 above.

and a social contract, as was advocated by Thomas Hobbes.[95] That justification is primarily oriented toward the question about how sin and its consequences are to be confronted. According to Luther's interpretation of the primeval history in the Bible, God created in Paradise — as original estates — the church and the *oeconomia* but not the *politia*.[96] The *politia*, which for us today is the state, is not an order of creation but rather an order of necessity. Correspondingly, the power of coercion is primary in the state. It alone hinders random actions; it alone restrains animal instincts, in situations where it is one against the other for survival; it alone can deal with Cain, the murderer of his brother; it alone subdues the battle of everyone against everyone else in a life-and-death struggle for mutual recognition. For this theological and political orientation, every time the law is broken it is like a dam breaking; the waters of chaos break in and threaten to devastate everything. This orientation — sadly — has become the most dominant within Lutheranism since the nineteenth century with respect to its effect on history.

A very different viewpoint is offered by the second orientation that has an optimistic view about natural law, which proceeds from the Aristotelian and Stoic tradition that assumes human beings originally got along well together and believes human beings can strive for a consensus that will eventually be cosmopolitan, a consensus of all peoples to be achieved by their powers of reason and that all people can follow in all aspects; rules being broken are the exceptions. This does not assume that one must battle chaos, but assumes a cosmos of peace and order and attributes to the human being an ability to live in peace and to use his freedom in a reasonable and socially acceptable way. This orientation can appeal for support from Luther as well, insofar as he not only makes a sharp distinction between the political estate, which is established because of sins and need, and the economic estate, which is an order of creation, since he could see that the two were interrelated as well and pointed out how the political estate is rooted within the economic or household estate. Thus, the explanation to the fourth commandment in the Large Catechism reads: "All other authority flows and spreads out from the authority of the parents."[97] And at another point: "The household is the source of all public affairs."[98] To this extent, Luther at times relativizes his strict theological assessment that the

---

95. Thomas Hobbes, *Leviathan* (London: J. M. Dent and Sons, 1950), I, c.13f., pp. 101-6.
96. Cf. 6.1 above.
97. *BSLK* 596.17–599.13; cf. LC I, 141, in *BC*, 405.
98. "Domus est fons omnium rerum publicarum" (WA 40III:220.4f.; on Ps. 127:1; 1532-33); cf. *LW* 15:5 ("Notes on Ecclesiastes," 1532). Cf. WA 47:854.7f. ("Sermon of September 29, 1539"): "Parentes sunt quell und born, ex quo venit weltlich regiment" [parents are the source and wellspring from which the temporal realm comes].

political estate had to be established because of sin. In that sense he comes close to the orientation of the Aristotelian and Stoic tradition with its identification of natural rights. The following table talk comment provides evidence to support this: "God created human beings so that they could get along together in a friendly and peaceful way."[99]

The present situation in the church and in theology, at least in Protestantism, with respect to the basic political approach, can be seen as a battle between these two orientations, with each position stated in its idealized typological form. It is easy to see which political options are linked to each and correspond to each.

Luther's understanding of the political estate is suitable for adopting and promoting the recommendation of a third way that is defensible for the present, which can go beyond the fact that the second orientation is deficient concerning a theology of sin just as the first orientation is deficient in its theology of creation.

If the state is responsible solely for dealing with sinfulness, and not with what the human being was like originally, that has disastrous consequences for one's understanding of the state: the state will tend toward being purely a police state. The idea that one must work through representatives will gain strength and will be reinforced. Opportunities to settle public matters by vote, to contribute to understanding the common will, are going to be distrusted in principle; one fears mob rule in such a system. But if the state were able to assume it was working with the original nature of the human being — even though one cannot deny that it is now perverted — then it could go about its business differently.

In the first place, the phenomenon of power would be perceived differently: not as that which because of sin sadly has to be established and exercised so that greater evil can be hindered, but — by contrast — also not as that which is evil in itself. It will be seen as that which is constitutive of what makes the human existence of human beings possible. This includes the fact that the human being is a form of life that hears and therefore — when responding — can speak, but who also must respond. Whoever can hear places himself under the power of the one to whom he listens, into the power of the one who speaks. The one who speaks, who addresses another, positions that person, deals with that person in relation to himself, and even exercises authority over him.

---

99. WA TR 6:266.23-25 (no. 6913). According to WA 40III:222.35f. (on Ps. 127:1; 1532-33), not only the economic estate but also the political estate was created at the same time as human beings were created ("leges et artes divina ordinatione cum homine concreatae").

As human beings we cannot be described as being symmetrical — for example, as those who have a pure and equal chance to speak — but rather on the basis of being asymmetrical: having the asymmetry that comes from sometimes hearing and then speaking, sometimes speaking and then hearing. It hardly needs to be mentioned that this does not describe a division into two distinctive groups, so that there is one that is alone responsible for speaking and another that alone is responsible for obeying. This lack of symmetry is even to be found in each individual human being. There is no human being in whom both would not be present — even though it could admittedly be in a changeable proportion, according to circumstances and situation.

As one who hears and speaks, like every other human being, I am one who has power over others and one over whom others have power. Only within this relationship between having power and needing to respond — and not somehow outside of it — does the human being have his dignity and his freedom. Freedom and dignity are not possessed by an individual alone, and one cannot even think about, to say nothing of have, freedom by distancing oneself from others. Instead, a human being's dignity and his freedom are located in the communal interchange between hearing and speaking, providing and acquiring, receiving and passing on, authority and critique thereof.[100]

From the time of its origin according to God's creative will, "freedom" as a form of interaction within community does not exist within a power vacuum, but in a relationship that views power as that which always seeks to benefit the life of the other, which shapes the relationship from the beginning, which practically creates it. Above all else, that is what gives physical and spiritual parenthood its dignity.

And yet such power no longer functions to promote life without disruption — and that is the second decisive aspect about it. The human being has essentially distorted and corrupted the original hearing and speaking, and along with it power, freedom, and dignity; he lives in a *statu corruptionis*. That assessment is not accorded its full value by those who follow the second orientation, or at the very least its importance is undervalued when applied to the history of mankind and its universal aspects. The power that creates and promotes life has been distorted to become a power that threatens and destroys life. *Distorted power is coercive force; force is the misuse of power.*

The biblical primeval history describes this misuse of power; it is depicted most clearly when a brother is murdered (Gen. 4). Corresponding to

100. Cf. Oswald Bayer, *Autorität und Kritik. Zu Hermeneutik und Wissenschaftstheorie* (Tübingen: Mohr, 1991).

this, the fifth commandment ("You shall not murder") is directed against the misuse of power in favor of its use to promote life[101] — just as all the commandments are orientated against the misuse of power and thus serve to promote freedom and life. With reference to justice, one should especially take note of the eighth commandment ("You shall not bear false witness against your neighbor!"). It deals with the power contained in someone's word that can be trusted and thus serves justice and the freedom that comes with it.

Because power is misused, because force is used in a distorted way, life cannot be preserved and promoted without governmental rule. *Whatever power is exercised because of force and whatever aims to stop the exercise of force, so that life can go well, is to be considered legitimate and responsible, accountable governmental rule, dominion.*

Political rule — even in a democracy, according to the root definition of the word — opposes naked force, prevents fratricide, aims to limit street justice and private recrimination. It is a huge cultural accomplishment when one can limit the use of force, its random explosiveness and its capriciousness.[102] One must also not forget, despite what has happened in the modern age as the totality of power has been concentrated in the state alone, that progress has been made against street justice and private recrimination and against the possibility that war could break out at any time, with everyone against everyone, since from the early modern age on the state has monopolized the use of force against others and justifies its use only when it serves the purposes of just order.[103]

Yet it must be said: "Legitimate physical use of force"[104] — not only something pejorative, such as brute force — cannot serve as the exclusive indicator that characterizes how order is properly maintained in the just state. It is used when all else fails — one should certainly not make a mistake about that and one ought not use it excessively, in an unreasonable way — but it is to be taken seriously. It is to be used not only as a threat but also in practice.

101. "We should fear and love God so that we do not hurt or harm our neighbor in his body, but help him and defend him in all bodily needs" (*BSLK* 508.31-34; cf. SC I, 10, explanation to the fifth commandment, in *BC,* 352).

102. It was first during Luther's lifetime that the right to carry on a feud was removed, by the Law of Perpetual Peace (1495); he never wished to see the guarantee of security within the political realm endangered — which is a main reason for his interest in preserving public order.

103. For Luther, what is just determines how something is to be decided, as is indicated by Reinhard Schwarz, "Christusgemeinschaft und Rechtsgemeinschaft — Theologie und Gesellschaft in Luthers Rede von 'Zwei Reichen,'" in *Herausforderung,* ed. Fernando Castillo and Heinrich Fries (Regensburg: Pustet, 1980), 9-27. Cf., e.g., WA 31I:201.16-18 (to Ps. 82:2; 1530).

104. Max Weber, *Staatssoziologie,* ed. Johannes Winckelmann, 2nd ed. (Berlin: Duncker & Humbolt, 1966), 27.

This does not mean that use of power becomes the norm; it is much rather *"ultima ratio."*[105]

It would be politically disastrous if the extreme case, if ordinances for special circumstances and emergency measures, if laws enacted principally because of a special need were used already or could serve as the model for establishing law and order within the state. In this regard, Luther's understanding of the state must be corrected. Even within this sinful, fallen world, that original power — that asymmetrical relationship between hearing and speaking that creates and promotes life — is happily not completely lost and extinguished, in spite of all its perversions and distortions. For this reason political order does not exist solely as force to be used against force. It is "dominion" insofar as it is more than just meeting force with force, when it assumes and can assume that the order for which one yearns and which one affirms is rooted within. The exercise of dominion in the just state is not rooted primarily even within the legitimate exercise of power in times of threat and need, but is affirmed also because its right to rule is acknowledged by its citizens. The exercise of dominion in the just state ought not be allowed to continue if it does not have the consensual affirmation of a large majority of its citizens, a moral consensus.

6.4. Love as Criterion

"Now over these three estates and orders comes the general estate of Christian love, in which a person serves not just the three estates, but also altogether every single person who has any need with every good action possible — such as to feed the hungry, give a drink to the thirsty, forgive the enemy, pray for all people on earth, suffer all manner of evil on earth, etc."[106] Here, in brief, Luther sets forth his teaching about the three estates in their relationship with love, which is set in motion by faith.[107]

Though the estates are relativized by their relationship with love, they are not all put on the same level. For Luther, placing love above the others and having to show how love is to be applied in some detail — though not exhaustively — demonstrate how each estate is related to the others as one lives in these various estates. Though the text of his *Confession* is quite short, it is not just by chance that love is constitutive when the estates are relegated

---

105. Max Weber, *Soziologische Grundbegriffe*, 4th ed. (Tübingen: Mohr, 1978), 81f.
106. WA 26:505.11-15; cf. *LW* 37:365.
107. Cf. further, chap. 13 below.

to relative status through the explanation about how love is to be at work in each one. This observation is also supported by the conclusion to the Table of Duties in the Small Catechism and in the command to love (Matt. 22:39).[108] This same connection between concise concentration in love and broad application living in the estates is found in the Augsburg Confession, article 16: it is right "to exercise love in all estates."[109] As with Luther's theology as a whole, the first commandment gets the last word as it gives the reason for and establishes the boundary of the Christian life: "One must obey God rather than any human authority" (Acts 5:29).[110]

---

108. *BSLK* 527.18f.; cf. SC VIII, 14, in *BC,* 367.
109. *BSLK* 71.12f.; cf. CA XVI, 5, in *BC,* 50 ("in talibus ordinationibus exercere caritatem").
110. *BSLK* 71.23-26; cf. CA XVI, 7, in *BC,* 50.

Chapter 7   The Human Being: In the Image of God

Paul gives a brief definition of the human being; concisely: a person is justified by faith.

One speaks theologically about the human being from three vantage points: he is first of all creature; second, he is that being whose nature as creature is perverted — and is thus a sinner; third, he is that being who has been brought out of the perversion of his nature as creature through Jesus Christ, so that he is made right again. With masterful conciseness Luther formulated the following theses concerning these three aspects in one single Latin sentence:

> 21. The human being is God's creation, consisting of flesh and a living soul, made from the very beginning in the image of God without sin, whose calling was to procreate descendants as well as to rule over the things and never to die.
>
> 22. [This creature] was subjected after Adam's fall to the power of the devil, which means, under sin and death — both of which are evil, which cannot be overcome by his own powers and which last forever;
>
> 23. only through the Son of God, Christ Jesus, can [the creature] be freed (insofar as he believes in him) and be given eternal life as a gift.[1]

Admittedly, because of the constrictions placed on these three aspects when all three modes of time are considered concurrently,[2] these three aspects can-

---

1. WA 39I:176.7-13. "21. Scilicet, quod homo est creatura Dei, carne et anima spirante constans, ab initio ad imaginem Dei facta, sine peccato, ut generaret et rebus dominaretur, nec unquam moreretur, 22. Post lapsum vero Adae subiecta potestati diaboli, peccato et morti, utroque malo suis viribus insuperabili et aeterno, 23. Nec nisi per filium Dei Iesum Christum liberanda (si credat in eum) et vitae aeternitate donanda." Cf. *LW* 34:138.

2. Cf. the introduction above.

not be distinguished completely from one another, as one might do by separating physical elements through the use of chemicals. This has already become clear, for example, when the teaching about the three estates was discussed, most clearly at the point where the first two vantage points — creation and sin — overlap with regard to the ethics of the state. Luther disputes with philosophy in the *Disputatio de homine* concerning the correct way to understand humanity. The dispute is not simply treated as a side issue; it is essential to Luther's understanding of theology. That is because, for Luther, there is never a mediating position. An academic *study of the inherent conflict* within these three aspects is constitutive for theological activity. This is shown already in the way the theses are arranged and divided. Theses 1-19 set forth, from a critical perspective, the way philosophy understands the human being; theses 20-40 treat the theological understanding of the human being, though not without including — critiquing — references to philosophy.

Luther's comments are in answer to philosophy and explain how he evaluates that tradition — with respect to anthropology, the teaching about the human being, and with reference to the philosophical definition of the human being as an *animal rationale*, as a reasoning life-form. Luther states his opposition to this philosophical formula that ruled the day and that came from the Aristotelian tradition with the following thesis (thesis 32): "In brief form, what Paul expresses in Romans 3[:28]: 'For we hold that a person is justified by faith, apart from works prescribed by the law' is the definition of the human being, which means that the human being is justified through faith."[3]

7.1. The Essence of the Human Being in Faith

Luther takes what for him is the central passage in the Bible, Romans 3:28 — concerning which he formulated no less than five series of theses![4] — as the definition of the human being: The human being is human *insofar as* he is justified through faith — *in that* he is justified by faith. Justifying faith for Luther is not something *about* a human being, no qualitative element, which comes only secondarily, as that which is accidental to the sub-

---

3. Here and in what follows the theses of the *Disputatio de homine* are from the Gerhard Ebeling translation (IL II, 294-97). Since a definition is involved in thesis 32, it would be more precise and to the point to translate it: "The human being is human in that he is justified by faith." Cf. chap. 5, n. 13 above.

4. LW 34:109-13, 113-20 (*Thesis concerning Faith and Law*, 1535); LW 34:151-53, 153-57 (*The Disputation concerning Justification*, 1536); WA 391:202-4 (1537).

stance. *Hominem iustificari fide* (a human being is justified by faith) is, instead, a *fundamental* anthropological thesis.[5]

To be human means to have undeserved existence, that which is purely indebted to another. Correspondingly, the main point is "about whether the human being is to be defined by his ability to reason or because he is designated as human on account of faith; thus, whether the existence of the world is guaranteed by the action of the human being or whether the existence of the human being in the world is to be believed as God's action toward him."[6] We have seen already how Luther interprets *creatio ex nihilo* (creation out of nothing): as continually new creation and as conservation of the world against nothingness and evil.

The existence of the human being is his elementary designation: one for whom life itself and whatever is necessary for life are given to him, guaranteed anew every second and not to be taken away — yet he cannot, even for a single blink of the eye, ever exist because of something that comes forth from within himself.[7] Waiting and yearning for that which is necessary for life: that is faith; at the same time, that is the very existence of the human being and all creatures, if this existence is guaranteed purely by goodness and purely because of mercy, against all threats. This is articulated in a classic way in the Small Catechism: "I believe that God has made me and all creatures . . . without any merits or worthiness in me."[8] As a created being, human existence is "justified-through-faith" existence. As "justified-through-faith" existence, it is created existence. For Luther, teaching about creation is to teach about justification, and teaching about justification means to teach about creation.

I am created "together with all creatures," thus, *within* the group of all fellow creatures, who also have their existence through faith alone, namely, through the faithfulness of God, just as we human beings have it. For admittedly, to make a further observation without advocating a false anthropocentric position — but against a widely held naive romanticism about nature that is advocated today — it is clear to see that we human beings also exist *over against* all the other creatures. It is also appropriate to speak theologically

5. Beyond this, justification can teach about the nature of every creature and not just that of the human being: undeserved, purely unmerited existence. Luther's central thesis in *De homine* was already discussed in this sense in chap. 5.1.1 above, and was further explicated in *mundum iustificari fide* — the whole world is justified through faith. The interpretation in this passage concentrates on the position of the *human being* within the world.

6. Gerhard Ebeling, *Lutherstudien*, vol. II/3, 544.

7. WA 18:662.12: "ut ne momento consistere suis viribus possint": "they cannot subsist for a moment by their own strength": *LW* 33:103 (*The Bondage of the Will*, 1526).

8. *BSLK* 510.33–511.5; cf. SC II, 2, in *BC*, 354.

about the fact that human beings have been placed into a special position; this corresponds to the initial question in the *Disputatio de homine,* which takes aim at the ancient definition of the human being as an *animal rationale,* as a "form of life furnished with the ability to reason."

Luther discusses this special status that is afforded to the human being over against the other creatures by referring to what theological tradition has termed the image of God *(imago Dei),* with reference to Genesis 1:26-28. Luther obviously does not start by referring to a quality that resides within the human being in and of himself; instead, he uses a relational term — a dignity that is imparted to me "without any merits or worthiness in me," which I receive first of all when I hear it, in order to be empowered to speak after hearing it; speaking is responding. The image of God consists in the ability that has been distributed to the human being to "re-spond." Luther says in his "Preface to the Psalter" (1528) that there is "no more powerful nor a more noble work for human beings than to speak, especially since the ability to speak is that which most clearly distinguishes the human being from other animals, more than the bodily form or other actions, since even a log can be made into the form of a man by means of the art of carving, and an animal can also see, hear, smell, sing, move about, stand, eat, drink, fast, be thirsty, suffer from hunger, frost, and harsh lodgings, just as a human being can."[9]

That reason is not something constructed by human beings and is not a human possession, but is a gift that has been given by an addressing word, can be seen more accurately as this is preserved in the Greek form of the philosophical definition of what it is to be human than is the case in the Latin: the human being is a form of life that has the Logos (ζῷον τὸν λόγον ἔχον).[10] To be sure, it is not clear here either to what extent the address comes to the human being from the outside; but one can at least hear in the word λόγος that reason is *comprehending reason* and does *not* come *apart from language.* Because the reference is directed toward hearing, the ability to reason by using language is distributed to a human being passively; for this reason the theological definition of the human being can be constructed only by using a verb in the passive. The ability of the *ratio* as *what is given* — not some type of *ratio* itself — is the characteristic mark of the *imago Dei.*

Hominem iustificari fide: Luther uses these three Latin words to formulate what is quintessential when describing the human being. *The human be-*

---

9. Heinrich Bornkamm, ed., *Luthers Vorreden zur Bibel,* 3rd ed. (Göttingen: Vandenhoeck & Ruprecht, 1989), 52; cf. *LW* 35:254 ("Preface to the Psalter," 1545/1528).

10. Aristotle, *Politics* 1.2.1253a.7-10, trans. H. Rackham, Loeb Classical Library, vol. 21 (Cambridge: Harvard University Press, 1990), 11.

ing has his nature as one who believes, just as his unnatural nature is not to believe, to be in sin.

7.2. Human Reason — "Almost Something Divine"

This thesis, *hominem iustificari fide* — the human being is human thereby, in that he is justified through faith — identifies what is of the essence before adding any conditions concerning what can be appropriately said about the human being as one who is in the likeness of God; using terminology from the secular world: concerning the dignity of the human being, concerning his *ratio* and his free will. How positively Luther spoke about the free will of the human being is often overlooked — the free will of the human being even has its own article in the Augsburg Confession: *De libero arbitrio* ("Concerning Free Will," article 18).[11] We are thus not to speak only about our will that is not free — namely, with reference to the salvation that we cannot, *Gott sei Dank,* create on our own.[12] We can speak about our free will as well, concerning the *liberum arbitrium* — namely, with reference to righteousness in relationship to the world *(iustitia civilis).* That is where free will has its proper place: "Even after Adam's fall, God did not take from reason this grandeur, but rather confirmed it."[13]

At the same time, a cardinal problem is addressed that affects every Christian ethic: the relationship between a general ethical system and Christian ethics. Is there something unique about Christian ethics? Let us reflect for a moment on the teaching about the three estates. In the *Confession* of 1528 Luther makes a remarkable distinction concerning how they are related: between what is "holy" and what is "saved." The estates are holy because they have been established by God; but we are not automatically saved therein. Even someone who lives in a holy estate can get lost. Luther emphasizes the fact that "certainly even the godless have many holy things, but they are [still] not thereby saved."[14] One must distinguish between "holy" and "saved."

---

11. "Concerning free will, it is taught that the human being has a free will in certain respects, that he lives in an external manner in an honorable way and can make choices among the things that reason can comprehend; but without the grace, help, and working of the Holy Spirit, the human being cannot be pleasing to God, fear God within his heart, or believe in him, or be able to cast from the heart the evil lusts that were within him at birth. Such things happen only through the Holy Spirit, which is given through the Word of God. For Paul says in 1 Cor. 2:[14]: 'the natural man comprehends nothing about the Spirit of God.'" CA XVIII; cf. *BC,* 50.

12. Cf. chap. 8.2 below.

13. WA 39I:175.20f.; cf. *LW* 34:137 (*The Disputation concerning Man,* thesis 9).

14. WA 26:505.20f.; cf. *LW* 37:365 (*Confession concerning Christ's Supper,* 1528).

In the *Disputatio de homine,* Luther makes these points still clearer when he adopts the schema of the four causes (theses 11-15), which played a huge role in the entire Aristotelian tradition; every aspect of the matter can be described by using these:

1. The efficient cause *(causa efficiens)* — whence does the matter come?
2. The material cause *(causa materialis)* — in what does it consist?
3. The formal cause *(causa formalis)* — as what does it exist?
4. The final cause *(causa finalis)* — toward what does it aim?

Luther grants a certain level of insight to the likes of Aristotle, Demosthenes, and Cicero in the areas of the second and third causes. He thinks these two aspects are handled most beautifully and in the best way possible by the ancient philosophers when discussing life in the world; they contain "certainly many holy things." But praise for the heathen orientation toward the world and their use of reason is not absolute: "But there is little question that philosophy does not know the efficient cause and the final cause as it relates to the human being. As regards the final cause, philosophy does not go beyond one's earthly journey; and it does not know that the efficient cause is God the Creator."[15] It also does not know *from whence* come the state and household estates either, *by whom* they are preserved, and *to what end* everything takes place. The *causa efficiens,* that the source is the creative hand of God, and the *causa finalis,* that of God's judgment and the fulfillment of the world, are both hidden from worldly philosophy.

It is thus the error of the philosophers, as it is of every godless person, to wish to be one's own *causa efficiens* and *finalis,* thus to be one's own creator and fulfiller in the estates of the state and the household. Even if they know something that is correct about them, the entire system that coordinates their life as a whole does not work as it should, since they themselves want to be in charge of the source of their existence.

The image of God for the human being consists in the fact that the individual is the representative *(vicarius)* of God and is the one responsible for carrying out his mandates on earth. Whoever is not satisfied with being an instrument of God and with being one who carries out his mandates destroys and misdirects the proper way to act in the image of God by glorifying himself instead, wrongly applying what was promised to him — the ability to reason by using language. A *homo politicus,* such as Cicero, speaks and acts in a good way; one cannot help but learn from him. But he does not act correctly

---

15. WA 39I:175.28-31; cf. *LW* 34:138 (theses 13-14).

in how he handles things, since he desires to praise himself by means of his deeds. Luther speaks shockingly in a play on words: "Haec ego feci. Ex hoc: feci, vere fiunt feces."[16] Fame, which is the highest that a Roman can strive to attain, is praise of self, and thus, *"feces,"* filth.

Appropriate actions within the estates of state and household are destructive when they become a medium and the material means for expressing oneself and justifying oneself. *Hominem iustificari fide absque operibus* — "The human being is human in that he is justified by faith and not by means of his works." That which is willed by God in terms of worldly activity is good if it is conceptualized within specific boundaries, when the human takes into account that he will come to an end and is cognizant of his finitude and fallibility. But as soon as temporal activity is conceptualized and saturated with justification of the self and praise of the self, when what is temporal is distorted and misdirected — for the very reason that it is no longer temporal in the proper sense, it is burdened instead by an ultimate claim to justify the self and thereby a claim to save oneself.

It has thus become clear that, and how, Luther conceptualizes the relationship between humanity in general and a Christian view of humanity, between a natural-philosophical ethic and a Christian ethic, as one that is fraught with conflicting elements. This conflict is not ameliorated by a proposal such as that offered by a Thomistic social ethic, with its view of relative independence and immanence, in which nature is exalted and completed in the end by means of grace. The pressure is also not taken away by postulating that God is the one who makes human freedom possible — as transcendental-philosophical thinking would have it. No amicable and peaceful coexistence is possible, where human nature and grace are positioned over or under one another. No separate parallel existence can be postulated for those who are heathen and those who are justified. The conflict remains and breaks out ever anew at the point where philosophy forgets that its appropriate responsibility deals with what is *within* this world and thus when it elevates itself instead and claims that it is in its own proper purview to define what is human.

From this perspective one can understand how Luther can characterize reason at one time as a "whore"[17] and can still call it *divinum quiddam,* "al-

---

16. WA 40III:222.34f. ("'I have made this,' says Cicero. But from this 'I have made this' [*feci*] come *Fäkalien* [feces]").

17. Cf. the philosophical theses of the Heidelberg Disputation (second thesis, including the reasons that substantiate it: WA 59:409.20–410.12; 1518); LW 45:39 (*The Estate of Marriage,* 1522); *LW* 37:221: "Here faith must blind reason. . . ." Cf. WA 51:123-134 (Rom. 12:3; preached on January 17, 1546).

most something divine," at another point.[18] There is no contradiction here, when one distinguishes between the *iustitia Dei* and the *iustitia civilis*, between the righteousness of God and temporal righteousness.

One must pay careful attention to this distinction. That is because — at least among those who have not read him and who judge him on the basis of some comment someone has made — Luther is put into the camp of those who denigrate reason. This moniker is hung on him because hardly any philosopher has taken any interest in him in decades[19] — in marked contrast to the massive attention afforded by the philosophical community to some, such as Augustine, Thomas, Schleiermacher, and Kierkegaard.

It is certainly true that Luther did, in actual fact, polemicize against reason in the harshest tones — namely, against the kind of perverted reason that claims for itself the ability to understand issues that deal with the *homo peccator* and the *Deus iustificans* and believes that it can make proper judgments in matters of sin, grace, and salvation. *For Luther*, ratio *always remains within the confines of the law and can never make its way to the gospel on its own.* Specifically, Luther spoke out against the way righteousness, as described in Aristotle's *Nichomachean Ethics*, was used in matters that dealt with sin and grace, as was done in the late Middle Ages, for example, by Gabriel Biel. If *ratio* wants to settle the matter by saying "You are what you accomplish," then it is valid to say *fides occidit rationem*,[20] "faith kills reason." It is only in this respect — in the soteriological realm, in regard to salvation — that Luther denies that reason and philosophy are competent.

As stated in the *probatio* to the second philosophical thesis in the Heidelberg Disputation: "apart from Christ," philosophers are just like those who engage in sexual activity outside of marriage. Just as sexual activity is "used appropriately only by someone who is married, so the only one who can philosophize rightly is one who is a fool, that is, a Christian."[21] For Luther the issue is about conceptualizing the right way to interact with knowledge. Whoever has let himself become a fool because of the message about

---

18. WA 39I:175.9f.; cf. *LW* 34:137 (thesis 4).

19. Cf. Oswald Bayer, "Philosophische Denkformen der Theologie Luthers als Gegenstand der Forschung. Eine Skizze," in Oswald Bayer, *Zugesagte Gegenwart* (Tübingen: Mohr Siebeck, 2007), 324-29.

20. WA 40I:359.7–373.2; cf. *LW* 26:226-35 (on Gal. 3:6 or Gen. 15:6; 1531).

21. WA 59:409.20f. ("The Philosophical Theses of the Heidelberg Disputation," 1518). The most important — and first — thesis reads: "Whoever wants to philosophize safely in Aristotle properly has to have been made a fool in Christ beforehand" (lines 3f.). In addition, 1 Cor. 3:18 is quoted in the *probatio* (lines 6f.): "Whoever among you thinks that you are wise in this age should become a fool so that he can become wise."

the cross does not seek to discover the nature of his existence through philosophical knowledge. Instead, he has actually been freed from that type of *perversion*. Thus, from within the context of love, he lets his knowledge bring benefit to the neighbor and what he needs. He does not seek his own honor and does not strive for the heights, but is enabled to cast his eyes toward the downtrodden;[22] for example, he sees how events unfold down below, from the perspective of the downtrodden. But if one comes at it from the perspective of sin, in unbelief, the Creator and the Judge are mistaken; reason misses the mark and plays blindman's bluff with God, so that it calls god that which is not God and does not consider God — on the cross and in the cradle — to be God.

It is all the more astounding that, in spite of sinfulness, reason can function as "discoverer and manager of the [liberal] arts, medical knowledge, jurisprudence, and all that humans are able to do with respect to wisdom, might, proficiency and grandeur,"[23] and not least of all that God uses such activities to protect this world that is passing away on behalf of the future he has in store. For "even after Adam's fall God did not rob reason of this grandeur," of its ability to exercise dominion (Gen. 1:28), "but rather confirmed it."[24] Within the earthly realm reason is in fact "a sun and a type of divine might, installed within this life, to have dominion over all these things [medical knowledge, jurisprudence, etc.]."[25] In this sense *ratio* is "discoverer," even "manager,"[26] ruler, queen. Purely within the bounds of *iustitia civilis*, since its boundaries are well-known, reason is also aware of what it can accomplish and not completely unaware of the dangers that lurk as well. It is freed from having to make absolute statements about everything and is freed thereby to find a sensible way to apprehend what is possible and necessary within the temporal realm and within history.[27]

---

22. Cf. Edgar Thaidigsmann, "Gottes schöpferisches Sehen. Elemente einer Sehschule im Anschluss an Luthers Auslegung des Magnificat," *NZSTh* 29 (1987): 19-38.

23. WA 39I:175.11-13; cf. *LW* 34:137 (thesis 5). German "translation" by Ebeling, *Lutherstudien*, 1, 16.

24. WA 39I.175.11; cf. *LW* 34:137 (thesis 9); cf. n. 13 above. With respect to this type of reason, wisdom as law does not convict one of sin; it functions instead in the sense intended concerning the *usus politicus legis* — according to Luther's shorthand description (*LW* 26:13-358, *Lectures on Galatians*, chaps. 1–4, 1535).

25. WA 39I.175.18f.; cf. *LW* 34:137 (thesis 8).

26. WA 39I.175.11; cf. *LW* 34:137 (thesis 5).

27. Is this use of reason apart from faith even possible? Only faith unburdens one from absolutes. Would not unbelief, *eo ipso*, weigh down what is temporal with soteriological concerns and thus pervert the use of reason?

7.3. ". . . Created Me Together with All Creatures"

How the human being is placed into the world as a creature — not isolated but within the realm of all creatures — is carefully articulated by Luther in his explanation to the first article of the Apostles' Creed in the Small Catechism, as this Old Testament scholar pays attention to detail when he describes proper order, just as wisdom literature does, by the careful way he arranges what he has to say:

1. Faith in God the Provider

a. Summary
"I believe that
    God has created me
    together with all creatures;

b. Development
The gift: secure existence
    ('body and soul':)
    he has given and still preserves
    for me body and soul;
        eyes, ears, and all members;
        reason and all senses;
    ('bread')
    in addition[:] clothing and shoes, food and drink,
        house and home, wife and child,
        fields, cattle, and all goods;
    (summary about 'body and soul,' and 'bread':)
        he richly and daily provides
        [me] with all necessities and nourishment
        for this body and life;
The gift: protection from nothingness
        shelters me against all danger;
        guards and protects me from all evil;
The Giver
and all this
[*positive*] purely out of fatherly, divine goodness and mercy,
[*negative*] all without my merits and worthiness.

2. The response
For all of this I am responsible to thank and to praise,
and because of this to serve and obey him.

3. The Amen

That is certainly true."

Using the example of formulas of faith and confession in the New Testament, Luther transforms what is normally the accusative object that follows after "I believe" into a subordinate clause, beginning with "that," which provides much room to expand; he uses the pronominal accusative "me," along with everything else, to give specific focus to that about which he speaks: "I believe that God has created me together with all creatures."

This designation is necessary and adequate for the person speaking. He would contradict himself if he were to go beyond the realm of what is said here by attempting to say something outside these parameters. "Except for this one alone, I consider nothing to be god, since there is no other one who could have created the heavens and the earth."[28] The Creator is unique; he excludes from consideration any other reason for the creation through any other being. For Luther, the consequence of this statement is that the word "Creator" signifies that none of us receive our lives from our own selves and that no one can guarantee the life he has received on his own.[29]

Though such exclusivistic and negating terms are used, and need to be, this is merely the reverse side of a fullness — the fullness of an existence that is not grounded in one's own efforts but solely in an existence that is guaranteed from without. This fullness can never be summarized exhaustively, but at least it can be hinted at by using an open-ended list of substantives:

> Body, soul, and life, body parts small and great, all senses, reason, and understanding and so forth, food and drink, clothing, nourishment, wife and child, domestic servants, house and home, etc., in addition all creatures for the needs and necessities of life . . . , sun, moon and stars in the heavens, day and night, air, fire, water, ground and what it produces and is capable of, birds, fish, animals, grains and all types of things that grow, as well as whatever else is provided for bodily and temporal goods, good government, peace, security.[30]

Luther does not let himself get lost in the plethora of things he itemizes in his lists; instead, he summarizes and presses forward on the basis of the notion

---

28. *BSLK* 647.43-46; cf. LC II, 11, in *BC,* 432. The explanation will include corresponding passages of the Large Catechism that will be discussed before the text of the Small Catechism is analyzed more precisely in terms of its syntax and semantics.

29. Cf. n. 31 below.

30. *BSLK* 648.14-26; cf. LC II, 13-16, in *BC,* 432.

that it is absolutely impossible that the world, and my life within it, could exist all by itself. His long lists serve to make clear "that not one of us, on our own, possesses that which we have or ever will get because of ourselves, nor will we be able to hold onto any of these things by our own power, no matter how small and insignificant they might be."[31]

Meditating on the catechism neither expects nor promises any intuitive knowledge; it does not take a discursive path either, which, once discovered and traversed, can be left as part of the past, as information that can be stored away, treasured, and retrieved from the storehouse of one's memories when one chooses to go there. It is rather "rumination" *(ruminatio)*,[32] lifelong learning, "remembrance,"[33] repetition; it is "to be practiced every day."[34] Even though Luther finds a pregnant and precise way to say it, one ought not to expect from Luther, even in his explanations of the parts of the catechism, a defining, comprehensive summary set of statements, but rather those that are suggestive, which set one's thinking and fantasizing in motion, which can be taken up for use and then taken still further, for which reason — as in the Small Catechism — they have a poetic character by necessity.

Theology cannot ignore the significance of the poetic shape of the explanation to the article on creation, if it is understood on the basis of linguistic analysis. Nothing in Luther's text is random and arbitrary; everything has its proper place. "The unending question about the Creator is treated at the same time according to its incomprehensibility."[35] Only what is most necessary is stated — but not too concisely; one needs to meditate on the breadth and fullness of the world within a space and with a rhythm that uses a sufficient number of words. The words of the text are arranged according to the setting in which human life is lived, which is broad but "not boundless"; "the human being would be lost in a place without bounds."[36]

---

31. *BSLK* 648.27-30; cf. LC II, 16, in *BC,* 432.

32. *Ruminatio* belongs to the nomenclature of the meditation tradition: cf. Martin Nicol, *Meditation bei Luther,* FKDG 34 (Göttingen: Vandenhoeck & Ruprecht, 1984; 2nd ed., 1991).

33. *BSLK* 650.11; cf. LC II, 23; *BC,* 433.

34. *BSLK* 549.7; cf. LC, first preface, 9, in *BC,* 381; cf. LC, first preface, 19, in *BC,* 382; LC, second preface, 4, in *BC,* 383.

35. Walther Killy, "Der Dichter," in *Luther kontrovers,* ed. Hans Jürgen Schultz (Stuttgart: Kreuz Verlag, 1983), 146-61, here 155.

36. Hans-Jürgen Hermisson, "Gottes Freiheit — Spielraum des Menschen. Alttestamentliche Aspekte eines biblisch-theologischen Themas," *ZThK* 82 (1985): 129-52, here 140. Cf. Evangelische Kirche der Union, ed., *Gott — Herausforderung der Kirche,* Votum eines Ausschusses der EKU (Neukirchen: Neukirchener Verlag, 1982), 33f.

7.3.1. Faith in God the Giver

7.3.1.a. Summary

The text is constructed as three sentences. The third ("That is certainly true") is the shortest. It is the only one constructed using third-person forms, which gives assurance, at the same time, of the objective nature of what is known and confessed in a subjective way. The second, longer sentence ("For all of this . . .") is constructed using the first person — as is the first sentence as well. The first sentence is the longest. That is the case admittedly only because of the long, tightly packed, and wide-ranging subordinate clause that emerges from the main clause, but it does not founder thereby. The principal clause, which is in the first person, is actually the shortest of the clauses and consists of only two words: "I believe . . ." But it does not let itself end right away with a period. Instead, following the grammatical pattern that one can observe in formulas of faith in the New Testament, which use an open clause that constitutes a matter, it automatically calls for an object and is related to that object. Faith is constituted by means of this relationship. There is no "absolute" faith.[37] Instead, it is related to a foundation, to a goal, to content; only faith that takes an object is faith.

Thus the subordinate clause states what is most important. One could recast it to be a main sentence: "I believe: God made me . . ." But instead, as formulated by Luther, it imprints a unique quality of movement on the text. It moves away from the "I" who is speaking, since the "I," in the nominative, right away becomes the object of the subordinate clause, "me," so that greater emphasis can be given to the dominant subject of the subordinate clause: "God" — linked to the predicate that belongs with its own predicate: "created." In parallel to the first accusative object, "me," the second accusative object, "all creatures," is not a simple addition and supplement, as has often been suggested; its positioning at the end of the clause gives it a particular significance. Coming as it does at the end of the clause, the speaking "I" referred to by the accusative object "me" finds himself safely tucked in within the whole host of all the creatures; the individual person does not find his Creator alone and in a direct encounter, but rather in the midst of a wide world.

But Roman Catholic opponents especially, supported by neo-Protestants, think they can detect in Luther a theologically questionable subjectivity and application of the truth about the faith at work. Paul Hacker has stated this

---

37. Contra Paul Tillich, *The Courage to Be* (New Haven: Yale University Press, 1975), 171-78.

most radically as he has taken up the role of prosecuting attorney in his 1966 book *Das Ich im Glauben bei Martin Luther* (English: *The Ego in Faith: Martin Luther and the Origin of Anthropocentric Religion* [condensed version], 1970). Starting on purpose with the Small Catechism, he sees Luther as the founder of the subjectivism that is advocated today, which seeks to dissolve all objective truth that stands in the way of the certainty one can achieve purely by self-assurance; Luther's radical way of "interpreting everything by how it relates to the 'I,'" supposedly disconnects "totally from the transmitted text of the Apostles' Creed."[38] "The 'I' turns back in on itself *in the very act of faith*"; Luther's faith is said to be *"reflexive."*[39]

Hacker did not read carefully enough. Otherwise he would have certainly noticed that Luther in fact specifically takes into account the reference to the relationship that is established by God when he addresses me with the words of promise and that he puts into words, but plainly not in such a way that causes one to turn in on the self, not so as to find a way to think oneself out of the relationship that is constitutive for being human in a most basic way in the midst of fellow creatures, but to see oneself placed into this larger setting from the very beginning. Luther's summary of the faith about creation that includes the phraseology "me together with all creatures" preserves the idea that all creatures have that same original relationship with the Creator, though this connection has been broken in recent times: reduced to that which is known and that which is unknown, to having private meaning and public validity, to understanding and explaining, to history and nature . . .

Since God has called me and all creatures into existence, he does not leave me alone; he makes sure that I am together with the other creatures. To be sure, from within the overall context of the catechism, but most importantly once again in the explanation of the first commandment, it can be shown that I am created not only together *with* the other creatures but in fact I come *through* them — most especially: through my parents. The fellow creatures are the medium, God works through them; they are the "means, through which God gives everything."[40]

---

38. Paul Hacker, *Das Ich im Glauben bei Martin Luther* (Graz, Vienna, and Cologne: Styria, 1966), 23. Hacker stands in a tradition that was strengthened significantly by Maritain: Jacques Maritain, *Trois Réformateurs. Luther — Descartes — Rousseau* (Paris: Plon, 1925), 1-75 ("Luther ou l'avènement du moi": enthronement of myself), especially 19; Luther is said to represent "une égoïsme métaphysique" (a metaphysical egoism).

39. Hacker, *Das Ich im Glauben bei Martin Luther,* 28. For a critique, see the review by Otto Hermann Pesch, *TRev* 64 (1968): 51-56.

40. *BSLK* 566.21f.; cf. LC I, 26, in *BC,* 389. Cf. the explanation of the fourth commandment: LC I, 130, in *BC,* 404; LC I, 149, in *BC,* 407.

Is Luther the founder of subjectivity in its present form? Luther stated it most succinctly: because of God I can, I ought to, I should also be in a relationship with myself — even though it is never *as* a relationship that I have with myself alone. Thereby it is at this point that the distinction between faith and unbelief comes into play. Unbelief wants to have it *as* a relationship with the self. But within faith the "I" discovers itself to be *in* a relationship with the self, which is transmitted within the framework of a larger connectedness, which is already assumed to exist when I perceive it. I do not need to figure it out and construct it on my own.

7.3.1.b. Development

The Gift: Secure Existence   Luther does not put a period at the end of the summary that he formulates. For this summary is inexhaustible and intends to remain that way, which corresponds to the matter at hand. Luther's overall approach, which unfolds and expands his first sentence, shows that Hacker's thesis that the truth about the faith has been made subjective has the wind taken out of its sails. If one notes how the words are formulated, it is clear to see in the way it is developed that the connection that links the two accusative objects, "me" and "all creatures," is constitutive for Luther's understanding of creation and that the inclusion of the word "all," in the way it is formulated, does not serve just as an addendum. In fact, if one counts up how many times the first-person pronoun is used in the entire text of the explanation and then compares that to the number of times "all" is used, it shows, to the surprise of those who object that Luther is involved in making the faith subjective, a striking preponderance of "all" formulations.

The praise of the Creator, who is the giver of all good things, does not take place in some sort of purely personal encounter with him; no immediate, direct relationship exists; instead, the relationship is essentially mediated through the things of the world. With such an understanding, Luther stands in opposition to Augustine, who did not seek to learn anything of importance except in regard to God and the soul.[41]

The human being in the Small Catechism is not, as in Caspar David Friedrich's "Monk on the Sea," the one who is alone, separate — not a tiny spark, which could be extinguished from an immeasurable distance. It also does not describe the human being whose religion is to be "Sense and Taste

41. "Deum et animam scire cupio. Nihilne plus? Nihil omnino" [I desire to know God and the soul. Nothing more? Absolutely nothing]. Augustine, *Soliloquia* 1.7.1; MPL 32:872.

for the Infinite."[42] Just the opposite: *belief in God the Creator gives sense and taste for the finite.* Within this faith the human being knows himself to be set within the framework of that which is proscribed by the physical elements — obviously not beyond danger and certainly not because of his own accomplishments. He is no lonely middle point within a lonely circle. Instead, he discovers from the outset — with "eyes, ears, and all members; reason and all senses" — that he is able to communicate.

He is able to communicate as a "body." It is not just by chance that this substantive noun is the first used when giving specificity to the summary statement. It starts out from a first circle that starts from within, not as that which characterizes one as all alone, but as one who is part of a wider community, in which I am joined together with all the other creatures through my senses. As this unfolds in a second stage, one strides into a second circle of life, which might be called the *extended body,* which I, in order to make an implicit connection to the explanation of the petition for bread in the Lord's Prayer, call the realm of "bread"; once again, it is not a circle of individuality, but describes what happens within community.

One might lament that Luther does not refer at this point in the Small Catechism, as he does in the Large Catechism,[43] to more expanded life circles, such as the cosmological and the political. But the explanation to the article on creation is not presented as being comprehensive; the explanation to the second table of the Decalogue, the petition for bread in the Lord's Prayer, and the Table of Duties are all there for the one who meditates on the catechism as a whole.[44] Luther concentrates on what is most necessary in regard to each topic; here, in the explanation to the article on creation, it deals with what is most elementary, with basic needs.[45]

To present and give special emphasis to what can be listed as most elementary, simple substantives are arranged one after another, in pairs of twos and threes; Luther learned this technique from the way Old Testament wisdom comes up with lists, as for example in Sirach 17:5 ("he gave them reason, speech, eyes, ears and understanding and knowledge"). "One must take seriously that more banal words and combinations of words than these hardly ex-

---

42. Friedrich Schleiermacher, *On Religion, Speeches to Its Cultural Despisers,* trans. Richard Crouter (Cambridge: Cambridge University Press, 1990/1799), second discourse.

43. Cf. n. 30 above.

44. On the subject, cf. Oswald Bayer, *Theology the Lutheran Way* (Grand Rapids: Eerdmans, 2007), 67-74 ("Catechetical Systematics").

45. The concept originates in cultural anthropology. Cf. Bronislaw Malinowski, *Eine wissenschaftliche Theorie der Kultur,* Suhrkamp Taschenbuch Wissenschaft 104 (Frankfurt am Main: Suhrkamp, 1975), especially 39ff., 118ff.

ist. But in the way they are arranged their necessity is brought out into the open, and one is shown the utter richness of that which one commonly uses every day."[46] The use of so many substantives tells the story of the fullness of guaranteed existence. But not exhaustively! One is presented with what has clearly been selected; the list of terms has gaps and can be expanded individually by the fantasies of the one who speaks and hears the text. Each listing begins with concrete terms; after the list has been started and the fantasy is set in motion, then it uses abstract terms, which come to a conclusion with a summary, which opens one up to think about it still more.

With regard to observations about the tense and type of action conveyed by the verbs, one notices that after it starts with perfects ("has created," and parallel to it, "has given"), only the present tense is used ("preserves," "provides," "shelters," "guards," "protects"); one can infer that the preceding perfects should be understood as present perfects.

The preponderance of terms clearly uses the present. This preponderance is not apparent in this text just by chance; it identifies Luther's understanding of creation in a substantive way. That the perfect is used at all, even though only marginally, accentuates the unmistakably factual nature of what is happening in the present. It also keeps one from mistakenly thinking that the Creator is present only at the moment when it says the Creator is present, since he provides the trustworthy relationship that impresses our life with the "natural" rhythms such as night and day, winter and summer. I, who am never in control on my own at any moment, as a creature among all the creatures, do not exist merely in an interminable "moment" in time.

If at first glance the explanation to the first article in the Small Catechism seems to be organized anthropocentrically and thus seems to be an example of modern thinking, which advocates a basic viewpoint for which "a principle of imitating the central perspective is characteristic,"[47] such an impression can be corrected to its very foundation by noting Luther's understanding of God, observing his unique way of expressing how God freely wills to be immanent and present in the world. "[T]hat which is new concerning modernism is in how it describes the march toward owning oneself" and in "absolutizing the self."[48] God the Creator fades to being little more than an idea of the necessary condition needed for human freedom. Luther's understanding of God has precisely the opposite impact: God the Creator is ines-

46. Killy, "Der Dichter," 155.

47. Dieter Jähnig, "Realisation," in Jähnig, *Welt-Geschichte. Kunst-Geschichte: Zum Verhältnis von Vergangenheitserkenntnis und Veränderung* (Cologne: Dumont Schauberg, 1975), 197-219, here 217.

48. Jähnig, "Realisation," 217.

capably present; he is present in what he is doing, in evil as well as in good. God is believed in and confessed here in the explanation to the article on creation as the one who categorically gives and bestows; he is believed and confessed in the response to his Word of promise: "*I*, I will give you enough!"[49]

The summary of what is provided in these two circles ("He richly and daily provides [me] with all necessities and nourishment for this body and life") — written in German by Luther in pairs of twos, each with the same number of syllables and with alliteration — is constructed with particular care and it leaves a deep impression. When we read it today, the question comes up, with reference to this summary and in connection with Luther's entire characterization of guaranteed existence, whether there is in fact an anthropocentric message, which has consequences that pose dangers to life that can still be detected and recognized today. Does not Luther foster such an anthropocentrism when he states explicitly in the Large Catechism that God the Creator lets me "be served by all creatures for the benefit and necessity of human life"?[50]

Even if we pause to reflect on such a sentence with care, because it would have been heard differently by the world of Luther's agrarian Wittenberg than by the world after Descartes, we must admit that an undeniable element of truth is at work in the question. A critical assessment of the question concerning what is to serve the human being ought not to lead in the direction that the world, as homeland, is to be plundered; he must be able to make use of the world in the way it is to be perceived correctly, so that he finds his place within it. Luther's statement that God the Creator "provides for all creatures to serve" me, as can be seen by the immediate context ("sun, moon, . . . day and night"),[51] demands that I do not think that everything that surrounds me is to be grabbed up greedily for my own possession, but leads first and last to thankful awe, which lets it be and recognizes what has been called into existence by God.

The Gift: Protection from Nothingness Astonishment concerning the guaranteed life would be flat and untrue if one did not recognize the ongoing possibility of threats to existence. The catechism speaks very briefly about this, but still in an unmistakable way. God the Creator is praised as the one who daily "shelters me against all danger; guards and protects me from all evil."

In spite of the brief treatment, the fundamental danger inherent for all life is depicted realistically. The emphasis that is given to each of the different

---

49. *BSLK* 560.40; cf. LC I, 4 (explanation to the first commandment), in *BC*, 387.
50. *BSLK* 648.19f.; cf. LC II, 14, in *BC*, 432.
51. *BSLK* 648.20-23; cf. LC II, 14, in *BC*, 432.

items in this artistically constructed explanation, which is certainly the result of careful reflection, suggests that such dangers, with forethought, deserve to be mentioned as having only a second order of importance, not a first order. The discussion starts by describing the fullness of life that is guaranteed — with a relatively expansive amount of detail. Only then is mention made of the nothingness of the nothing that hides itself, appropriately with only one set of parallel expressions. "Nothing" does not go back as far in time as existence; in no way do the two have equal weight. There is no almighty power to be attributed to the power of chaos that breaks forth in evil.

The Giver As is characteristic of Luther's theology, the theme is developed first of all with God's action mentioned as *event*. Only in a second step — by means of an adverbial designation, added to the verbs — is the *reason* for such action stated: "and all this purely out of fatherly, divine goodness and mercy." The fact that God guarantees existence makes him good; the fact that he protects from nothingness makes him merciful. These are thus for Luther the two focal points for his understanding of the faith in God as Creator: his gift-giving "goodness" and his "mercy"[52] that protects from evil, even to the point that he rescues from the power of death; not just redemption, but creation itself is a work of mercy by the triune God.

Using what is formally an exact parallel to what has just been added to the verbs that describe the gifts, Luther inserts a further adverbial description: "all without my merits[53] and worthiness." By means of a strict syntactic parallelism he uses artistic rhetoric at this point to intensify the effect of the way and the means by which God and the human being — I myself — are interrelated, that is, knowledge of God and knowledge of myself.

The human being who believes thus speaks in a *via negationis* — not about God but about himself and at the same time about his fellow creatures. Representing the entire creation, the human being confesses that this goodness and mercy come without cause, being caused only by what goes on internally within itself. Coming without cause and coming only because of itself negates every other reason, every claim that the self can claim to be the reason for creation. One significant reason for saying this is that seeking to trust in one's own performance, setting my hopes on "my own merits and worthiness," and the resultant concerns reveal their fascinating and shocking pow-

---

52. The eulogy in 2 Cor. 1:3-11 illustrates the nature of God's mercy and power to save from and through death.

53. The German noun *(verdienst)* can be singular or plural ("without all my merits"); the Latin translation construes it as plural.

ers, their self-produced idols and nothingnesses, and they bring "danger" and "evil." The Creator guards and protects from that in that he himself cares — he alone and no other beside him.[54]

7.3.2. The Response

Insofar as faith confesses that God is categorically the Giver, it itself is also the response — to the Word of promise to provide, the response to God as a Word that has come already to the faith at a previous time, which gives it reason to believe. Luther does not just suggest by implication that one ought to thank and praise, as something one would simply expect would happen after the preceding articulation of the faith in God the Creator is presented. Instead, the second sentence of the explanation makes it explicitly clear that such a response is necessary: "For all of this I am responsible to thank and to praise, and because of this to serve and obey him." This describes everything about the human being that needs to be stated. He sees himself defined by a word that is addressed to himself, which calls him into life. His calling now is to respond; but he also must respond.

The first aspect of the response is to praise and to thank. More specifically, to respond means to praise that which faith produces, through which God is given what is appropriately owed to him in a productive way.[55] To this belongs giving to others what has been given. "Thus we are also to give and loan our goods and allow them to be taken, not only to friends but also to enemies and not let the matter rest there but even give ourselves over to death, for friends as well as for enemies, and to think of nothing else than that we are only to serve others and be useful with body and goods in this life."[56] The answering response includes an ethos of giving and of love.

7.3.3. The Amen

Luther's basic problem was the problem concerning certainty. What can stand powerfully against threats, against the constant threats to existence, against the agonizing struggle?

---

54. Cf. the stanza on creation in Luther's creedal hymn: *EG*, #183, 1 ("Wir glauben all an einen Gott" = "We All Believe in One True God"). *LSB*, #954.

55. Cf. below n. 60.

56. WA 17II:206.15-19 (*Fastenpostille*, on Eph. 5:1-10; 1525).

With an emphatic conclusion to the explanation, "That is certainly true," the issue of certainty is resolved by seeing that it is given as a gift. This last sentence refers back to the first and clearly points out how one is to evaluate the character of what has been said to this point: it is an assertion, true and certain speech. Its truth and certainty are given by the Word. If creation is viewed as address, one is provided with the certain response of the human being and the need of the human to give such a response.

7.4. The Human Heart — a Place for Making Pictures

The human being is *animal rationale, habens cor fingens*[57] — a being furnished with reason that has a heart,[58] which imagines, makes pictures, invents. Luther came up with this ingenious formula, which goes into further detail about the orientation of the *ratio* by concentrating on the aspect of the imagination, in the lecture on Genesis 8:21 ("The inclination of the human heart is evil from youth"; cf. Gen. 6:5), at the same time he was crafting the theses *De homine* of 1536. As had been stated in the theses, Luther makes use of the traditional definition of the human being as an *animal rationale*, which is constructed on a formal level on the basis of the principles of definition set forth by Aristotle. According to those rules, first comes the identification of the most obvious overall concept (the *genus proximum*), and then come the differentiating markers for the special cases to be sketched out *(differentia specifica)*. In this case it means: the general term *animal* (living being) is defined more explicitly by the differentiating term *ratio* (reason); the human being is that form of life that is able to reason, that has reason.

Luther expands the one-dimensional orientation of this traditional anthropological formula, which concentrates on what it means to be rational in connection with Genesis 8:21, when he adds *"habens cor fingens"*: the human being has a heart, which can invent, which can imagine, which can make pictures. There are thus *two* basic powers that drive the human being — his *rational* consciousness and his *utopian* consciousness. The one defines the intellectual interaction with the world of human beings and is primarily oriented toward the present; the other is located in the realm of the imagination, which focuses primarily on the past and the future — interpreting the past and projecting into the future. Luther's definition can be

---

57. WA 42:348.38; cf. *LW* 2:123 (*Lectures on Genesis*, chaps. 6–14, 1536).
58. Cf. Johannes v. Lüpke, "Herz," in *RGG*, 4th ed., vol. 3 (2000), cols. 1695-97.

made more precise yet: the human being does not only *have* an inventive heart; but rather he *is* a *cor fingens*. The human being as one who can speak is a heart, which continually produces images and idols. The power of imagination fabricates images — sketches of goals for life, of happiness, as well as images of fears about disaster. They are all rational remembrances, diagnoses, prognoses, guided by images, by images of what is good, of what makes life successful, and are images that the human heart has imagined and produced, by pictures of fear and hope, which once again are grounded in certain experiences.

Luther's definition of the human being as an *animal rationale, habens cor fingens* has its theological validity within *creation,* but is to be understood first of all, on the basis of Genesis 6:5 and 8:21, as a theological description of *sin* — which corresponds to Luther's work with the problem of natural theology in connection with his interpretation of Jonah 1:5 and the first commandment in the Large Catechism. In an exactly parallel way, Calvin says: "The fantasy of the human being is a factory that works ceaselessly to make idols."[59]

This is correct if the circumstances of the sinful situation are at issue. But at the same time, that which identifies what is appropriate to the creation in this formula still remains: even in faith I am *cor fingens,* in that I praise God by letting God be God, in that I, when I — in spiritual, spirit-motivated (Col. 3:16) creativity — accord to him what is appropriate to him. The *cor fingens* is at work even in a poetic song of praise, but in the sense that it offers thanks. Thus Luther's famous phrase *fides creatrix divinitatis* is to be understood as follows: the faith is the creator of the deity, to be sure, *non in persona sua, sed in nobis*[60] — not in and of itself, but in us. *We make God to be God, in that we give to him what is due to him; we let God be God.*

Can one therefore characterize the imagination of the human heart as "creative"? If God works through the creature, is the creature then creative? Based on an understanding of *creatio ex nihilo* in terms of a theology of justification — God's unblemished creation — one ought to use the concept of being creative only in reference to the Creator himself. That corresponds to the observation that the Hebrew word for "create" is never uttered in connection with a human being, but only with reference to God. Thus the creatures are indeed coworkers, but not those through whom creation is transmitted or

---

59. ". . . hominis ingenium perpetuam . . esse idolorum fabricam." Calvin, *Institutes of the Christian Religion* 1.11.8; cf. 1.5.12.

60. WA 40I:360.5f.; cf. *LW* 26:227 (on Gal. 3:6, 1531).

co-creators. We are *cooperatores Dei,* but not *concreatores*[61] — no co-creators with God, but his coworkers.

But what happens when the human being wants to be his own creator, when he wants to be in charge of himself down to the depth of his being, down into the root of his existence?

61. WA 47:857.35 (sermon on St. Michael's Day, September 19, 1539). Cf. *LW* 33:242-43 (*The Bondage of the Will,* 1526).

Chapter 8   Sin and the Bound Will

Scripture describes the human being:
curved in on himself apart from God,
that he looks out for himself in all things.

8.1. The Perversion of the Human Being in Unbelief: Sin

Luther offers his definition of the human being as *animal rationale habens cor fingens* in connection with a theological discussion about sin — corresponding to the text he interpreted from the Primeval History: Genesis 8:21, with reference to Genesis 6:5. The imaginations, the fantasizing, the designs of the human heart do not take place in reality and in practice in the way the Creator willed it to be and for the purpose that he empowered it — to praise God and to acknowledge him — but instead always in a distorted form, with the construction of idols, with images of false gods. The human heart is no neutral producer of images but produces on its own only images of false gods.

This topic is discussed in an instructive way in the eleventh section of the tractate *On the Freedom of a Christian;*[1] it is a key text for expressing Luther's teaching about sin:

Faith exercises its power in that it honors the one in whom it believes with the most faithful and highest belief, that is, it considers the person to be believed to be a true and worthy human being. No other honor is comparable to that belief about the truth and righteousness by means of which we honor one whom we believe. What greater thing can we attribute to an in-

---

1. The German text of the tractate *On the Freedom of a Christian* is not simply a translation of the Latin version; instead, two independent versions are involved; equal attention must be accorded to both. A translation of the Latin text is offered in what follows, which is more extensive and precise than the German version.

dividual than truth, righteousness, and virtually unconditional goodness. And, by contrast, it is the most horrible insult when one spreads an opinion about someone or is suspicious about a person that he is a liar [*mendax*] or is unrighteous, which we do when we cannot trust him [*non credimus ei*]. This is how the soul acts in faith when it believes steadfastly in the God who makes promises, considers him to be one who is true and righteous, and cannot attribute anything greater still to God than this belief. This is the highest honor accorded to God, to attribute to him truth and righteousness, and to give him everything that is to be believed [or: which is believable]. This is the way the soul shows itself to be ready for all of his [believable] will; it is here that it hallows his name and lets whatever happen that God chooses to do to it, as it pleases him, because it holds firmly to the promise of God and does not doubt that he is a true, righteous, wise God, who acts, ordains and gives care according to what is best. And is not such a soul, by means of its faith, obedient to God in all things? Which commandment will thus be extra, so that it will not need to be fulfilled in complete obedience? Which fullness would be fuller than obedience in all things? And this does not take place through works, but only through faith.

By contrast, what rebellion [*rebellio*], what unbelief [*impietas*], what insult [*contumelia*] is greater than not believing in his promise [*non credere promittenti*]? How is this anything other than either to make God a liar or else to doubt that he is true [*dubitare veracem esse*]? Does this not say that one attributes truth to oneself, but to God, instead, the lie and nothingness [*mendacium et vanitatem*]? Does the human being not negate God and judge himself to be an idol in his heart [*et seipsum sibi Idolum in corde erigit*]? Of what use are the works then, which are performed from within such unbelief, even if they were the works of an angel or an apostle? It is right of God that he includes everything not within wrath or within lust but within unfaith [*in incredulitate;* Rom. 11:32], so that they do not flatter themselves by thinking that they can fulfill the law by chaste and mild works of the law — for these are political and human virtues — [*ut sunt politicae et humanae virtutes*] and assume that they would be saved thereby, because they are conceptualized within the framework of the sin of unbelief, so that they either seek mercy or are condemned by means of righteousness.

But where God sees that truth is attributed to him and that he is honored with such an honor that comes through faith in our heart, of which he [alone] is worthy, he then responds in return and honors us, and thus attributes to us truth and righteousness because of this faith as well. It is faith, namely, that makes truth and righteousness, in that it gives God his due; for this reason, in response, God gives honor to our righteousness.[2]

8.1.1. Basic Definition

With exceptional clarity, Luther explains here what "sin" is according to its essence: unbelief. If the nature of the human being consists of hearing and believing,[3] then perversion rumbles along by not hearing, by *dis-obedience*, in unbelief and in sin. As has been seen already when viewing faith, consideration of unbelief and of sin shows that it does not deal with some sort of quality, as if something were added to the substance of "human" at a later time, but that it offers the definition of the entire human. It is not just something about him but rather involves his very nature.

Sin means: not to trust God's promise, to say: Does God actually do what he promises?[4] Has God really said? Luther calls this *"disputare de deo."*[5] The faith that is tempted can also dispute with God and thus express doubts — in the very fact that it brings its questions to God as laments. But this doubt becomes unbelief when it separates itself from the relationship with God and expresses itself with a view toward justifying the self and stabilizing the self. Whoever thinks he can fulfill his own life by his own efforts, whoever wants

---

2. WA 7:53.34–54.20. The briefer German version reads: "When one man believes in another, he does so because he holds him to be duteous and trustworthy, which is the greatest honour that one man can pay another. On the other hand, it is the greatest insult if he holds him to be loose, untruthful, or shallow. Thus also, if the soul firmly believes in God's word, she holds Him trustworthy, good, and righteous; and thereby she pays Him the greatest honour in her power. For then she acknowledges Him to be in the right, obeys His law, and honours His name, and lets Him do with her what He will, because the soul has no doubt that He is good and trustworthy in all His words. Further, no one can show God greater disrespect than not to trust Him. By lack of reverence and faith, the soul holds Him to be incompetent, deceptive, and shallow, and, as far as she is concerned, she disclaims Him by such unbelief. She sets up in her heart a false god of her own imagination, as if she understood better than He. But when God sees that the soul acknowledges Him to be true, and honours Him by her faith, He honours her in return and holds her to be devout and trustworthy on account of such faith . . . this is not done by those who have no faith, even though they are busily concerned doing many meritorious works." Translation by Bertram Lee Woolf in *Reformation Writings of Martin Luther* (London: Lutterworth, 1952), I, 362-63; cf. the explanation to the first commandment in LC I, in *BC*, 386-92.

3. Cf. chap. 7.1 above.

4. Cf. *LW* 1:160-62 (on Gen. 3:6). The sin was not the eating of the fruit; it lay in calling God's Word into question, in doubting him.

5. WA 42:118.11-32; cf. *LW* 1:157 (on Gen. 3:4-5).

to guarantee his own existence, will no longer have need for hearing and responding — by praising, lamenting, and petitioning.

Luther arrives at his concept of sin completely on the basis of belief in the promise, in that he considers it to be a perversion of such belief (cf. Rom. 14:23). As a point of departure, he expresses what it means to believe in the God who is encountered on the basis of his promise, in the eleventh section of *On the Freedom of a Christian*. Then the opposite of faith is demonstrated by direct contrast and it is thus shown: what sin is. When one does not believe in God, it means to consider him unreliable, as one who cannot be considered worthy of trust, and thereby to make God out to be a liar. With such a move the human attributes the truth to himself, but lies and nothingness to God. Whoever does such a thing negates God and is thus an atheist — whether in an abstract and theoretical sense or, as is more usually the case, in the realm of what one practices, by acting in a way that does not trust God or considers God to be of little account (Ps. 14:1).[6] One who is godless elevates himself, on the basis of his *cor fingens,* to be his own idol, by making an image of an idol in his heart.

Faith and unbelief are more than merely explanations about reality. In both cases, concerning both faith and unbelief, something actually *happens:* the judgment of God makes a determination about the existence of the human being; the judgment of the human being concerning God makes a determination as well — though admittedly not about the nature of God; it determines something about the human being instead. It is like what takes place in a relationship between those in love: what is affirmed by the other when I hear "I love you" affects my being. When I hear this and believe it, I really am the beloved one. But if instead I do not believe it, then I am not that beloved one. *Reality is constituted by one's assessment.* Sin has a qualitative nature and is not simply a deficit, as if something good is lacking, so that one minimizes the intensity of one's being or speaks merely of a "disinclination" and "inhibition concerning the knowledge about God."[7] Luther does not quantify. For him there is no smooth transition. He sees only a qualitative difference; there is only the one or the other: either faith or unbelief.

6. Martin Luther, *The Bondage of the Will,* trans. Henry Cole (Grand Rapids: Eerdmans, 1931), 29: "All have a darkened heart; so that, even if they know how to speak of, and set forth, all things in the Scripture, yet, they cannot feel them, nor know them: nor do they believe that they are the creatures of God, nor any thing else: according to that of Psalm xiv, 1. 'The fool hath said in his heart, God is nothing.'"

7. Friedrich Schleiermacher, *Der christliche Glaube nach den Grundsätzen der Evangelischen Kirche im Zusammenhange dargestellt,* ed. Martin Redeker, vol. 1, 7th ed. (Berlin, 1960), §62.66 (341.355 and elsewhere).

8.1.2. Differentiation within the Basic Definition

Practically all the pertinent biblical terms — especially those from the Old Testament — are gathered together in the Latin text of *On the Freedom of a Christian: peccatum, rebellio, mendacium, vanitas.* At the root of it the following holds true: in sin the human being finds himself in contradiction to the nature that God has determined for him, in contradiction to what the God who made him said about him at creation. This contradiction manifests itself as follows:

a. in failing to hit the mark (חטא, חטאה). When one misses the mark, the human being makes a purely errant stab when trying to reach out to God,[8] and instead of hearing a living and enlightening Word, which creates communication (John 1:4), he conceptualizes only a mute and unfeeling idol that one produces on one's own. Such an errant stab is, at the same time:

b. a *perversion* (עון; *perversio*) of the originally guaranteed communion. As regards this perversion, the human being is certainly not completely without connection and relationship, but the relationships with his Creator and his fellow creatures become relations fraught with tension; the relations become disproportions. The sinner lives no longer — to add to the problem — *in* a relationship with the self, as would correspond to what was determined when he was created, but rather *as* one in a relationship with the self. No matter what confronts him, he relates it to himself; in everything he looks for what is in his own best interest (cf. Phil. 2:4).[9] This response can even take place completely within the framework of pious intentions — even when speaking about God. But in this type of relationship with the self, God is no longer heard as the one who is over against the creature; God is merely given the functional task of being the vehicle for the human who seeks to find "myself" and seeks self-realization, and the relationship deteriorates in this way to the point that the sinfulness of the self claims that the self is absolute. Sin is thus distorted communication, a false relationship.

c. Within and by means of this distortion of the relationship, rebellion (פשע; *rebellio*) against the Creator comes next; when the word *rebellio* is used, the true nature of the will, the true nature of sin, is explicit: the human being does not want God to be God. This understanding of sin as *rebellio* is articulated in the classic sense in thesis 17 of Luther's *Disputatio contra scholasticam*

---

8. Cf. Luther on Jon. 1:5; cf. chap. 6, n. 51 above in context.

9. Cf. the critical presentation in Theo Dieter, *Der junge Luther und Aristoteles. Eine historisch-systematische Untersuchung zum Verhältnis von Theologie und Philosophie*, TBT 105 (Berlin and New York: De Gruyter, 2001), 80-107: "Luther's concept of the '*quaerere quae sua sunt*' ('to strive for his own') as a definition of the sinner."

theologiam (1517): "By nature, the human being cannot will that God be God [which is what Scholastics such as Duns Scotus and Gabriel Biel specifically affirm]; instead, he would like it [if he only could!] if he himself would be God and that God would not be God."[10] The sinner seeks to be under his own power right down to the very roots of his existence, in radical fashion to provide for his own life, to create himself by his own effort. But in that sense the human being does not want the promise and gift of God that discloses everything in the world, together with God's judgment about his existence — "You are mine!" — to be true. He puts in its place his own judgment and that of others about himself, and thus doubts the truth of God's Word and falls thereby back upon himself, upon his "proud and desperate heart" (Jer. 17:9). In *superbia,* in self-glorifying obstinacy and pride, I place too high a value on myself as creature; in *desperatio,* in despair and doubt, I falsely assess what I am as a creature.

d. In such a relationship, in which he is turned in on himself, in which he makes God out to be the liar, the human being himself falls into *lies* and into *deception* (אָוֶן; *mendacium*), and along with that into what cannot be trusted, breaking promises, misusing language (שָׁוְא; ματαιότης), acting treacherously. But where one's word is broken, life is no longer safe; thus lying and murder belong together (John 8:44).

8.1.3. Turning Away from God; Curved in on the Self

When considered altogether, sin can be understood as *aversio a Deo,* as — intentional, freely willed — turning away from God.[11] The human being, who can live in any sense of the word only because the Spirit of the Creator has turned toward him beforehand (Gen. 2:7; Job 33:4; Ps. 104:27-30), turns himself away from God and turns exclusively to himself. In contrast to the nature that God has determined for him, as an ecstatic (i.e., outward-looking) being — through faith in God, through love for one's fellow creatures[12] — the sin-

10. "Non 'potest homo naturaliter velle deum esse deum,' Immo vellet se esse deum et deum non esse deum" (the Bonn edition, 5, 321; here, reading differently from *LW* 31:10 ["It is false to state that the will can by nature conform to correct precept. This is said in opposition to Scotus and Gabriel [Biel]"], the polemical nature of the thesis is thus evident; the statement of Biel and Scotus is built right in and refuted by it). Cf. thesis 30 as well *(rebellio)*.

11. Cf. chap. 6.2.3 above. Cf. WA 44:472.38 (on Gen. 42:6-7): *aversio a deo* ("aversion of God").

12. WA 7:38.6-10 (*Von der Freiheit eines Christenmenschen,* 1520; concluding thesis of the German version).

ner curves back in on himself. In being curved back in on himself *(incurvatio in se ipsum)*,[13] he cuts his ties with life, which consists in receiving from others and giving to others. The relationship with the self, which originally involved being in harmony in the relationship with God and the world, changes now so that the self is isolated and made into an absolute. The human being, who is made by nature to respond by looking outward, ends up entrapped now in the endless downward spiral of a circle, talking to himself ceaselessly and to those who are like him, and spends his time doing nothing but being completely absorbed in his own existence in an arrogant and hybrid way. At the same time, the sinner draws his fellow creatures in, so that they have to suffer (Rom. 8:18-23).

Sin is interruption, even a complete breakdown, of the comprehensive process of communication that starts with receiving and continues by giving to others unconditionally, which is what humans were created to be. The original sin of unbelief thus brings with it ingratitude, greed, hoarding for oneself, not being willing to give anything to others.[14] It is only because of God's preserving grace, because he continues to carry on his work as the Creator, that one can give thanks that life goes on at all and does not devolve into nothingness instead. In sin, in spite of sin, yes, even through sin God preserves the creation[15] for the future that he has in store for it. The grace of God even preserves the sinner, but that is not yet enough to save the sinner.

13. This apt expression, found even in his latest work, first appears in the lectures on the Psalms (1513-15): WA 3:212.36. It is then explicated for the first time in the lectures on Romans (1515-16). Cf. especially *LW* 25:345 (on Rom. 8:3): "[Scriptura] hominem describit incurvatum in se adeo, ut non tantum corporalia, sed et spiritualia bona sibi inflectat et se in omnibus quaerat" [Scripture describes the human being curved in on himself so that he uses not only physical but even spiritual goods only for his own purposes and looks out for himself in all things]. Cf. 258:27f. (on 3:21) and 304.25–305.6 (on 5:4).

14. Cf. chap. 5.2.1 above.

15. Cf. *LW* 34:137 (*The Disputation concerning Man*, thesis 9; cf. chap. 7.2 above). Through reason God preserves a tolerable order that under certain circumstances might actually cause offenses to be perpetrated. In his remarks on the fourth commandment in the Large Catechism, Luther states that God governs the world when one scoundrel kills the other (LC I, 154, in *BC*, 408). And yet, the way reason works and the way the "invisible hand" is concurrently at work to limit evil by evil simply cannot be reconciled by us. Attempts to reconcile them — even in variant forms that are pious — lead to cynicism. Before our death and before the world comes to an end, as long as we live only by faith and not by sight, no intelligent perception into the way God governs the world will be provided to us and there will thus be no justification of evil as "the *cunning of Reason*" (Georg Wilhelm Friedrich Hegel, *Reason in History*, trans. Robert S. Hartman [New York: Liberal Arts Press, 1953], 44). God's overall rule within the temporal realm is hidden and is also often alien to faith, which laments concerning God's hiddenness and yet believes he is ruling, in spite of appearances to the contrary.

With reference to this understanding of sin, what Jesus Christ's work of salvation entails can be stated already: it is that communicative event by which the world that is curved in and distorted, because it is closed in on itself completely, is saved and is thereby opened once again to be able to receive, to praise, and once again to give to others. The "happy exchange," the exchange of gifts, is the successful communicative event between the sinning human being and the justifying God.[16] God frees me from my self-imprisonment and opens for me communication with him and with fellow creatures once again.

From the perspective of being freed in this way, the sin from which I am torn away is shown to be a radical bondage: the human being who is curved in on himself is forced to misuse the freedom he is given by the Creator and is thus radically in bondage. Kierkegaard, in his *The Concept of Anxiety* (1844), with the subheading "A Simple Psychologically Orienting Deliberation on the Dogmatic Issue of Hereditary Sin" (in English: ed. and trans. Reidar Thomte [Princeton, 1980]), provided a classic demonstration of how freedom and bondage are intertwined within one another — both within each individual and within the history of humanity as a whole.

When one looks at the way one analyzes this diagnosis of humanity, there is an unavoidable conflict between philosophical and theological — especially reformational — anthropology. If philosophy — at any rate, that which is based on the type practiced by Erasmus of Rotterdam — conceptualizes bondage in such a way that it thinks one can escape from it, but also that bondage itself can even be conquered, Luther's realistic concept of sin by contrast demonstrates the fact that the human being has already gambled away his basic freedom and has forfeited it and can no longer win it back on his own. Thus the reformational concept of sin leaves "open the factual self-contradictory nature of human freedom, because the bondage of sin can be understood only as an appearance of freedom, as a slavery that is chosen by the self (John 8:34)."[17]

The question about understanding what sin entails is thus inextricably bound up with the question about the freedom of the human being, or, stated another way, about whether his will is free or bound.

---

16. Cf. chaps. 2.2 and 10.2.

17. Joachim Ringleben, "Freiheit VII. Dogmatisch," in *RGG*, 4th ed., vol. 3 (2000), 317-19, here 317. The sinner commits such sins "based on his own impulse and with a will that is ready to desire such actions": WA 18:634.25; cf. 635.12f. (*The Bondage of the Will*; 1525).

8.2. The Bound Will

Sigmund Freud speaks about three insults that characterize human love for the self: the "cosmological" insult, which is connected with Copernicus's name; the "biological" insult, which is linked to the name of Darwin; and in the third place what he himself adds to the list and calls the "psychological" insult, which is to be attributed to narcissism, which advocates the position that "mental processes are in themselves unconscious and only reach the ego and come under its control through incomplete and untrustworthy perceptions." Such an explanation is the same as saying that "the ego is not master in its own house."[18]

By contrast, in spite of his teaching about the radical nature of evil, Kant says: "Two things are required for inner freedom: being one's own *master* in a given case *(animus sui compos)* and [habitually] ruling oneself *(imperium in semetipsum)*, that is, subduing one's affects and *governing* one's passions."[19] Freud's insight suggests that this understanding of freedom leads to disappointment. That the ego is not lord in its own house was admittedly not first discovered by psychoanalysis — which Freud knew as well, since he refers to Schopenhauer. To be sure, the "unawareness" of spiritual existence is already referred to in the psalms. Psalm 19:12 says: "But who can detect their errors? Clear me from hidden [unknown to me] faults." Psalm 90:8 declares that what is unknown comes to light only when in the presence of God: "You have set our iniquities before you, our secret sins in the light of your countenance." Luther's understanding of the human being is determined decisively by this insight and discovery; corresponding to this, Augsburg Confession, article 11, declares that it is not even possible to recount all of one's sins and supports the statement by a reference to Psalm 19:12.[20]

Such a recounting is not possible because we are not able to know ourselves in regard to that which is most decisive — not only that we cannot know

18. Sigmund Freud, "A Difficulty in the Path of Psycho-Analysis," in *The Standard Edition of the Complete Psychological Works of Sigmund Freud,* trans. James Strachey, with Anna Freud (London: Hogarth Press, 1968), 17:140-43, here 143.

19. Immanuel Kant, *The Metaphysics of Morals,* trans. Mary Gregor (Cambridge: Cambridge University Press, 1998), 166.

20. CA XI, in *BC,* 44. Cf. CA XXV, 7-8, in *BC,* 72: "Concerning confession, it is taught that no one should be compelled to enumerate sins in detail. For this is impossible, as the psalm [19:12] says: 'But who can detect their errors?' And Jeremiah [17:9] says: 'The human heart is so devious that no one can understand it.'" Cf. further, Apology of the Augsburg Confession IV, 65, in *BC,* 187 (apology to article 11); SA III, 3, 18-19, in *BC,* 315; SA III, 7, in *BC,* 321, and as early as in *LW* 40:296, *Instructions for the Visitors of Parish Pastors in Electoral Saxony* (1528).

ourselves in an intellectual, Socratic sense of not knowing, but that we are not able to know ourselves in the elementary sense that the will is not able to know. The prophet Jeremiah, in the spirit of the psalm that was cited, says: "Who can understand his heart?" (Jer. 17:9). For Luther, this question posed by the prophet unlocks the nature of the human being. To formulate it more appropriately, it probes the mystery of the human being. In a rather free rendering, Luther articulates the meaning of this passage by using Augustine's description of sin as *superbia* and *desperatio,* as pride and despair: "The heart is proud and desperate — who can understand it?" That means: we are withdrawn from our self, hidden, not our own lord. We are not even lord of our consciousness — to say nothing of our unconscious nature — not lord of our conscience, not lord of the images and dreams that fascinate and frighten us; instead, we are most radically bound. Who knows his own heart, that "is deeper than all [else]" (Jer. 17:8, according to the Septuagint), down to its deepest foundation! Whoever wants to reach down to its foundation will fall into a chasm.

Melanchthon, who came to Wittenberg from Tübingen in 1518 and was immediately won over to the cause of the Wittenberg Reformation, begins his *Loci* of 1521 with a section devoted to the human being *(De hominis viribus adeoque de libero arbitrio (Concerning the Powers of the Human Being, Especially concerning Free Will),* in order to show his colors and to state that the human being is not lord in his own house. To be sure, it cannot and ought not be denied that there is "a certain freedom for external works" within the powers of human reason — "as you yourself can discover, that it is in your power to greet a person or not to greet him, to wear this clothing or not put it on, to eat meat or not to eat it." "By contrast, the inner emotions are not under our control. For through experience and custom we experience the fact that the will, under its own impulse, cannot do away with love, hate, or other emotions; one emotion is overcome by the [other] emotion."[21] Whoever can maintain "that it is the nature of the will to fight against emotions or that it can conquer emotions, whenever reason admonishes or decides it," has succumbed to an illusion. In the inmost being, in the heart of the human being, in the center of his will, "the fount of emotions,"[22] the human being is not free; "there is nothing less under his control than his heart."[23] Only when it is changed by the Spirit of God is it free to think what is good and to do it.

---

21. Philipp Melanchthon, *Loci communes* (1521) (Gütersloh, 1993), 1.42 and 44; cf. *The Loci Communes of Philipp Melanchthon* (1521), trans. Charles Leander Hill (Boston: Meador Publishing Co., 1944), 76, 77.

22. Melanchthon, *Loci communes* 1.46.

23. Melanchthon, *Loci communes* 1.65, 43 (sentence structure reversed): ". . . nihil minus in potestate sua esse quam cor suum" [there is nothing less within his power than his heart].

Correspondingly, Luther identified what is essential to his radical teaching about sin with his statement about the bondage of the will in the Heidelberg Disputation of 1518: "The free will, after the fall into sin, is a matter of a bland, empty title" — little more than a word that does not correspond to any reality.[24] This Heidelberg Disputation thesis XIII is the embryonic cell that gave birth to the dispute with Erasmus in *De servo arbitrio (The Bondage of the Will)*. Since this thesis was cited as one of the forty-one "Errors of Martin Luther" in the papal bull *Exsurge Domini* of June 15, 1520, which threatened him with the ban, Luther defended it intensively and extensively in the same year (1520) in article 36 of his *Assertio omnium articulorum,* his *Affirmation of All the Articles of Martin Luther That Were Condemned in the Most Recent Bull of Leo X.*[25] Erasmus referred to this article in his Diatribe (Debate) on article 36.[26] He wrote *De libero arbitrio (On Free Will)* in 1524, to which Luther wrote his reply in *De servo arbitrio* (1525).

This document, which Luther identified in later reflection as his most significant writing, along with his catechisms,[27] was an assault on the humanistic portrayal of the human being, as advocated by Erasmus. According to it, the human being is made of three parts: spirit, soul, and flesh. As it is described in Erasmus's *Handbook for a Christian Soldier (Enchiridion militis Christiani),* the spirit allows us to be gods, but the flesh, with its desires and baser emotions, moves us to be animals. What stands in the middle is the soul, not tending one way or the other on its own, which could sink down to follow the animal instincts or could also reach toward what is above, turning to what is godly, which can thus decide to choose what is good or what is evil. It is thus fitting to say that the soul has a free will. Empowered by this freedom, the human being can fight against the flesh and for the spirit. Erasmus thought he could use Paul, who does indeed talk about a battle between spirit and flesh, but something completely different is meant thereby: that, namely, as Luther emphasizes, "the entire human being [is] both, spirit and flesh, who fights with himself until he becomes completely spiritual."[28] Faith and unbelief, God and idol are locked in a battle with one another. Such an under-

24. "Liberum arbitrium post peccatum res est de solo titulo": *LW* 31:48 (Heidelberg Disputation, 1518).

25. WA 7:142.22–149.7.

26. On this title, cf. Thomas Reinhuber, *Kämpfender Glaube. Studien zu Luthers Bekenntnis am Ende von De servo arbitrio,* TBT 104 (Berlin and New York, 2000), 6f.

27. *LW* 50:173 (letter to Wolfgang Capito on July 9, 1537).

28. Heinrich Bornkamm, ed., *Luthers Vorreden zur Bibel,* 3rd ed. (Göttingen: Vandenhoeck & Ruprecht, 1989), 192; ("Vorrede zum Römerbrief," 1522; in English, "Preface to the Epistle of St. Paul to the Romans"); cf. 184.

standing of Paul moved Luther to disagree sharply with both the Scholastic theologians and the humanism advocated by someone like Erasmus, which he did by using the anti-Pelagian writings of Augustine.

The stumbling stone for Luther was Erasmus's thesis that "it is within the power of our freedom to turn our will toward grace or to turn away from it — just as we are free to open our eyes to see the light that shines upon us or to do the opposite, to close our eyes to it."[29] Parallel to this, Erasmus says: "As regards *liberum arbitrium,* we understand the power of the human will as that with which the human being can turn himself toward what leads to eternal salvation or can turn away from it."[30] Erasmus certainly did not attribute to the human being the ability to redeem himself. Everything for him is grace: creation, redemption, and the consummation of the world; all this lies within the power of God alone. The free will that is attributed to the human being is the ability to turn toward the grace, which is just a *perpusillum,*[31] just a puny thing, just a single tiny droplet within the wide and broad sea of grace, that Erasmus wanted to preserve as a possibility and as an action that the human being could perform: to affirm the Word of grace and not to act against it. If one does not allow for this puny little thing, Erasmus would argue, on the one hand it would eliminate any human responsibility, and any ethical demand with it; on the other hand, human evil would have to be attributed to God. Thus to deny that puny little part that the human being can play in his salvation would destroy both human responsibility and the image of God as a God who is nothing but a good and gracious God.

Luther disagrees with Erasmus as vociferously as possible: "You do not reflect on how much you attribute to free will when you use this reflexive term 'oneself' or 'himself.' When you say: he himself can turn [toward salvation], you thereby exclude the Holy Spirit with all his powers, as if he were superfluous and unnecessary."[32] Such turning toward salvation, which is what faith is, is in no way the work of the human being; it is the work of God alone[33] — just as the divine promise that creates faith is solely the work of God, which no one can keep from being fulfilled and completed, precisely be-

29. Desiderius Erasmus, *De libero arbitrio* διατριβη *sive collatio,* in *Ausgewählte Schriften,* ed. Werner Welzig, reprint of 2nd ed., vol. 4 (Darmstadt, 1995), 2a.11; cf. *Erasmus-Luther Discourse on Free Will,* trans. Ernst F. Winter (New York: Frederick Ungar, 1961), 28-29 (cf. n. 26 above).

30. Erasmus, *De libero arbitrio* 1b.10. For the opposite view, cf. Luther in *LW* 33:112-13 *(The Bondage of the Will).*

31. Erasmus, *De libero arbitrio* 4.7f.; *Erasmus-Luther Discourse,* 85.

32. WA 18:665.13-16; cf. Luther, *The Bondage of the Will,* 129.

33. "Faith is God's work in us that changes us and gives us new birth from God, John 1[:13]" (Bornkamm, *Luthers Vorreden zur Bibel,* 182).

cause God is almighty.[34] He does not only hope to, but he can also accomplish whatever he promises (Rom. 4:21).

If salvation were not completely and solely under God's control, if I would have even the slightest role in making it happen, even if I would be relying on myself at this one point alone — which is, to be sure, the fulcrum of Archimedes, then an uncertainty would creep in that would wreck the certainty of salvation and everything that goes with it. This is what Luther confesses at the end of his dispute with Erasmus, in that he uses this confession to summarize the main point of his entire work:[35]

> I confess it to be true about myself: If there were any way it could happen, I would not wish to have free will given to me or that there would be anything left under my control, by means of which I could busy myself with matters of salvation, not merely for the reason that I would not be able to survive because of so many temptations and dangers, against so many demons that storm against me, since a demon is more powerful than all human beings and no single human being could be saved, but because I, even if there were no dangers, no temptations, no demons, would still be forced to exert my efforts in regard to what is uncertain and would have to stab about in the air; for my conscience is never going to be certain and confident, whether I would have done enough for God even if I were to live forever and were to perform works. For with every work that was completed that fearful doubt would remain about whether it pleased God or whether he would expect something more yet, as can be demonstrated by every experience with works righteousness and as I, to my own misfortune, have learned all too well for so many years.
>
> But now, since God has removed my salvation from my will and has taken it up into his will, not because of my actions or accomplishments, but because of his grace and mercy (Rom. 9:16), he has made a promise to rescue me, so that I am confident and certain that he is trustworthy and that he will not lie to me and, in addition, that he is so mighty and power-

---

34. Cf. Luther, *The Bondage of the Will*, 44: "For if you doubt, or disdain to know that God foreknows and wills all things, not contingently, but necessarily and immutably, how can you believe confidently, trust to, and depend upon His promises?"

35. This "confession" at the conclusion of the tractate can also be used to evaluate its individual arguments critically. Cf. Luther himself on the use of the word *necessitas*: "Optarim sane aliud melius vocabulum dari in hac disputatione quam hoc usitatum Necessitas, quod non recte dicitur, neque de divina, neque humana voluntate" (*The Bondage of the Will*, 40: "I could wish, indeed, that we were furnished with some better term for this discussion, than this commonly used term, *necessity*, which cannot rightly be used, either with reference to the human will, or the divine").

ful that no demon and no vexatious powers can position themselves to defeat him or tear me away from him. "No one," he says [John 10:28-29], "will snatch them out of my hand, since the Father, who has given them to me, is greater than all of them." Thus it happens that, even though it might not be everyone, yet there will still be some, even many, who will be saved, whereas by means of the power of the free will [of human beings] precisely none would be saved, but we would all be lost along with everyone else.

Thus we are also confident and certain that we are pleasing to God, not by means of the accomplishment of our works but because of the graciousness of his mercy, which has been promised to us, and if we do less or act in an evil way, that he will not reckon it against us but that he will forgive us in a fatherly way and make things better. That is the boast of all the saints concerning their God.[36]

Concerning that which the human being is and seeks to be, it is obvious that one cannot discuss the issue without having the most difficult questions concerning the teaching about God rise to the surface. If, as Luther sets forth against Erasmus with all the passion of the heart and all the sharpness of the spirit, God is the one who works everything in everyone with all his power, does he then bring about not only salvation but also disaster? Not only faith, but also unbelief? Not only that which is good but also that which is evil? Or instead: ought God not to be kept separate from evil? Is evil to be attributed solely to the human being and to his will, who thus — in any case at least a little bit — has to be free: must have the freedom to choose either that which is good or else that which is evil? Again and again such an idea was suggested and there were links back along a long chain of philosophical and theological traditions, to which Erasmus hooked himself up as well.

This train of thought seems so correct that, after Luther's death, on the evangelical side — with Melanchthon! — further discussion once again took place concerning the thesis Erasmus had set forth for discussion, that the will has the tiniest ability to turn toward grace and salvation or can turn to reject it. This occasioned what has been called the "synergistic controversy," which was mediated in the Formula of Concord.[37] As has been stated, the point of

36. WA 18:783.17-39 (in essence a translation according to Bruno Jordahn, in *Martin Luther, Ausgewählte Werke,* ed. Georg Merz, vol. 1 of the supplementary series, 3rd ed. [Munich: Kaiser, 1954], 243-46). On this, cf. Reinhuber, *Kämpfender Glaube.*

37. Formula of Concord, epitome, II, in *BC,* 491-94. Cf. Walter Sparn, "Begründung und Verwirklichung. Zur anthropologischen Thematik der lutherischen Bekenntnisse," in *Bekenntnis und Einheit der Kirche. Studien zum Konkordienbuch,* ed. Martin Brecht and Reinhard Schwarz (Stuttgart: Calwer, 1980), 129-53.

contention concerns whether the human being cooperates in any way in his salvation — or can even go down to the level: what role he plays in receiving salvation. Yet one must ask about what reasons Melanchthon had later in life when he brought up for discussion the question about the manner and way one participates in receiving salvation, concerning how he went about it. If faith, as for Luther, is in forgetting the self completely, then such a question simply never becomes a topic of interest.

The contention that the human being has the ability to turn toward the grace that is offered, or else to turn away from it, as one finds the issue treated in the later Melanchthon, is of no consequence. For the fact that Melanchthon differentiated law and gospel decisively and continually during his whole lifetime places central emphasis on the fact that one must of necessity differentiate the action of God from the action of human beings. In the realm of the law, even the sinner can act in such a way externally that his works do contribute to human beings having the ability to live together, and for that reason they are termed good even when they do not have value before God — who, in contrast to human beings, can see the heart (1 Sam. 16:7) — which means: such civil and temporal works cannot establish and justify my existence.

Even though both Luther and Melanchthon express thanks when they affirm a "universal" humanity, including the humanity of non-Christians as well, as a gift from God that is at work incognito by grace to preserve humanity, just as surely they speak against this same humanity whenever and wherever it seeks to express itself as an absolute. For they view the human being as one who cannot bring about the justification of his existence on his own, who cannot probe the depths of his own heart, who cannot forgive himself his own sins, and who cannot free himself from fear of the future. The human being must be freed from these very concerns — and along with that from his doubts and his hubris, from his arrogance that causes him falsely to perceive his end. But this does not happen by means of the law but by means of the gospel alone, through which God's Spirit creates faith and turns the heart around "from the outside in," renewing it — so that I can become congruent with what my final end is to be and so that I can live in a temporal setting no longer burdened and oppressed by my longing for eternity and by my own claims about salvation, but that I can arrive at a sense of and a taste of final things.

To be freed in this way seems to the obdurate and deluded human being to be an offense against his own self-love. That is indeed what it is — in any case, in the sense that Elisabeth Cruciger, who was alive at the time of Luther and Melanchthon in Wittenberg, speaks of in a prayer: deliver the old man over to death, so that the new man can live. "The new man can differentiate faith — namely, the certainty that God cares for him — from his own work and his own efforts, which he must carry out on his own, 'as if no God is there.'"[38] If one keeps this distinction in mind, one has a way to assess and to evaluate what is done in areas such as psychoanalysis. The clarification of what is in the unconscious should not, as Freud practiced it, be done on the basis of the "Logos," by evaluating human reason,[39] but is to be placed within the arena of faith, because the human God (John 1:14) "came to his own home" (1:11). For this reason what comes is not an offense but rather a glorious freeing: one need not be lord in one's own house.

8.3. The "Inherited" Sin

As has been emphasized already, the will is not bound with reference to activities that are carried out within the world and within the realm of the freedom that humans have when making decisions, in regard to the *liberum arbitrium* that was confessed and taught by Luther, as well as by Melanchthon when he crafted the Augsburg Confession (article 18). The will is bound, however, as regards the *reason for existence* for the human being, insofar as this is determined by present human perversion — brought on by sin, by unbelief. *Alea iacta est,* the die is cast — as the sinner must admit: "Behold, I was conceived in sin, and in sin my mother bore me" (Ps. 51:5). For the entire tradition, including for Luther and for the Augsburg Confession (article 2), this verse is the classical supporting text for what is called "inherited" sin — a passage so offensive and obviously so unacceptable to modern sensibilities that it has been quietly excised from the new *Evangelisches Gesangbuch.*[40] The stone of stumbling has thus now been removed from the liturgy, and thus from the public conscience of the congregation, though it could give one an occasion to raise questions and to think critically. There is no doubt that such thinking about sin is still necessary. For the psalm text and the term "inherited sin" have been linked in the history of theology and piety, since the time of Augustine, to issues of biological transference; "inherited sin" was passed on exclusively during sexual relations.

But the truth of the matter is falsified thereby. Luther got it exactly right.

38. WA 15:373.3; cf. *LW* 45:317-31 ("Exposition of Psalm 127, for the Christians at Riga in Livonia," 1524).

39. Sigmund Freud, "The Future of an Illusion," in *The Standard Edition of the Complete Psychological Works of Sigmund Freud,* 21:54.

40. *EG,* p. 727.

In his *Confession* of 1528, he emphasizes the exact wording: "not: my mother conceived me by acting sinfully, but rather: I, I, I was conceived in sin."[41] Even though, according to the grammar, "my mother" is the subject and "I" am the object, Luther reverses the order of words in his explanation, so that my nature as subject, as a person, and as one who cannot get out of my own responsibility, as one who has the nature of a sinner, is beyond all doubt: "My mother bore me in sin . . . , which means that I [!] grew from sinful seed in my mother's womb, which is what the Hebrew text means."[42]

The extensive passage that brings out most prominently that I am imprisoned in original sin in all its fullness and in all its radical nature establishes the constitutive connection between the inherited sin and the bound will:

> For I confess and know how to demonstrate from Scripture that all human beings come originally from one man, Adam, and from this individual, by means of birth, the fall, guilt, and sin come along with it and are inherited, which evil this Adam accomplished in Paradise by means of the devil's evil, and that in this way, along with him, all are born together in sin, live and die, and would have to be judged guilty of eternal death, if it had not been that Jesus Christ came to help us and took such guilt and sin upon himself as an innocent lamb, paid for us by means of his suffering, and still stands in on our behalf daily and steps in for us as a faithful, merciful mediator, savior and unique priest and bishop of our souls.
>
> At this point I reject and condemn as plain error all teaching that praises our free will, as such, that strives to go against this very help and grace of our Savior Jesus Christ. For since apart from Christ death and sin is our lord and the devil is our god and sovereign, there can be no power nor might, no wisdom nor reason, by means of which we can prepare for ourselves or strive for righteousness and life, but we must be deluded and imprisoned and must belong to the devil and sin, so that we do and think what pleases them and what goes against God and his commandments.
>
> I thus also condemn the new as well as the old Pelagians, who did not want to consider the inherited sin to be sin, but rather a weakness or mistake. But because death comes to all human beings, inherited sin cannot be a

41. WA 26:503.31f.; cf. *LW* 37:363 (*Confession concerning Christ's Supper,* 1528).

42. WA 26:503.30-34; cf. *LW* 37:363. Luther remains within the framework of traditional concepts in other passages where he teaches about original sin (cf. Paul Althaus, *Die Theologie Luthers,* 6th ed. [Gütersloh: Gütersloher Verlagshaus, 1983], 144; Bernhard Lohse, *Luthers Theologie in ihrer historischen Entwicklung und in ihrem systematischen Zusammenhang* [Göttingen: Vandenhoeck & Ruprecht, 1995], 268f.).

weakness, but it must rather be considered an exceedingly great sin, as Saint Paul says: "The wages of sin is death" [Rom. 6:23] and, elsewhere: "The sting of death is sin" [1 Cor. 15:56]. David says the same thing, in Ps. 51[:5]: "Behold, I was conceived in sin, and in sin my mother bore me, not: my mother conceived me by acting sinfully, but rather: I, I, I was conceived in sin."[43]

The threefold repetition, "I, I, I," as stated so expressively in the text of the *Confession,* should not be ignored. One cannot express more intensely one's nature as subject, one's inability to escape responsibility, and one's accountability for the sinful "I." In spite of what is conveyed by the term "inherited sin," it is of course better, and less open to misunderstanding, to speak of "original sin" — corresponding to the common Latin expression *peccatum originale* or *peccatum originis:* sin of origin. To be sure, Luther understands "origin" also as a historical beginning point, but chiefly in the sense of a definition of one's basic nature, as that which characterizes every human being: *Each one confronts himself already in original sin; at the same time, each one is responsible for it.* Thus Luther says that we carry along our original sin "from our parents"; yet it is "not in any way less to be attributed to us than if we had done it ourselves."[44]

8.4. Ridden by the Devil

My will is like that of all human beings — inescapably in actual fact — already completely bound and imprisoned. The human being is an animal to be ridden, which is ridden in any case — either by the devil or else by God. As regards matters of salvation, Luther does not think neutrality is possible. "The human will is thus placed into the middle as a beast of burden; if God sits on it, it desires to go where God wants to go. . . . If Satan sits on it, it desires and goes where Satan wants to go. And it does not have it in its power to consider that it will go to one of the two riders or to seek one out, but the riders themselves do battle in order to hold fast to it and to possess it."[45] But at

43. WA 26:502.25–503.32; cf. *LW* 37:362-63.

44. WA 17II:282.14-21. *Festpostille;* 1527/"Evangelium am Tage Mariä Empfängnis." Luke 11:27-28. Cf. *LW* 1:161 (*Lectures on Genesis,* chaps. 1–5, 1535-36): "As Satan acted then, so he does now."

45. WA 18:126.23-28; cf. Luther, *The Bondage of the Will,* 74. Cf. *LW* 33:70. *LW* 40:144-223 (*Against the Heavenly Prophets in the Matter of Images and Sacraments — Part Two,* 1525). On the history of the imagery, cf. Reinhuber, *Kämpfender Glaube,* 46 n. 135: Scholasticism was already aware of the imagery of the horse that was ridden, but used it in the sense that the animal cooperates (free will) with the rider (grace); cf. Alfred Adam, "Die Herkunft des Lutherwortes vom menschlichen Willen als Reittier Gottes," *LuJ* 30 (1963): 25-34.

the same time — and this goes most deeply against our customary logic — this inescapable necessity and factual situation is in no way determined by necessity from some distant location, that one has to be a sinner, as a destiny or a fate. Concurrently, sin has the same point of origin and is the original deed of every human being. For this reason he is guilty and must bear responsibility. Luther thus says in his interpretation of the story about the fall into sin, that it would be the highest level of sin if one were to insult God by accusing him and holding him accountable as the originator of sin.[46] This corresponds to Augsburg Confession, article 19: "Concerning the origin of sin it is taught by us: Although God the Almighty created all of nature and preserves it, it is still the distorted will [alone] that works sin in all evil and contempt for God, as it is the [original] will of the devil and all godless people that at the very moment when God pulls away [or has pulled away] his hand, it turns away [or has turned away] to malice, as Christ says in John 8[:44]: 'The devil [as also every godless person] speaks lies according to his own nature.'"[47]

In reality the human being is not free not to sin; he cannot do anything else. But at the same time he acts willfully, with self-determination, autonomously, and is therefore answerable for sin — not only for this or that concrete sin in action or in thought, but also for inherited sin, original sin. It is a "synthesis of destiny and guilt."[48]

It is obvious that the questions about evil and the origin of sin have not been resolved adequately yet. The questions will go deeper yet in the next chapter.

46. "Hic ultimus gradus peccati est Deum afficere contumelia et tribuere ei, quod sit autor peccati" [This is the last step of sin, to insult God and to charge him with being the originator of sin]. WA 42:134.8f.; cf. *LW* 1:179.

47. *BSLK* 75.1-11; cf. CA XIX, in *BC*, 52; cf. the variant in *BSLK*, p. 75, lines 19-22, with the citation from Hos. 13:9: "O Israel, dein Verderben ist aus dir, aber deine Hilfe steht allein bei mir" [O Israel, your transgression is from you yourself, but your help is with me alone]. This conforms to the maxim from someone who set the Augsburg Confession to rhyme: "Vom freien Willen weiß der Christ, / dass dieser nicht vorhanden ist — / zum Guten nämlich! Doch zum Bösen / ist er vorhanden stets gewesen" [Lit.: The Christian knows about free will / that this is not available / for good things. But to evil / it is always available].

48. Werner Elert, *Morphologie des Luthertums*, vol. 1, 3rd ed. (Munich, 1965), 25; cf. *The Structure of Lutheranism*, trans. Walter A. Hansen (St. Louis: Concordia, 1962), 29; cf. Reinhuber, *Kämpfender Glaube*, 220 n. 606.

Chapter 9   God's Wrath and Evil

To seek God apart from Jesus Christ — that is the devil.

With reference to God's wrath, one must differentiate between God's understandable wrath and his wrath that is completely impossible to understand.[1]

9.1. God's Understandable Wrath

The Bible speaks about an understandable wrath of God. The theological view of the Deuteronomistic History, which gives shape to large sections of the Old Testament, uses the schema of the correspondence between guilt and punishing wrath: the people are disobedient to God's law, God's wrath comes down upon the Israelites, they perform acts of repentance; but then another disobedient king comes to power and the sequence of events is repeated. The understandable wrath of God is the reverse side of his love. God is jealous on behalf of his people because he wants the best for Israel — even if this becomes plain to Israel at times only in retrospect.

    Luther explains this understandable wrath of God in the Jonah commentary of 1526, which we have come to know already: Jonah fled from God and evaded his obligation. But he first became conscious of this wrath in that moment when the person responsible for the storm at sea was sought. While Jonah slept,

---

1. On this important distinction, cf. Thomas Reinhuber, *Kämpfender Glaube. Studien zu Luthers Bekenntnis am Ende von De servo arbitrio*, TBT 104 (Berlin and New York, 2000), 91-202.

there is no repentance, no reflection. Jonah could have gone on sleeping his whole life long. And if God had forgotten his sins, he [Jonah] would certainly never have thought about it again. That is indicated here in [the book of] Jonah, that he slept so deeply and soundly in the middle of the storm, and that down below in the depths of the ship, as if it should be said: He is completely deluded, hardened, sunken down, in fact dead, and that he lies in the situation of having an unrepentant heart, would also remain forever in that condition, and would be destroyed. For sin does not permit one to sense that an ability to do good could stir within the human heart — whether it be that of free will or reason. There he lies and snores in his sins, hears and sees nothing, and does not feel what God's wrath is doing and undertaking above him either. But as the sailor awakens him and encourages him to call on his God, then something else begins to happen: Then he recognizes that God is coming after him with punishment and has not really forgotten his sins; then the conscience is aroused, then the sin returns once again and comes alive. That is where "the sting of death is sin" [1 Cor. 15:56] and that points to the wrath of God, at which point not only the ship, but the whole world is too small.[2]

That which was suppressed comes to the surface and the conscience awakens. Within all the chaotic drama this remains a completely understandable event: even in the midst of all this there is communication between God and human being. Jonah, and with him every human being, can interpret what confronts him; he hears God's voice thereby, which can be understood — even though it is not the voice of his grace. With reference to the fact that God can be understood when he speaks in wrath, Old Testament scholars speak of the "sphere of actions that bring about consequences": sin and punishment, action and consequences are perceptibly related; they are interconnected, one with the other, in a way that can be understood.

But what about the wrath of God that cannot be understood? One cannot mistake the fact that this is discussed in biblical texts as well — most especially in the psalms of lament. Yet it is most surprising that God's wrath is often incalculable, fearsome, and incomprehensible, that it thus cannot be explained as something understandable or at least not as something that can be comprehended as a measured response to a specific mistaken action. That is the problem for the book of Job and is also the problem that Luther wrestled with in his biblical lecture on the book of Job, but most especially in *De servo arbitrio*.

2. WA 19:209.28–210.10; cf. *LW* 19:58.

9.2. God's Incomprehensible Wrath

Martin Luther, the "Old Testament scholar," could not avoid speaking about God's incomprehensible hiddenness. In a famous passage in *De servo arbitrio*, he deals with it as follows: "One must dispute in a different way about God and God's will insofar as he is preached, revealed, presented to us and is worshiped by us, than we do about God insofar as he is not preached, not revealed and presented, and is not worshiped by us. Insofar as God thus hides himself [*sese abscondit*] and does not want to make himself known by us, we have nothing to do with him. Here, namely, that proverb is true: what is above us does not concern us."[3] Luther distinguishes this *coldly distanced* hiddenness of God in his reformational theology[4] very strictly from that hiddenness in which God, in the weakness of the suffering and death of his Son, is *present in a saving way* and "preaches, reveals, and presents"[5] himself in the message of the cross, so that we can hear and understand and comprehend him as the God who was crucified and who became a human being; more specifically, this is also to be distinguished from God's all-consuming, terrifying hiddenness, in which his incomprehensible wrath works, in which I cannot hear him any longer, or at least cannot "understand" him any longer, but can "hear" only in terror and experience him as oppressive, fearsome, sinister. This aspect of the hiddenness cannot even be conceptualized and described in an orderly way at all. Because of this, *Deus absconditus* (hidden God) is not one name or attribute for God among others, never one of the personal names of God, but is always a problematic concept and a concept that talks of what is on the edge; but that, as such, does not mean it is to be avoided; the way it is still used will have to be made properly clear.

In essence, for Luther and for us there are two major questions that speaking about this dark side of God, this *Deus absconditus*, make unavoidable. First of all: Is God also at work in the sinner (9.2.1)? We encountered this problem already in the last chapter and will have to deal with it more specifically here. If one reflects further on the issue at this point, one comes to the

---

3. WA 18:685.3-6; cf. *LW* 33:139. What is meant is the pseudo-Socratic dictum *Quae supra nos, nihil ad nos* [things above us are no business of ours]. In another passage (cf. chap. 4, n. 54 above), Luther totally disallows this dictum. Cf. WA 43:458.35–463.17 (on Gen. 26:9; 1540-41).

4. Luther had not yet come upon this distinction in his prereformational theology (Oswald Bayer, *Promissio. Geschichte d. reformator. Wende in Luthers Theologie*, FKDG [Göttingen: Vandenhoeck & Ruprecht, 1971; 2nd ed. Darmstadt: Buchgesellschaft, 1989], 62f., 340).

5. WA 18:685.3f.; cf. *LW* 13:139. On the hiddenness of the revealed God, which brings deliverance, see WA 18:633.7-23; 639.2f.; 689.22-24.

question about predestination (predetermination): Did God really determine from eternity that some human beings would be damned?[6]

The second question (9.2.2), which is occasioned by the discussion about *Deus absconditus*, is: Does God also work in evil, but in that which is not thereby sin *(malum extra peccatum)*?

9.2.1. God's Complete Efficacy Even in the Sinner

Because Luther desired to remain true to what is connected with the certainty of salvation,[7] he maintained the following about God's omnipotence and complete efficacy:

> God accomplishes everything altogether. Nothing takes place apart from him. Nothing takes effect apart from him. That is because of what his nature as almighty entails, as Paul says to the Ephesians [1:19].[8]

> But I do not call that power almighty [as the Occamists do] in which he [God] fails to do many things that he can do; instead, this speaks of that actual, efficacious power in which he powerfully does everything in everything. Scripture understands him as almighty in just this way. And I would say, based on this omnipotence and this foreknowledge of God, that the dogma of free will is destroyed down to its roots.[9]

> Free will is a completely divine attribute [*plane divinum nomen*], which can be attributed to no one else; it is appropriate to none other than to the divine majesty. This majesty is consequently able to and actually does accomplish (as the psalm [135:6] sings) everything the Lord pleases in heaven and on earth.[10]

---

6. One might say that this is the specifically "Christian" question about the *Deus absconditus*.

7. Cf. especially *LW* 33:288-89. Cf. chap. 8 above, quoted at n. 36. Cf. Rom. 4:21.

8. WA 18:709.10-12; cf. *LW* 33:175.

9. WA 18:718.28-31; cf. *LW* 33:189.

10. WA 18:636.28-30; cf. *LW* 33:68. Cf. Joachim Ringleben, "Freiheit VII. Dogmatisch," in *RGG*, 4th ed., vol. 3 (2000), 317-19: "Since the human will apart from grace is left to the inescapable omnipotence of the divine will [*LW* 33:37], the more it simply pursues itself as will [33:150-52], the more it is bound in its condition" — at least with respect to the relationship with God. Cf. also Paul Althaus, *Die Theologie Martin Luthers*, 6th ed. (Gütersloh: Gütersloher Verlagshaus, 1983), 105-7; in English, *The Theology of Martin Luther*, trans. Robert C. Schultz (Philadelphia: Fortress, 1966).

In a passage cited already from Augustine, Luther advocates in his teaching about creation that God is deeper within me than I am within myself (*interior intimo meo*),[11] in the most absolute way possible,[12] so that the concept of God and of the human being as entities that stand opposite one another as independent becomes problematic. If God is one who works within me, speaks, prays (cf. Gal. 4:6), and thinks — is he then not also the one who commits sin in me?

But is this not contradicted by what Luther says in his interpretation of Genesis 3:13, when he maintains: "This is the highest level of sin, to insult God and to attribute to him that he is the originator of sin"?[13] But how can both be maintained at the same time: that God is not the originator of sin, and yet that he is the one who continues to create, as the *Deus actuosissimus,* who works everything in everything, and thus also must make sin happen?

Luther sees no other possibility than to attempt the following high-wire balancing act: "God, however, cannot act in an evil way, even though he does work evil through evil; for he himself, who is good, cannot act in an evil way and yet he uses evil as a tool that cannot escape his power, carrying evil forward and making it work."[14] In this regard, Luther uses the following illustration: if the hatchet is jagged, it can produce only damaged goods, even if the carpenter works with it in the proper way.[15] The situation can possibly become clearer still in the following illustration: water flows incessantly — but at the wrong mill. To be sure, such illustrations have limited applicability. It could always be asked in response why the carpenter does not sharpen the hatchet or why the miller does not pay attention so that the water flows properly. But that is not the point of the illustrations. Luther speaks in opposition to the "idle" gods of the Epicureans[16] to make the point that God is not inactive:[17] God is

---

11. Cf. chap. 5, n. 27 above.

12. In all creatures God is "more deeply, more inwardly, more present than the creature is to itself" (*LW* 37:60 [*That These Words of Christ "This Is My Body," Etc., Still Stand Firm against the Fanatics,* 1527]).

13. Cf. chap. 8, nn. 46-47 above.

14. "Deum tamen non posse male facere, licet mala per malos faciat, quia ipse bonus male facere non potest, malis tamen instrumentis utitur, quae raptum et motum potentiae suae non possunt evadere." WA 18:709.23-31; cf. *LW* 33:176.

15. *LW* 33:176.

16. Luther came to know the "idle" gods of the Epicureans by way of Cicero, *De natura deorum* 1.51, 115, 121, 123; 2.59.

17. Cf. WA 14:109.21 ("Sermons on Genesis," 1523-24): "God was not idle after he created. It was due to the word of God that the creatures increase"; *LW* 3:337-38 (on Gen. 20:6-7, 1539): "For God is no idle talker. Whatever he says is important and profitable"; WA 47:795.2f. (sermon of June 15, 1539): "God is not idle; wherever his word is, there is also his work."

not idle; instead, he is "incessantly active."[18] His ability to create is not inhibited; it never ceases to work and is by its nature a beneficent power, even when it is misused through the *perversio* of sin.[19] "The evil lies within the tools, which God does not allow to stand idle, so that evil indeed has effect as a result of God's own impetus."[20] Even the criminal has his power to be alive and his intelligence from God; God's creative power works on in his life and in his actions. "Because God moves and accomplishes everything, he by necessity moves and accomplishes things also in Satan and in the godless. He works in them such as they are and as he finds them. This means: since they are turned away from God and are evil, and are forcibly taken along by the impetus of the divine almighty power anyway, they do only that which is at enmity with God and is evil."[21] Thus Luther can still talk about where evil gets its *power,* its might — namely, from the almighty God. He is still at work, even though it is against his original intention.

But that by no means provides the answer to the question about evil's *overall* source and capability. Where does evil come from?[22] It is obvious that the only theological answer one can offer comes in connection with the actual fact of sin: "Sin came into the world through sinning."[23]

9.2.2. Evil or the Evil One; "God as Devil"

Just the concept of a power of God that works within the sinner is difficult enough for what one teaches about God. Yet, everywhere one looks, there is evidence for the *perversio* of what is good because of the power of sin — even though it cannot be proved, but simply because it is seen in actual fact. For anyone who wants to consider it when reflecting on the question about theodicy,

18. WA 18:747.25; 711.1; cf. *LW* 33:233, 178: *actuosissimus.*

19. Cf. Rom. 7:12-20.

20. ". . . mala fiunt, movente ipso Deo": WA 18:709.32f.; cf. *LW* 33:176.

21. WA 18:709.21-24; cf. *LW* 33:176. Cf. *LW* 33:177: "God cannot lay aside his omnipotence on account of man's aversion, and ungodly man cannot alter his aversion." "Läßt Gott Hitler seinen oder Seinen Willen tun?" (Theodor Haecker, *Tag- und Nachtbücher 1939-1945,* ed. Heinrich Wild, 2nd ed. [Munich, 1948], 75).

22. "Si quidem deus est, unde mala? Bona vero unde, si non est?" [If there is a God, whence the evil? If there is none, whence the good?] (Boethius, *The Consolation of Philosophy,* trans. Richard Green [New York: Bobbs-Merrill, 1962], p. 1; bk. 1).

23. Rudolf Bultmann, *Theologie des Neuen Testaments,* 9th ed. (Tübingen, 1984), §25, 251 (in English, *Theology of the New Testament,* trans. Kendrick Grobel, 2 vols. [New York: Scribner, 1951-55], 1:252), borrowing from Søren Kierkegaard, *Der Begriff Angst, Gesammelte Werke,* vol. 11f. (Düsseldorf: Diederichs, 1965), 29: "Sin came into the world through one sin."

the question about the righteousness of God in light of evil, the issue arises on whether God works within evil in a way that is not sinful, whether he sends suffering that is without cause and without guilt *(malum physicum)*.[24]

God is quite certainly not only the one who punishes in a measured way — as Jonah experienced it and as God is depicted in the Deuteronomistic History and at some points in the prophetic literature; he also allows what is incomprehensible to take place. Whereas God can be met in a verbally comprehensible way on the basis of the law when he punishes, the hidden God does not allow himself to be addressed directly; he is certainly the subject matter of the lament, but he is not directly the addressee.

The decisive point in regard to the experience of the *Deus absconditus* does not lie simply in the experience of evil but in the fact that evil is imperceptibly mixed within the good, thus in what is equivocal and uncertain: God "works life and death and everything in everything": "The God who is hidden in his majesty does not lament death and does not abolish it, but he works life, death, and everything in everything. For in that realm he has not defined himself by means of his Word but has preserved for himself freedom over all things."[25] God's terrifying hiddenness, experienced as equivocal and uncertain, lies in the fact that he accomplishes evil *as well as* good (Lam. 3:38), life *as well as* death, light *as well as* darkness (Isa. 45:7), happiness *as well as* misfortune (Amos 3:6). For us, beauty and cruelty are inextricably intertwined in nature and history.

Such intertwining is depicted graphically in a most impressive way by HAP Grieshaber in his portrayal of Jacob's battle at the Jabbok (Gen. 32). In contrast to the most well-known depictions of this scene of Jacob's battle with God — by Rembrandt, on to Gauguin, and finally by Chagall — Grieshaber uses a watercolor sketch, with the two figures so wrapped up with one another, so intertwined and wedged together, that the observer cannot distinguish the one from the other, even after studying it for a long time. To start with, one cannot be immediately sure that there are two figures; there could be more. Only when one starts to count the feet — which are not placed anatomically where they belong either, comparable to Picasso's *Guernica* — does

24. Gottfried Wilhelm Leibniz in his *Essais de Théodicée* of 1710 differentiates among three types of evil *(mala):* "Metaphysical evil consists in simple imperfection; physical evil in suffering, and moral evil in sin" (trans. Artur Buchenau, 2nd ed., PhB 71 [Hamburg: Meiner, 1968], 110f.). According to Leibniz — as well as Augustine and Thomas — evil is permitted by God so that good may come of it; the imperfection of one part serves the greater perfection of the whole.

25. "Caeterum Deus absconditus in maiestate neque deplorat neque tollit mortem, sed operatur vitam, mortem et omnia in omnibus. Neque enim tum verbo suo definivit sese, sed liberum sese reservavit super omnia." WA 18:685.21-23; cf. *LW* 33:140.

HAP Grieshaber, "Jacob Wrestles with the Angel"
Watercolor illustration, 1977, for *Angel of History*, © 2003 VG Bild-Kunst, Bonn

one see that it depicts *two* persons. They are together, conjoined by segmentation and yet mixed, by fragmentation and yet intertwined. The colors used in the watercolor increase the confusion. The equivocal and uncertain nature of the event, which catches my attention — *that* is the *Deus absconditus.* Clarity comes only at the end of the story. Only upon reflection does Jacob recognize that it was God with whom he fought (Gen. 32:31-32) — and then the sun rises upon him. Up to that point, it could have been a demon, a dark power, a big "It": God as devil.

It is anything but self-evident that this neuter "It" can become a personal "You." Theology cannot start without further ado by speaking about God as "You" — and Luther does not start this way either. The almighty "You" brings comfort only after it is contrasted with the almighty "It."[26] The almighty God is not merely to be praised. For God's omnipotence brings with it for us more than one interpretation. "Almighty" is not as clear an attribute of God as is his love; instead, it is a metapredicate with many meanings.[27] This means: the omnipotence of God's love is not to be identified for us and for our experience in the same way as that almighty power that works in his terrorizing hiddenness.

The experience of this terrorizing hiddenness is so oppressive and unavoidable that the question is posed: Does God work not only indirectly, *in* evil, or does he also work *evil*, directly? But then how could he be distinguished from the devil?

From many texts in the New Testament — most especially in the Synoptics — it rings in our ears that God stands in opposition to evil or to the devil, along with all the demons. Jesus confronts them in the name of God, wages battle against them, and defeats them. "But if it is by the finger of God that I cast out the demons, then the kingdom of God has come to you" (Luke 11:20). "I watched Satan fall from heaven like a flash of lightning" (Luke 10:18).

By contrast, Satan appears in the texts of the Old Testament only marginally, as the figure that stands in opposition to God (1 Chron. 21:1, though not in 2 Sam. 24:1; Job 1–2; Zech. 3:1-2). That which stands in opposition to the merciful and gracious God, the power of annihilation and destruction of life, is shockingly attributed to Yahweh himself — as in Genesis 22:1; Exodus 4:24; Isaiah 45:7; Amos 3:6; Lamentations 3:1-19; Job 6:4; 12:13-25; 16; 19. The Old Testament scholar Martin Luther takes such texts seriously when he — as a

---

26. Cf. Dietrich Bonhoeffer to Eberhard Bethge, February 21, 1944: "God meets us not only as Thou, but also 'masked' in the 'It,' and at bottom what is involved in my question is how we find the 'Thou' in this 'It' (fate), in other words, how 'fate' actually becomes 'leading.'" Dietrich Bonhoeffer, *Letters and Papers from Prison* (New York: Macmillan, 1971), 217.

27. Cf. Oswald Bayer, "Eigenschaften Gottes, V. Christentum," in *RGG*, 4th ed., vol. 2 (1999), cols. 1139-42.

Christian — maintains: "To seek God apart from Jesus Christ — that is the devil."[28] More pointedly yet: "God cannot be God [unless] he has to be a devil first of all."[29] The human is terrified. In any case, such talk stands diametrically opposed to one-sided talk that speaks only about a "loving God." If the God who promised you on oath "so acts, as if he is not concerned about you at all,"[30] and hides his yes inside a no,[31] then the thought intrudes that God is merely playing with humans, that he is just as frivolous and unreliable as one could infer about the nature of the devil according to Luther.

Luther's harsh way of talking about the devil is to be understood in its essence as follows: the devil, the most embittered enemy of the human being, who attacks and oppresses these very human beings constantly and everywhere, is nothing other than a mask of the almighty God in his terrifying hiddenness. The deepest temptation is that in which God himself becomes my enemy and in which I can no longer distinguish God and the devil, so that I, as Luther says, "do not know whether God is the devil or the devil is God."[32] We come to Luther's chief question once again, which has to do with certainty of salvation: Who or what assures me about how I am in my relationship with God? How does one come to the necessary clarity without denying contradictory experiences of the world, of one's self, and even of God?

Luther holds tightly to God's goodness, to his almighty power, and *at the same time* to his unity — and this precisely because of the certainty of salvation. He would have sooner allowed for logical inconsistencies than weaken the might and goodness of God or even go further yet and deny his unity.

Both Gnosis and Manicheism came to the point that they denied the unity of God at the time of the early church: God appears in such teaching as one who is in principle good, positioned against one who is in principle evil. Marcion constructed a dualism when he separated the Creator of the world from the Redeemer — and correspondingly the Old Testament from the New Testament. This solution is not possible for Luther. He argues as follows: if one denies to the generic name *(nomen appellativum)* "God" the dark power of that terrifying hiddenness, then God would no longer be God; then a

---

28. WA 40III:337.11: "extra Iesum quaerere deum est diabolus" (on Ps. 130:1; 1532-33).

29. WA 31I:249.25f.; cf. *LW* 14:29-32; 14:31 (on Ps. 117:2; 1530).

30. In the words of Paul Gerhardt (*EG*, #361, 9; *LSB*, 754, "Entrust Your Days and Burdens" [not all stanzas are translated]).

31. Cf. Luther's sermon on Matt. 15:21-28: WA 17II:203.32f. (*Fastenpostille*, 1525): it is a matter of seizing and holding the "Yes, deep and hidden beneath and above the No, with firm faith in God's Word, just as this woman does."

32. WA TR 5:600.11f.; cf. Reinhuber, *Kämpfender Glaube*, 56-62.

power would be next to him or opposite him that would have no master. Because of God's *unity,* one cannot avoid speaking about the *Deus absconditus* — only this is not yet for us the triune God. When we are no longer under way in the struggle of faith, but live by sight, this enormously sharp and painful difference between God's terrifying hiddenness and his manifest love, which has been revealed by the Holy Spirit through the Son, will be taken away, defeated, and made to disappear.[33] But, in contrast to this God who will be revealed completely, the one who comes to us before the eschaton has not yet disappeared, but is the one who is acting to make us into something, as the *Deus absconditus* who seizes us; he remains so dark and hard to figure out that he could be confused with the devil. He does not allow himself to be addressed directly. *"Deus absconditus"* is no attribute *(nomen proprium)* and can never be used in the vocative voice.

9.3. The Concept of Omnipotence and Form of Address

9.3.1. The Stronger and Weaker Concepts of Omnipotence

God works life and death, good and evil, everything in everything — this thesis is not an overstatement, to be ignored or at least relativized, when examining Luther's writings in their entirety. This most important statement provides one with a foundational element of Luther's whole theology — as also of the Bible that Luther claims to interpret.

At the same time, one need not be surprised that Luther's stronger concept of omnipotence has always been treated as offensive. What follow are two more recent attempts to make what is so offensive into something milder, by using what can be called a "weaker" concept of omnipotence (a and b), and a third, classic attempt, which advocates a stronger concept of omnipotence — though in a highly questionable form (c). Over against these it will be possible to present (9.3.2) the way in which Luther speaks of the devil/the *Deus absconditus,* more specifically: how he deals with him.

9.3.1.a. "Permission": Universal Talk about a Suffering God

The first attempt is an effort to soften or to give up completely on the concept of omnipotence. It is thus often said that God does not cause evil, but simply lets it happen. But such talk about the bland "permitting" *(permissio)* of evil

33. Cf. chap. 15 below.

is too harmless. It assumes the possibility of a power vacuum or even that there is an independent power that is in opposition. At the very least, it assumes that the human being has freedom to stand up against God.

If the concept of omnipotence is weakened in this way, it can lead to giving up the concept altogether, as happens with a philosopher such as Hans Jonas: God appears as one who is absolutely and completely impotent. According to Jonas, the way God is portrayed "becomes the questionable responsibility of the human being to fill in the picture, to be saved or destroyed by means of what the human being does in relation to himself and to the world," so that "our course of life becomes lines in the divine face."[34] We "can heal and harm, nourish the deity or let him starve, complete his picture or disfigure it: and the scars of the one are as lasting as the brightness of the other."[35]

This God is delivered completely into the control of the human being. His "omnipotence" thus becomes the possession and responsibility of the human being. Since the question about omnipotence cannot be displaced that easily, it now simply changes its place, so that Jonas, as also Dorothee Sölle[36] and those who follow them, can do no more than emphasize the ethical power, the reasonable efforts, and the responsibility of the individual human being and of humanity as a whole. Suffering will allow itself to be pushed back a few steps if Christians all decide together that they will listen to the cry of those who suffer and participate in their hurts. This movement gains potency because of the impotence of some suffering people. In humanism of this type, which is correspondingly also grounded in a theology of the cross, the impotent God remains as a symbol for our unending responsibility to love; he remains a postulate.

One might say that Jonas turns the belief that humans are in the image of God into the total and absolute description about humanity. Not only is the well-being of the world entrusted to the human being, but its salvation is as well — and thereby the human becomes "god." The differentiation between *iustitia Dei* and *iustitia civilis,* the righteousness of God and civil righteousness, falls by the wayside. Even statements of Bonhoeffer from his *Letters and*

---

34. Hans Jonas, "Unsterblichkeit und heutige Existenz," in Jonas, *Zwischen Nichts und Ewigkeit,* KVR 165 (Göttingen: Vandenhoeck & Ruprecht, 1963), 44-72, here 58. Cf. Jonas, *Der Gottesbegriff nach Auschwitz. Eine jüdische Stimme,* Suhrkamp Taschenbuch 1516 (Frankfurt am Main: Suhrkamp, 1987), 23.

35. Jonas, "Unsterblichkeit," 59.

36. Dorothee Sölle, *Leiden,* 6th ed. (Stuttgart: Kreuz Verlag, 1984), 183: "Christ has no other hands than ours." Cf. 217 (the perspective of a complete solidarization of the good will of all human beings). In English, *Suffering,* trans. Everett R. Kalin (Philadelphia: Fortress, 1975).

Papers from Prison[37] are read within this conceptual framework. But what is missed in this view is that Christ on the cross was not just impotent, that he thus became one with the millions who have suffered, but that, with the communication of attributes[38] of God and man, both impotence and omnipotence are intertwined on Golgotha.

9.3.1.b. The Wrath of God as the Opposite Side of His Love

The second attempt seeks to take the central teaching of the Christian faith seriously, that God is love. In essence: the power of the Holy Spirit lets human beings peer into the heart of God the Father by looking at him through Jesus, as Luther summarizes it when he teaches about the Trinity in the Large Catechism,[39] which is a precise commentary on that central teaching.

However: Can love be turned into a principle? Luther denies the possibility. Turning love into a principle makes it a form of enthusiasm, which impatiently does away with the difference between faith and seeing — in the assumption that the terrifying hiddenness of God, which is so contradictory to his love, is already in the past. Since the time of Schleiermacher,[40] and then most especially under the influence of Karl Barth, many have advocated the view that darkness and evil have been rendered impotent ever since Jesus' death on the cross on Golgotha. In the final analysis, whatever confronts us today as evil is nothing, is mere appearance,[41] since the world has been reconciled to God ontologically already — with particular recourse to 2 Corinthians 5:17-21.

But the reality of evil is no longer taken seriously by this solution; one might say in a nuanced way that evil has been robbed of its impact by a questionable application of Christology. The christological perfect ("It is fin-

---

37. "Human beings go to God in his distress" ("Christen und Heiden," in *Widerstand und Ergebung* [Munich: Kaiser, 1970], 515). "God is powerless and weak in the world and precisely and only in this way is he with us and helps us" (to Eberhard Bethge, July 16, 1944; *Widerstand und Ergebung*, 534). For English translation, see above, n. 26.

38. Cf. chap. 10.4 below.

39. LC II, 62, in *BC*, 439.

40. On the topic, cf. Hans Walter Schütte, "Die Ausscheidung der Lehre vom Zorn Gottes in der Theologie Schleiermachers und Ritschls," *NZSTh* 10 (1968): 387-97. Schleiermacher advocates avoiding any talk about God's emotional state. Theodosius Harnack wrote in opposition to Schleiermacher and Ritschl in *Luthers Theologie mit besonderer Beziehung auf seine Versöhnungs- und Erlösungslehre,* 2 vols. (Erlangen: Theodor Blaesing, 1862, 1886); a second edition was published during the Luther renaissance by Kaiser Verlag, in 1926-27.

41. Plato had already argued in similar fashion, in order to hold fast to language about the unity and goodness of God (cf. Oswald Bayer, *Theology the Lutheran Way* [Grand Rapids: Eerdmans, 2007], 4-6).

ished": John 19:30) is turned into a perfected Christology. All of theology gets a serene face thereby. But it is questionable whether and how one can make love into a principle that stands the test in real situations of need, and correspondingly in pastoral care.

9.3.1.c. Double Predestination

The third attempt is no longer so prominent in the modern age, but it belongs systematically at this point. It deals with the way Calvin spoke of double predestination. He does this in systematic fashion in his discussion about the *gemina praedestinatio*, double predestination. God appears here as the one who already determined, before time began, that a certain person would be saved and that another would be damned.

This attempt is based to a certain extent on Romans 9–11 and demonstrates significant systematic rigor as well. And yet, with Luther, one needs to reflect critically on the *form of speech* this type of theology takes: speech that is framed logically, as double predestination is, risks going beyond the limitations imposed by the human situation; it also does not correspond to what the Christian faith has to say about the agonizing struggle and about God's passionate entry on behalf of sinful humanity. Luther spoke about the *Deus absconditus* and about predestination from a completely different perspective than did Calvin, less systematizing and more oriented toward pastoral care: the dark, terrifying hidden God is not to be treated in any way as parallel to the one who reveals himself; the former is much more the subject matter for the lament, which I can direct only to the God who has been revealed in Christ and who can be addressed.

With respect to predestination Luther uses a different form of speech than does Calvin: in faith I can confess with thankfulness that I was predestined to salvation — and not something like: "I am (hopefully) predestined, and for that reason I believe."[42] It is very important to Luther that one avoid

---

42. Calvin, *Institutes of the Christian Religion,* ed. John T. McNeill, trans. Ford Lewis Battles, Library of Christian Classics (Philadelphia: Westminster, 1960), III, 21-24, especially 21.1, 5, 7 (pp. 920-22, 926-29, 930-31); 22.10 (pp. 943-46); 23.1, 4 (pp. 947-49, 951-52); 24.4, 6-8 (pp. 968-70, 971-75). In 21.7, n. 1 (p. 968), Calvin cites and agrees with Luther's writings on the subject, including *De servo arbitrio,* among others. But he comes to the opposite conclusion in 24.3: we must certainly seek to be confident about our election in the gospel, "for if we try to penetrate to God's eternal ordination, that deep abyss will swallow us up. But when God has made plain this ordination to us, we must climb higher, but the effect [that is, faith] does not overwhelm the cause [that is, the election]." In the same section Calvin praises the *verbum externum* (the external Word), but then describes it as nothing but a canal that leads to the source that lies behind it, and not as the matter itself.

causal thinking and the linear perspective that is suggested thereby. He thinks within the framework of confession and of what is contingent, on the basis of the Christ event, without trying to reflect back to that time that existed before the rupture in the ages. The Lutheran way of confessing, that I am predestined to salvation by faith, thus has its concrete setting in life and sings in light of the cradle: "Before I was even born, / then you were born for me; / and made me your very own, / before I knew you, chosen."[43]

Each of the three attempts summarized here has logically deductive arguments on its side; at the same time, each one is indefensible from an exegetical and systematic perspective. Each seeks to hold onto God as one who is *understandable,* and thus each comes to a theologically questionable definition of the relationship between God's *omnipotence* and *goodness.*

9.3.2. Form of Speech

Luther speaks neither of the *Deus absconditus* nor about the devil in a constitutive way, by using the form of speech that makes a statement. It is indeed the nature of evil that it does not allow itself to be understood, defined, or explained. Correspondingly, Luther does not theorize about the devil; he does not dispute with him either, but greets him by shaking his fist, just like the iron fist on the shield of Gottfried of Berlichingen, or he throws the legendary ink bottle at him. He can also drive him away with music and with joyous fellowship with friends.

There is hardly a page in the Weimar edition of Luther's works where Luther does not do battle against the devil. That this battle is one of the chief marks to identify his theology was noted already in the title of the introduction, "The Rupture between Ages,"[44] so much so that the issue in Luther's distinction between and arrangement of what is "hidden" and "revealed" does not deal with speculative thinking, which tries to make bearable what is unbearable. The question posed by theodicy cannot be "resolved" by any means. Discussion about the hidden God has much more to do with an immediate "setting in life" — within the lament. Discussion concerning the hidden God is wrung out from the agonizing struggle, in the form of a lament.

43. Paul Gerhardt, "Ich steh an deiner Krippen hier," *EG,* #37, 2 (in English: "O Jesus Christ, Thy Manger Is" [*LSB,* #372]). Therefore: "non esse inquirendum de praedestinatione Dei absconditi" (WA 43:463, [3-17] 11f.; on Gen 26:9; 1540-41). Cf. n. 3 above.

44. Cf. further Reinhuber, *Kämpfender Glaube,* 56-62: "Luthers Rede vom Bösen und von den Dämonen in heutiger systematischer Verantwortung."

To summarize: Luther's teaching about God, for reasons of certainty about salvation, holds steadfastly to speaking both about God's goodness and about his omnipotence and thus chooses to forgo the notion that one can understand God fully. Luther admits that God cannot be understood completely; the omnipotence, even of the hidden God, and the goodness of the revealed God, in whom one believes, can both be preserved thereby.

9.3.3. The "Three Lights"

Luther knows that he finds himself in the midst of a dilemma and admits this openly. At the end of *De servo arbitrio*,[45] he thus speaks about three lights: the light of nature, the light of grace, and the light of glory. The first shines on all humanity,[46] the second shines on believers, and the third is what believers hope as they await the eschaton, the judgment of the world as the consummation of the world. Only when this third light shines will it be demonstrated that God acted justly and understandably, also in the events and occurrences that are incomprehensible to us in the here and now, which are hidden from us, and which seem to be completely unjust.

a. Whoever wants to understand the order of the world by using his natural reason, the *"light of nature,"* wants to identify and establish a clear relationship between action and consequences — as did Job's friends, about whom Luther says: "[They] have such a worldly and human way of thinking about God and his righteousness, as if he were just like humans and his justice is exactly like the world's justice."[47] The judgment of the empiricists is just as much in error as that of the rationalists. "If one examines the judgment of human reason and follows it, one is forced to say either that there is no God" — then God is cleared of blame in theodicy, because it has been demonstrated that he does not exist — [48]

> or that he is unjust. . . . For look how the wicked succeed but the just are defeated; the mother of proverbs, which shows what is meant by every proverb and by experience, declares: "The bigger the crook, the bigger the take." "In the houses of the godless," Job says [12:6; cf. 21:7], "excess reigns."

45. *LW* 33:288-92.
46. Cf. chap. 6.2 above.
47. Heinrich Bornkamm, ed., *Luthers Vorreden zur Bibel*, 3rd ed. (Göttingen: Vandenhoeck & Ruprecht, 1989), 60 ("Vorrede zum Buch Hiob," 1524). Cf. *LW* 35:251.
48. Thus Stendahl (cf. Walter Sparn, "Mit dem Bösen leben," *NZSTh* 32 [1990]: 207-25, here 221).

And Psalm 73[:12] laments that the sinners in the world have an overabundance of riches. Listen up, does not every person think it is wrong that those who are evil are blessed with many things that bring happiness and those who are good are afflicted terribly? But it is obvious everywhere that this happens in the world. At this point the best of the best have denied that God exists and they invent the idea that happiness drives everything blindly, as for example the Epicureans and Pliny. Move on to Aristotle; he thinks that his original being [= God], to free himself from suffering, sees nothing except himself alone as the cause, since Aristotle believes that it would be too burdensome for God to look upon so much suffering and so much unrighteousness. But the prophets, who believed that God does exist, are caught up in the question about whether God is unjust, and are tempted and sorely troubled, as were Jeremiah, Job, David, Asaph, and others.[49]

b. Even belief in righteousness by faith remains a belief that experiences agonizing struggle. God's goodness and love cannot be demonstrated; the question about whether God might indeed be unjust cannot be done away with — especially not by the one who believes. Since God's love cannot be demonstrated, cannot be positioned safely beyond all doubt, whoever believes lives in the agonizing struggle. Faced with God's hiddenness, he takes flight to the promise, in which God does reveal himself; he flees into the *"light of grace,"* the *lumen gratiae,* into the "light of the gospel, which alone is powerful in Word and in faith."[50] The other way to flee, to deny God and to speak of blind destiny and luck, is not a possibility for faith.

c. As the book of Job intends in the end to say nothing other than that "God alone is righteous,"[51] the same is true of Luther's last word in *The Bondage of the Will.* It is not in seeing and knowing, but only in the hope of faith that one can believe it is true: the *"light of glory . . .* will show that God, whose judgment [in the present] is only incomprehensible righteousness, is most righteous and is completely obvious righteousness, about which we can only believe in the meantime."[52] Such wrestling with the question about theodicy does not resolve what is stated in the lament, but it does keep it alive and thereby watches concurrently with passionate hope for the consummation of

---

49. WA 18:784.36–785.10; cf. *LW* 33:291. On the reference to Aristotle, *Metaphysics* 12, see Oswald Bayer, *Freiheit als Antwort* (Tübingen: Mohr, 1995), 36f., especially n. 36, as well as chap. 5, n. 58.

50. WA 18:785.20; cf. *LW* 33:292.

51. Preface to the book of Job, in Bornkamm, *Luthers Vorreden zur Bibel.* See n. 47 above.

52. WA 18:785.35-37; cf. *LW* 33:292.

the world. At that time God himself will finally act with justice, and the lament will get its answer without an agonizing struggle.[53]

But when all is said and done, Luther cannot prove this in answer to Erasmus; he can only believe and confess. A God whom I do not understand — not just in every aspect but also in this painful aspect — is no subject who can offer proof; he is an anonymous power, who oppresses me, from whom I flee away — right to the shining face of the Father who is revealed in Christ. It is valid "against God to press toward God and to call out."[54] This movement never becomes a principle for Luther; unlike the certainty of salvation, it never becomes something one can know for sure. For Luther the unity of God is not a matter of thinking but of confession.

Theodicy is not, as Leibniz thought, to be brought before the forum of reason, which can understand and judge, so that one can dispute or reflect *about* God; as Job experienced it, it is much more about a dispute *with* God — summoning God against God (Job 16; 19); one appeals to God against God. The only speech that is legitimate is the careful form of speech that recognizes there are boundaries and that concerns the experience of the terrifying hiddenness of God. Such speech is appropriate to the lament, in which it is proper "against God to press toward God and to call out": to the God revealed in the gospel. Only through Christ does the Holy Spirit let one see into the heart of God the Father. Only in this way will he be experienced as love. But to turn this understanding into a theological principle would make it a form of enthusiasm, which impatiently does away with the difference between faith and seeing — supposing that the terrifying hiddenness of God and the way it contradicts his love have been left in the past already.

---

53. In his teaching about the lights, Luther distinguishes the problem of theodicy, which he takes to be "resolved" by the light of grace and can thus be endured by faith, from the problem of predestination, which for him goes much deeper: Why is faith given to some and not to others? But one must wonder whether these two questions, with all their ramifications, can actually be distinguished in this way, or whether — precisely with respect to the eschatological hope of faith — we must speak of the "open wound of theodicy" (cf. Oswald Bayer, *Autorität und Kritik. Zu Hermeneutik und Wissenschaftstheorie* [Tübingen: Mohr, 1991], 201-7). We can in fact believe and hope *that* God will remove suffering and will actually transform the past at the time of the consummation of the world. But the unresolved question of *how* still awaits a solution; this problem causes most agonizing struggle for believers as well.

54. WA 19:223.14-17; cf. *LW* 19:72 (*Lectures on Jonah*, 1526): natural reason "cannot surmount the obstacle posed by this wrath, it cannot subdue this feeling and make its way to God against God and pray to Him. . . . Therefore when Jonah had advanced to the point of entreating God, he had gained the victory." Cf. WA 5:204.26f. (*Operationes in psalmos*, 1519-21): "ad deum [revelatum] contra deum [absconditum] confugere" [to flee to God against God].

Chapter 10   "Through the Son, Our Lord":
God as Mercy and Love

He said to His beloved Son:
"It's time to have compassion.
Then go, bright jewel of My crown,
And bring to all salvation."

Within the course of this presentation, this chapter — corresponding to Luther's own theology — marks the turning point, the radical shift from sin, death, and the devil toward God the Father who, through Jesus Christ, the Son, our Lord, reveals himself by the Holy Spirit as the one who is merciful and loving. Claim is made for a radical change and turning point, which does not take place merely within the presentation of theological teaching, and also not just within the experience of the believing human being, but which took place beforehand within God himself. The overthrow within God himself, from wrath to love as the condition that makes the "happy exchange" between Christ and the sinner possible, carries with it fundamental consequences for the entire Christian teaching about God, most of all with respect to speaking about the Trinity. This can be demonstrated paradigmatically in a central text of the Reformation: in Luther's hymn of liberation: "Dear Christians, One and All, Rejoice."[1]

10.1. "Dear Christians, One and All, Rejoice"

What does the Christ event mean for Luther with respect to speaking about God's being?

---

1. *EG*, #341. The printed version is "Dear Christians, One and All, Rejoice," *LSB*, #556. [Trans.: The detailed study is based on a literal translation of the German text, without attention to poetry and rhyming.] The time of origin is disputed. It was probably first published in 1523, though evidence of its existence dates initially to 1524. WA 35:422-25.

According to the Greek way of thinking, what belongs to the essence of God as essence itself is immortality, impassibility, and along with it the inability to experience emotions, which is known as apathy. The deepest conflict with Greek metaphysics and ontology must of necessity come at the point where the biblical texts are taken with utter seriousness. What is ontologically unthinkable is described in Hosea 11:7-11, which ancient metaphysics would reject as mythology: an "overthrow," a change within God himself: God is not the one who is identical with himself, who corresponds to himself: "My heart has changed within me; my remorse grows powerfully, I will not execute my fierce anger; I will not again destroy Ephraim; for I am God, not a human being" (vv. 8-9).[2]

Martin Luther experienced, preached about, reflected about, and sang about this God, the God of passionate mercy — most concentrated in the song "Dear Christians, One and All, Rejoice."

The form of this text is not superficial as regards its content. *What* is said can obviously be said only in an appropriate way in this manner: as a song, as praise, in which the story of liberation from deepest need is narrated. That which is "doxological" speaking about God is demonstrated here in a paradigmatic way. With respect to the description of the form of this text as a whole, which certainly appeared already in 1523, we can begin with the superscription included in one of the first printings: "A Song of Thanks for the Most Magnificent Act of Kindness That God Has Shown Us in Christ."[3] Luther, who is rooted deeply in the psalms, understandably uses the formal elements from these ancient prayers of Israel and the church: description of need, description of liberation.

At first glance the song seems to be that of just one individual. And yet it was sung by the congregation. In the first stanza the other Christians who are present are encouraged to sing. The reason and circumstances of this song of praise, Spirit-inspired, are extolled as events that have taken place "for us" (1:5).[4] The summons to praise (1:1-4) and its short summary of the reason (1:5-7) are both cast in the *we* form. And the rest of the story that is described in detail in nine long stanzas consistently uses the first-person *singular,* but only after the introductory stanza summarizes the story in anticipatory fashion. It is thus certainly incorrect — because of what happens in the introductory stanza — to suggest that this is about an individual "I" who is isolated

---

2. On the topic, cf. Jörg Jeremias, *Der Prophet Hosea,* ATD 24/1 (Göttingen: Vandenhoeck & Ruprecht, 1983), 143-47 ("overthrow of the will within God"). Cf. Jeremias, *Die Reue Gottes* (Neukirchen-Vluyn: Neukirchener Verlag, 1975), 52-59.

3. WA 35:423.

4. References to the hymn include stanza and line numbers, separated by colons.

from the congregation. As in the creed, the "I" of every Christian speaks here
— in fact, in stanzas 2 and 3, it is the "I" of every human being.

The gospel is praised. This is composed, right down to the smallest detail,
in parallel with the definition of the gospel that Luther had framed just before
this (1522) in his "Preface to the New Testament."[5] In that work, as well as in
what is admittedly a still sharper way in this hymn, the gospel is described as a
two-part story: as the story of a lament that has been heard, which, as light
through a magnifying glass, concentrates on Romans 7:24 and 25a: "Wretched
man that I am! Who will rescue me from this body of death? Thanks be to
God through Jesus Christ our Lord!"

The two parts of this story are arranged following the lament and response paradigm that we know from the psalms, such as Psalm 22, juxtaposed
— but with no transitional element. The need that is described comes to an
end with no way out; the narrative breaks off at the deepest point of the journey that has been made without any hope for liberation; it pitches headlong
into the abyss. There is no hint of any hope of an imminent turn of events or
of the hope suggested by Adorno, that "the completed negativity, once comprehended by the eye, [crystallizes] to become the written mirror of its opposite."[6] Should one agree: "But where danger is, that which saves grows there as
well" (Hölderlin)?[7] No! There is absolutely no negative dialectic at work here.
The pious proverb simply does not apply here, in its present cursory form:
where the need is the greatest, there God is the nearest. The rupture cuts
through completely.

The search for one's identity, the human search that seeks its identity everywhere it can, is experienced here in a dreadfully perfect circle in which one
is caught within oneself, in which the person who is caught up in himself no
longer even cries out to God. Where the word "God" appears in the song —
only one single time: "Free will against God's judgment fought" (3:3) — it is
identified there as the reason for and substance of hatred. The "I" that is speaking at that point is turned toward God, if at all, only in hatred, as Tilmann

5. *LW* 35:360 and 358 ("Preface to the New Testament"); cf. chap. 4.4 above.

6. Theodor W. Adorno, *Minima Moralia. Reflexionen aus dem beschädigten Leben* (Frankfurt: Suhrkamp, 1973), 333f., the last aphorism: "Zum Ende," 334.

7. Friedrich Hölderlin, the hymn "Patmos," in *Sämtliche Werke, Große Stuttgarter
Ausgabe*, ed. Friedrich Beissner, vol. 2/1 (1951), 165-72, here 165, 3f. Cf. Ernst Bloch, *The Principle
of Hope*, trans. Neville Plaice (Cambridge: MIT Press, 1986), 122. "'Where there is danger there is
rescue'; this line of Hölderlin's indicates simply the positive dialectical turning point for which
fear of the place of death disappears." Martin Heidegger, *Die Technik und die Kehre*, opuscula 1
(Pfullingen: Neske, 1962), 5-36: "Die Frage nach der Technik," 28-36, and (37-47: "Die Kehre")
41-43, likewise refers to this verse from Hölderlin.

Moser writes in a curse of God in his *Gottesvergiftung*[8] — in a hatred that is not far from becoming anonymous, as in modern literature, in which one states opinions without so much as uttering the word "God" at all, finding other objects and directing one's attention to others who can be addressed, most especially other human beings: hell is other people (Sartre).[9]

1:1. Dear Christians, one and all, rejoice,
  2. With exultation springing,
  3. And with united heart and voice
  4. And holy rapture singing,
  5. Proclaim the wonders God has done,
  6. How His right arm the vict'ry won.
  7. What price our ransom cost Him!

PART 1

2:1. Fast bound in Satan's chains I lay;
  2. Death brooded darkly o'er me.
  3. Sin was my torment night and day;
  4. In sin my mother bore me.
  5. But daily deeper still I fell;
  6. My life became a living hell,
  7. So firmly sin possessed me.

3:1. My own good works all came to naught,
  2. No grace or merit gaining;
  3. Free will against God's judgment fought,
  4. Dead to all good remaining.
  5. My fears increased till sheer despair
  6. Left only death to be my share;
  7. The pangs of hell I suffered.

PART 2

4:1. But God had seen my wretched state
  2. Before the world's foundation,
  3. And mindful of His mercies great,
  4. He planned for my salvation.

8. Tilmann Moser, *Gottesvergiftung* (The poisoning of God) (Frankfurt am Main, 1976). Cf. Oswald Bayer, *Gott als Autor. Zu einer poietologischen Theologie* (Tübingen, 1999), 65-72: "Ichfindung als Gottesfluch" [Discovery of the "I" as curse of God].

9. Jean-Paul Sartre, *No Exit and Other Plays,* trans. Stuart Gilbert (New York: Knopf, 1947), 47: "Hell is other people."

5. He turned to me a father's heart;
6. He did not choose the easy part
7. But gave His dearest treasure.

5:1. God said to His belovèd Son:
2. "It's time to have compassion.
3. Then go, bright jewel of My crown,
4. And bring to all salvation.
5. From sin and sorrow set them free;
6. Slay bitter death for them that they
7. May live with You forever."

6:1. The Son obeyed His Father's will,
2. Was born of virgin mother;
3. And God's good pleasure to fulfill,
4. He came to be my brother.
5. His royal pow'r disguised He bore;
6. A servant's form, like mine, He wore
7. To lead the devil captive.

7:1. To me He said: "Stay close to Me,
2. I am your rock and castle.
3. Your ransom I Myself will be;
4. For you I strive and wrestle.
5. For I am yours, and you are Mine,
6. And where I am you may remain;
7. The foe shall not divide us.

8:1. "Though he will shed My precious blood,
2. Me of My life bereaving,
3. All this I suffer for your good;
4. Be steadfast and believing.
5. Life will from death the vict'ry win;
6. My innocence shall bear your sin,
7. And you are blessed forever.

9:1. "Now to My Father I depart,
2. From earth to heav'n ascending,
3. And, heavn'ly wisdom to impart,
4. The Holy Spirit sending;
5. In trouble He will comfort you
6. And teach you always to be true
7. And into truth shall guide you.

10:1. "What I on earth have done and taught
   2. Guide all your life and teaching;
   3. So shall the kingdom's work be wrought
   4. And honored in your preaching.
   5. But watch lest foes with base alloy
   6. The heav'ly treasure should destroy;
   7. This final word I leave you."

[Trans. What follows will employ literal renderings from the German.]

If one looks for one single basic foundational text that Luther would have used to describe the descent into the hell one descends into when seeking knowledge of the self (stanzas 2-3), among all the biblical texts[10] that have been used in some way here, one would turn to Romans 7:7-24. This lament — of the old man, who has also dragged the rest of his fellow creatures along with him to destruction (Rom. 8:18-25), a situation that is apparent only because one becomes aware of the new man (Rom. 7:25a) who can stand in for the old man — is not so radical an idea that it is given voice for the first time only in the modern experience of the human being, who is weighed down in an effort to find his identity. Instead, the appropriate language for putting these experiences into words is provided, for the very first time, by that lament of Paul and by the way Luther expresses it in an appropriate fashion.

The story about the journey to hell, as one becomes aware of the self, describes the movement within the essence of the self, which closes itself in upon itself — so tightly that the air goes out of the "I," but at the same time his sickness does not lead to death; it eternally tortures him with being caught in himself. In this ontology that describes the essence of the self, the law works by condemning and eternally killing, confining me inescapably within myself and — in the midst of a completely lost humanity and an entire world drawn down with it to destruction — holds me as tightly as I hold onto myself by the deeds that I myself have done. *This ontology of the essence of the self is thus an ontology of self-justification.* It wears an even more terrifying face today than it did at Luther's time, which treated Aristotle in a positive way as it taught about sin and grace — or even at the time of Aristotle himself, whose metaphysics of self-realization was an expression of a human being as a pious person within the entire cosmos and within the body politic, who was not yet caught within his own nakedness.

---

10. With respect to the exact references to biblical texts that Luther uses, cf. Martin Brecht, "Erfahrung — Exegese — Dogmatik. Luthers Lied 'Nun freut euch, lieben Christen gmein,'" *NZSTh* 32 (1990): 94-104.

If the lament of the old man, as expressed in stanzas 2 and 3 of the song, is still centered on the experience of God's understandable wrath, the darkness about God is given still further expression for modern man in that the experience of God is anonymous. Concerning the experience of the law, the theodicy question, together with the incomprehensible wrath of God in the present, takes shape in a completely different form. Whether at Luther's time or today, however, the human being finds himself caught, without any chance to be free of God, in this godlessness.

The rupture between the first and second parts of the hymn of liberation described in this story is so deep that it cannot be measured; one cannot find adequate terminology to conceptualize it on the basis of the experience of the law, nor by the modern experience of suffering.[11] There is no way to find common ground between the two parts of this story. The problem of finding some common ground to negotiate a transition is not just within the realm of the human being and his world. It is hard even to conceptualize a unity within God: in the law — he speaks against me, so that I can only hate him and his judgment with my whole heart (3:3); in the gospel — he speaks on my behalf, so that I can do nothing but love him through his Son by the power of the Spirit, with my whole heart.[12]

Customary ways of thinking — when one is seeking a guiding principle for describing identity as the unity one seeks in one's essence or consciousness — cannot resolve the tensions; the resolution can be set in motion and can be described by the gospel alone. How this happens, happened, and will happen is depicted in the second part of the story (stanzas 4-10) — which is more important not only in a superficial sense. It does not describe a reality that merely coexists, one that is identical with one's own nature. Instead, it describes a change, a turning, in fact: an unheard-of "overthrow" (Hos. 11:8).

Some have attempted by various means to tone down the proclamation that this overthrow has taken place and have tried to make it seem plausible

---

11. Georg Büchner, *Dantons Tod*, act 3, scene 1, in *Complete Works and Letters*, trans. Henry J. Schmidt (New York: Continuum, 1986), 96: "One may deny evil, but not pain; only reason can prove the existence of God, our feelings rebel against it. Mark this, Anaxagoras: why do I suffer? That is the rock of atheism. The smallest twinge of pain — and it may stir up only a single atom — makes a rent in Creation from top to bottom."

12. This corresponds to the equally sharp contrast that characterizes Luther's report concerning his reformational discovery — the turning point in his life and theology — as he reports it in his preface to the first volume of the complete edition of his Latin writings (1545) (cf. chap. 3 above): *LW* 34:336-37 ("Preface to the Complete Edition of Luther's Latin Writings"), especially 336: "I did not love, yes, I hated the righteous God who punishes sinners."

— even by advocating the teaching about eternal predestination.[13] Or they have turned to a salvation-historical construct that seeks to attenuate the breakdown of the traditional notion of time and eternity by a chronological understanding of time. In the same way, they have used existential interpretation with great effect. Both alternatives — that God became man because it was necessary to bring to reality an eternal decision about predestination and that this is God's reaction to human sin — are rendered impotent by Luther's hymn. Luther's alternative describes an inexpressibly hard paradoxical and harsh new beginning: "But as God grieved in eternity . . ." (4:1), in which he intertwines present time and eternity by using the imperfect narrative tense, but bursts beyond both alternatives at the same time and offers something else to think about.

It is not insignificant that one is to reflect on the nature of Jesus Christ by means of a *story*. Each story admittedly has its own unique time structure. A variety of perspectives can be used to tell a reader or hearer about someone else — depending on how time and sequence are handled. Thus if we ask about the nature of Jesus Christ, we cannot help but notice that various time frames are used. One also cannot ignore the way time frames are used by the *narrator* to tell the story. The speaker in the song is explicitly an "I." In the second section, which is our focus at this time, a completely different "I" speaks, very different from the "I" in the first part. The one who was turned in on himself in a deadly confinement and is at a distance speaks there. Here it is an "I" that is constantly in the dative — in the *dative of having been given a gift.* As one who has his existence by God's giving, the "I" is constituted completely by means of a conversation: not as one speaks to himself under the strictures of seeking his own identity as a human being while curved in on himself because he is caught up in sin. Instead, this happens in conversation, in a conversation that has been initiated by someone else and that has a future because of the relationship with this one — indeed, *in* him.

This "I," which we call the "new I" (in sharp contrast to the old, completely uncommunicative existence of the "I" who is curved in on himself in a hellishly close conversation with himself), lives by means of and in what is thoroughly *communicative being.* In the person of Jesus Christ God gives himself to us without hesitation and without restrictions, wholly and completely, with everything that he is and does, with what he has and is able to do:

---

13. This does not preclude talking of eternal election as such, but rather that it can be constructed a priori — as if the theologian sat in on God's secret cabinet meeting. A posteriori — on the basis of the confession of faith — the confession of one's *being elected* takes on a totally different tone and status. Cf. chap. 9.3.1 above.

"He let it cost him his best" (4:7); "he acquired it at great cost" (1:7). He opens himself up in such a way that he allows us to partake of the fullness of his being and takes us up into fellowship with him in that he sacrifices himself for us.[14] The nature of God as the nature of Jesus Christ is a valid promise and gift that is guaranteed in testamentary fashion.

As a preliminary conclusion we can assert: in Luther's hymn of liberation, by means of the Spirit-inspired praise to God by the congregation (stanza 1), as an anticipatory answer to the lament of the old and lost man (stanzas 2-3), God's gift of himself in his Son is described as the liberation of the human being who has sunk into the depths of hell; he is brought into discussion with God from the outset, as one who is receiving a gift "passively." The lament of the human being, which is not addressed any longer to God, is heard from within eternity — admittedly so that this response and salvation take place historically, through God becoming a human being and dying. And then this is communicated to us historically as well, concentrated in the physical means of the Word in baptism and in the Lord's Supper. The discussion between Father and Son, Son and Father, is not within the realm of an abstract thought about trinitarian and theological speculation, but is described from the very beginning as an event that brings benefit to the sinner, as "mercy." The entire nature of God is understood as a surrender of himself in the promise, which the Son gives to the human being caught in death: "Hold fast to me . . . ; I myself give myself completely for you . . . !" (stanzas 7-10).

The story that tells of the saving actions of the triune God (stanzas 4-10)[15] differentiates itself from speculation about the Trinity that ignores existence at every turn; all three modes of time are used by the narrator to draw the one who has been given a gift into the story of God's Word, work, and nature from the outset; the gift is not given to him only when he comes to the second stage. The dative, as a *dative of having been given a gift,* is constitutive: "he wanted to let me be helped" (4:4); "he turned to me the Father's heart" (4:5); "be the salvation of the poor"; "help him"; "slayed bitter death for him"; "let him live with you" (5:4-7); "he came to me on earth" (6:2); "spoke to me"; "it will now come true for you"; "I give myself completely for you"; "I will do battle for you"; "I am yours" (as if to say: I am united with you; 7:1-5); "all that

14. Cf. *LW* 37:366 (*Confession concerning Christ's Supper,* 1528).

15. Part 2, which develops the summary that was stated in brief in stanza 1, lines 5-7, furnishes the reason and object for the praise and is constructed as follows: after a further summary exposition (stanza 4), the event *within the Godhead* (stanzas 5-6) is depicted and is then followed by what takes place on the *outside* (stanzas 7-10). This part addresses, extends to, and concretely involves me.

I suffered for your good" (8:3); "now I will be your master" (9:3); "I want to give you the Spirit" (9:4); "I leave all that for you to the end" (10:7).

That I myself am drawn in, in my own being, into God's action of salvation, into his mercy, does not square with what one can describe as part of the nature of the human being. One cannot simply remember such matters intellectually; they do not simply come to one's mind as a purely inner manifestation of the Holy Spirit. They come to me, to the one who is telling the story, by means of which I can identify myself as a Christian, when I use the text of the song as it is grounded in the biblical witness. It is the substance of what belongs to all in the community. It comes more powerfully still when it is concentrated in the physical Word and work of baptism, the Lord's Supper, and the absolution, and when biblical texts are preached in such a way that they focus on the same issues. Thus the key to understanding the story of salvation is without question in stanzas 7 and 8. Luther uses their basic structure to assert the same gifting Word that was spoken in the final discourse of Jesus at the Lord's Supper in the Gospel of John: *I for you!* In this way God makes a promise to me as the Father who binds himself to me through the Son by the Holy Spirit, giving himself completely for me, making it possible for me to participate in his nature. As stanzas 7 and 8 make dramatically clear, this takes place in a "happy exchange and battle"[16] — in an exchange of human sin and divine righteousness, which at the same time is a "battle," a conflict with the power of the old world: with the "enemy" (7:7; 8:1-2); with the "devil" (2:1; 6:7); with "death" (2:2; 3:4, 6; 8:5); with "sin" (2:3, 7; 7:6); with "hell" (3:7). Forgiveness of sins is not what it means to Schleiermacher — an enlightenment and empowerment of one's consciousness of God. In a reality that goes far beyond one's consciousness, it describes how all the powers of destruction that are at enmity with God and humanity are overpowered.

In stanzas 7 and 8, Luther puts into words especially what he stated in his tractate *On the Freedom of a Christian* (1520); one should pay especially careful attention to him at this point. The christological teaching about the two natures is given its sharpest focus in the teaching about the communication of attributes — the teaching about the reciprocal participation of the unique attributes *(idiomata)* of the divine and human nature in the one person Jesus Christ.[17] It articulates what is necessary for the sinner to communicate with the Holy God. This communication that has taken place in the Word made flesh and in the faith that God has created has an "inner side." The viewpoint

---

16. WA 7:25.34 (*On the Freedom of a Christian*, 1520).

17. Cf. 10.4 below. Cf. Oswald Bayer, "Das Wort ward Fleisch. Luthers Christologie als Lehre von der Idiomenkommunikation," in Oswald Bayer, *Zugesagte Gegenwart* (Tübingen: Mohr Siebeck, 2007), 126-64.

advocated by salvation history, which uses a chronological framework, depicts this as a preexisting "prehistory." But one cannot make this "inner" history of the *promise* and *giving-forth* of God to me, in the midst of all the believers, into a historical event that can be described by using the past tense (even though in its definitive essence, as something that happened, it has to be told using this tense!) — just as little as one can design a construct that describes a timelessly intelligible relationship.

Typically, the attempts to speak of God, as triune, founder between the description of the timeless relationship between Father, Son, and Spirit, on the one hand, and the assumption that there are ages — which follow one another in point of time — of the Father, of the Son, and of the Holy Spirit, on the other hand. Others follow another approach and attempt to coalesce speculation about the inner relationship with historical events. But what is not actually taken seriously in all such attempts is God's nature — as one who gives gifts and promises them in a testament, in which he gives himself to us completely: he communicates himself to us in a definitive way.

Luther's hymn "Dear Christians, One and All, Rejoice" shows which elements are central to the teaching about the Trinity, or more specifically: for the proper determination of its *place* within systematic theology as a whole. Teaching about the Trinity concentrates on nothing but the *gospel,* on how liberation took place: the freedom that Christ acquired and brought to us, which he promises and imparts to us through the Holy Spirit by the Word.

If teaching about the Trinity concentrates on the pure gospel and nothing but the gospel, one cannot attribute the law that kills to the triune God, pure and simple. Whoever confesses that the one who speaks *against* me in the law and the one who speaks *for* me in the gospel, in fact who intervenes on my side, is one and the same, utters the paradox of a miracle that cannot be robbed of its power by articulating the assumption that God is sufficient in and of himself. Luther's hymn of liberation, as it depicts the rupture between stanzas 3 and 4, points to an unprecedented issue with which theology must grapple.[18]

This problem is normally ameliorated by making the law that kills, the idea that God "hates" me and allows me "to sink" "to hell" (stanza 3), to be naturally predicated as something that the triune God does. But if the doctrine of the Trinity, as articulated only in the second part of the hymn of lib-

---

18. This topic has been further elaborated by Christine Helmer, *The Trinity and Martin Luther: A Study on the Relationship between Genre, Language, and the Trinity in Luther's Works (1523-1546)* (Mainz: P. von Zabern, 1999); Helmer, "God from Eternity to Eternity: Luther's Trinitarian Understanding," *HTR* 96 (2003): 127-46.

eration (stanzas 4-10), reflects only and specifically on the gospel — being nothing other than God's mercy and his love — and if the destiny of the lost human being is not to be attributed merely to the perversion of his own personal freedom, if that fallen human being is still in a relationship with "God," even in this perversion, then it is *unavoidable that one must distinguish a "generic" doctrine of God and anthropology from a doctrine of the Trinity* and that neither can be allowed to intermingle with the other; if the analysis is correct, the break between stanzas 3 and 4 makes that necessary.

Such a "generic" doctrine of God describes the non-Christian human being, who stands nevertheless under God's demand and accusation. It asks what it means to deal with the omnipotence of God outside the relationship with Jesus Christ, outside the love of the triune God;[19] it asks about what Luther's hymn of liberation articulates in stanzas 2 and 3.

One of the grandiose blunders in the more recent history of philosophy and theology seeks to describe this omnipotence within a trinitarian theological framework. This blunder goes so far as to bring about a darkening, indeed a displacement, of the gospel, which can be studied only from a trinitarian perspective. Whoever wishes to go further and distinguish "generic" teaching about God and anthropology from the doctrine of the Trinity, within the framework of and aided by the doctrine of the Trinity, must of necessity turn the doctrine of the Trinity into generic teaching about God. But the removal of the distinction between the doctrine of the Trinity and generic teaching about God can be expected only at the eschaton and will correspondingly be a topic for this presentation of Luther's theology only in the final chapter. It is a matter for a concluding doxology, for the ultimate song of praise.[20]

10.2. The "Happy Exchange"

We examine further the way the triune God communicated and continues to communicate himself in Christ as the one who brings mercy and love by letting another classic text guide us. Luther speaks impressively about the "happy exchange,"[21] about a transfer, and uses for this the biblical marriage

---

19. God's love can be experienced only where, through the Son in the Holy Spirit, he opens "the most profound depths of his fatherly heart and his pure, unutterable love" (LC II, 64, in *BC,* 439).

20. For more detail on the distinction between teaching about the Trinity and teaching about God in general, cf. chap. 15.2.2 below.

21. WA 7:25.34; cf. *Freedom of a Christian,* trans. Bertram Lee Woolf, in *Reformation Writings of Martin Luther* (London: Lutterworth, 1952), 363.

metaphor, and the way it is used, to characterize the mystique of the bride. This is expressed paradigmatically in *On the Freedom of a Christian,* section 12: faith "binds the soul with Christ, just as the bride with the bridegroom. By means of this secret (as the apostle teaches [Eph. 5:32]) Christ and the soul become one flesh."[22]

> What takes place here now is the utmost delightful theatrical play, not only to depict the communal relationship, but a theatrical play that depicts a war that results in liberation: that of the victory, of the salvation, of the liberation. Since Christ is namely God and human in one and the same person, who not only has not sinned, not died, and is not damned, but instead neither can sin, nor die, nor be damned, and because his righteousness, his life, his salvation is unconquerable, eternal, almighty — because, I say, such a person becomes one with the sins of the bride, her death and her hell because of the engagement ring of faith, and in fact makes them his own, and acts in no other way than as if they are his own and as if he himself had sinned — going through great exertions, dying, and descending into hell — so that he could overcome everything and, because sin, death, and hell could not swallow him up, everything therefore is swallowed up in him ["absorbed," 1 Cor. 15:54] by means of a battle between two that awakens astonishment. For his righteousness is spread out over the sins of all, his life is stronger than every death, his salvation is more invincible than any hell. In this way the believing soul is freed from all sins by the dowry; its faith in Christ, its bridegroom, is safe in the face of death, and is protected from hell, because the eternal righteousness as well as the eternal life and salvation of its bridegroom Christ are all given to it as a gift. Thus he creates for himself a magnificent bride without spot or wrinkle, since he purifies her in the bath with water through the Word of life [Eph. 5:27, 26], that is, through what is worked through faith, which comes through the Word, through life, through righteousness, and through salvation. Thus he betroths himself to her in faith, in mercy and compassion, in righteousness and judgment, as it is stated in Hosea 2[:19-20].[23]

The main key for understanding this passage is found in the biblical citations. They are not just ornamental; they do not illustrate a set of circumstances that could exist even without them. Instead, they are essential; in fact, the passage is

---

22. WA 7:54.3f.; cf. *LW* 31:351. The Latin reads: "[Fides] animam copulat cum Christo, sicut sponsam cum sponso. Quo sacramento (ut Apostolus docet [Eph. 5:32]) Christus et anima efficiuntur una caro."

23. WA 7:55.7-23 (translation of the Latin version).

constructed on the basis of these texts and their contexts. It is not by chance that Luther uses the parenesis directed toward marriage partners in Ephesians 5:21-33 and that text from the Old Testament that there is used to make the essential point: Hosea 2 and its overall context (Hos. 1–3), according to which the marriage of Hosea to a prostitute, as a symbolic action of a prophet, is used by Yahweh to promise anew his faithfulness to his faithless people; his relationship to Israel, even in light of the breakdown of the faithfulness and of the judgment that is deserved, is renewed and endures *in an incomprehensible way.* As no other biblical book, the book of Hosea proclaims that Yahweh's relationship with Israel — "I am the Lord, your God!" — is a relationship of love and is comparable to marriage. When the Song of Songs, a collection of worldly and sensuous love songs, is taken up later into the canon and is interpreted in terms of the relationship between God and his people, in the relationship of God to the church, as well as the *unio* of God and the individual human being, the basic reason that this can happen is provided by the book of Hosea. To be sure, there are other metaphors here and there that speak of close personal connections, which are used to describe the relationship between God and his people — such as the "son" ("Out of Egypt I called my son"; Hos. 11:1) or a foundling (9:10). But the marriage metaphor remains dominant. It, and the erotic vocabulary connected with it, creates and nurtures the personal description of communion with God in the history of biblical interpretation, most particularly when the "mystical bride" theme is used.

The urgency and potency of the address in the gospel preamble to the Decalogue — "I am the Lord your God!" — have their source in the language of love. The interactive relationship is not one of domineering force; instead, love is promised: "I am yours, you are mine!" (cf. Hos. 2:19-20). But a declaration of love can still be taken as an irritant and as foolishness and can be scorned. That did not happen for the first time because of the cross of Jesus Christ. In like manner, Hosea presents Yahweh as a lover, whose people have found "other events and powers, figures and truths" (First Thesis of the Barmen Theological Declaration [1934]) to be more interesting, more important, more real, and more necessary than he is: "Yet I have been Yahweh your God ever since the land of Egypt; you know no God but me, and besides me there is no savior!" (Hos. 13:4; cf. *BSLK* 60:35f.: "Look here and let me alone be your God and never seek any other"). What happens to the lover is shown as the text continues: "When I fed them they were satisfied; they were satisfied, and their heart was proud; therefore they forgot me" (Hos. 13:6).

The people betrayed the love; only judgment and death are to follow (Hos. 13:7-9): "So I will become like a lion against them, like a panther I will lurk for them beside the way. I will meet them like a bear robbed of her cubs, and will tear open their hardened heart and I will devour them like a lion; the wild animals will tear them apart. Israel, I will bring you to disaster; for your salvation is with me alone."[24]

God's mercy stands opposite God's wrath. Luther gives full weight to what makes this brand-new start so incomprehensible. He does not use the way the law operates and what it declares, attributing sin to a person and driving that person into destruction, into the hell of damnation, to convey the way the gospel operates and what it declares; he lets the rupture stand. On the other side of that rupture, the gospel begins afresh with a second, new, and final message from God: "The different message comes in this way."[25]

The effect that the law creates is not surprising. One has no trouble understanding what it means to rely on oneself and on one's own deeds; the action-consequences relationship has its own logic. But the gospel is absolutely, completely incomprehensible. That God rescues one from, and brings one safely through, the deserved judgment is a miracle. Law and gospel cannot be plausibly intertwined together; their existence is hard and fast in opposition to each other. The gospel is literally a paradox: it stands against that which the sinner can reasonably expect; it stands against damnation.

It is thus not surprising that the communion between the sinning human being and the God who justifies through Jesus Christ by the Holy Spirit is incomprehensible; it is stupefying — astonishing — which does not lead one to be calm and at peace. Rather, it is described by Luther as a "stupendum duellum"[26] — as a duel that arouses astonishment, as a duel like the one Jacob engaged in at the Jabbok (Gen. 32). That this deadly confrontation between God and humanity ends joyfully, that the dispute between God and humanity is a "happy exchange,"[27] is a miracle. The one who has escaped from judgment and death cannot be sufficiently astounded about this.

"The love of God does not find one worthy of its love to be present already, but [first] creates it."[28] In this sense God is "God and no mortal" (Hos.

24. Cf. Luther's express reference to it in *LW* 31:348. But when God turns his heartfelt mercy toward the people who have fallen completely into judgment and ruin — going against himself and his own righteousness (Hos. 11:8) — he thus rescues from death. This happens by virtue of the same type of love that takes place in creation out of nothing, *creatio ex nihilo*.

25. WA 7:24.9f.; cf. *LW* 31:348.

26. *LW* 31:352: "a mighty duel," italics added. Cf. Uwe Rieske-Braun, *Duellum mirabile. Studien zum Kampfmotiv in Martin Luthers Theologie*, FKDG 73 (Göttingen, 1999).

27. Cf. n. 16 above. Only from the perspective of the end can it be said that the exchange is "happy," and thus a joyful one.

28. WA 1:354.35; cf. *LW* 31:41 (Heidelberg Disputation, thesis 28, 1518): "Amor dei non invenit, sed creat suum diligibile."

11:9). For: "human love comes for one who holds another worthy of love [already]."[29] By contrast, the justification of the ungodly (Rom. 4:5) is nothing less than a resurrection of the dead and creation out of nothing (4:17).

God's action of salvation cannot be described in any other way; it uses intense wording and takes place on the edge and at the point of the rupture, as

> [that] happy exchange, in which the rich, noble, righteous bridegroom Christ takes as spouse the poor, shamed, evil little whore [cf. Hos. 1–3] and acquits her of all evil, decorating her with all good things. Thus it is not possible that the sins will damn her; now they lie upon Christ and have been swallowed up by him. She thus has such a rich righteousness from her bridegroom that she can survive once again against all sins — even if they would lie upon her. Paul speaks about this in 1 Cor. 15[:57, 55; cf. Hos. 13:14]: "Praise and thanks be to God, who has given us such a conquest in Christ Jesus, in which death is swallowed up, together with sin."[30]

The passage cited from *On the Freedom of a Christian* is placed within a context in which Luther states three times in a row what is meant by the *unio* of "Word" and "soul," about God and the human being in faith. It deals with a single action of speaking and action-causing speaking, which — because it is so important to Luther, since it is so miraculous — he tries to describe with a series of ideas that view the event from three different vantage points: in the third (in section 12) he uses the *comparison to marriage*, which we have observed already; in the first (in section 10) he uses the imagery of *unifying iron with fire*, a topic from the history of the christological teaching about the two natures. Surrounded by these two that match up nicely together, section 11 refers to the act of *reciprocal recognition of the justifying God and the sinning human being*, whom God justifies in the confession of sins (i.e., conferring upon him righteousness).[31]

The sinner does not remain opposite God, condemning himself and not communicating with God, and thus in a deadly confrontation between the two; the wonder of fellowship with God comes instead: that happens by force

---

29. WA 1:354.35f.: "Amor hominis fit a suo diligibili." Cf. *LW* 31:41.

30. WA 7:26.4-12; cf. *LW* 31:352.

31. Cf. chap. 2.2 above. The way this mutual recognition takes place is explained here just as in Luther's explanation of the first commandment in the Large Catechism. That God and faith, Word and faith belong together (LC I, 3, *BC*, 386), just as idolatry and unbelief do, in the faulty alliance of what one might call an unholy marriage, certainly does not actually denote an identity without distinctions; community is determined by a distinction in eternity: the distinction between Creator and creature. *No relationship without distinction!*

of the *unio personalis* in the joyful play of that "happy exchange" and transfer, that "happy transaction," that "economy of salvation," "in which the rich, noble, righteous bridegroom Christ takes as spouse the poor, shamed, evil little whore."

10.3. "I Believe That Jesus Christ . . . Is My Lord"

As we turn now to Luther's explanation to the second article of the Apostles' Creed in the Small Catechism, we take up once again the themes that were discussed in both of the preceding sections.

> I believe that Jesus Christ,
> > true God, born of the Father in eternity,
> > and also true man, born of the Virgin Mary,
> is my Lord;
> > who has redeemed me, a lost and condemned person,[32]
> > acquired, won from all sins,
> > from death and from the power of the devil;
> > not with gold or silver,
> > but with his holy, precious blood
> > and with his innocent suffering and death,
> > so that I might be his own
> > and live under him in his kingdom and serve him
> > in everlasting righteousness, innocence, and blessedness,
> > just as he is risen from the dead,
> > lives and reigns in eternity.
> That is certainly true.[33]

10.3.1. Faith in Christ the Lord

The overall construction of this text corresponds rather carefully to the explanation of the first article, which we have studied extensively in regard to an-

---

32. Cf. *LW* 12:311, on Ps. 51, 1532: "The proper subject of theology is man guilty of sin and condemned, and God the Justifier and Savior" [subiectum Theologiae homo reus et perditus et deus iustificans vel salvator]. Cf. chap. 2.2 above.

33. *BSLK* 511.23-38; cf. SC II, 3, explanation of the second article of the creed, in *BC*, 355. [Trans.: the translation of the explanation to this article is very literal so as to follow the author's train of thought.]

thropology in connection with the teaching about creation.[34] We must be clear once again that the chief element for the correct understanding of this entire explanation is shaped by the statement according to which "faith is nothing other than an answer and a confession of the Christian to the issue that is posed by the first commandment."[35] This means: "I believe" — *credo* — is something I can say only because I have been addressed by the promise: "I am the Lord your God!" In fact, it constitutes the relationship. I have been created and placed into a communion thereby. I can say "I believe that Jesus Christ . . . is my Lord" only because God's introduction of himself and of his name has come before my faith came and has preceded it. The *kyrios* title, a title used for God and God's own personal name since the time of the Septuagint, is used to address Jesus Christ in the New Testament: "My Lord and my God" (John 20:28; cf. 1:18).

One must ask at the same time about what this identification of the human being Jesus with the almighty God declares. But first we must examine the overall construction of Luther's explanation more carefully: "I believe" has an object, which is at the same time its basis; faith is never "absolute" faith; it is always a completely relational matter; it is faith that is *related* to its basis and content:[36] "I believe *that* . . ." In the explanation to the first article, the summary of the entire matter is offered right at the very beginning ("I believe that God has created me together with all creatures"). The same is true here as well — matching the acclamation of Thomas in John 20:28: "my Lord" (cf. Phil. 2:11). One reaches the high point of the entire explanation in this acclamation;[37] it would be possible, as in Philippians 2:11, to end the sentence with a period right there. But the catechism needs to articulate in *what way exactly* Jesus Christ is Lord. What exactly does this title state? What exactly does this title, this name, say, this divine name?

"My Lord" is the high point of the "that" statements, which go in many directions. Grammatically, it is dependent upon "I believe," but one could easily be led to interpret it as its own main clause: "I believe: Jesus Christ is my Lord. . . ." Grammatically a subordinate clause, semantically it states the

34. Cf. chap. 7.3 above.

35. *BSLK* 647.36-38; cf. LC II, 10, explanation of the first article of the creed, in *BC*, 432.

36. Cf. Philip Melanchthon, *Capita* 1519/20, CR 21:36: "Faith that is specifically related to the *promissio* is justifying faith" [Fides proprie relata ad promissionem est fides iustificans].

37. The Large Catechism clearly states that the concentrated use of the *Kyrios* title is deliberate: "This article is very rich and far-reaching, but in order to treat it briefly for children, we shall take up one phrase and in it grasp the substance of the article so that everyone may learn from it, as we have said, how we are redeemed. We shall concentrate on these words, 'in Jesus Christ, our LORD'" (LC II, 26, in *BC*, 434).

main point: the reason and the goal — the object — of faith. In this way it functions as the main clause. In that sense "my Lord" is not only the high point but also the fulcrum and the cardinal point. This is the point that gives definition to what goes before it ("true God") and to the subordinate clause that follows ("who . . . me"), right to the very end. Both sections explain what is meant by the title "Lord" in the way they are arranged.

10.3.2. Christ's Nature Is His Work — Christ's Work Is His Nature

The teaching of the ancient church on the two natures, which Luther accepts completely, is not for Luther idle speculation and observation that there are two "natures" that each exist independently as separate entities and remain so. Instead, *as such* this teaching is already soteriology; it teaches already about salvation by its very nature. The teaching about the two natures declares and explains what is involved only within the framework of the work of Jesus Christ, his office, his function: Jesus Christ is God *in the fact that* he is true God and at the same time true man, that he "has redeemed me, a lost and condemned person." He is not somehow, primarily, first of all, someone who in his nature as subject or substance as God and man is a substantive being, a "God-man," and only secondarily — materially, logically, temporally, or in whatever manner — treated as redeemer as well, so that one could speak about a "subject" Jesus Christ who has the "predicate" "redeemer." No, his nature is actually his work and his work is his nature. He is — in a way that differs from us — identical with that which he does.

Correspondingly, the relative clause "who has redeemed me, a lost and condemned person" is not to be understand as a subordinate clause that describes something accidental, but as a subordinate clause that conveys something essential. The subordinate clause does not describe what "my Lord" is as something in addition to what his nature as Lord is already, but rather how he has this nature of being Lord already *in his essence* of being this Lord; it explains the essence of his nature as Lord; it tells what constitutes his being Lord. This interpretation is supported by the way it is articulated in the Large Catechism: "That is now the high point of this article, that the little word 'Lord' simply means the same as 'Redeemer,' which means: the one who has brought us from the devil to God, from death to life, from sin to righteousness, and preserves us thereby."[38]

This title of majesty, "Lord," is thus interpreted satisfactorily on the basis

---

38. *BSLK* 652.25-30; cf. LC II, 31, in *BC*, 434.

of the verb "redeem" (λυτρόω: purchase release for one who is imprisoned, set free by paying the price of redemption). Stated the other way around, the event — which is the event of Easter that can be described and interpreted as an overthrow and as a qualitatively new designation — is solidified in the title, in the substantive, in order to establish and maintain the irreversible validity of what happened once and for all. But the relative clause that describes the essence of the matter is formulated so that the character of the substantive — which describes an event that occurred in history — is not overlooked and mistaken: "who has redeemed me, a lost and condemned person, acquired, won from all sins, from death and from the power of the devil . . . with his holy, precious blood and with his innocent suffering and death." In this way the uniqueness of what takes place "under Pontius Pilate" is emphasized and unmistakably removed from the realm of myth. That Christ is Lord from all eternity — but that such a relationship comes to us in a specific way only as the action of salvation unfolds[39] — is anchored in the unique historical event of the crucifixion and resurrection. The customary disjunctions between an eternal nature and a temporal coming into existence swirl around together and are intertwined within one another, are woven and interlaced: eternity now never again exists apart from time, and time is never again apart from eternity.[40]

All the specifics about the divine action of salvation are arranged under the core term "redemption."[41]

Jesus Christ's work of salvation, which is conveyed to us and appropriated for us in the "happy exchange," cannot be abstracted from his "per-

---

39. Cf. LC II, 27, in *BC*, 434, in the context of LC II, 27-28, in *BC*, 442: ". . . has become my Lord." Cf. also the acclamations in the Yahweh Kingship Psalms ("Yahweh is king/has become king").

40. The question about whether God became flesh to show his reaction to human sin follows a thought pattern that overemphasizes a linear, chronological schema. Instead, the incarnation, by which God is most deeply engaged in human sin, is at the same time an answer that was given beforehand, hearing the complaint before it was uttered: "Then God moan[ed] in eternity" (verse 4, line 1, literally rendered, of "Dear Christians, One and All, Rejoice"). Such a statement is impossible for common logic. It implies the expressed interlacing of time and eternity as well as that of the past, present, and future.

41. Cf. the corresponding passage in the Large Catechism: "The remaining parts of this article simply serve to clarify and express how and by what means this redemption was accomplished — that is, how much it cost Christ and what he paid and risked in order to win us and bring us under his dominion. That is to say, he became a human creature, conceived and born without sin, of the Holy Spirit and the Virgin, so that he might become Lord over sin; moreover, he suffered, died, and was buried so that he might make satisfaction for me and pay what I owed, not with silver and gold but with his own precious blood. And he did all this so that he might become my LORD" (LC II, 31, in *BC*, 434).

son." One goes astray theologically if one either speaks only speculatively about the "person" of Christ or discusses his work of salvation only in terms of the historical effect it has. Neither Christology nor soteriology can be understood apart from the other, neither the "person" nor the action of salvation.

And yet different aspects are described by the same content when Luther speaks about the doctrine of the two natures or about the saving work of Christ. For as little as he knows anything about "God in himself" or "faith in itself,"[42] with reference to salvation, just as little does he find it sensible theologically to speak about "Christ in himself." We encounter Christ, and God through him, in truth only when we encounter him from within the horizon of the question about salvation.

10.4. Communication of Attributes and Facing Outward

The hymn of liberation "Dear Christians, One and All, Rejoice," the tractate *On the Freedom of a Christian,* and Luther's explanation of the second article of the creed each speak about the human being who believes as one who has been given a gift, one who is purely and solely reliant on the person and work of Christ, and who is thus a radically dependent being who now faces outward. The believer lives no longer in himself, but in Christ (cf. Gal. 2:19-20). Being curved in on oneself and finding one's own ground of being, seeking to establish one's own identity, is now overcome.

The nature of Jesus Christ in faith is a specific nature "for me" *(pro me)* — not for me as an isolated "I" that looks egotistically to save myself. Instead, it applies to me "together with all believers";[43] it thus describes an existence "for us" *(pro nobis),* the gift of God that is "for [all of] you" *(pro vobis)* — the gift of the Father through the Son given by the Holy Spirit — promised, appropriated, and transmitted.

The human being as sinner cannot experience an identity that achieves the happiness he hopes for, but suffers instead the painful experience of being separated. Correspondingly, the forgiveness of sins is no conciliatory way to be raised up so as to achieve identity inside oneself; one's identity is transposed into another, into one who always remains alien: into the alien righteousness *(iustitia aliena)* that is given as a gift of Jesus Christ. In addition, the sinner who is now justified to become a new man must continue to have a re-

---

42. Cf. chap. 7.3.1.a above.
43. *BSLK* 512.11f.; cf. SC II, 6, in *BC,* 355 (explanation to the third article; cf. chap. 11).

lationship with the old man. He lives in that relationship in the — concurrently painful — tension between faith and sight.

The transaction of justification in God's presence brings with it a contradiction to the desire of the human being to find an identity by which he seeks to bring peace to himself in a moralistic and metaphysical way; his striving for wholeness is crushed. He cannot establish a continuity of any kind across the rupture; not even his experience of the world and of the self gives him a chance to detect any continuity. Instead, he is created completely anew and continues to find his identity outside himself, in another, in one who is foreign: in the one who has taken his place in a happy exchange and transfer of human sin and God's righteousness. The criterion for truth is provided by this event, in which Jesus Christ takes another person's place with a propitiatory death, on the basis of which *theology, concerning both premodern metaphysics of substance and the modern metaphysics of subject, can be evaluated only critically,* since these approaches to life do not permit one to think in a way that looks beyond the self and to find my identity outside myself.[44]

This identifies the decisive point of contention in the conflict between reformational theology and modern thinking: theology must ask what it means that the righteousness of Christ, which has been appropriated to me, which has been given to me as my own, is and remains a *iustitia aliena* — a gift from someone else, by whose life I live (Gal. 2:19-20). But how ought theology to handle this paradox that goes against every way we conceptualize how to establish one's identity?

This question, which is so difficult and yet so decisive, finds its answer in Luther's description of the relationship between Christology and soteriology, in the phrase that has been presented already: "the happy exchange." That the human being who sins becomes clean with the righteous God, in that the human being is wrenched away from sin and is furnished with the righteousness of God, includes the presupposition and enduring implication that God and man have been united in one person, which means they are together in a communicative event, which reaches out in a human way to the sinning human being, but simultaneously does not leave him alone with his own kind, but delivers God and his righteousness to him. It is exactly this christological and consequently soteriological point that is conceptualized in the teaching about the *communication of attributes.* In a short form, it is articulated in the text that has already been refer-

---

44. For a more detailed treatment, cf. Bayer, "Das Wort ward Fleisch," especially V.a and b, and VI.c.

enced from *On the Freedom of a Christian,* section 12: "Namely, because Christ is God and a human being in one and the same person . . . , everything thereby [namely, sin, death, and hell] is swallowed down by him,"[45] absorbed.

The christological concept of the communication of attributes was indeed known in theological tradition from the time of the early church on, but it had only marginal meaning.[46] Luther was the first one to place it into the center of Christology, indeed, in that of theology as a whole. For him the communication of attributes is articulated and becomes the central concept for describing and articulating the person of Jesus Christ and the work that was completed by him — neither the person nor the work is ever to be isolated from the other! This concept intends to say that the *general* attributes of the human being take part in the divine nature in the *concrete* person Jesus Christ and that the reverse is true as well: in Christ, the human being, God suffered, died, and was victorious over death; in Christ, who is God, the human nature has become omnipresent, omniscient, omnipotent.[47]

In a very compact way and with great specificity Jörg Baur has described what is involved with Luther's concept of the teaching about the communication of attributes as a complete, christologically new definition that has meaning both for the human being and for God, and he shows in what sense Luther stands in ongoing conflict on this point with modern thinking about identity:

> In Christ God and the human being exist no longer so that one stands over against the other as a discrete entity, but they communicate unimpeded with one another. . . . The work of Christ in proclamation, acts of healing, and miracles, in suffering, cross, resurrection, ascension, and expectation of his arrival in an epiphany is not the achievement of an isolated super-subject, but is the concrete explication of his communicative nature in dismantling what is old in the rebellious world of sin, the law, and death. . . . This transfer of the human ground of existence into Christ and into the tri-une [God] happens *"solo verbo,"* through God who always comes in a con-

45. "Cum enim Christus sit deus et homo eaque persona . . . ," in the context of lines 7-23, quoted above in German translation, n. 23. Cf. *LW* 31:361-62.

46. Cf. Bayer, "Das Wort ward Fleisch," III.

47. It was chiefly concerning this issue that conflict arose between Zwingli and Luther; Luther stated his position in two great treatises on the Lord's Supper (*LW* 37:13-150 [*That These Words of Christ "This Is My Body," Etc., Still Stand Firm against the Fanatics,* 1527] and *LW* 37:161-372 [*Confession concerning Christ's Supper,* 1528]). On the subject in detail, cf. Jörg Baur, "Ubiquität," in *TRE* 34 (2002), 224-41.

crete way as one who addresses and makes promises, who takes away from the person the trust that he had up to this point that was grounded in the self and thus awakens faith as the fulfillment of what awakens one to life that is directed totally outward.[48]

Such direction toward that which is outward and such openness strike the modern person who relies on himself and on his own narcissism as offensive.[49] The truth of the faith that opens one up to what is beyond the self stands in contradiction to reliance on the self and to being closed in on the self. This means that the Christian existence looks outward in two ways. This can be said on the basis of the communication of attributes that is rooted in Christology. At the end of Luther's tractate *On the Freedom of a Christian,* he articulates this outward thrust impressively: "This is now our concluding thesis: A Christian man does not live in his own self, but in Christ and in his

---

48. Jörg Baur, *Das reformatorische Christentum in der Krise* (Tübingen: Mohr-Siebeck, 1997), 17f.

49. The modern age is wary of falling into Docetism (God in a seemingly human body). But Christ ought not to be thought of as a *Gattungs-individuum,* simply as a representative of the human species. "Jesus Christ is neither an idealized human being nor is he the mythical cipher to demonstrate what one would suppose the divine-human nature of the human species would look like. He is the event in which the Creator's presence among all creatures now turns to take on identity within a single human life, by which the rebuke of the law turns into the Yes of the gospel" (Jörg Baur, "Der reformatorisch-lutherische Rechtfertigungsglaube angesichts der Herausforderung durch das neuzeitliche Selbstbewusstsein," in *Aufbruch und Orientierung,* ed. Joachim Heubach, Veröffentlichungen der Luther-Akademie Ratzeburg [Erlangen: Martin-Luther-Verlag, 2000], 99-110, here 109f.). Finally, the idea of Adoptionism (God selects a particular human individual) seeks to avoid both Docetism and mistaking Jesus Christ as representative of the human species. But it is just as misleading to say: in the incarnation "the Creator who was previously absent does not draw near to a particular individual, Jesus of Nazareth, in a unique way. Rather, the one God discloses in himself the difference between the one who sends and the one who is sent, between Father and Son, and brings humanity into the one who is sent, into the unity of a single life, and does so in such a way that humanity can take part in the deity because humanity is taken up into the life of the divinity of the Son, even within the circumstances of the distortions that lead to the end of life; at the same time the divinity is affected by all the realities of being human. Jesus Christ, as person, is thus the event of the communication between the deity who gives of himself and the humanity that has been taken on; what follows is the infinite openness to which and upon which those who are distorted are 'drawn' to one another. . . . Through the God-Man, and in him, the sinner who is removed from himself in faith, now has his new place as one who is placed outside himself. Salvation is thus not primarily that one who was previously used to doing evil is now qualified all over again, as one who will customarily do good, but that the subject has been pulled away from himself. He is given a new place on the basis of baptism, the Word, and faith. As early Luther said: [*LW* 25:322]: 'Man rather than sin is taken away'" (Baur, 107). *LW* 31:371.

neighbor — or else he is no Christian. [He lives] in Christ by faith, in the neighbor through love: By means of faith he is drawn above himself into God; conversely, he lets himself be drawn down in love to his neighbor and remains at all times in God and in his love."[50]

50. WA 7:69.12-16; cf. *LW* 31:371. Cf. the *Kirchenpostille,* 1522 (on Titus 3:4-7): "All Christian teaching, work, and life [are] briefly and clearly stated with all the words one needs with these two: FAITH and LOVE, through which the human being is placed between God and his neighbor as a means, which receives what comes from above and distributes it down below, and is just like a barrel or pipe, through which the spring of divine goodness ought to flow onto other people, without being impeded . . . , since the divine nature is nothing other than pure beneficence and, as Paul says here, friendliness and happiness about other people, which daily pours out its good things with overflowing measure on all creatures" (WA 10I/1:100.8–101.2).

Chapter 11 God's Presence: The Holy Spirit

The Holy Spirit is not a skeptic.

11.1. "I Believe": "The Holy Spirit Has Called Me through the Gospel"

As we turn now to discuss the question about appropriation, better yet: about the presentation and addressing of the saving work of Jesus Christ — which means his "person" as well — we can start by asserting the following: such a conversion is not achieved by "one's own reason or strength," but is attributable solely to God's work in us. It is the work of God the Holy Spirit. "No one can say 'Jesus is Lord' except by the Holy Spirit" (1 Cor. 12:3). Luther uses this Pauline statement, more than any other, when he explains the third article of the Apostles' Creed in the Small Catechism:

> I believe
> 1. that I cannot by my own reason or strength
>   believe in Jesus Christ my Lord
>   or come to him;
> 2.1. but the Holy Spirit has called me
>   through the Gospel,
>   enlightened with his gifts,
>   sanctified and kept in the true faith,
> 2.2. just as he calls the whole Christian church on earth,
>   gathers, enlightens, sanctifies,
>   and preserves it with Jesus Christ in the true, one faith;
> 2.3. in which Christian church, daily, he richly
>   forgives all sins for me and all believers

and on the last day will raise me and all the dead
and will give me with all believers in Christ an eternal life.
That is certainly true.[1]

If one notes in the wide-ranging subordinate clause, in the "that" clause, that the subject changes from "I" to "the Holy Spirit," then one can divide this explanation into two parts: the first part (1) states what the believing and confessing "I" *cannot* do; the second part (2) explains what the Holy Spirit gives the believer, what the believer partakes in now. This positive side of what is stated negatively at first offers three aspects: that which is for the individual person (2.1), then what is for "the whole Christian church" (2.2), and finally what is specifically superimposed upon both aspects, which impressively applies ("just as") these benefits by showing how they apply equally (2.3).

11.1.1. "I Believe That I Cannot . . ."

If one reduces the first part to its syntactic framework, a paradox is uttered: "I *believe* that I *cannot* . . . believe" (cf. Mark 9:24)! *I* cannot do it, namely, "not by my own reason or strength" — which is parallel to the way it is formulated in the explanation to the first article of the Apostles' Creed — "all without my merit and worthiness." Faith is the work of the Holy Spirit in the believer. No matter how coming to faith, or being in faith, is experienced, whether subjectively, biographically, psychologically — faith is the work of God and not of the human being. As for whatever is involved in salvation, our will is bound — which is good for us![2]

When I confess that I *cannot* "believe by my own reason or strength," that excludes every understanding of faith that is linked to a human predisposition. No faith is grounded in the self and is thus an "absolute" faith;[3] instead, there is only a faith that is created outside one's own self, grounded outside the self, a faith grounded outside the center of one's being, a faith that in this sense is determined by its content. It has its basis in the object: "Jesus Christ, my Lord," through whom, as his Son, God conveys himself as Father through the Holy Spirit and allows himself to be addressed. Faith is in fact completely an act of trust, but it is a trust that is grounded and connected. If I do not

---

1. *BSLK* 511.46–512.13; cf. SC II, 6, in *BC*, 355. [Trans.: the translation of the explanation to this article is very literal so as to follow the author's train of thought.]

2. Cf. the conclusion of *De servo arbitrio*, where Luther confesses that he would not choose to have free will, even if it were possible, since the certainty of salvation can be grounded only in God himself — not in the human subject (cf. chap. 8.2, n. 36 above).

know the one in whom I place my trust and what I entrust to him, then the faith relationship — no matter how sincerely and earnestly it may be — remains empty and aimless.

Luther's explanation to the first commandment in the Large Catechism thus does not call attention primarily to the preparedness of the human heart, to observe one's striving, as such, but from first to last it deals with *that upon which* I can place my trust; *from whence* I can promise myself good things, in fact, the best of things; and *whom* I may address for deliverance in all times of need, because saving mercy and good things that guarantee my existence are *promised*: "*I*, I want for you" — this is how Luther explains God's self-revelation (Exod. 20:2; cf. 3:14), his personal name — "to give enough and to deliver from all needs; only let your heart not hang on or rest on any other."[4] One is reminded here of what Luther said in his interpretation of Jonah 1:5: the sailors' prayer of faith, which showed that they all knew about God, ought not be any less intensive and upright than the faith of the Christian; but the sailors do not have a "certain God" and thus they also have no certain faith.[5]

11.1.2. ". . . but the Holy Spirit"

The second part brings about the sharp turn from the "I," which from the outset "cannot believe in Jesus Christ, my Lord," toward the Holy Spirit, who gives me this faith; the confession of one's own inability to believe is radicalized to the extent that the Holy Spirit now becomes the subject.

11.1.2.a. ". . . Has Called Me through the Gospel"

The first element of the statement already offers the central thesis of the entire explanation: "The Holy Spirit has *called* me through the gospel." This call is bound together with baptism, an event that happened once for all time but that has an ongoing effect; it is never in the past. Its ongoing effect is expressed likewise by the use of the present perfect tense, with the words "enlighten," "sanctify," "preserve." The Holy Spirit does not do his work only when he brings one to faith, but also works by faith to make sure the believer continues in and remains in the faith; one might say that he does not work

---

3. Cf. chap. 7, n. 37 above.
4. *BSLK* 560.40-42; cf. LC I, 4, in *BC*, 387.
5. Cf. chap. 6.2 above.

only deistically, by merely giving the initial spark; he guides and preserves the Christian life at every moment. Some of the links in the chain of the *ordo salutis* (especially that which was constructed by using Rom. 8:29-30), advocated at a later time by Lutheran orthodoxy and pietism[6] — calling, enlightening, sanctifying, and preserving in the faith — appear already here, at least the words do, but not yet in the later sense that steps are prescribed to identify the temporal sequence of a process; instead, more correctly, they describe the various aspects of one and the same justifying action of the Holy Spirit.

In a way that differs from the Small Catechism, the explanation in the Large Catechism is dominated by the verb "sanctify," which is used only in reference to God. If the human being is sanctified, it means that God himself sanctifies him, in that God delivers himself to the believer as the holy one, the one who alone is holy. God himself is holy; and the one he addresses and thus creates becomes holy in that way as well.[7] In this way he imparts his holiness, which he does not desire to keep for himself.

In what way, then, does the Holy Spirit come to us? How and in what way does he impart himself? The Spirit works faith in the human being inwardly, but never apart from means, never without the external "physical Word."[8]

In light of the primal human drive[9] for extraordinary religious experience, as immediate experience of the Spirit, it is certainly not obvious to everyone that Luther would formulate the central thesis for his understanding of the Holy Spirit as "The Holy Spirit has called me through the *gospel.*" This means: although the Holy Spirit cannot be apprehended, he is not an incomprehensible fluidity, but comes in a clearly specific Word that can be heard.[10] The gospel has the form of a Word that can be heard, which has been promised to me by another human being; it has the form of the Word that can be heard, which can be seen and discerned in the sacrament. According to Lu-

6. Cf. Johann Anselm Steiger, "Ordo salutis," in *TRE* 25 (1995), 371-76.

7. According to the testimony of the New Testament and Reformation teaching, all members of the communion of believers are "holy." Their holiness is based on the holiness that is promised to them by God: "You shall be holy, for I the Lord your God am holy, says the Lord your God" (Lev. 19:2). *This concept of what it means to be "holy" is applicable to all Christians, and is thus catholic and not elitist, as in the Roman view.*

8. CA V: the teaching of those is rejected "who teach that we obtain the Holy Spirit without the external word of the gospel through our own preparation, thoughts, and works" (*BC*, 40).

9. Cf. 4.6.3 above on the Smalcald Articles: "Enthusiasm clings to Adam and his children from the beginning to the end of the world" (III, 8, 9, in *BC*, 323).

10. On the inseparability of Spirit and Word: "By the word of the Lord the heavens were made, and all their host by the breath of his mouth" (Ps. 33:6), and "the words that I have spoken to you are spirit and life" (John 6:63).

ther's *Confession* of 1528, sermonic words, baptism, and the Lord's Supper are the "three means or ways in which he [the Holy Spirit] comes to us."[11]

The Holy Spirit is no apparition but is a being that speaks.[12] He calls: with power in words and power in deeds, at the same time, as Romans 4:17 says about God: he calls for things that do not exist that they might come to be. The Holy Spirit is the *spiritus creator* — as in Luther's adaptation of the hymn from the Middle Ages: *Veni creator spiritus,* which is titled "Come, Holy Ghost, Creator Blest."[13] This creative power of God is identical with the gospel. Gospel is consequently not only the description of something that happened but is part of this happening, the saving act of God in its own right; it is the δύναμις θεοῦ — the power of God, which saves (Rom. 1:17).

In addition to the work of the Holy Spirit being "to call," three verbs are added: "enlighten," "sanctify," "preserve." I am called *to* the true faith, I am sanctified and preserved "*in* the true faith." Verbs that describe a point in time and those that have a durative aspect are intertwined within one another. "Enlightenment"[14] in the New Testament can refer to the inner aspect of a call that took place once upon a time; in fact, in the book of Hebrews (6:4; 10:32) it is a baptismal term. But at this point Luther uses it in the sense that it is identified as one of the charisms — as one of the "gifts" of the Spirit[15] — which is interpreted in what takes place in one's life and in the context of the congregation. In the same way one can speak of "sanctification" as something that has happened once upon a time, in which a person becomes the possession of God (1 Cor. 6:11), but it can also be used with reference to an entire process that unfolds throughout life, in which baptism is effective.[16] Correspondingly, Luther's *On the Councils and the Church* (1539) states that the Holy Spirit "does not [work] only" through a call that comes just once, but "through sin being swept out each day and through the [daily] renewal of life, [so] that we do not remain in sin, but can and ought to lead a new life in all manner of good works and not in the

---

11. WA 26:606.10-12. Such holding fast to the external, physical Word soon brought the Lutheran Reformation into conflict with what is currently identified as the "left wing" of the Reformation, thus with Spiritualists and Anabaptists; some of the evangelical free churches can be traced to a greater or lesser extent to that movement.

12. Cf. Mark 6:49-50: Jesus is no φάντασμα (phantom), but "he *spoke* to them and *said,* 'Take heart, it is I; do not be afraid.'"

13. Rabanus Maurus, *LSB,* #498, 499, 1.

14. Cf. 2 Cor. 4:6 and the *claritas interna* in *De servo arbitrio* (chap. 4.6.1).

15. Cf. the seven gifts of the Holy Spirit (Isa. 11:2), and further 1 Cor. 12–14; Rom. 12; Eph. 4:7-11 (especially v. 11).

16. "Sanctify," as used in "sanctified and kept in the true faith," more likely ought to be construed as durative, and thus not as in 1 Cor. 6:11.

old, evil works."[17] The durative aspect is clearest when "preserves" is used
— but this preservation is also nothing other than protection from nothingness, which continues to be renewed, and from unbelief. God, the Holy
Spirit, as Creator, preserves me ever anew — and thus in an ongoing fashion — in life and in faith.

11.1.2.b. ". . . Just as He Calls the Whole Christian Church on Earth"

This present tense is to be understood in a durative sense. One might compare this with the Augsburg Confession, article 7: because of the call of God, it
cannot be otherwise than "that at all times . . . a holy Christian church exists
. . . and remains."[18]

It is most noteworthy that and how Luther places these two aspects of the
individual and the community on an equal level; in the Latin translation, for
"just as" it reads *quemadmodum* ("just as," "in such a way as"). Putting the
two aspects on the same level states that the way an individual becomes a
Christian, which means through the faith that comes to him (Gal. 3:25), is no
different from the way the church as a whole comes into existence, the way
the Christian church as a whole is constituted on earth. Stated the opposite
way: the church is constituted no differently than the individual Christian.
Based on the logic of the matter, they are equal in their origin and in their
function. The same way they function and originate is demonstrated in the
impressive way the same verbs are used to describe the *ecclesia;* Luther had already used the same verbs when he described how the faith of the individual
Christian is constituted "through the gospel": call, enlighten, sanctify, preserve. The verb "gather" is admittedly used here in addition, since it makes
sense only with reference to the collective subject "Christian church." This
corresponds to the addition of the adjective "one" (*unica*)[19] to "in the true
faith": the true faith, in which the call by means of the gospel is taken to be
true, is the one, and the only one, that unites all Christians.

One cannot overestimate the importance of what Luther does when he
uses the same vocabulary to describe how an individual believer is constituted and how the church at large is constituted. It signifies that the church,

---

17. WA 50:625.26-28; cf. *LW* 41:144 *(On the Councils and the Church)*. Cf. 143-44: the Christian people "have the Holy Spirit, who sanctifies them daily, not only through the forgiveness of
sin acquired for them by Christ (as the Antinomians foolishly believe), but also through the ab-
olition, the purging, and the mortification of sins."

18. ". . . ecclesia perpetuo mansura sit" *(BSLK* 61.3; cf. CA VII, 1, in *BC,* 42).

19. *BSLK* 512.7f.; cf. SC II, 6, in *BC,* 355.

"the whole Christian church on earth" — which means the "universal" and, in the original sense of the adjective, the "catholic" church — according to its essence does not come into existence through the gospel either *before* or *after* the individual Christian is called. Luther thus understands the church neither in the Roman Catholic sense of an institution for salvation nor in the modern-collegial sense of a society. For him the church is neither a legal institution that presumes faith created by the gospel, the external form of which has a spiritual dignity, nor an association constructed in a secondary manner, which arose at its point of origin through people joining one another and making an agreement among those who were already like-minded comrades; in this — collegial — sense the church is not a *congregatio*.

"The Holy Spirit has called me through the gospel" — me individually, but not in an isolated sense; instead, he addresses me as one in the midst of the "whole Christian church on earth," which corresponds to the explanation of the first article: "created me together with all creatures." Just as a person needs in life those who are fellow creatures — above all else one's parents — and cannot live alone, so the believer cannot believe all alone either. Though it is true that the believer has direct access to God "through the gospel" and does not need the holder of an office such as a priest or pope to be the go-between any longer, it is also true that the faith does not come into existence apart from its being transmitted in a historical, physical way, not apart from a mother or father in the faith, and it cannot survive without being embedded in the congregation that prays on behalf of all others. The Word precedes faith. In *this* sense Luther can speak of the church as "mother."[20]

11.1.2.c.   ". . . in Which Christian Church, for Me and All Believers, He . . ."

This last section of the wide-ranging subordinate clause says something about what is true for both aspects, though each is treated separately in what precedes: the personal, individual aspect as well as what applies to the entire Christian church; that both are dealt with on the same level comes out most impressively once again. The "Christian church" or "the Christian people," which is what Luther liked to say instead of "church,"[21] and the faith of the individual are both — on an equal level — the work of the Holy Spirit.

The Holy Spirit remains the subject even in the closing section of the explanation, in which Luther touches on those elements of teaching of the faith

---

20. Cf. chap. 12.2, nn. 34-35 below.
21. Cf. *LW* 41:142-46, and LC II, 47 (explanation of the third article of the creed), in *BC*, 437.

that are listed in a simple sequence in the Apostles' Creed: forgiveness of sins, resurrection of the dead, and life everlasting. They are all works of God, carried out by the Holy Spirit who makes alive, which we either believe already and are able to experience or believe in and hope for at the end of our life, when the world comes to an end. This perspective gives shape to the topics that will be discussed after the chapter on the church,[22] in chapters 13–15: the life of the Christian in the world (faith and good works), the differentiation between that which is temporal and that which is spiritual (two types of authority), and the consummation of the world.

11.2. Lively Spirit — Trustworthy Word[23]

11.2.1. Against the Spiritualists ("Enthusiasts")

God has now permitted his holy gospel to go [forth] in such a way that he deals with us in two ways. One way is externally, the other is internally. In an external sense he deals with us by means of the spoken Word of the gospel and by means of external signs, as they come in baptism and sacrament. Internally he deals with us by means of the Holy Spirit and faith, together with other gifts. But all this takes place in such a way and [in] such an order that the external elements ought to and need to come first and the internal aspects come afterward, through the external elements; he decided it in this way that he would not give any human being the inner elements except by means of the external ones. For he does not desire to give anyone the Spirit, nor faith, without the external Word and sign that he has instituted for this.[24]

The title of this treatise *(Against the Heavenly Prophets in the Matter of Images and Sacraments)* points out the nature of the conflict that occasioned it. In this regard, Luther directed his remarks against Andrew Carlstadt, Wittenberg preacher, professor, and Luther's doctoral adviser, who originally allied himself with Luther but was then attracted to mystical and spiritualizing ideas and ended up contending that Christ was not physically present in the Lord's Supper. Since that brought into question the certainty of salvation for Luther, he reacted sharply in this document. It is not heavenly, hidden wisdom and specula-

---

22. Chap. 12.

23. The following threefold typology reflects and supplements what was developed in chap. 4.6 from the perspective of biblical authority.

24. WA 18:136.9-18; cf. *LW* 40:144-223 (*Against the Heavenly Prophets in the Matter of Images and Sacraments — Part Two,* 1525); cf. the relation between what is "external" and "internal" in the *Confession* of 1528 (*LW* 37:366); it is much the same in the Smalcald Articles; cf. 11.2.2 below.

tion that lead to salvation, but rather holding fast to what is stated in the clear Word, in preaching and sacrament, which all can hear and see. "What then?" he writes against Carlstadt. "The Word, the Word, the Word, you, O lying spirit, hear it as well; the Word does it! For [even] if Christ had been given and crucified for us a thousand times, it would all be for naught had not the Word of God come and distributed it to us and given it to me as a gift and said: You shall do this, take and have it for yourself."[25] The external Word is important not only as a means of mediation and for external, ecclesiastical reasons — to prevent disorder and the multiplication of offices because of some supposedly higher revelations — but also because I would know nothing without it, what it is that happens by means of the Holy Spirit, his works and his gifts. If the Holy Spirit calls only "through the gospel," but the gospel is gospel only as it is distinguished from the law, then the distinction between law and gospel is decisive with respect to the teaching about the Holy Spirit, about pneumatology, as well. Thus the work of the Spirit is, first of all, to sharpen the law and to bring about God's judgment against sin; only then does the Spirit work through the second and final Word of God, the gospel, in that he forgives sin and creates faith: "In the first place, before all works and things, one hears the Word of God, in which the Spirit punishes the world on account of sin, John 16[:8]. If sin is recognized, then one hears of the grace of Christ. The Spirit comes [once again] in the same Word and gives faith, where and to whom he will.[26] After that the killing [of the old Adam] takes place, and the cross, and the works of love."[27] This last element corresponds to sanctification and preservation in the true faith, which was discussed in the Small Catechism.

Against the Spiritualists and their way of calling upon the Spirit, Luther makes the point that the Spirit comes only in the Word of the gospel as the one who brings Christ, and thus brings life and blessedness.

11.2.2. Against Rome

In the Smalcald Articles, Luther takes not only the Enthusiasts to task in a most surprising way, but at the same time also the enthusiasm of the Roman

---

25. WA 18:202.36–203.2; cf. *LW* 40:146. The famous couplet of the Silesian mystic Angelus Silesius (*Cherubinischer Wandersmann* 1.61) is similar and yet quite different, since it is directed toward what is internal: "Were Christ a thousand times in Bethlehem born / and not in you, you'd be forlorn." On Luther's distinction between "acquiring" and "distributing," cf. chap. 12.2.3 below.

26. Cf. CA V, in *BC*, 40.

27. WA 18:139.20-25; cf. *LW* 40:149.

papacy; he does this with the sharpest polemic possible: "For the papacy is also pure enthusiasm, when the pope boasts 'all rights are in the treasury of his heart'[28] and everything that he judges and commands concerning his church is to be Spirit and right, even if it is above and against Scripture or the spoken Word. That is all of the old devil and the old serpent, which made Adam and Eve into enthusiasts as well and drew them away from the external Word of God toward [enthusiastic] spiritualism and into their own arrogance."[29] As with the Enthusiasts' movement,[30] the papacy supported itself on "external words" — but its own words.

11.2.3. Against Erasmus

Just as Luther introduced the external nature of the Word that creates faith into the discussion against Carlstadt's spiritualizing, against the skepticism of Erasmus he crafted the *assertio:* "Abolish the assertions and you have abolished Christianity."[31] Erasmus had said he did not like *assertiones* — solid, certain statements, affirmations — and would rather move about in the realm where one could construct hypotheses and in the realm where one could ponder how to compare opposing theses.[32] Luther countered: "The Holy Spirit is not a skeptic and has written nothing doubtful or just in the realm of opinion into our hearts, but rather assertions that are more certain and more trustworthy than life itself and all experience."[33]

28. *Corpus Iuris Canonici, Liber Sextus* I, 2 c. 1. Cf. *LW* 44:202, 203 (*To the Christian Nobility of the German Nation,* 1520).

29. *BSLK* 454.7-15; cf. SA III, 8, 4-5, in *BC,* 322: the allusion is to Gen. 3:1: "Did God say . . . ?" Luther sees pure enthusiasm at work even in the papacy (*LW* 31:392, *Why the Books of the Pope and His Disciples Have Been Burned by Martin Luther,* 1520; cf. chap. 4, n. 63 above); he bases that assessment on the way the pope uses Scripture, which he states in the thesis that "the pope has the power to interpret and to teach Holy Scripture according to his will and allows no one to interpret it otherwise than he wants. He thereby puts himself above God's word, dismembers and destroys it." (On how much of Luther's diagnosis still applies today, cf. chap. 4.6.2 above.)

30. SA III, 8, 5-6, in *BC,* 322. In SA III, 8, 9-11, in *BC,* 322-23, Luther offers an unexcelled caustic summary of the worldwide and primal human phenomenon "enthusiasm."

31. "Tolle assertiones, et tulisti Christianismum": WA 18:603.28f.; cf. *LW* 33:21.

32. Cf. Thomas Reinhuber, *Kämpfender Glaube. Studien zu Luthers Bekenntnis am Ende von De servo arbitrio,* TBT 104 (Berlin and New York, 2000), 6-8.

33. WA 18:605.32-34; cf. *LW* 33:24. The Latin reads: "Spiritus sanctus non est Scepticus, nec dubia aut opiniones in cordibus nostris scripsit, sed assertiones ipsa vita et omni experientia certiores et firmiores."

11.3. External Word and Modern Spiritualism

Faith comes by hearing (Rom. 10:17) — by hearing the Word. Faith comes from the promise in which Jesus himself, and God's righteousness through him, is opened for me, brings me back to my homeland in the midst of the congregation, into Paradise, and makes me into a new person. The Augsburg Confession advocates Luther's theology when it speaks in article 5 of establishing the service — the "instituting" — of the Word, thus identifying the office of the Word, by means of which we receive the faith that justifies: "So that we acquire this faith, God established the office of the Word, the gospel and the sacraments. Through this means God gives the Holy Spirit, who creates faith in those who hear the gospel, where and when he wills. The gospel teaches that we have a gracious God by means of Christ's efforts and not because of our own merits, if we believe it."[34] As it rejects an immediate and unmediated — "enthusiastic" — understanding of the Holy Spirit, the article articulates God's coming in a *verbum externum,* an "external Word."[35]

Article 5 is the most important article in the Augsburg Confession. It provides the decisive point for understanding the article on justification (article 4), as well as an understanding about new obedience, good works (article 6); it is the tip of the scale. The "establishment" of the Word is the fundamental "institution."[36] The whole world hangs on this, not just the church or even a denomination. It is the institution and the event from which comes faith, which allows us to comprehend that the world is the creation, even after one goes through the judgment; it is the institution and the event from which faith comes, faith as belief in the one who "gives life to the dead and calls into existence the things that do not exist" (Rom. 4:17).

Is the Word really to be treasured so highly? Ought one not to ask questions about how to verify it and about its authority? Should one not investigate its tangible and material history? Is it then not "just" evidence of an event, a deed, which needs to be distinguished from this word?[37] Ought one not to correct the beginning of the Gospel of John, "in a Faustian way": "In the beginning was the deed"?[38]

---

34. *BSLK* 58.2-10; cf. CA V, in *BC,* 40.

35. CA V, 4, in *BC,* 40 ("others who teach that we obtain the Holy Spirit without the external word of the gospel through our own preparation, thoughts, and works"). Cf. n. 8 above.

36. The New Testament root for that particular concept of institution appears especially in 2 Cor. 5:18-19 (v. 18: "given"; v. 19: "[en]trusted"; Latin: *dare* and *ponere.* Cf. Eph. 4:7-14 [*dare*]).

37. Of course, the distinction between "acquiring" and "distributing" should be kept in mind; cf. chap. 12.2.3 below.

38. Johann Wolfgang Goethe, *Faust,* line 1237.

Treasuring the Word that highly, as Luther does in his theology, was just as offensive to many of Luther's contemporaries — the spiritualists, the Roman papacy, and Erasmus — as it is for many in the modern era. To further sketch Luther's profile of the Spirit who has bound himself with the external Word, I will bring Luther into a dispute in what follows with widely unrecognized modern spiritualism.

The external Word — what is meant in the common but unfortunate formula "Word and sacrament" — should really be identified more appropriately as preached Word as sacrament and sacrament as Word: Jesus Christ himself in concrete form, in which he allows himself to be heard and apprehended, in which he delivers himself "physically." Based on the Christ event, it is also meant as constitutive of the way he communicates and integrates himself in the believer; God's friendliness toward humans allows itself to be "tasted" (Ps. 34:8).

Since not only believers but also unbelievers encounter God's goodness and mercy in a physical way, and since such experiences take place as opening, appropriating, offering, communicating, and giving, irrespective of the disposition of the person who serves the gift and irrespective of the disposition of the person who is receiving it and taking hold of it[39] — the value of such an act ought not to be diminished because the "external Word" has an institutionalized quality. Instead, it is much more than that which establishes justifying faith; it does not allow itself to be taken over; in fact, it prevents such a takeover. By contrast, modern subjectivism still seeks to establish its guiding principle, or at least to discover it — even if it is in the feeling of absolute dependence — within the believer himself. Modern and neo-Protestant subjectivity — the position of the spiritualists, the ravers, and the enthusiasts, which was rejected by the Augsburg Confession — justifies itself by appealing to the validity of an "inner" word against the physical, external Word.

It is not appropriate to identify "the correlation between the external and internal word" with the help of the modalities of "possibility" and "reality," by suggesting that the "external Word" makes something possible and the "inner word" brings to reality a "new awareness of the self."[40] The "external" way God comes to us in the Holy Spirit, in which God conveys himself, is basically

---

39. ". . . nec pendere ex dignitate ministri aut sumentis" (*BSLK* 63.37f.: Wittenberger Konkordie; 1536). See FC SD VII, 16, in *BC*, 596: "its power does not rest upon the worthiness or unworthiness of the minister who distributes the sacrament, nor upon the worthiness or unworthiness of the one who receives it."

40. Against Wilfried Härle and Eilert Herms, *Rechtfertigung. Das Wirklichkeitsverständnis des christlichen Glaubens*, Uni-Taschenbücher 1016 (Göttingen: Vandenhoeck & Ruprecht, 1980), 119-21.

different from a possibility that is yet to be ratified and yet to be realized; it is an *empowerment*. Nor is the gospel, the power of God (Rom. 1:16), as the "external Word," a reality that one seeks in order to make something possible; it is a power that establishes its own reality.

Modern reason and subjectivity may indeed recognize, in certain aspects, the need for "means of salvation" *(media salutis)* and assent to them. But they clearly do not affirm an external "means" as a necessary *foundation*, but only as a useful and functionally comprehensible *trigger point*. Preaching, baptism, and the Lord's Supper are all seen, in this view, as necessary institutional elements that get something started, which sets the process of adaptation in motion and keeps it on track. If it states in Augsburg Confession, article 5, that to achieve such justifying faith, God established the office of the Word *(institutum est)*, gave the gospel and sacrament,[41] such an "institution" is taken at the same time to be a whetstone on which subjectivity can sharpen itself. In *this* sense, what is institutional, what is established, what is grounded, what has been provided already beforehand, is still seen as indispensable in the neo-Protestant view. Modern and neo-Protestant subjectivity need what is external and outward in order to have the necessary support for one to have a relationship, to be able to work hard, in order to have something that allows one to assimilate and apply.

But this subjectivity, with its consumer-oriented greediness, is the enemy of the "external Word" on which Luther stands. Whoever agrees today with Luther's understanding of the Holy Spirit, according to which he binds himself to the external Word, and is in agreement with it, must be ready for the hard task of a fundamental critique of modern subjectivism.

The dispute shows up with particular sharpness and clarity at the point where — as with Hegel — the Reformation faith and its freedom are identified with the subjectivity of modernism. Hegel claimed that he found — in Protestantism — Christianity as universally valid, so that he could negate the "external Word" according to his particular view of its nature as institution and in its opposition to the spiritual, as expressed in what is sensual.

Impressive evidence for this is provided by the numerous passages in which Hegel reflects on the Lord's Supper and concurrently on the complete appropriation of what God integrates into believers there, as he assigns everything external to the realm of enjoyment and consumption. "All externality in relation to me is thereby banished, just as is the externality of the Host: it is only in communion and faith that I stand in relation to God."[42] According to

41. Cf. n. 34 above.
42. *Hegel's Lectures on "The History of Philosophy,"* trans. E. S. Haldane and Frances H. Simson (London: Routledge and Kegan Paul, 1896), III, 149.

Hegel, "the life of the spirit" consists "in being turned back within itself in the particular content which appears as another; while spirit is not free if it allows this other-being, either unassimilated or dead, to exist in it as something foreign."[43] "This is the great principle" of the Reformation and of the Lutheran confession, "that all externality disappears in the point of the absolute relation to God; along with this externality, this estrangement of self, all servitude has also disappeared."[44] "Luther's simple doctrine is that the specific embodiment of Deity — infinite subjectivity, that is true spirituality, Christ — is in no way present and actual in an outward form, but what is essentially spiritual is obtained only in being reconciled to God — *in faith and spiritual enjoyment.* These two words express everything."[45]

Against such an "Enthusiasm" that emphasizes what is internal and what is remembered, the Augsburg Confession and the Smalcald Articles[46] insist that the justifying faith that comes in the promise of the gospel, and the *alien* righteousness *(iustitia aliena)* of Christ that comes with it only in this manner, must always receive proper emphasis. This alien righteousness never becomes the individual person's own possession. What applies to him, what is appropriated to him, and what is imparted to him can never use his own internal powers to reflect on it, to remember what it is about, make its truth something that is one's own possession. Being turned inward in this way would stand in contradiction to the communal relationship that the gospel creates. As the external and physical Word, as a voice, as a call, cry, lament, and praise, briefly: in its own nature as what is articulated verbally and externally, the gospel does not allow itself to be drawn in or taken back as one's own private possession without friction and without sound; instead, it guards against that. The Christian is never certain of the freedom that his faith entails, never certain because of what happens within the self, but apprehends it on the basis of an external, verbal Word that is articulated in open battle.

The markers that identify this externality can be detected in the Lord's Supper. Four aspects can be detected as interacting within it. Constitutive is first of all (a) *the social and concurrently natural-cultural moment* when common eating and drinking take place. By this present, actual, physical, participatory, and also observable process and because of its relationship to the Words of Institution of Jesus Christ that are quoted, as he gives a gift, only by hearing can one be told of (b) the *new covenant,* the creation that is brought

43. *Hegel's Lectures,* 154.

44. *Hegel's Lectures,* 150.

45. Georg Wilhelm Friedrich Hegel, *The Philosophy of History,* trans. J. Sibree (New York: Dover, 1956), 415 (cf. n. 42 above).

46. Cf. 11.2.2 above.

back home, the definitive communal relationship between God and humanity. This eschatological communion does not take place without the physical assembly of those who become and have become part of the communion (c) through the *performative* Word that has been addressed to them — through bread and wine — which (d) gets its *power* because of the resurrection of the crucified Jesus.

If the external nature of the faith depends on the "external" Word, as discussed here, faith is established in an external sense and not by relying on oneself — in which what is experienced would show a person what is possible but that the individual would have to make it real on his own — the public nature of constituting the faith does not make sense at a time when religion has become a private matter.[47]

On the one hand, one cannot simply quit differentiating between general, communal openness and the private freedom of the individual, in terms of opinions, conscience, and faith; the differences have been clarified through painful and passionate experience; in spite of all the conflict between public and private, the two are correlates and empower and support one another. But, on the other hand, the Christian faith cannot follow the formula that religion is a private matter if it is to function in the sense known in the Augsburg Confession, that what takes effect happens through the "external" Word and that understands itself to be continually grounded in it. Externality, verbal expression, and openness are constitutive for the Word that creates faith and for the Spirit that works thereby. But one cannot avoid conflict about the form that it is to take — admittedly "not by using human power, but only by using the Word."[48]

---

47. Informative in this regard is the controversy between Christian Thomasius and Valentin Ernst Löscher concerning the privatization of faith. In Thomasius's view of religion as a private matter (Hans Hattenhauer, "Christian Thomasius," in *Die Aufklärung. Gestalten der Kirchengeschichte*, ed. Martin Greschat, vol. 8 [Stuttgart: Kohlhammer, 1983], 171-86, here 182), Löscher saw the "detachment of the spiritual from the temporal," as the "surrender of the external for the sake of a pure inwardness" (Martin Greschat, "Valentin Ernst Löscher," in *Orthodoxie und Pietismus. Gestalten der Kirchengeschichte*, vol. 7 [Stuttgart: Kohlhammer, 1982], 287-300, here 297). Cf. further Gottfried Hornig, "Die Freiheit der christlichen Privatreligion. Semlers Begründung des religiösen Individualismus in der protestantischen Aufklärungstheologie," *NZSTh* 21 (1979): 198-211.

48. *BSLK* 124.21; cf. CA XXVIII, 21, in *BC*, 94: "sine vi humana, sed verbo" [not with human power but with God's Word alone]. Cf. the position of Johann Gerhard: "He wants neither a total privatization of religion . . . nor coercive rule over faith and conscience" (Jörg Baur, "Johann Gerhard," in *Orthodoxie und Pietismus*, 99-119, here 116).

11.4. The Triune God Gives Himself Completely in the Spirit

Luther's theological testament, his *Confession* of 1528, which provides the kernel of the Augsburg Confession, shows with unsurpassed clarity how the third article of the Apostles' Creed is to be understood as trinitarian; it shows at the same time that the secret of the revealed God can be disclosed only by means of the Holy Spirit:

> These are the three persons and one God, who has given himself to us completely, with everything that he is and has. The Father gives himself to us with heaven and earth and all his creatures, so that they can serve us and be useful. But this gift became darkened and useless because of Adam's fall. For this reason the Son also gave himself to us completely, gifted us with all his works, suffering, wisdom, and righteousness and reconciled us with the Father, so that we, once again alive and righteous, might recognize and have the Father with all of his gifts. But since this grace would not be useful to anyone if it were to remain hidden, and could not come to us, the Holy Spirit comes; he also gives himself to us utterly and completely. He teaches us how to recognize this wonderful deed of Christ, which is shown to us, helps us to receive and to maintain it, how to use it and share it in a useful way, to multiply and to promote it. This he does internally as well as externally: internally through faith and other spiritual gifts, but externally by means of the gospel, by means of baptism and the Sacrament of the Altar, through which he, as through three means or ways, comes to us and works the suffering of Christ in us and lets it serve for salvation.[49]

The key verb is "give." In these few verses the verb "give" or the substantive "gift" appears seven times; in addition, the related words "give as a gift" and "distribute" appear as well, along with the related verbs "have," "receive," and "maintain." The theology of the Holy Spirit, just as the entire theology of the Trinity, is *a theology of categorical gift.* God is categorically the one who gives: the *Father* does not just give some particular things — namely, life and the world; he gives us himself in this creation. In the same way the *Son* gives himself to us — and at the same time gives us the Father once again in a new way, whose face was obscured from our view because of sin. The *Spirit* finally is nothing other than the opener and distributor of this self-giving of Christ — and thereby that of the Father as well. We recognize and love God the Father through Jesus Christ in the Holy Spirit.

49. WA 26:505.38–506.12; cf. *LW* 37:366 (*Confession concerning Christ's Supper*). Cf. chap. 5.1.1 above. The corresponding section in the Large Catechism is almost identical: LC II, 38-39, in *BC*, 436. On the Trinity, cf. chap. 15.2-3 below.

Chapter 12   The Church

Where the Word is, there is the church.

The central article of the Augsburg Confession, as pointed out in the last chapter, is article 5. It is central not only because it refers back to article 4 on justification and because it describes how the Spirit comes and brings salvation, namely, by means of the external Word that can be comprehended by reason; it is central also because it is the starting point for everything that follows — first of all because the themes discussed in articles 7 and 8 draw out the ecclesiastical consequences of the reformational discovery of the distinction between the law and the "promise-delivering" gospel, as well as because they identify what these reformational insights have to say about the church itself.

In the reformational sense, as mentioned already, the church is to be understood neither in a juridical way, as an institutionalized place of salvation, nor merely collegially as an association. On the one hand, it is not essentially tied to certain holy sites, holy times, holy persons, and holy rites; on the other hand, it also does not exist in a Platonic sense, in the ideal form of a community of citizens, which is what the Reformers were soon accused of making it by those whose thinking was Roman.[1] The church is neither "as visible as the

---

1. LW 39:218 (*Answer to the Hyperchristian, Hyperspiritual, and Hyperlearned Book by Goat Emser in Leipzig — Including Some Thoughts regarding His Companion, the Fool Murner,* 1521): "Since I had called the Christian church a 'spiritual assembly,' you mocked me as though I wanted to build a church just as Plato built a city which is nowhere." In the Apology of the Augsburg Confession (IV, 20, in *BC*, 177), Melanchthon protests against the insinuation that the Reformers dreamed of a "Platonic city." In Lutheran dogmatics the question of the *Platonica civitas* was a standard topic. Cf., e.g., Leonhard Hutter, *Compendium locorum theologicorum* (Wittenberg: Jobi Wilhelmi Fincelli, 1610), locus XVII.1.

Republic of Venice"² nor just "internally" hidden within the individual, which is a widely held misunderstanding in neo-Protestantism.³

What distinguishes the reformational understanding of the church? The well-known tripartite typology of Ernst Troeltsch — institutionalized place of salvation ("church"), opposition congregation ("sect"), and free association of like-minded individuals ("mysticism") — which he develops in his "social teaching of Christian churches and groups,"⁴ does not provide an instrument that can help one to comprehend the uniqueness of Luther's understanding of the church. The most important aspect of this topic is provided by the orientation furnished by the reformational turning point in Luther's theology — his discovery of the Word as a means of grace.⁵

2. Roberto Bellarmini, *Disputationes de controversiis christianae fidei adversus huius temporis haereticos* (Ingolstadt: ex typographia Adami Sartorii, 1593), III.2.

3. Luther's (incorrect) translation of Luke 17:21 ("das Reich Gottes ist inwendig in euch" = "the kingdom of God inside you") is used not only by Ernst Troeltsch (*Die Soziallehren der christlichen Kirchen und Gruppen* [Tübingen: Mohr, 1912; reprint, Aalen, 1961], 868, 968, 986 [in the first two passages as a description of "mysticism," in the last as a characterization of his own position in the concluding section of the total work]), but also by contemporary representatives of liberal Protestantism. The revised Luther Bible of 1984 correctly translates *mitten unter euch* ("in your midst").

4. Cf. the "conclusion" of Troeltsch, *Die Soziallehren der christlichen Kirchen und Gruppen*, 965-86.

5. Precisely at this point Troeltsch sees the "sociological problem of Protestantism" (*Die Soziallehren der christlichen Kirchen und Gruppen*, 427-512) and of Lutheranism in particular: the Word as such is not strong enough or specific enough to bring consensus regarding church structure. Luther's real contribution involved a genuine idea about what is religious and inward; it offered a concept of grace that was not sacramental and that was apprehended directly (432-39). He was thus still captive to a type of "church," admittedly no longer one that was a "hierarchical and sacramental church," but to a "Scripture and preacher church; and yet, with respect to its members, an institution set over them as that which, by virtue of being supernatural, instituted and led by God, is what makes them to be members of the church" (449). Nevertheless, its sociological and organizational weakness has always compelled the churches of Lutheranism to rely on the rule of the sovereign (450f., 466-72). Luther "wants to unite the objectivity of the institution and the subjectivity of personal Christianity in his concept of 'Word' and 'faith' as the basic powers that constitute the church. Given the difficulty of uniting these opposites, it is not surprising that this concept of the church goes beyond what was intended originally, accenting now the one [the institutional aspect], now the other [the mystical and individualistic] aspect" (467). "No sociological organization can endure without the use of force. . . . At this point Luther radically corrects his initial idealism," for which Troeltsch refers particularly to the debates with the Anabaptists (471). Though he is correct in some of what he detects here, one must question the way he understands the purely inward Word and the purely outward understanding of the institution (cf. n. 3 above).

12.1. The Office of the Word

Corresponding to the discovery referred to here, the shortest definition of Luther's understanding of the church reads as follows: *Ubi est Verbum, ibi est ecclesia* — "Where the Word is, there is the church."[6]

Everything that makes the church the church is contained in the "Word": the *preaching* of the gospel, its visible and tangible form in the *sacrament,* and the *Holy Spirit* by the gospel, whose office is to sanctify. The Holy Spirit who is given in the Word is the one who makes a human being into a Christian and makes a gathering of Christians into the church.[7] For this reason, where the Word of God is, there the church is. Everything that Luther otherwise has to say about the church and everything that follows in this chapter is nothing but an unfolding of this basic axiom.

With classic conciseness, as has been mentioned several times already, Augsburg Confession, article 5, says everything necessary about the office of the Word as that which establishes the church — fully in the sense of Luther's theology: "In order to obtain such [justifying] faith, God established the preaching office, provided Word and sacrament. . . ."[8] Against one's first impression — which the use of the word "preaching office" seems to imply at this point — this does not speak just about the office of pastor, as an office that is limited to those who are ordained; that topic receives attention first in article 14, which says "that no one in the church should teach pub-

6. WA 39II:176.8f. (*Promotionsdisputation von Johannes Macchabäus Scotus,* 1542). Cf. WA 7:721.9-14 (*Ad librum eximii Magistri Nostri Magistri Ambrosii Catharini . . .* , 1521): "To be sure, the gospel is of greater importance than the bread and baptism as the single, most certain and most important sign [*symbolum*] of the church, for only through the gospel is the church conceived, formed, nourished, generated, trained, pastured, clothed, adorned, strengthened, armed, and preserved; in short, the entire life and nature of the church is grounded in the Word of God, as Christ says [Matt. 4:4]: one lives 'by every word that proceeds from the mouth of God'" [. . . cum per solum Euangelium concipiatur, formetur, alatur, generetur, educetur, pascatur, vestiatur, ornetur, roburetur, armetur, servetur, breviter, tota vita et substantia Ecclesiae est in verbo dei . . .].

7. When Luther went against Cajetan at Augsburg in 1518, he insisted on a particular and discrete faith, the *fides specialis,* which could be attributed to the clear word of the *promissio,* which could give one complete assurance; Cajetan countered: "This means a new church is constituted" [Hoc enim est novam Ecclesiam construere]. Thomas de Vio Caietanae, "Utrum ad fructuosam absolutionem . . . ," in *Opuscula Omnia,* from the edition in Lyon, 1575 (Hildesheim: Olms, 1995), 111a, 7f. Cf. Oswald Bayer, *Promissio. Geschichte der reformatorischen Wende in Luthers Theologie,* FKDG (Göttingen: Vandenhoeck & Ruprecht, 1971; 2nd ed., Darmstadt, 1989), 194-97.

8. *BSLK* 58.2-4; cf. CA V, 1, in *BC,* 40. Contrast CA V, XIV: 12.2.4 below ("The Office Connected with Ordination").

licly or preach or administer the sacraments without a regular call."[9] Article 5 does not deal specifically with the office of the pastor, but rather with the *ministerium evangelii* in its most basic sense, which means it is about the office of the Word, as it has been entrusted to everyone who is baptized. According to 1 Peter 2:9, everyone who has been baptized is empowered and obligated to proclaim the act of deliverance that God accomplished through Jesus Christ. The Word does not depend on the office; instead, the office depends on the Word that issues its call — just as every office in the church depends on the Word that issues its call. The Word even caused the creation; it also caused the *new* creation, the communion of saints. The Word is thus never the possession of the church or in any way built into the church or arranged on the basis of the church; instead, it is the *foundation* of the church.[10]

According to Luther's theology, in actual fact the Word cannot be esteemed too highly. Isaiah 55:10-11 plays an important role in this regard in both Luther's theology and in the Confessions:[11] "For as the rain and the snow come down from heaven, and do not return there until they have watered the earth, making it bring forth and sprout . . . , so shall my word be that goes out from my mouth; it shall not return to me empty, but it shall accomplish that which I purpose, and succeed in the thing for which I sent it." That is the *promissio* that accomplishes what it promises.

Luther takes this understanding of the Word seriously — even to the point of contending for the faith of a child in baptism *(fides infantium)*,[12] which seems so offensive to modern consciousness. How can a newborn child already be able to believe? But Luther expresses this completely from within the Word — obviously without attributing to the Word a magical or automatic power:[13] God's Word is *verbum efficax,* an efficacious Word. It never returns void, but it does what it says.[14] According to Luther's theological understanding of the Word, faith is already there in the nursing child, even if it

9. *BSLK* 69.2-5; cf. CA XIV, in *BC,* 46.

10. On the other hand, Roman Catholic reference to Christ as the original sacrament and the church as the foundational sacrament (cf. Gunther Wenz, "Sakramente I. Kirchengeschichtlich," in *TRE* 29 [1998], 663-84, here 681; Eberhard Jüngel, *Wertlose Wahrheit* [Tübingen: Mohr-Siebeck, 1990], 311-34) allows the Word as foundational category to be almost totally omitted.

11. Cf. Apology of the Augsburg Confession XIII, 11, in *BC,* 220. Cf. Leonhard Hutter, *Compendium locorum theologicorum,* locus XVII.2.

12. Cf. further 12.2.1.c below. Cf. especially "Von der Wiedertaufe an zwei Pfarrherrn" (1528): WA 26.144-74 and the exposition of Matt. 19:13-15: WA 47:326.29–337.31 (1537).

13. Cf. 12.2.1.b below.

14. On the specific shape of the Word as promise and as Christology, cf. especially chaps. 3 and 10 above.

shows itself in a way that can be described in a conscious and psychological sense only later. Yet the Word aims to create just such a faith; it aims to be understood correctly and comprehended consciously in faith.[15]

The universal meaning of the office of the Word, which is at the center of the discussion in Augsburg Confession, article 5, becomes clear when we clarify for ourselves that it involves the reestablishment of the corrupted order that the church had *when created*.[16] Church is not just something particular, but it refers to a completely renewed humanity, a "new creation" (2 Cor. 5:17). What was said to humans in Paradise — you may take and eat from everything (cf. Gen. 2:16) — and what was said about individuals lost in unthankful disregard of the gift, is promised and given in a final sense for all time to human beings in the new covenant (1 Cor. 11:24): "Take and eat — this is my body for you."[17]

12.2. The Marks of the Church *(Notae Ecclesiae)*

What such a comprehensive understanding of the Word means for constituting, for understanding the basic elements, and for setting parameters for the church — even in regard to contemporary reflections on regional churches and ecumenical matters — is set forth by Melanchthon, just as Luther had articulated it, in Augsburg Confession, article 7:

> It is also taught [by the reformational congregations] that [it can be no other way than that] one holy, Christian church also exists and remains for all time, which is the gathering of all believers, in which the gospel is preached in purity and the holy sacraments are administered according to the gospel. For this is enough [*satis est*] to have true unity in the Christian church, that the gospel is preached harmoniously there according to the correct understanding of the gospel and that the sacraments are administered in accord with the divine Word. And it is not necessary, for true unity in the church, that ceremonies following an exact form are used in every place, which are by human design, [but rather] as Saint Paul says in Eph.

---

15. This is the way it was articulated by Luther's doctoral candidate Johannes Macchabäus Scotus (cf. n. 6 above): "Where the Word is, that is, the Word rightly understood and apprehended in faith . . ." [Ubi est verbum, id est, recte intellectum et fide apprehensum]; WA 39II:159.18f.

16. Cf. chap. 6.2 above.

17. On the subject: Oswald Bayer, *Theology the Lutheran Way* (Grand Rapids: Eerdmans, 2007), 86-93.

4:[4-5]: "one body, one Spirit, just as you were called to the one hope of your calling, one Lord, one faith, one baptism."[18]

Here — based on what is articulated as foundational in article 5 — what establishes the church, how it is to be recognized, and what one can infer about its unity are unfolded on the basis of the Word. It is to be recognized in the pure preaching of the gospel and in the right administration — meaning according to Scripture — of the two sacraments, baptism and the Lord's Supper. These three — preaching the gospel, baptism, the Lord's Supper — are the marks of the church *(notae ecclesiae);* since baptism and the Lord's Supper are nothing other than particularly clear forms of preaching the gospel, all three together form the one and only, foundational and nonnegotiable characteristics of the church: characteristics of recognition and, at the same time, characteristics of its nature.

Without such distinguishing characteristics, there is no church. But one is not forced to understand these three distinguishing characteristics in an exclusive way — so that nothing further can and ought to be said about the church — as is shown in Luther's massive ecclesiastical writing *On the Councils and the Church* (1539)[19] and in *Against Hans Wurst* (1541).[20] In these writings he lists additional characteristics to identify the church, in one case seven and in the other case ten; moreover, they have a somewhat differentiated systematization and order. In addition to the three chief characteristics *preaching, baptism, and Lord's Supper,* further characteristics are placed afterward and subordinated. In *On the Councils* the fourth is *confession and absolution;* the fifth is the *offices,* which are understood as positions of service (of which one — obviously the most important — is the pastoral office);[21] the sixth is *prayer and praise of God,* including confession (concerning which Luther also included that one would "publicly teach the catechism");[22] and, in conclusion, the seventh is *cross and suffering* on account of the gospel.

Even though the latter four are not as important as the first three, they certainly grow from them and describe the life of the Christian congregation. The three characteristics of the church identified in Augsburg Confession, article 7,

---

18. *BSLK* 61.2-17; cf. CA VII, in *BC,* 42.

19. *LW* 41:9-178; third part, 143-78. The word "church" in Luther's title, *Von den Konziliis und Kirchen,* does not denote a plural — which is unthinkable for Luther! It is a matter of the old *n* ending of the singular (cf. *BSLK,* introduction, ix).

20. *LW* 41:185-256.

21. The relevant reformational term reads "Service of the Divine Word" *(ministerium verbi divini).*

22. WA 50:641.24; cf. *LW* 41:164.

thus ought not to be treated in isolation — as happens so often today, either to justify a freewheeling personal brand of Christianity or to justify a shabby regional-church brand of communal living; *satis est* does not mean: "nothing more ought be included." What is enough to describe the foundational elements calls for further clarification and is open to further description.[23]

In *Against Hans Wurst* such further description is set forth in view of life in one's community in general and, for example, what is considered a correct understanding of marriage in relation to the *notae ecclesiae;* in the document that deals with the councils, matters of life in community are articulated in an addendum that goes into further detail about the three estates.[24]

Because different arrangements of the *notae* exist, it is clear that the concentric schema from the center outward was not sharply delineated. As a rule of thumb, one can say: the further the identifying marker is down the list, the less important its comments about ecclesiology. When one deals with an issue such as suffering or having a good marriage, it is not quite as clear that one can detect that the church of Christ is present as is the case with Word and sacrament. Even the heathen can live in a good marriage; that and to what ex-

---

23. In this connection (cf. also 12.2.3 and 5 below) (with Paul Philippi, "Diakonie und Sakrament. Erwägungen über das Verhältnis von Praktischer Theologie und Ekklesiologie in einer 'Kirche des Wortes,'" in *Diaconica. Über die soziale Dimension kirchlicher Verantwortung,* ed. Jürgen Albert [Neukirchen Vluyn: Neukirchener Verlag, 1984], 130-48, here 140f.), it should be pointed out that the current ecclesiological debate often opens with the *in qua* and fails to take into account the actual entity that the phrase more properly defines, that is, the congregational assembly *(congregatio).* On the other hand, Trutz Rendtorff decisively pleads for the "minimalist" understanding of Augsburg Confession, article 7: "[W]hat is alone decisive is that, at the level of the *visibilitas ecclesiae,* the freedom for which Christ has set us free requires no other universal characteristics than the presence of those institutional offices of mediation that make it possible to attain justifying faith" ("Theologische Probleme der Volkskirche," in *Volkskirche-Kirche der Zukunft? Leitlinien der Augsburgischen Konfession für das Kirchenverständnis heute. Eine Studie des Theologischen Ausschusses der VELKD,* ed. Wenzel Lohff and Lutz Mohaupt [Hamburg: Lutherisches Verlagshaus, 1977], 104-31, here 122). "How does the church live now as an institution of freedom? When it allows freedom to be free" (130). This, of course, opens a place for saying but does not articulate how the *congregatio* achieves its *constructive* shape. On the other hand, the *congregatio* can in no way be regarded as presupposition for the Word — as per the Roman Catholic solution. Instead, the Word implies it is self-evident that it exists; for the Word is a Word that addresses and implies that those who are addressed are gathered together as living beings. "God's word cannot be without God's people, and conversely, God's people cannot be without God's word. Otherwise, who would preach or hear it preached, if there were no people of God? And what could or would God's people believe, if there were no word of God?" *LW* 41:150. This dual sentence is obviously symmetrically constructed, but with respect to its content is to be understood as asymmetrical.

24. *LW* 41:176-78. With reference to the way a particular believer will conduct his life (146-47), Luther already drove home the significance of works as fruits of faith.

tent a marriage of Christians is a good marriage is demonstrated in regard to the central and fundamental characteristic that identifies the church: the Word of God.[25]

When additions are made to the three central characteristics that identify the church, it points out that the Word does not remain alone, all by itself, but penetrates the life of the individual Christian, the congregation, and the world, to preserve each of them — or to use a modern slogan to describe what happens: orthopraxy.[26] Luther places a lot of weight on this: they can also be, as it says in the treatise on the councils, "external signs, by means of which one can recognize the holy Christian church, namely, that the Holy Spirit makes us holy also with respect to the other [the second] table of Moses."[27] A specific ethic can also serve as a distinguishing characteristic of the church.

Admittedly, it is often demanded today that orthopraxy should be understood as a replacement for the traditional *notae ecclesiae*. It is said that there is too much speaking and teaching, that the *actions* of the church are more important and are also expected by the community at large.[28] But in and of itself, Luther would say, orthopraxy does not provide a clear *nota ecclesiae*, since "even some heathen are so practiced in such works and clearly at times seem to be holier than Christians."[29] The *notae* that are connected with the

25. Cf. chap. 6.3.1 above.

26. Cf. chap. 13 ("Faith and Good Works") below.

27. WA 50:643.6-8; cf. *LW* 41:166. The reference is to commandments four through ten, which deal with life together in a social community; in Lutheran tradition they are identified with the natural law that everyone — even unbelievers — carries in the heart (cf. chap. 13.4.3).

28. Cf., e.g., Peter Steinacker, *Die Kennzeichen der Kirche. Eine Studie zu ihrer Einigkeit, Heiligkeit, Katholizität und Apostolizität* (Berlin: De Gruyter, 1981), 19: "The change [in the perspective of his study] over against the tradition can perhaps be detected in the fact that the study no longer gives such central place to the congregation that meets for worship as the starting point for its understanding of the church. As important as this point is, it simply does not match the way contemporary evangelical Christians live their life. . . . Is not the 'church' present wherever people act and think in Jesus' name in such a way that we would describe as indicative of the characteristics of the church?" At best, one can recognize the worship service among the *notae* of the Augsburg Confession, but not the church; according to Steinacker, this can evidently exist without a word being spoken. With its claim to be a new *nota ecclesiae*, the "Konziliare Prozess für Frieden, Gerechtigkeit und Bewahrung der Schöpfung" [the conciliar process for peace, justice, and the protection of the environment] is frequently brought into the discussion.

29. WA 50:643.28f.; cf. *LW* 41:167. Of course, the actions of the heathen "do not issue from the heart purely and simply, for the sake of God, but they search for some other end because they lack a real faith in and a true knowledge of God" (167). Cf. chap. 7.2 above for the distinction between "holy" and "saved." Motivation for action cannot be unequivocally recognized from the outside and is thus disqualified as a possible *nota ecclesiae*.

second table cannot thus "be so clearly observed"[30] as are "the seven chief elements of the Holy of Holies,"[31] which have been treated already. No human action, not even the action of one who has been justified, is in principle removed from the realm of ambiguity in interpretation;[32] one must always connect such actions with the unambiguous characteristics of Word and sacrament. For these are not just *external* signs among other signs that help one to recognize where the church is; they are at the same time characteristics that point to what is the *nature* of and what is *constitutive* of the church: they *create*, they constitute the church. It is not as if a church that is already constituted is recognized only by means of Word and sacrament, but rather: that which causes them to be recognized causes them to be constituted at the same time.

The Holy Spirit does not come to these *notae ecclesiae* as an additive; he is at work within them. The sanctifying Spirit of God is at work in the Word that creates the church. One's view is not thus directed in the first instance to the individual who has been sanctified, or to the members of the church, but to the one who sanctifies and his Word: "For God's Word is holy and sanctifies everything that it touches."[33]

Thus the Holy Spirit and the church are intimately related in Luther's conceptualization. The classic formulation concerning this connection is recorded in the Large Catechism:

> So learn to understand this article in the clearest way possible. When one asks: What do you mean with the words: "I believe in the Holy Spirit"? then you can answer: "I believe that the Holy Spirit sanctifies me, as his name states." But in what way does he do this, or what is his manner and means to accomplish this? Answer: "through the Christian church, forgiveness of sins, resurrection of the flesh, and life everlasting." For in the first place he has a special congregation in the world, which is its mother, which produces and carries every Christian by means of the Word of God, which he reveals and sets in motion, which enlightens and fires up hearts, so that they can comprehend, take hold of, rely on and remain with it.[34]

---

30. WA 50:643.27; cf. *LW* 41:167.

31. WA 50:642.32f.; cf. *LW* 41:165-66.

32. This is clear in the present with respect to the discussion about the problem of "just war." Cf. also Oswald Bayer, *Freedom in Response: Lutheran Ethics; Sources and Controversies* (Oxford: Oxford University Press, 2007), 242-44.

33. WA 50:629.3f.; cf. *LW* 41:149. See chap. 11, n. 7 above.

34. *BSLK* 654.46–655.8; cf. LC II, 40-42, in *BC*, 436.

We see: Luther can by all means speak of the church as "mother" — in the sense that the church is the arena in which the Word of God reaches me and creates faith.[35]

The *notae ecclesiae,* which describe how the Word of God that establishes the church makes it happen, are the means used by the Holy Spirit. Luther calls them *Heiltümer.* He makes use of a traditional term but assigns to it the exact opposite meaning. *Heiltum* at his time was a technical term used for "relic"; in some churches there were thousands of relics — as for example in the castle church in Wittenberg, the Foundation of All Saints. Already in the Ninety-five Theses Luther calls for reduction of and concentration on these items: the only *Heiltum,*[36] the Holy of Holies of the church, by means of which it is sanctified, is the "most holy gospel"[37] — to which then is added — according to a logical arrangement (even though they exist at the same time) — seven or more shrines, which have been mentioned already.

We now take a closer look at the most important of these *Heiltümer,* or marks that distinguish the church.

12.2.1. Baptism

The central place of the Word, also as regards the understanding of baptism and the Lord's Supper, was not something that Luther understood from the outset. It took much theological work in order to arrive at this insight, which almost goes without saying today as one of the core beliefs for Lutheranism.

The general approach of the baptismal sermon of 1519 shows that Luther was still following the Augustinian tradition, characterizing the understanding of baptism by using the three-part framework of sign, thing signified, and faith *(signum, res, fides).* But when he goes into detail in the specifics, the reformational turning point that resulted in the discovery of that specific concept of promise[38] begins to provide powerful application.[39]

---

35. A parallel formulation in the Large Catechism reads that the Holy Spirit "first leads us into his holy community, placing us in the church's lap, where he preaches to us and brings us to Christ" (II, 37, in *BC,* 435-36).

36. It is important (beyond the German language) that one distinguish etymologically between "to heal" *(sanare),* "to make holy" *(sanctificare),* and "to bring salvation, to save" *(salvare);* in his treatise on the councils Luther considers the second and third meanings to be closely related (*LW* 41:149).

37. Thesis 62 in *LW* 31:31.

38. Cf. chap. 3 above.

39. *LW* 35:38 (*The Holy and Blessed Sacrament of Baptism,* par. 15, 1519). Cf. Bayer, *Promissio,* 257.

a. From that time on the central insight, which shapes the discussion in the catechisms as well, starts with the Words of Institution. "What is baptism? Answer: Baptism is not just plain water, but it is water connected with God's command and connected with God's Word."[40] The sign certainly belongs to it as well, but one cannot just meditate on water alone — possibly by reflecting on the danger it can bring, its power to cleanse and to give life — if one seeks to recognize the essence of baptism.[41] Instead, the element is saturated through and through and comprehended in the biblical Word: based on the commission to baptize in Matthew 28 as well as the promise of baptism in Mark 16:16: "The one who believes and is baptized will be saved; but the one who does not believe will be condemned."

b. The *faith* consists in submission to what is given in the sacrament: forgiveness of sins. "What does baptism give or profit? Answer: It works forgiveness of sins, delivers from death and the devil, and gives eternal salvation to all who believe what the Word and promises of God declare [Mark 16:16]."[42] Faith does not make the sacrament,[43] but the Holy Spirit creates faith by use of the sacrament. All who desire the forgiveness of their guilt are admitted to the sacrament — not only those who have achieved a certain level of confidence. "Whoever believes and is baptized" — a statement of holy justice — "that one will" *eo ipso* "be saved." This does not occur at some random time, who knows when, but takes place in the very moment the sacrament is bestowed. For the sacrament does not depend upon the human individual who exercises an office; then I would never be sure of salvation. Instead, the work of God and the work of the human being who serves the divine Word in the sacrament are "one and the same" work, as Luther emphasizes in *De captivitate*.[44]

This identification is a stumbling stone for modern spiritualistic thinking, which differentiates strictly between God and human being, Word of God and human speech.[45] Does this not betray magical thinking? This objec-

40. *BSLK* 515.24-27; cf. SC IV, 1-2, in *BC*, 359.

41. This describes the limit to the possibilities of what one teaches about the meaning of symbols.

42. *BSLK* 515.36–516.2; cf. SC IV, 5-6, in *BC*, 359.

43. On the problematic nature of Luther's reference to what Augustine says, according to which the sacrament is an effective sign of grace, not because it occurs, but because it is believed, cf. Bayer, *Promissio*, 178f., 202, 268.

44. *LW* 36:62-63 *(On the Babylonian Captivity of the Church):* "Therefore beware of making any distinction in baptism by ascribing the outward part to man and the inward part to God. Ascribe both to God alone. . . . [God as] Doer and the minister are different persons, but the work of both is the same work."

45. Provisionally diagnosed by Luther as *distinctio metaphysica*. "We will neither give place

tion can be answered by referring once again to the Augsburg Confession, article 5: the activity of God the Holy Spirit remains safely *beyond the disposal* of human beings, in the realm of *ubi et quando visum est Deo* (where and when God chooses); but at the same time, there is no doubt about the *certainty* of his coming in the Word. If the gospel is heard as gospel, then the Spirit is there as well and forgives sins; then the sacrament works faith: "If you believe, then you will have."[46]

c. The third question about baptism in the catechism reads as follows: "How can water do such great things? Answer: It is certainly not water that does these things, but the Word of God, which is in and with the water, and faith that trusts this Word of God in the water; for without the Word of God the water by itself is simply water and no baptism; but with the Word of God it is a baptism, that is, a gracious water of life."[47] The entire argumentation is based upon Mark 16:16 and therefore on the basis of *Word and faith.* Baptism is a transference of life in God, the Lord; whoever believes this Word has eternal life. Without baptism no faith, without faith no baptism.[48]

No baptism without faith. Faith is described in the baptismal liturgy that is appended to the catechism in the Baptismal Booklet,[49] with respect to dealing with baptism of children,[50] as follows: The infant is asked: "Do you believe in God, the Father almighty," "in Jesus Christ, his only Son," "in the Holy Spirit"? "Do you wish to be baptized?" The infant answers through the

_____

to them nor concede this metaphysical and philosophical distinction and difference that has been spun from reason: the human being preaches, threatens, punishes, frightens, and comforts, but the Holy Spirit does the work; to say it the other way, the servant baptizes, absolves, and offers the Supper of the Lord Christ, but God purifies the heart, and forgives the sins. Oh no, by no means; this we conclude: God himself preaches, threatens, punishes, frightens, comforts, baptizes, offers the Sacrament of the Altar and absolves" (WA TR 3:673.31-36; no. 3868, May 10, 1538).

46. In his sermon on baptism *(LW* 35:38, *The Holy and Blessed Sacrament of Baptism)* and in his treatise on freedom (*LW* 31:348-49), Luther transposes the sentence of holy law of Mark 16:16 into this promise (cf. chap. 3.2.2 above). Cf. Bayer, *Promissio,* 200f.

47. *BSLK* 516.11-19; cf. SC IV, 9-10, in *BC,* 359.

48. In this way Luther assumes no external perspective in which he might assert that "one comes to faith, another does not," and then starts to look into the reasons for this difference, let us say to predestination or to free choice. Instead, he always speaks of the sacrament from the perspective of the one who needs it for his own faith.

49. The Baptismal Booklet, 1-25, in *BC,* 371-75.

50. Luther is not a biblicist. He knows that infant baptism is neither explicitly commanded nor forbidden in the New Testament and that it came into general use only in the fourth century. He does not interpret it as *literally* biblical, but *in the sense of* the Bible. One should chiefly keep in mind those passages that speak of the efficacy of the Word (e.g., Isa. 55:10-11; Ps. 33:4) and of prevenient grace (Rom. 5:6, 8).

mouths of the sponsors: "Yes."[51] That is *fides aliena,* faith in which one stands in for another, into which the child should and ought to grow. The corresponding admonition to pray is rendered as follows in the present-day liturgy: "Therefore pray, dear parents and sponsors, that your child will come to his (her) own faith and will be able to rejoice in his (her) own baptism."[52] The parents and sponsors are duty-bound in this way to do everything in their power to help the child come to his own faith, which he will claim as his own and for which he himself will be answerable.

For modern, individualistic thinking — even for many pietistic and free-church Christians — such a faith in which one stands in for another is difficult to comprehend, if one can do so at all. Luther takes his stand here in the tradition of the healing miracle recorded in Mark 2,[53] according to which a lame man was brought to Jesus by friends and he forgave him his sins, "when he saw their [!] faith" (Mark 2:5). This ought not to be misunderstood in the sense of someone who acts as a trustee or in the sense of a healing and salvation that takes place automatically; it comes from the insight that faith always comes to me through other people, who stand in on my behalf and make intercession. Faith that stands in on behalf of another and includes intercession builds a bridge to one's own faith.[54]

d. The fourth baptismal question in the Small Catechism proves that Luther did not think of baptism as an isolated act, but that it decidedly includes the *Christian life* that proceeds from it as well: "What does such baptism with water mean? Answer: It means that the old Adam in us should be drowned and die through daily contrition and repentance, along with all sins and evil desires, and that daily a new self should come forth to live before God in righteousness and purity forever."[55] Since baptism not only creates one's existence

51. *BSLK* 540.19-42; cf. The Baptismal Booklet, 19-31, in *BC,* 374-75.

52. *Kirchenbuch für die evangelische Kirche in Württemberg,* pt. 2, *Die heilige Taufe,* special edition (Stuttgart: Quell Verlag, 1989), 27.

53. *LW* 36:73-74.

54. This does not mean that infant baptism is performed casually or in a way that is external and ritualistic. To prevent such a misuse, for example, Luther insists in his baptismal booklet that "fine, moral, serious, upright priests and godparents" ought to be chosen (*BC,* 373). This recommendation appears to be in tension with his usual pathos against the Donatists (cf. CA VIII). The difficult question regarding possibly refusing to baptize emerges here as well. Is it commanded for situations where there is no recognizable intent by the parents to bring up the child as a Christian? Or, in view of the *fides aliena* of the entire Christian community, does *in dubio pro infante* apply (in doubtful cases, act for the benefit of the child)?

55. *BSLK* 516.30-38; cf. SC IV, 11-12, in *BC,* 360. Cf. *BSLK* 706.6-18: "If you live in repentance, you walk in baptism, which not only signifies such a new life, but also produces, begins, and exercises it. For therein are given grace, spirit, and power to overcome the old man, so that the new

as a Christian, but also preserves it, it has an impact on my entire biography. With respect to the individual life of the one who is baptized, one might say incidentally, the concern of the modern age is properly addressed as the individual is seen as unique and in a certain sense as an irreplaceable being. This is shown, not in the least important sense, in that the child is called by name: one is not baptized just in the sense that one is an example of the species known as human, but as a unique individual, with whom God has a particular history.

e. That the Christian life is defined at all times by the baptism that occurred once for all time is shown by Luther's understanding of *penance:* for him, this is not something like a substitute for a baptism that has ceased to be in force — an interpretation that would correspond to a tradition that goes back to Jerome, which explains penance as a plank to which one can cling, to be saved when a ship breaks up in a storm.[56] Instead, confession is a return to baptism.[57] A Christian believer never develops beyond baptism, as long as he or she lives, no matter how much one has grown, no matter how much one has learned, and no matter what changes one has experienced. For in baptism one already has everything that comes with the name of God. This ship is unsinkable. It can certainly happen, to stick with the imagery employed by Jerome, that I could go overboard at some time. But by means of the lifesaver of the Word and faith I am hauled back aboard ever and again into this ship.[58] This understanding shows why a second baptism is senseless. God made his promise once for all in baptism — no matter at what age it is carried out for

man may come forth and become strong. Therefore our baptism abides forever; and even though someone should fall from it and sin, we nevertheless always have access thereto, that we may again subdue the old man. But we must not again be sprinkled with water" (cf. LC IV, 75-78, in *BC,* 466).

56. WA 6:527.12-22: "poenitentiam appellat secundum post naufragium tabulam, quasi baptismus non sit poenitentia" (*LW* 36:58: "he terms penance 'the second plank after shipwreck,' as if baptism were not penance"). Cf. Hieronymus, *Epistula* 130.9 *(ad Demetriadem de servanda virginitate),* MPL 22:1115.

57. WA 6:572.16f.: "via ac reditus ad baptismum" [a way and a return to baptism] (*LW* 36:124).

58. Cf. LC IV, 80-82, in *BC,* 466: "I say this to correct the opinion, which has long prevailed among us, that baptism is something past that we can no longer use after falling back into sin. . . . Indeed, St. Jerome is responsible for this view, for he wrote, 'Penance is the second plank on which we must swim ashore after the ship [baptism] founders,' [the ship] in which we embarked when we entered the Christian community. This takes away the value of baptism, making it of no further use to us. Therefore it is incorrect to say this. The ship does not break up because, as we said, it is God's ordinance and not something that is ours. But it does happen that we slip and fall out of the ship. However, those who do fall out should immediately see to it that they swim to the ship and hold fast to it, until they can climb aboard again and sail on it as before."

the individual. God does not lie. In this regard baptism takes on an indelible character *(character indelebilis)* — irrespective of what happens later in the life of the person who is baptized. It is not a guarantee of salvation, but it is the action of God in the life of this person, which continues to have its effect and behind which I can never go — just as I remain a child of my parents my whole life long, no matter what happens between us.

f. Not the least important aspect of baptism is *the renunciation of the devil (abrenuntiatio diaboli)*, which takes up considerable space in the Baptismal Booklet liturgy mentioned above.[59] Today it has been shortened to the formula: we "renounce the devil and all his works and nature."[60] And even this is eliminated by many pastors, because it appears to be offensive to speak of the devil at such a beautiful family festival. But one must include the renunciation of the evil one, since it must be made clear that no human being lives in neutral space. I am always being attacked from all sides: I belong either to the triune God or to other lords and powers.[61] Baptism is no harmless ritual; it is a battle against evil. Pastor, parents, sponsors, and the congregation ought to "throw everything that they have into the fight for the child against the devil and to act in such a manner that they make this so important that it is no fun for the devil."[62]

12.2.2. Confession and Absolution

It is noteworthy that the article concerning confession is placed between baptism and the Lord's Supper in the Small Catechism.[63] In our congregations, of course, we hardly hear anything anymore about private confession, and even congregational confession — "public confession" — in connection with the Lord's Supper is often used in a watered-down form; this is a terrible loss for Protestant piety and faith. The revival movement of the nineteenth century can be understood as an answer to this having been lost.

At the outset, Luther vacillated about whether confession should be considered a third sacrament. Against the Roman tradition — when he wrote *On the Babylonian Captivity of the Church* — he reduced the number of sacraments from seven to two, with the argument that something could be considered a

59. The Baptismal Booklet, 8, 11, 15 (exorcism), 18-22 (actually: *abrenuntiatio*), in *BC*, 373-75.

60. *Kirchenbuch für die evangelische Kirche in Württemberg*, 28.

61. Cf. chap. 8.2 and 8.4 above.

62. *BSLK* 537.22-25; cf. The Baptismal Booklet, 7, in *BC*, 372-73.

63. SC IV, 15-25, in *BC*, 360-61. On the other hand, in the Large Catechism, "A Brief Exhortation to Confession" follows the section on the Lord's Supper (*BC*, 476-80).

sacrament only if there was a clear biblical institution by Christ with reference to Word and sign. As regards confession, there is only a Word (Matt. 16:19; 18:18; John 20:22-23), but no material sign is added. Thus it became, in relation to baptism — as a return to it[64] — what one might call "sign number two and one-half," as an evangelical sacrament. "What is confession? Answer: Confession embraces two parts. First, that one confesses one's sins; the other, that one hears the absolution or forgiveness from the one who hears the confession, as if one receives it from God himself and as one does not indeed doubt, but truly believes that his sins are thereby forgiven before God in heaven."[65] In this way, when a human being assures me of the forgiveness of sins in the name of God, God himself has forgiven me in that very act and at that very moment. The human word is not just an indication of the divine Word, but it is actually the Word of God.[66] God's Word comes *as* a human word — that is its humiliation. Just as God becomes human in Mary's womb, thus he comes to the sinner in the Word, which is spoken to him by another human being in the name of God. Luther considers that this other human being is not only the ordained person who holds that office, but is any baptized person.[67]

12.2.3. The Lord's Supper

Just as with his understanding of baptism, Luther himself did not discover immediately after the reformational turning point how the Words of Institution would give him a point of orientation, which would give shape to his reformational teaching from the ground up. In his sermon "The Blessed Sacrament of the Holy and True Body of Christ, and the Brotherhoods" (1519),[68] he was still following the Augustinian tradition, as he was doing at the same time with respect to baptism, and was using the three-part framework of sign, thing signified, and faith.[69] The most important element at that point is the

64. Cf nn. 56-58 above.

65. *BSLK* 517.10-17; cf. SC IV, 16, in *BC,* 360. The Large Catechism ("A Brief Exhortation to Confession," in *BC*) places great emphasis on the asymmetrical relation of the two parts: absolution as a work of God is "surpassingly grand" (p. 477). Therefore we should "keep the two parts clearly separate. We should set little value on our work ('when I lament my sin and desire comfort and restoration for my soul') but exalt and magnify God's Word" (par. 18; interior quotation from par. 15; p. 478).

66. Cf. nn. 44-45, and chap. 3.2 above.

67. Cf. 12.2.5 below.

68. *LW* 35:49-73.

69. Cf. Bayer, *Promissio,* 226-41. For a critical view, cf. Ursula Stock, *Die Bedeutung der Sakramente in Luthers Sermonen von 1519* (Leiden: Brill, 1982).

concept about communion that is developed most especially on the basis of the image of the body; Dietrich Bonhoeffer, in his *Sanctorum Communio,* expanded further on this with his — not unproblematic — formula "Jesus Christ existing as community" in an impressive way.[70]

From the time he wrote *A Treatise on the New Testament, That Is, the Holy Mass* (1520),[71] in a way that corresponds to his reformational understanding of *promissio* and faith, he began with the Words of Institution. In the same way, his explanation of the Sacrament of the Altar[72] is constructed exactly parallel in his Small Catechism to his explanation of baptism: the Sacrament of the Altar, it is thus defined, "is the true body and blood of our Lord Jesus Christ — under the bread and wine for us Christians, to eat and to drink, instituted by Christ himself."[73] This is followed by an extensive citation of the Words of Institution,[74] by which the three questions that follow are to be answered: "Of what value is such eating and drinking?"; "How can physical eating and drinking do such great things?"; "Who then receives such a sacrament in a worthy manner?" There is thus a question concerning the matter itself *(res)* and the efficaciousness *(efficacia)* of the meal, as well as the worthiness *(dignitas)* of the person who receives it. In each case, the answers are completely "based on the words, through which it [namely, the sacrament] is instituted by Christ";[75] they are thus established neither simply because the rite has been completed nor because of the simple subjective attitude of the person who receives the sacrament.

Luther does not concentrate on the threefold repetition of the two phrases "given for you" and "shed for the forgiveness of sins"[76] just by chance.

---

70. Dietrich Bonhoeffer, *Sanctorum Communio. Eine dogmatische Untersuchung zur Soziologie der Kirche* (1930), vol. 1 in *DBW*, ed. Joachim von Soosten (Munich: Kaiser, 1986); in English: *Dietrich Bonhoeffer Works,* vol. 1 (Minneapolis: Fortress, 1998). The formula is not unproblematic, since it does not sufficiently differentiate Christology and ecclesiology (cf. the corresponding exposition in Bayer; cf. n. 69 above). Paul Althaus, *Communio sanctorum* (Munich: Kaiser, 1929) (incorporated into Althaus, *Die Theologie Martin Luthers,* 2nd ed. [Gütersloh, 1963], 254-78), sets the Lord's Supper sermon of 1519 within the wider context of Luther's theology. Unfortunately, right to the present, Lutheran theology has not really detected the correctness and the importance of the concept of community that Luther articulated in 1519, particularly in connection with his correlation of the doctrine of the Lord's Supper, with its orientation to God's Word and human faith, and the doctrine of the church, as this relates to the Words of Institution and that thus correlates Word and faith.

71. *LW* 35:79-111.

72. SC V, 1-10, in *BC*, 362-63.

73. *BSLK* 519.41–520.2; cf. SC V, 2, in *BC*, 362.

74. SC V, 4, in *BC*, 362: 1 Cor. 11:23-25 with insertions from the Synoptic traditions of the Lord's Supper (Mark 14:22-24; Matt. 26:26-28; Luke 22:19-20).

75. *BSLK* 708.3-5; cf. LC V, 1, in *BC*, 467.

76. *BSLK* 520.24-26, 34-36; 521.6f.; cf. SC V, 6, 8, and 10, in *BC*, 362-63.

God's turning toward the sinner, the promise that creates faith, empowered by the death and resurrection of Jesus Christ,[77] cannot be summarized any more succinctly and specifically than by using these words. This must be stated clearly as a critique of the depersonalizing speech about the "bread of life" or the diminution of the Lord's Supper to become a generic lovefest.[78] The Lord's Supper is not some diffuse celebration of life but is defined in a precise way in its essence by means of the connection between the Word of Christ that has effective power and the faith.

a. Thus, the question about the value of eating and drinking is answered by Luther when he says "that in the sacrament, forgiveness of sins, life, and salvation" are not only "shown" and stated, but that "through such words such things are given."[79]

b. How can such gifts become effective? Once again the Word is brought to the fore, and faith proceeds from it: "Eating and drinking by themselves accomplish nothing, but the Words that are there: 'given for you' and 'shed for the forgiveness of sins.'" "Whoever believes these words has exactly what they say and what they express, namely, 'forgiveness of sins.'"[80]

c. Is faith not presupposed thereby? No, Luther answers. The appropriate "preparation" for the meal is located nowhere else than in the faith that is first created by these words: "He is truly worthy and well prepared who has faith in these words: 'given for you' and 'poured out for the forgiveness of sins.' But whoever does not believe or doubts these words is unworthy and unprepared."[81]

This does not say: the true body and the true blood of Jesus Christ would not be there either, except for our faith! They are there, they are present, they are distributed, given, and taken by means of the power of the

---

77. WA 9:660.32–661.1 (Easter sermon, 1521): "'Take and eat.' These words embrace all the mysteries of death and resurrection. These words — 'this is my body' — say this much: I will die now and yet remain alive; I will make an eternal testament so that your sins will be forgiven. He thus shows that he will not die but remain alive, for he makes it himself, gives it himself, fulfills it himself and distributes it [himself]. He does not say to Peter: 'You distribute it,' but he himself says: 'Since I have it, I myself will give it to you, will leave it behind [for you] and afterward die, yet I myself distribute it and thus remain alive.'"

78. The gifting Word, which is christological, is not to be separated from the concrete *narratio*, the historical narrative of the Lord's Supper tradition.

79. *BSLK* 520.24, 26-28; cf. SC V, 6, in *BC*, 362. "Life and salvation" is to be construed in the fully eschatological sense: the Lord's Supper effects deliverance from the last judgment — from perishing eternally (cf. chap. 15.1 and 15.3 below).

80. *BSLK* 520.33-36, 38-40; cf. SC V, 7-8, in *BC*, 363.

81. *BSLK* 521.4-9; cf. SC V, 9-10, in *BC*, 363. The only "condition" for participating in the Supper is that one knows and faithfully accepts the Words of Institution: LC V, 2, in *BC*, 467.

Words of Institution. Wherever God's almighty Word is, which does "great things,"[82] by means of which the heavens and the earth were created, it never happens that "nothing at all" is there, but what exists there is exactly that which this Word says: my body and blood for you for the forgiveness of your sins.

Christ's body and Christ's blood, the new covenant that comes with the elements, and the eternal communal relationship with God are all there; they are present in a tangible sense because of what happened at that time and place — under Pontius Pilate, on Golgotha. The eternal treasure that was "acquired" then and there is "distributed" here and now.[83] This happens when the Lord himself *unites, by speaking,*[84] his body and his blood with the bread that we eat and the wine that we drink — not that the bread is transformed to become his body and the wine to become his blood; instead, the person who receives it is transformed: the sinner becomes the righteous one, so that he lives no longer for himself but for him who died and has been raised for us. By promising to give his body that was given over into death in this gifting Word, uniting bread and body by speaking — "This bread is my body, given for you!" — the resurrected Lord distributes, at the present time, the eternal treasure that he has acquired, and he uses the mouth and the hand of a human being to accomplish it.[85]

12.2.4. The Office Connected with Ordination[86]

As has been mentioned already, it is substantively erroneous to identify article 5 with article 14 of the Augsburg Confession. The office of the Word in article

---

82. *BSLK* 520.32; cf. SC V, 7, in *BC,* 362.

83. Cf. *LW* 40:213 (*Against the Heavenly Prophets in the Matter of Images and Sacraments — Part Two,* 1525); *LW* 37:192 (*Confession concerning Christ's Supper*). Cf. LC V, 28-29, in *BC,* 469, and frequently.

84. Cf. *LW* 37:192.

85. On the relationship between the four dimensions of the Supper (the social, covenantal, performative, and effective), cf. chap. 11.3 above.

86. On the entire section cf. Harald Goertz, *Allgemeines Priestertum und ordiniertes Amt bei Luther,* Marburger Theologische Studien, vol. 46 (Marburg: N. G. Elwert, 1997); Dorothea Wendebourg, "Das Amt und die Ämter," *ZevKR* 45 (2000): 5-37. The Roman Catholic discussion has a chief point of reference in the Dogmatic Constitution of the Second Vatican Council regarding the Church (*Lumen Gentium* II, 10), especially: "But the universal priesthood of believers and the priesthood of service, that is, the hierarchical priesthood, are, of course, distinguished according to their nature and not merely according to their rank. Yet they are ordered with respect to one another."

5 is dealt with according to its fundamental depth and universal breadth: the restitution of the corrupted order of creation: the church. The corrupted creation is renewed in baptism. All of the baptized are priests.

Thus one must first speak about the general priesthood or, stated another way, the priesthood of all believers. In that connection we can observe what is meant by the two requirements that stand out in article 14: *publice docere* (to teach publicly) and *rite vocatus* (a regular call).[87]

At the same time, these two requirements also function to show how Luther specifically distinguishes the pastoral office from that priesthood that can be attributed to every baptized person according to 1 Peter 2:9.

a. A document that had great effect, in the public realm as well, which one might call the Magna Carta for Luther's understanding of the *priesthood of all believers,* is titled *The Address to the Christian Nobility of the German Nation concerning the Reform of the Christian Estate;* it was one of the major reformational publications in 1520. The Roman papacy, the "Romanists," according to Luther's impressive polemic, had three walls around them, "by means of which they have protected themselves up until now, so that no one can reform them, which has resulted in Christendom as a whole having fallen horribly."[88] The first wall: when one tries to press against the Romanists with temporal might, they respond that temporal powers have no rights against her; much rather, spiritual power is on a higher level than temporal power. The second wall: if one sets out to convince by means of the Holy Scripture, they respond in opposition that no one besides the pope has the right to interpret the Bible. Finally, the third wall: if one threatens them with calling a council, they invent the answer that no one can call for a council except the pope.[89]

In response to this, Luther demonstrates the correctness of his concept of the general priesthood:

> One notices that pope, bishop, priest, and people in the cloisters are assigned to the spiritual estate, whereas princes, lords, those who work with their hands and in the fields are assigned to the temporal estate, which is indeed a fine fabrication and distortion. And yet no one ought to let himself be intimidated thereby, and for the following reason: All Christians are

87. "De ordine ecclesiastico docent, quod nemo debeat in ecclesia publice docere aut sacramenta administrare nisi rite vocatus." CA XIV, in *BC,* 47: "Concerning church order they teach that no one should teach publicly in the church or administer the sacraments unless properly called."

88. WA 6:406.21-23; cf. *LW* 44:126 (*To the Christian Nobility of the German Nation,* 1520).

89. Cf. *LW* 44:126.

in reality in the spiritual estate, and there is no difference among them, except for that which concerns the office.[90]

For the one that has crawled out from baptism can celebrate that baptism, which itself already dedicates one to be priest, bishop, or pope, even though it is not proper for everyone to exercise the duties of such an office.[91]

b. "All Christians are in reality in the spiritual estate, and there is no difference among them, except for that which concerns the office." This *distinction* between all who are baptized, all who are in the spiritual estate, and that particular one who holds the pastoral office is clarified by Luther with the clear distinction that is rooted in the terms *sacerdos* and *minister* — as for example in the document that is particularly helpful in this regard, titled *De instituendis ministris Ecclesiae (Concerning the Installation of Servants of the Church)* from 1523; there it reads: "The priest [i.e., the believer] is not the same as the elder or the minister [i.e., the officeholder]; that one is born [in baptism, through water and the Spirit]; this one is made so [by means of the *vocatio*] to exercise the office."[92] Clearer still: "It is true that all Christians are priests, but not all are pastors. For in addition to the fact that one is a Christian and a priest, he must also have an office and a role that he is instructed to perform in the church. The call and the command makes one a pastor and preacher."[93]

The "call" — the Latin equivalent, *vocatio*, is used today also for those who have a call from the church to serve as religious teachers in the German public schools — makes the pastor and preacher, makes one a *public* servant of the Word of God *(minister verbi divini).*

The reason for the unique nature of the church office as the public proclamation of the Word and administration of the sacraments is simple: what can be done by *all* because of the power of one's baptism cannot be exercised by everyone at the same time; otherwise, chaos would result.[94] Luther bases this view

90. WA 6:407.10-15; cf. *LW* 44:127. On this point Luther appeals to 1 Cor. 12:12ff.

91. WA 6:408.11-13; cf. *LW* 44:129. Hans-Martin Barth, *Einander Priester sein. Allgemeines Priestertum in ökumenischer Perspektive* (Göttingen: Vandenhoeck & Ruprecht, 1990), 29-53, has more closely analyzed the relevant texts in which Luther discusses the universal priesthood.

92. WA 12:178.9f.; cf. *LW* 40:18 ("Sacerdotum non esse quod presbyterum vel ministrum; illum nasci, hunc fieri").

93. WA 31I:211.17-20; cf. *LW* 13:65 (on Ps. 82, 1530).

94. *LW* 44:128: "Because we are all priests of equal standing, no one must push himself forward and take it upon himself, without our consent and election, to do that for which we all have equal authority. For no one dare take upon himself what is common to all without the authority and consent of the community." Cf. *LW* 44:127-28.

on 1 Corinthians 14:40: "All things should be done decently and in order" — as is stated in the Augsburg Confession: with an orderly procedure *(rite)* with a regular call. This is stated again, just as clearly, in *De instituendis ministris Ecclesiae:* "For even though all Christians hold these [rights] in common, it is not permitted that anyone, empowered by his own authority, can step in the middle and grab that which belongs to everyone for oneself alone. . . . Instead, this properly constituted community will become convinced that one [or more], as seems good to the congregation, is to be elected or chosen, who will exercise this service publicly in the name of all who have this same right, so that disgraceful disorder does not arise among the people of God."[95]

c. It is thus clear in what way *ordination* to the pastoral office, without prejudice as regards its importance and seriousness, is not a sacrament according to a Lutheran understanding. This does not imply that the pastoral office was not "instituted by God"; Luther articulates that emphatically in the document to the nobility.[96] This institution by God (cf. Eph. 4:11-12) does not stand for Luther in contradiction to the installation by the congregation and its representatives.[97]

12.2.5. The Other Offices

It has become clear that, for Luther, the office connected with ordination, the specific pastoral office, has a connection with the office of the Word[98] that is given to all the baptized and presents just one special — admittedly the most important — concretion of this fundamental institution. So it is apparent that the pastoral office cannot be isolated and ought not to be isolated from the other offices in the church that are likewise grounded in that fundamental institution, the office of the Word. Each baptized person, female and male —

95. WA 12:189.17-25; cf. *LW* 40:34 (*Concerning the Ministry,* 1523). The statement in *LW* 41:154 (*On the Councils and the Church*) is a close parallel: there must be offices of bishops and pastors or preachers, since "the people as a whole cannot do these things, but must entrust or have them entrusted to one person. Otherwise, what would happen if everyone wanted to speak or administer, and no one wanted to give way to the other? It must be entrusted to one person, and he alone should be allowed to preach, to baptize, to absolve, and to administer the sacraments."

96. *LW* 44:176-77. Melanchthon comes up with a similarly wide definition of the sacraments: *BSLK* 293.42–294.49 (Apology of the Augsburg Confession XIII).

97. *LW* 36:113: "The priests . . . are ministers chosen from among us" [ministri sunt ex nobis electi]. Nevertheless, they are called by God: Deus vocat nos omnes ad ministerium vocatione per hominem estque divina vocatio (WA 40I:59.4f.; Grosser Galaterkommentar; on Gal. 1:1; 1531-35).

98. CA V, 1-3, in *BC,* 40.

by means of baptism — has an office, a charisma.[99] In *On the Councils and the Church* Luther mentions as the fifth characteristic the "offices," with one, to be sure the most important, being the pastoral office.[100] The sixth characteristic for him is prayer and praise of God, within which is included the confession of faith and that one "publicly teaches the catechism."[101] Prayer — which is commanded and entrusted to every baptized person — is thus a *nota ecclesiae;* most especially, the Lord's Prayer has great ecclesiastical meaning (see Luke 11:1). In addition to this comes the catechetical calling of the parents[102] and teachers, and furthermore, the musical gifts (cf. Col. 3:16) and the diaconal competencies, by means of which the baptized serve one another, and encourage, fortify, and strengthen others in the faith.

Everything that can be unfolded in this connection can be summarized paradigmatically in the "mutuum colloquium et consolatio . . . fratrum":[103] in the mutual conversation and the consolation that brothers and sisters offer one another. In this regard, Luther refers to Matthew 18:19-20 ("Where two or three are gathered together in my name, there am I in the midst of them"). Concerning this central passage for the theology of the congregation, he says in another place, in a sermon, that Christians should find the "community of the forgiveness of sins" not only in the public worship service "but also at home in the house, in the field, in the garden. Wherever even just one comes to another, there he should bring along comfort and deliverance." I should

> pour out my sadness to the one who is close to me and ask him for comfort. What that person then gives and promises to me as regards comfort is to be affirmed by God in Heaven as well. On the other hand, I should also comfort and say to another person: dear friend, dear brother, why do you not let go of your affliction? It is certainly not God's will that you experience a single bit of suffering. God allowed his Son to die for you, so that you need not mourn but that you can be joyful. Therefore be of good courage and be comforted; you will do a service and that which is pleasing to God, and you ought to kneel down with one another and pray the Lord's Prayer, which is certainly heard in heaven, for Christ promises: "I am in

99. Cf. especially 1 Cor. 12–14 and Rom. 12. Luther takes up the Pauline idea of the body, particularly in his Lord's Supper sermon of 1519 (cf. nn. 68-70 above).

100. WA 50:632.35–633.11 (1539); *LW* 41:154.

101. WA 50:641.24; cf. *LW* 41:164.

102. Luther intended the Small Catechism above all for the home; see the introductory comments preceding parts I-V and the appendixes, in *BC,* 351, 354, 356, 359, 362, 363, and 364.

103. The "mutual conversation and consolation of brethren": SA III, 4, in *BC,* 319.

your midst" [Matt. 18:20]. He does not say: "I will see it. I will hear it," or "I will come to you," but "I am there already."[104]

12.3. The Hiddenness of the Church

Even as the church is constituted and defined by external signs that can be heard and seen, it is at the same time a matter for faith — which is admittedly true about every element of the confession of faith: also that the natural world is a creation (Heb. 11:3), that the historical person Jesus is at the same time the Christ, that the cross is a power of God: all this is "foolishness" (1 Cor. 1:18–2:16) to the natural human being. Thus the church is also not objectively a matter for verification: *Abscondita est ecclesia, latent sancti* — "the church is hidden, the holy ones are kept out of sight."[105]

The holiness of the church is not openly visible, "like items for sale at a market." This citation, from the second preface to the Revelation of Saint John (1530), is particularly instructive within its context:

> The topic ("I believe in one holy Christian church") is a matter of faith as much as any other. Thus reason cannot detect it, even if one uses magnifying glasses. The devil can certainly cover it over with scandals and by means of various parties, about which you must be vexed. In the same way, God can also hide it under maladies and all kinds of shortcomings, so that you end up becoming a fool and would come to the wrong conclusion about it. It is not to be visualized, but believed. But faith deals with that which a person cannot see, Heb. 11[:1]. And it also sings the song with its Lord: "Blessed is the one who takes no offense in me" [Matt. 11:6]. A Christian is even hidden from himself, so that he does not see his holiness and his virtue, but sees in himself nothing but lack of virtue and a lack of holiness. And you, a rough-hewn smarty, want to see Christianity with your blind reason and impure eyes?
>
> In conclusion, our holiness is in heaven, where Christ is, and not in the world, visible to the eyes, like items for sale at a market. Thus let scandal,

---

104. WA 47:298.2-19 (Matt. 18–24 interpreted in sermons; 1537-40).

105. WA 18:652.23; cf. *LW* 33:89. In his early ecclesiological writings Luther actually speaks of "two churches," one external and the other internal (*LW* 39:70, *On the Papacy at Rome*, 1520), which is "not the physical gathering, but is a gathering of the heart in one faith" (WA 18:293.3f.). Yet because of the threat of spiritualism, he soon quits talking in such a dualistic way. On Luther's ecclesiology in the polemical writings between 1519 and 1521, cf. Carl Axel Aurelius, *Verborgene Kirche* (Hannover: Lutherisches Verlagshaus, 1983), especially 21-59.

party spirit, heresy, and maladies be, and let them accomplish what they will. If the Word of the gospel alone remains pure in our midst and we hold it dear and valued, then we will not doubt that Christ is by and with us, even when things are at their worst. Thus we see here in this book [of the Revelation] that Christ, through and beyond all plagues, animals, evil angels, is still nearby and with his holy ones, and finally prevails.[106]

Important observations can be made from this passage:

a. The question about the church, dealing with ecclesiology, provides for Luther the key to understanding the Revelation of Saint John. After he had criticized the book in his first preface in 1522, as obtuse, and said it obscured the witness to Christ — though he noted clearly that this was his own personal judgment[107] — he continued to discover more and more parallels between the church of the sixteenth century and that persecuted community of Christians who lived at the end of the first century, who are addressed by this book. It seemed that there were phases in history when the *hiddenness of the church* became a special topic for discussion and in which some other books of the Bible — as the book of Daniel — began to speak as well, which were otherwise not much valued.

b. "The topic ('I believe in one holy Christian church') is a matter of faith as much as any other. Thus reason cannot detect it, even if one uses magnifying glasses." The condition of the church, as it appears to the eye, often gives reason for annoyance. But one ought not to be surprised by such a state of affairs, if the true church is hidden; if it were not so, it would not be stated in the Confession of Faith. Luther and the other Reformers frequently turned in this regard to Hebrews 11:1.[108] "Now faith is the assurance of things hoped for, the conviction of things *not* seen."[109]

---

106. Heinrich Bornkamm, ed., *Luthers Vorreden zur Bibel*, 3rd ed. (Göttingen: Vandenhoeck & Ruprecht, 1989), 230f. (= *LW* 35:399-411, "Preface to the Revelation of St. John [II]," 1546/1530).

107. Cf. Bornkamm, *Luthers Vorreden zur Bibel*, 218f. (= *LW* 35:398-99, "Preface to the Revelation of St. John [I]," 1522); cf. chap. 4.5 above.

108. Cf. *LW* 39:221.

109. In the Apology of the Augsburg Confession, to articles 7-8, Melanchthon articulates the relationship between the hiddenness and the visible nature of the church by way of the example of its catholicity, and thus its universality: "This article has been presented for a very necessary reason. We see the endless dangers that threaten the destruction of the church. There is an infinite number of ungodly persons within the church itself who oppress it. This article in the Creed presents these consolations to us: so that we may not despair, but may know that the church will nevertheless remain; so that we may know that however great the multitude of the ungodly is, nevertheless the church exists and Christ bestows those gifts that he promised to

c. A reason for the hiddenness of the church is because of *sin and the devil:* "The devil can certainly cover it over with scandals and by means of various parties, about which you must be vexed. In the same way, God can also hide it under maladies and all kinds of shortcomings, so that you end up becoming a fool and would come to the wrong conclusion about it." This argumentation touches on Luther's reflections concerning the *Deus absconditus:* in specific situations one cannot separate the work of the devil and that of the hidden God.[110] Correspondingly, the church is also hidden within its opposite. She also takes part in sin. Just as the individual believer always remains a *peccator* (sinner), the same holds true for the church: she is holy and a sinner at the same time *(simul sancta et peccatrix),* in fact a *magna peccatrix;*[111] she confesses as much just by the very fact that she prays the petition concerning the forgiveness of sins in the Lord's Prayer.[112]

Augsburg Confession, article 8, reflects on this problematic relationship with reference to the question that surfaces again and again concerning the (most possibly) pure community: it happens again and again "in this life [that there are] many false Christians and hypocrites, even manifest sinners, who remain among the pious."[113] But the sacraments still do their work, and it is important to take note of that.

d. A further reason for the hiddenness of the church is found in the fact that I, as a Christian, *have been separated from myself:* "A Christian is even hidden from himself, so that he does not see his holiness and his virtue, but sees in himself nothing but lack of virtue and a lack of holiness. And you, a rough-hewn smarty, want to see Christianity with your blind reason and impure eyes?" Whoever attempts to arrive at some objective statement to describe his situation as a Christian or his election gets into the realm of speculation or falls headlong into the abyss of temptation concerning predestination. But it is comforting that even one's own existence as a Christian, "even hidden from himself," can be left alone and that one can place trust in Christ — corre-

---

the church: forgiveness of sins, answered prayer, the gift of the Holy Spirit. Moreover, it says 'church catholic' so that we not understand the church to be an external government of certain nations. It consists rather of people scattered throughout the entire world who agree on the gospel and have the same Christ, the same Holy Spirit, and the same sacraments, whether or not they have the same human traditions" (VII and VIII, 9-10, in *BC,* 175).

110. Cf. chap. 9.2 above.

111. WA 34I:276.7f. (Easter sermon of April 9, 1531). Cf. *LW* 26:109: "Est quidem Ecclesia sancta, tamen simul peccatrix est" [The church is indeed holy, but she is a sinner at the same time]; on Gal. 2:11; 1535.

112. WA 34I:276.3, 8f., 21f. (Easter sermon of April 9, 1531).

113. *BSLK* 62.5-7; cf. CA VIII, in *BC,* 42.

sponding to the Word in Colossians 3:3, that "your [new] life is hidden with Christ in God." As far as this affects the life of the congregation, it means that one ought not to judge the relationship between God and fellow Christians — not as if faith had no meaning, but because this measuring stick *(canon fidei)* is a matter for God alone. One is to deal with fellow Christians on the basis of the measuring stick of love *(canon caritatis):* I should assume the very best about a fellow Christian,[114] "be a Christ" for him by praying on his behalf and bearing his burdens.[115] But I have to speak against him — as Luther did most especially over against the papacy — whenever he *teaches* the faith in a false way. "It is a matter for love to endure all things [1 Cor. 13:7] and to soften all matters. By contrast, it is a matter of faith to endure nothing at all and not to be soft toward anyone."[116] This distinction between faith and love, thus with respect to the teaching and the person of the fellow Christian, is extremely helpful in situations that deal with conflicts in the church.

e. "In conclusion, our holiness is in heaven, where Christ is, and not in the world, visible to the eyes, as items for sale at the market. Thus let scandal, party spirit, heresy, and maladies be, and let them accomplish what they will. If the Word of the gospel alone remains pure in our midst and we hold it dear and valued, then we will not doubt that Christ is by and with us, even when things are at their worst." In spite of its hiddenness, the church is no spiritualistic phantom. Instead, the Word and the other identifying characteristics[117] show *that* there is on earth, at all times, a holy Christian church and that this also remains.[118] Only *where* its borders are to be found and *who* belongs to her in individual cases cannot be described perfectly according to human decision. But the desire for such objectivity is to be rejected by those who believe in the promise, the *promissio:* Christ is with all of you, with you individually.

f. ". . . that Christ, through and beyond all plagues, animals, evil angels, is still nearby and with his holy ones, and finally prevails." This hiddenness of the church is not established only because of human sin, in the hide-and-seek that the devil plays, and in the fact that the Christian is hidden from himself, but finally and most particularly in the *eschatological structure* of our faith and life. That Christ "finally prevails" will be seen by all eyes only at the end of days. Only then will the church be hidden no longer.

---

114. *LW* 33:88.
115. WA 7:35.35; cf. *LW* 31:367.
116. WA 40II:48.13f.; cf. *LW* 27:38 (on Gal. 5:9-10; 1531).
117. Cf. 12.2.1-5 above.
118. CA VII, in *BC*, 42; cf. Apology to Articles VII-VIII.

Chapter 13 Faith and Good Works

Behold how love flows forth from faith.

The topic of "faith and good works" brings us to one of the most important pivot points for theology: the relationship between dogmatics and ethics. How does what we believe relate to what we do? Should do?[1] Can do?[2] Ought to do? Do we on our own do anything because of our own power? Or is it God the almighty, instead, who works in us and thus ought to be the subject of ethics (cf. Eph. 2:10)? What role does Luther set forth on this, particularly as it relates to freedom, which is foundational in ethical discussions today?

13.1. Faith as the Source of Good Works

The seminal discussion concerning Luther's reformational insights about the relationship between faith and works is found in the excursus *De fide et operibus (Concerning Faith and [Good] Works)* in the second set of lectures on the psalms (on Ps. 14:1; 1519-20).[3] Both major reformational writings discussed in detail in this chapter are rooted in this excursus: *Treatise on Good Works* and *On the Freedom of a Christian,* both written in 1520.

The *Treatise,* which is considered the first statement of an evangelical ethic, clearly places faith before works. One's special attention is drawn to the faith — but, and that is the point, not to faith in and of itself but to faith as

---

1. To state the essence of the ideal typology for Kant's prescriptive ethics.

2. To state the essence of the ideal typology for Schleiermacher's descriptive ethics.

3. WA 5:394.16–408.13. Cf. Wilhelm Maurer, *Von der Freiheit eines Christenmenschen. Zwei Untersuchungen zu Luthers Reformationsschriften 1520/21* (Göttingen: Vandenhoeck & Ruprecht, 1949).

the fulfillment of the first commandment, or more specifically: faith as trust in God's promise "I am the Lord, your God!" In the Large Catechism Luther expounds this promise: "*I, I will give you enough* [in my goodness] and [in my mercy] I will help you out of all need!"[4]

For what reason is faith, as trust in God's promise, given priority over all works? In what way does it alone make all works good? Because it alone — and thus God alone, who establishes faith — breaks open the nature of the sinner as one curved in on himself; only he can loosen the fist that is clenched so tightly, so that my existence on behalf of others becomes natural once again and takes place with "passion and love." The imagery of receiving and passing on to others brings us to the foundational motif of Luther's understanding of God, that of categorical gift: through the Son, God in the Spirit gives himself to us as Father, in every sense of the word,[5] so that we do not hoard and keep for ourselves what is given to us, which is what we do as sinners, but instead we pass it on to others: "For through this knowledge we get passion and love for all the commandments of God, since we see here how God gives himself completely, with all that he has and is able to do, to give us help and support for keeping the Ten Commandments: the Father gives all creatures; the Son gives all his works; the Holy Spirit gives all his gifts."[6] Since faith is the motivator, in fact, even more: since it is the mover that gives the reason for action, as the power and might to open oneself and to give on to others that which has been given, it can be identified by Luther as the *opus operum*,[7] the "work of all works." That would seem to be a paradoxical way to phrase it. It can be understood correctly only if *opus* can be understood in different ways in different situations: faith is that work *of God (opus Dei)* that makes *human* works *(opera hominum)* good; as Luther says, it is the "master worker and the chief in charge."[8] If faith, as the fulfillment of the first commandment, is placed prior to and is foundational for all the works that are fulfilled in the other commandments, then it is stated at the same time that the first commandment itself has priority over and is foundational to all other commandments, that, as we shall see in just a moment, it forms the matrix for the exposition of the Decalogue.[9]

---

4. *BSLK* 560.40f.; cf. LC I, 4, in *BC*, 387.

5. LC II, 67-70, in *BC*, 440; cf. *LW* 37:366 (*Confession concerning Christ's Supper*, 1528).

6. *BSLK* 661.35-42; cf. LC II, 69-70, in *BC*, 440.

7. WA 5:396.32 (cf. n. 3 above).

8. WA 6:213.14; cf. *LW* 44:34 (*Treatise on Good Works*).

9. This description of the context in which the subject is set — *to pay attention to the first commandment* from the perspective of faith — is an interpretation of the author, for which he naturally can appeal to the beginning of the excursus in the commentary on Ps. 14:1 (WA

When Luther, in his *Treatise on Good Works*, starts with strict reference to the words of the Ten Commandments, he goes against the human ordinances — what he calls "ceremonies"[10] — which have darkened the clear will of God. A good work is not what human beings can conceptualize and value; instead, what fulfills the command of God should be identified as a good work. Luther bases his observations on Matthew 19, where Jesus, in answer to the rich young man's question on the way to be saved, does not identify any particular work but refers to the Ten Commandments that were known by all. But the highest good work is faith, as is stated at the very beginning of the *Treatise*[11] with reference to John 6:28-29: "This is God's work, that you believe in him whom he has sent." "For all works must take place within this work [namely, within faith] and the good things that flow into these deeds [from faith][12] receive their worth from that faith, as a loan."[13]

Luther directs his attention against those theologians who demand good works but who are weak in matters connected with the question about the certainty of salvation. According to Luther, the best works do me no good if I do not know how I am doing in my relationship with God. Without faith the best work is dead: "All these works [namely, praying, fasting, being in a monastery, etc.] go outside the faith; they are thus nothing and completely dead: For as your conscience is related to God and believes, thus so are your works that proceed from it. Now [for the Roman] there is no faith, no good conscience toward God, thus the head of all good works is chopped off, and all their life and worth is nothing."[14] And yet a misunderstanding follows hard on the heels of this statement: "But it happens that whenever I accentuate faith to such a great extent and reject such works that do not proceed from faith, they accuse me of forbidding good works, at the very point where I yearn to teach about correct, good works of faith!"[15]

When he teaches about good works, Luther is interested in discussing the traditional two-tiered description of ethics, that of the commandments

---

5:394.20ff.), as well as to Luther's explanation of the first commandment in the Large Catechism. In the *Treatise* Luther begins with faith, without immediately giving particular accent to the special position of the first commandment. But cf. *LW* 44:30 (par. 9), and n. 21 below.

10. Cf. the second part of the excursus on Ps. 14:1: WA 5:405.6–408.13.

11. WA 6:204.25-28; cf. *LW* 44:23.

12. With the term *einfliessen* (to flow into) Luther makes reference to the Roman teaching of *gratia infusa* (grace that is poured in), which has its origin in the Augustinian concept that a mediating substance delivers the grace.

13. WA 6:204.31f.; cf. *LW* 44:24.

14. WA 6:205.6-10; cf. *LW* 44:24.

15. WA 6:205.11-13; cf. *LW* 44:24.

(praecepta) and "evangelical counsels" *(consilia evangelica).*[16] The church in the Middle Ages resolved the tension between the high level of expectation involved in the call to follow especially what the Sermon on the Mount demanded, over against the demands of the laws that seemed to be easier to fulfill, by teaching that the common people were expected to obey the commandments that seemed easier and that the monks and nuns were to fulfill the more difficult ones on behalf of others. Luther, by contrast, takes faith as the criterion of *every* good work, whether it involves matters of daily work or "singing, reading [the Bible and edifying literature], playing the organ, celebrating the mass, praying at matins, vespers, and other hours of the day, endowing churches, altars, cloisters, and furnishing them with bells, precious gems, vestments for mass, jewelry."[17] "For if he [e.g., the believer] senses in his heart the confidence that it pleases God, then the work is good, no matter even if it is so insignificant as to pick up a straw. If this confidence is not there, or if he doubts it, then the work is not good, even if it would waken all the dead and the person would let himself be burned [as a martyr; 1 Cor. 13:3]. Paul teaches this in Rom. 14[:23]: 'Whatever does not proceed from faith is sin.'[18] From faith, and from no other work, what we call Christian believers are named, as being the chief work" — not somehow originating in the human being,[19] but in God! "For all other works can be done by a heathen . . . as well. But to trust confidently that he is pleasing to God is possible only for a Christian, who is enlightened and fortified by grace."[20]

To conceptualize faith now as fulfilling the first commandment, as "faithfulness" and as "confidence in the depth of the heart," without which there is "otherwise no good work that one can do enough to fulfill this commandment,"[21] is absolutely one of the most important theological insights of Luther, the foundational significance of which can hardly be valued too highly. The turning point for Luther's understanding came already in 1520, as set forth in the Small Catechism (1529), to treat the first commandment as the preamble and matrix within which one was to interpret all the command-

---

16. Cf. Thomas Aquinas, *STh* I/II q. 108 a. 4.

17. WA 6:211.15-17; cf. *LW* 44:32.

18. Luther and Melanchthon take Rom. 14:23 as the basis for their teaching about sin as such. In his excursus on Ps. 14:1 Luther alters the negative formulation of Rom. 14:23 to the positive formulation that all good works come from faith (WA 5:394.16ff.).

19. Following Fichte, Rudolf Bultmann distinguishes deed and work: faith is the "free deed of [human] decision" ("Gnade und Freiheit" [1948], in Bultmann, *Glaube und Verstehen*, vol. 2 [Tübingen: Mohr, 1952], 149-61, here 157), but it is not man's work.

20. WA 6:206.9-18; cf. *LW* 44:25.

21. WA 6:209.33-35; cf. *LW* 44:30.

ments that follow. Before Luther, the Ten Commandments were generally understood as a collection of statements, one added to the next. But that is handled differently in the Small Catechism: it starts off with the first commandment, with the statement in the absolute: "We should fear and love and trust God above all things." In the explanation to the rest of the commandments, Luther repeats this statement, in each case in the absolute, and — with an ingenious grasp of the issue! — specifically emphasizes the reason with a consecutive clause: "We should fear and love God so that we [to use the example of the fifth commandment] do not hurt or harm our neighbor in his body, but help him and care [for him] in all bodily needs."[22] It should be emphasized that it deals here with a consecutive clause, thus describing a consequence — and not in the sense of a final clause that intends something to be fulfilled only later; the "that" is thus not to be understood deontologically as a moral obligation, but as has been pointed out, as a consecutive, as an internal natural consequence. Faith — with an inner necessity — cannot help but be active in love; all good works spring from and "flow"[23] from faith. Thus the fulfilling of the faith in works is not a temporal or psychological consequence, but is a consequence that proceeds logically from the nature of faith.

Chiefly because of 1 Corinthians 13:13, but also with respect to Romans 13:8-10, the question is posed about how love and faith relate to one another. Is not love the power that first makes faith effective? In any case, this was the judgment of the Scholastics in their interpretation of Galatians 5:6, according to which faith achieves the form it was meant to have for salvation and its fulfillment by means of love; in this sense one speaks of *fides caritate formata:* faith must first be formed through love. Is love not thus, according to 1 Corinthians 13:13, to be accorded higher honor than faith? Luther warns about such an attempt to tear the two apart, one from the other, in order to arrange them in a hierarchy of importance: "Now it has been stated above that such a confident faith brings with it love and hope; in fact, if we view it correctly, then love is the first to come forth or is even there at the same time with faith. For I would not be able to trust God if I were not to think that he wants to deal with me favorably and graciously; because of this I am gracious toward him in response and am thus moved to trust him heartily and to hope for all good things from him."[24] But all "who [want] to move God to be favorable by means of many good works (as they call them)" hope "to buy his grace at the same time . . . , as if he were a peddler or day laborer, who would not be willing

---

22. *BSLK* 508.31-34; cf. SC I, 10, in *BC*, 352.
23. WA 6:210.1; cf. *LW* 44:30, which reads "proceed."
24. WA 6:210.5-9; cf. *LW* 44:30.

to part with his grace and favor without getting something in return."[25] To state this in thesis form, briefly, Luther's preface to the Letter to the Romans says "that the human being is justified without works, even though he does not continue without works, if he has become righteous."[26] Love does not get added to faith at a later time, in order to make it complete.[27] Much rather — which is how the Greek phraseology of Galatians 5:6 can be translated — the faith goes forth in love with the energy that is its own and that is within itself; as *faith* it is active in love.[28] This is not immediately apparent so much in specific works, but rather in a basic way of living that goes through and through in all that a Christian does and does not do. "Because the human being, according to his nature, cannot exist for a single moment without acting or failing to act, suffering or fleeing (for life never rests, as we see): now then, get started, whoever wishes to be pious and wants to be filled with good works, and start practicing in all life and works at all times. . . . That person will then discover how much he has to do and that it is rooted in all things completely in faith and he can never be lazy, since even being lazy has to take place as a work that exercises faith."[29] It states in the definition that must be considered classic, which Luther offers in the preface to the Letter to the Romans:

> Faith is a godly work in us which changes us and brings us alive anew from God, John 1[:13], and kills the old Adam; it makes of us a completely different human being in our heart, courage, senses, and all powers, and brings the Holy Spirit along as well. Oh, it is a living, creating, active, powerful thing, this business about faith, so that it is impossible that it does not do good deeds incessantly. It does not ask whether there are good works to be done; instead, even before one asks, it has accomplished them and is always doing them.[30]

---

25. WA 6:210.19-22; cf. *LW* 44:31.

26. Heinrich Bornkamm, ed., *Luthers Vorreden zur Bibel*, 3rd ed. (Göttingen: Vandenhoeck & Ruprecht, 1989), 187 (= *LW* 35:374).

27. This is the scholastic articulation of the *fides caritate formata*, which is based on Gal. 5:6 (Thomas Aquinas, *STh* II/2, q. 4.3; cf. III q. 49 a. 1, ad 5). The Council of Trent supports this teaching (*Kompendium der Glaubensbekenntnisse und kirchlichen Lehrentscheidungen*, ed. Heinrich Denzinger and Peter Hünermann, 39th ed. [Freiburg: Herder, 2001], 1531 and 1648).

28. On Luther's understanding of Gal. 5:6, cf., above all, his treatise on freedom: "faith goes to work with joy and love" (*On the Freedom of a Christian*, WA 7:34.32f. and 7:64.35-37; cf. *LW* 31:365), his disputation *De veste nuptiali* (WA 39I:265-333; cf. Matt. 22:11-12), and his commentary on the passage: *LW* 27:28-31 (*Lectures on Galatians*, chaps. 5–6, 1535); for further passages, cf. WA 59:721, n. 10.

29. WA 6:212.32–213.1; cf. *LW* 44:34.

30. Bornkamm, *Luthers Vorreden zur Bibel*, 182 (= *LW* 35:370).

The righteousness of faith, which is worked by God alone, which is thus only to be suffered and received by the human being, is thus highly active, and precisely because of its passive nature it is active because of the work of God. In no way can it exist without works. In the Heidelberg Disputation, Luther said, "I wish to say that 'without works' is to be understood thus: not that the righteous does nothing, but that his works do not create for him any righteousness; instead, the righteousness [that is entrusted to him] produces works."[31] Luther's ethic thus has not been comprehended sufficiently by either Kant or Schleiermacher,[32] though it is much closer to the approach taken by the latter: "Thus love flows out of faith."[33] "Good works will never make a good, pious man, but a good man produces good, pious works."[34]

13.2. Free for Servanthood

In practice, faith does not express itself with the same intensity in the lives of Christians. For this reason Luther identifies four groups of human beings in his *Treatise:* those who, because of the faith, do the will of God spontaneously, without the law; those who still need the admonition of the law so that they do not misuse freedom by sinning; the evil, who without the force of the "political" use of the law would go way beyond what they ought; and finally those who are still children in the faith and still need works as a measure of support until they arrive at a complete reformational understanding of the faith.[35]

31. WA 1:364.6-8; cf. *LW* 31:55-56 (Heidelberg Disputation, 1518).

32. Cf. nn. 1-2 above.

33. WA 7:66.7; cf. *LW* 31:367 ("Ecce sic fluit ex fide caritas"). Cf. 44:30.

34. WA 7:32.5f.; cf. *LW* 31:361. Cf. Matt. 7:18. In contrast to Luther, from the time of his exposition on Colossians (1527) on, Melanchthon tended more toward a prescriptive ethic. This is his formulation of article 6 of the Augsburg Confession: "that such faith *should (debeat)* yield good fruit and good works and that a person *must (oporteat)* do such good works" (CA VI, 1, in *BC,* 40, italics added). In the disputation *De fide* Luther cites Melanchthon but then corrects him in a substantive way: "We confess that good works must follow faith, yes, not only must, but follow voluntarily, just as a good tree not only must produce good fruits, but does so freely" (*LW* 34:111, *Thesis concerning Faith and Law,* 1535). John Calvin gives special weight to progress in one's good (Christian) life (the "third" or "pedagogical" use of the law as its most important use): John Calvin, *Institutes of the Christian Religion* 2.7.12 and 3.6.1.

35. *LW* 44:35. The fourth group "must be led back to faith again in a kindly manner and with gentle patience, just as a sick man is nursed. For the sake of their conscience they must be allowed for a while to go on clinging to some works and to perform them as necessary for salvation, as long as they grasp faith properly. Otherwise, if we try to tear them away too suddenly their weak consciences may be utterly shattered and confused, and consequently they end with neither faith nor works" (44:36-37).

The first-named group, who are truly free in the faith, are also now free to put themselves under the law for the sake of others; Luther at this juncture points to Paul's argumentation in Romans 14, with reference to the relationship between the "strong" and the "weak."

The law is not done away with but is fulfilled. "Everything that you do [proceeds] from the heart. But no one gives someone such a heart, except for the Spirit of God. He makes the law acceptable for human beings, so that he gets one to desire the law in the heart, and from this point on not because of fear or force, but one does everything because of a free heart."[36] Christian or *evangelical freedom is that freedom through which the conscience is free of works — not in the sense that none take place but in the sense that one does not rely on any of them.*

Luther never tires of emphasizing the freedom and spontaneity of the new obedience, of the way one who is reborn hears and acts. He summarizes the relationship between faith and love in *On the Freedom of a Christian* in the twofold thesis: "A Christian is a free lord over all things and is subject to no one. A Christian is a ready servant of all things and is subject to everyone."[37] The Christian is not a species of human being or a religious human being, but is simply human as a freed human being. In faith he lives outside of himself: in God — freed from having to seek his identity and having to make himself what he is on his own. This is how he can make it happen that he is servant of all.

In the entire document concerning freedom, Luther does not intend to do anything else than to explain one single sentence of Paul: "Because I am free with respect to all, I have made myself a slave to all" (1 Cor. 9:19). Not although I am free, but *because* I am free. Luther claims at the same time that he can explain the text in Romans that speaks of fulfilling the law through love: Romans 13:8-10. With faith one receives the freedom to serve in love,

> so that, from now on, we have no law and are not in debt to anyone else in any way except to love [Rom. 13:8]; we do good to our neighbor in the same way as Christ did for us through his blood. For this reason, all laws, works, and commandments that demand of us that we can serve God do not come from God. . . . Yet the laws, works, and commandments that are demanded of us for the sake of serving the neighbor, they are good, we should do them, so that we are to obey temporal power in its sphere of authority, follow, and serve, feed the hungry, help the needy.[38]

36. Bornkamm, *Luthers Vorreden zur Bibel,* 179 (= *LW* 35:367).
37. WA 7:21.1-4; cf. *LW* 35:344.
38. WA 12:157.6-14 (a letter to the congregation of the city of Esslingen; 1523).

The fulfillment of the law by exercising love does not lead one beyond the relationship of being responsible for one another; this will stand until the end of the world — and with it the conflict, indeed the battle, of everyone against everyone else for mutual recognition. But there is a decisive element in this battle that goes counter to the "fight to the death" being fought in world history. It is decisive insofar as God himself, who is free in the absolute sense, because of his riches, became poor on our behalf in the history of Jesus Christ, so that we through his poverty might be rich. This is what Paul extracts from the well-known events in the Christ hymn in Philippians 2:6-11, when he writes 2 Corinthians 8, 9; Luther follows him. Because of what happened in the story of Jesus Christ, and because of the turn of events occasioned in those events in the battle of various definitions of how to attain justification, the Christian — by being brought through, beyond the death of the old Adam — is retrieved and thereby made righteous. "Righteousness is now such faith and is called 'God's righteousness' or 'that which avails before God' because it is God's gift and prepares the human being by giving to everyone that for which he is responsible. For through faith the human being is without sin and receives the desire to fulfill God's commands. In this way he gives God the honor due him and pays him what he owes him; but he serves the other human being at no charge, wherever he can, and thus also pays everyone."[39] Thus faith that is energized in love cannot distance itself from the relationship in which each one has responsibility for the other and thereby cannot distance itself from the battle among various definitions of how to be justified; in a certain sense it lives out its relationship within that battle. The forensic structure of reality — existence as judgment, existence in mutual recognition — is not thus rendered null and void; in the way just mentioned it is fulfilled. In this sense the Old Testament and the ancient Near Eastern wisdom tradition — world order as faithfulness to the communal relationship and righteousness — is enhanced in the concept of love and brought to its fulfillment. Luther does not offer a narrow interpretation of Paul, as is maintained in a commonly held misunderstanding of his theology and of Augsburg Confession, article 4. That the law is fulfilled in love, that righteousness is fulfilled in mercy, expands its impact and applies to the widest social and worldwide relationships.

13.3. Metaphysical Advance? — Ethical Advances

Faith does not ask "whether good works are to be done but rather, before one even asks, it has been done already and is always at work. But whoever does

---

39. Bornkamm, *Luthers Vorreden zur Bibel*, 183; cf. *LW* 35:371.

not do such works is a faithless human being."[40] That seems to be the statement of Pietism, Methodism, the Holiness Movement, and even James (James 1:22-25; 2:17, 20); they wonder about the status of faith if it does not show itself to be as active as Luther expects. Is faith recognizable in deeds? Or must I also believe the faith?

As was already at issue concerning a way to verify baptism on the basis of the life that follows,[41] one ought to be warned at this point as well, as Luther warns, about advocating extreme positions. We are cautioned against following the position advocated at times in Calvinism, that of the *syllogismus practicus*[42] — concluding that the faith is present or held seriously on the basis of the works — because of the ambiguity of all human action. Such inferences lead one only into uncertainty and legalism. It would be just as wrong — viewed from the opposite side of the issue — to separate faith and works completely, one from the other, as libertines do.[43]

Luther differentiates two viewpoints. Viewing the matter as a whole is decisive: no matter what still happens and how the events of life turn out   a person who believes is completely justified. Added to that fact, subordinated and considered subsequently, is the special aspect:[44] growing in holiness in the pietistic sense, becoming more holy as a process.[45] To be sure, Luther can also talk about growing in sanctification, as regards "sins being swept away each day and life being renewed, so that we do not remain in sin, but that we can and ought to lead a new life with all manner of good works."[46] "Progress means nothing but beginning anew, again and again. Beginning without progressing, however, is retreat."[47] But this process of sanctification cannot be assigned grades. Believing means that one is removed from being in charge of oneself and responsible for one's own judgment. And judgment for the works still lies ahead for us. If this is not taken into account, then one's observations

---

40. Bornkamm, *Luthers Vorreden zur Bibel*, 182; cf. *LW* 35:370.

41. Cf. chap. 12.2.1 above.

42. Cf. Heidelberg Catechism, question 86.

43. Cf. Konrad Hilpert, "Libertinismus," in *RGG*, 4th ed., vol. 5 (2002), cols. 325-26.

44. On the distinction between the total and partial aspect, cf. Wilfried Joest, *Gesetz und Freiheit. Das Problem des Tertius Usus bei Luther und die neutestamentliche Parainese* (Göttingen: Vandenhoeck & Ruprecht, 1951; 3rd ed., 1961), 55-82.

45. In expounding the catechism's explanation of the third article, a distinction was drawn between the punctual aspect and durative aspect in sanctification (chap. 11.1.2 above).

46. WA 50:625.26-28; cf. *LW* 41:144 *(On the Councils and the Church)*.

47. WA 4:350.14; cf. *LW* 11:152-553 *(First Lectures on the Psalms*, 1513; on Ps. 119:88; 1513-15). In Luther's writings this sentence actually becomes a topos. On its precise understanding, cf. Theodor Dieter, *Der junge Luther und Aristoteles. Eine historisch-systematische Untersuchung zum Verhältnis von Theologie und Philosophie*, TBT 105 (Berlin and New York, 2001), 317-25.

about oneself can lead to a pious version of being curved in on the self *(incurvatio in se ipsum)*. The sanctified individual as such does not deserve recognition; one should take note of God, who sanctifies and who uses his Word as the means of sanctification.[48]

Luther's understanding of creation and history prohibits a philosophy of history that fits into this point of view; it particularly stands opposed to the modern view of progress. That does not mean that the justified person goes around in circles and cannot take any steps in a particular direction. Just the opposite is the case. In the relationship of the new man versus the old man there is in fact progress. In *On the Freedom of a Christian* it says: "We begin and make progress in that which will become complete in the life to come."[49]

With respect to ethics, with a view toward our works, our actions, our political engagements, there are certainly advances — even if there is no progress in the absolute sense. Advances in the ethical sense are thus unburdened by metaphysical constraints. The kingdom of God does not come because one works at making the kingdom of God happen; it has been prepared for a long time already (Matt. 25:34), as Luther points out impressively in *De servo arbitrio*.[50] The idea of making progress no longer fits salvation thinking. Religious fascination that applies a distorted view of salvation is abandoned. Fanaticism in the political realm can be abandoned as well. Unburdened by the question of salvation, one can say that ethical advances take place in the realm of worldly progress; they do not take place in the name of what is absolute and total, but rather in small yet definite steps.

Actual advances in the worldly sense can "be satisfied with that which is present [and] at hand" and does not need to "master and control" the matters and circumstances "that deal with the future."[51] This differentiation between ethical progress and metaphysical progress has been forgotten in the modern era. One must wonder whether and in what way Pietism has brought this about. If one forgets this distinction, it means that the meaning of baptism has been forgotten as well.

Baptism draws the dividing line between the old and the new world. Ethical advances can come only when one returns to one's baptism. We can assure ourselves that there will be advances in what is actually good, and not just good but the absolute best; such advances come with repentance and a return to baptism. A world thus described sees that the alternatives of opti-

48. Thus chap. 11.1.1 above.

49. WA 7:59.31; cf. *LW* 31:358.

50. Cf. chap. 15, n. 11 below.

51. Bornkamm, *Luthers Vorreden zur Bibel*, 81 (= WA DB 10II:106.8f. ["Vorrede auf den Prediger Salomo"; 1524]).

mism and pessimism — grim fear of the future or euphoric hope for further evolution of the cosmos and its potential to improve — have been destroyed, since it is true that God the Creator unceasingly does new things.

In this skepticism in regard to the Enlightenment view of progress and to pietistic efforts of striving for sanctification by working to bring the kingdom of God to reality, it is appropriate to live in history in such a way that we recognize that we are determined by the distinction of law and gospel. The Formula of Concord, the Lutheran confession of 1577, says the following in connection with the way to deal with the relationship between justification and sanctification, with respect to how the law applies to one who is reborn: "These two sermons [law and gospel] stand next to each other in the church of God, always and at all times, from the beginning of the world, and are to be applied with proper distinction" and are "to be applied consistently until the end of the world."[52]

Luther always accented the fact that the law is not to be preached to Christians, insofar as they have been made righteous by the gospel; but it is to be preached to them insofar as they are sinners and thus belong to the old world. In the same way the Formula of Concord, article 6, vigorously seeks to articulate "what the gospel does, creates, and effects for the new obedience of the believer and what at this point, as regards the good works of the believers, the office of the law is,"[53] what the function and task of the law entail. In this way this Lutheran confession returns again and again to the old man, in order to emphasize the function of the law with reference to that nature. For "the old Adam hangs on," even now, to the Christian.[54] The old Adam is "the obstinate donkey, fixing for a fight," against whom the new man wages "constant battle."[55] The "Christian" and "true believer" is no different, insofar as he is old man, from the "unbeliever, non-Christian, and unrepentant person"![56] The *same* law applies to the "believer . . . no less than to the godless."[57]

A particularly pressing question comes up with respect to modern thinking that poses the problem about how, in the spontaneity of new obedience, sanctification can be kept from leading to enthusiasm; it is not enough to point to the enduring validity of the law for the old man. The gospel must be

52. *BSLK* 959.33–960.1.23-26; cf. Formula of Concord, Solid Declaration V, 23, 24, in *BC*, 585-86.

53. *BSLK* 965.31-34; cf. Formula of Concord, Solid Declaration VI, 10, in *BC*, 589.

54. *BSLK* 964.39-42; cf. Formula of Concord, Solid Declaration VI, 7, in *BC*, 588.

55. *BSLK* 969.14-17; cf. Formula of Concord, Solid Declaration VI, 24, 23, in *BC*, 591. Cf. Gal. 5:17.

56. *BSLK* 969.43-45; cf. Formula of Concord, Solid Declaration VI, 26, in *BC*, 591.

57. *BSLK* 967.25; 968.1; cf. Formula of Concord, Solid Declaration VI, 19, in *BC*, 590.

taken with the same seriousness, but given priority in regard to its content. For the new man to have a relationship with the old man, more than anything else he must stay alive. But for this he is constantly pointed to the promise of the gospel and the "alien" righteousness of Christ that is given him therein. This applies to him as that which has validity, is appropriate, and is distributed to him but never in the sense of what is his own, so that he can think of it as something that comes from within himself and that he can remember as his own. Such reliance on the self, even such reliance on the self that applies to the pious man, who wants to see his growth in faith and love, would stand in contradiction to the community into which the gospel takes its place.

So that the person who is reborn and renewed does not turn back to himself and thus to a view of the self that either doubts or is arrogant, the law that punishes and kills such self-will is necessary, but the gospel is even more necessary, which does not let such thoughts come to him at all. The spontaneity of new obedience is protected from enthusiasm in that it is not appropriate to talk of it as something that the self possesses or that is egotistical about salvation as something that is my own, as is the case with the delusional "self-arrogance";[58] it is to be apprehended as a present and gift of another, which empowers me to live life (Gal. 2:19-20).

13.4. Freedom

13.4.1. "You Are Called to Freedom!"

Luther renewed this call to freedom that comes from the New Testament, and specifically from Paul, and applied it anew with its full authority and strength.

A conscience that is not burdened or concerned needs the law; it needs to be aroused so that it becomes more aware of the law's demands. But to free the confused, fearful, and burdened conscience and to help it see clearly and have confidence — one must not drum in rules, norms, and laws and threaten punishment. Such a conscience can be helped by the gospel alone, through the freedom that is provided by what takes place in what happened through Jesus Christ and what is distributed and offered by Jesus himself in his Word and meal. Luther agrees with the call to freedom uttered by the apostle Paul, who wrote to the Galatians: "For you were called to freedom!" (Gal. 5:13). "For freedom Christ has set us free. Stand firm, therefore, and do not submit again to a yoke of slavery" (Gal. 5:1).

58. *BSLK* 454.15; cf. SA III, 8, 5, in *BC*, 322.

294

Many of Luther's contemporaries immediately agreed vociferously with Luther, but they did not always hear and take seriously what was included in this call to freedom and how the sentence in Galatians continues: "You were called to freedom, brothers and sisters; only do not use your freedom as an opportunity for self-indulgence, but through love become slaves to one another. For the whole law is summed up in a single commandment: 'You shall love your neighbor as yourself'" (Gal. 5:13-14).[59]

Luther's summons to freedom got a hearing once again during the Enlightenment. He was implored by Gotthold Ephraim Lessing in his dispute with the Lutheran head pastor in Hamburg: "Luther, you! — Great, misunderstood man! And not more misunderstood by anyone . . . than by the short-sighted stubborn people who, with your slippers in their hand, call others to follow down the path you set forth but dawdle along the way at the same time. — You loosed us from the yoke of tradition: who will release us from the unendurable yoke of the letter of the law!"[60]

This voice and many similar voices uttered the question: Was Luther the banner bearer for freedom in the modern age, a spiritual pioneer of the French Revolution, as this was understood by Hegel and, though in a changed sense, by Karl Marx as well?[61] Was Luther a revolutionary or a conservative? It holds true for him as for hardly another person: "Tangled up among the parties in favor and hatred, the picture of his character vacillates in history."[62] To take one example, in the German Democratic Republic he was first considered a "lackey of those in power"; by the time of the celebration of his birth in 1983 he was almost treated as a "comrade."[63] What then is Luther: lackey of

59. Cf. LW 44:400 (*Judgment of Luther on Monastic Vows*, 1521).

60. Gotthold Ephraim Lessing, "Eine Parabel — Nebst einer kleinen Bitte, und einem eventualen Absagungsschreiben an den Herrn Pastor Goeze, in Hamburg, 1778," unveränderter photomechanischer Ndr. Der 3. von Franz Muncker durchgesehenen und vermehrten Auflage der Ausgabe Karl Lachmanns von *G. E. Lessings sämtlichen Schriften*, vol. 13 (Berlin: De Gruyter, 1897), 102, 4-9. (Cf. Heinrich Bornkamm, *Luther im Spiegel der deutschen Geistesgeschichte*, 2nd ed. [Göttingen: Vandenhoeck & Ruprecht, 1970], 210f.) Hegel praises Luther in similar fashion: "It was with Luther first of all that freedom of spirit began to exist" (*Hegel's Lectures on "The History of Philosophy,"* trans. E. S. Haldane and Frances H. Simson [London: Routledge and Kegan Paul, 1896], III, 148).

61. Cf. Oswald Bayer, "Marcuses Kritik an Luthers Freiheitsbegriff," in Bayer, *Leibliches Wort. Reformation und Neuzeit im Konflikt* (Tübingen: Mohr-Siebeck, 1992), 151-75, here 157-60.

62. Friedrich Schiller, *The Robbers and Wallenstein*, trans. F. J. Lamport (New York: Penguin Books, 1979), 168. On the conflict surrounding Luther's relationship to the ages, cf. the introduction above.

63. Cf. Peter Hölzle, "Vom Fürstenknecht zum Genossen? Martin Luther im Kulturerbe der DDR," *EK* 16 (1983): 595-97.

the princes or comrade? Revolutionary or conservative? Was he an advocate for freedom or for law and order? For keeping things as they are or for change? For subjectivity or for the institution?

13.4.2. Following Christ Evangelically

A key text to resolve this question is that particular text — having been articulated at first, and not just by chance, in a sermon — that sets forth theses published May 9, 1539, titled *Concerning the Three Hierarchies*.[64] These theses represent the chief historical and systematic points for Luther's ethic as no other text; it is astounding that they have been accorded little notice to this point by scholars in general — to say nothing of their light treatment by those who study Luther.[65] In an artful way the motifs and analogies that are loosely connected or are treated only individually elsewhere are intertwined in one place. One's attention is drawn here to the question about the compatibility of freedom and service, freedom and institution, subjectivity and society.

With respect to these theses, Luther's accomplishment as an ethicist can be summarized in the following thesis: *Luther brought the distorted truth of the vows taken by the monks — the truths of poverty, of chastity, and of obedience — to the fore once again.*

What type of poverty is appropriate to the gospel?[66] What type of chastity is appropriate to the gospel?[67] What type of obedience is appropriate to the gospel?[68] No ethical issues and problems are beyond the range of these questions. The question about poverty involves the question about possessions, property, work; it is the question about the economic dimension of the world and our life. The question about chastity involves the issues that surround sexuality, marriage, and family — the way one deals with elementary human necessities and resources in working with others in a way one cannot avoid but which still finds it necessary to recognize differences in gender.

---

64. WA 39II:39-91 (cf. the introduction, n. 8).

65. To my knowledge the theses were treated in a monograph only by Rudolf Hermann, "Luthers Zirkulardisputation über Mt 19,21," *LuJ* 23 (1941)[!]: 35-93, reprinted in Hermann, *Gesammelte Studien zur Theologie Luthers und der Reformation* (Göttingen: Vandenhoeck & Ruprecht, 1960), 206-50. Cf. now: Volker Stümke, "Einen Räuber darf, einen Werwolf muss man töten. Zur Sozialethik Luthers in der Zirkulardisputation von 1539," in *Subjektiver Geist. Reflexion und Erfahrung im Glauben*, ed. Klaus-Michael Kodalle, Festschrift for Traugott Koch (Würzburg: Königshausen und Neumann, 2002), 207-28.

66. WA 39II:40.8-15 ("Von den drei Hierarchien," theses 17-20, 1539).

67. WA 39II:39.20-22 (thesis 10); cf. WA 39II:44.1-4 (theses 89-90).

68. WA 39II:40.38-41 (theses 31-50); cf. WA 39II:43.26-29 (theses 82-83).

Living with other human beings also involves obedience, if a human being is human in the sense that he is addressed and thus can hear and can also speak and offer an answer; being human means hearing. But this means he is related to all other human beings and to the one who addresses him through creatures, to God. Thus the word "obey" identifies a human being's basic standing before God, but also his standing in the world and in relation to himself. "In the world" means: in the realm of justice and in both its social and political connection, in the widest sense, even to the point of responsibility for fellow creatures.

Thus all the realms included in the relationship with God, the world, and the self are dealt with in the three vows of the monks. The parallel to the structure of what is taught about the three estates is obvious.[69] We first direct our attention to the aspect with which Luther begins his disputation theses of 1539: the topic of poverty.

Luther begins by discussing Jesus' encounter with the rich young man, as described in the Gospel of Matthew. Jesus speaks to the young man, who says he has kept all the commandments from his youth up: "If you wish to be perfect, go, sell your possessions, and give the money to the poor, and you will have treasure in heaven; then come, follow me!" (Matt. 19:21). It deals with complete obedience, with fulfilling the will of God completely, with the radical nature of what it means to follow.

Francis of Assisi once heard this word and became a begging monk. Francis and his order, with its "Franciscan poverty," provoked a following in history, and still does in our day. For us Francis of Assisi is an attractive figure who is worthy of love. Because of the ecological crisis many Christians, as well as many non-Christians, have been moved to reflect on his life. But Luther takes this much-respected Francis to task — in fact, in such a sharp way that we are left feeling uncomfortable: "Saint Francis was a good young fellow, but rough: he was unlearned and lacked experience with Holy Scripture. For neither he nor his brothers have kept this rule of Christ in the proper way."[70] Why? Because they lived as mendicant friars instead of by the work of their own hands — and had to live this way if they wanted to stay alive — which is different from what they would have accomplished and possessed by their own effort.

It is indeed hypocrisy and lies that they offer when they say that they have sold and left everything, for they do have to live — whether it comes now

---

69. The teaching about the three estates was set forth in chap. 6 in its relationship with a theology of creation and a fundamental anthropology; at issue here is the soteriological question with respect to freedom and its relationship with ethics.

70. WA 47:338.15-17 (Matt. 18–24 interpreted in sermons, 1537-40).

from that which is given to them by others or whether it comes from that which they accomplish by their own efforts. . . . But since they eat, drink, clothe themselves and live, they have indeed not sold everything, but they have and use all of it. That is indeed a completely splendid notion, to live lazily and confidently by means of the goods of others! And based on poverty or on "having left everything" they do the same thing as what is otherwise commonly called "possessing."[71]

"If they want to abandon and sell everything, in the sense that the monks mean it, they must leave this world altogether."[72] They have to take their lives. Then they will have abandoned everything. "They must go out and wander where no one lives, eats, drinks, clothes themselves, dwells, in order to really leave everything. For life: what you live, eat, drink, what you wear, the place, the hour, and everything like that: everything that you have in your possession is yours — by the very fact that it is used."[73] With this same sharpness, which Luther uses to speak against the mendicant orders, he also thinks of the hypocritical frugality by which the Cynic Diogenes lived in the barrel.[74] Luther's reflections deal with the roots of human existence, going in fact so deep as to deal with existence in this world in general, with sober reflection on this as he considers what happens as a result. As he considers critically his own previous life as a monk[75] — also in a mendicant order — it does not deal simply with a random question, but rather with an issue that goes to the heart of the Christian faith and life: concerning following Jesus Christ in space and time, dealing with what it means to be a Christian in the world.

The monastic movement, which to a great extent was rooted in the story of the rich young man, considered following Jesus to be wrapped up in the attempt to stay faithful to the vows of poverty, chastity, and absolute obedience. To do that, Luther said, the monks and nuns would have to desert the world altogether, which they were unable to do. For they have houses, the cloisters, in which they live; they have something to eat, to drink; they have clothing.[76]

Luther put the Anabaptists in the same category with the monks and nuns, whom he polemically called "Enthusiasts."[77] These were people who initially allied themselves with Luther, Christians who came out of the Reforma-

---

71. WA 39II:39.23-40, 3 ("Von den drei Hierarchien," theses 11-14, 1539).

72. WA 39II:40.8f. (thesis 17).

73. WA 39II:40.10-13 (theses 18-19).

74. Cf. WA 47:360.9-27 (Matt. 18–24 interpreted in sermons).

75. WA 47:349.32-35.

76. WA 47:352.18–353.8.

77. WA 47:345.26-32.

tion, who sought with all earnestness to lead a life that followed Jesus Christ, in a most consequent and radical way, and wanted to fashion their lives solely on the basis of the Sermon on the Mount. They refused to take an oath and to serve in war, and some did not marry either; they were not willing to hold any political office. Christians were not to take on any duties in their towns if they were really true Christians and really wanted to follow their Lord.[78]

Luther held the same views against the enthusiasm of the Anabaptists as he did against the monastic movement. Luther's ethic cannot be understood — as is true of his theology as a whole — without his critical and polemical opposition to these two groups and to the understanding of discipleship they considered to be correct. Luther thought the one group was like the other, even though they were in sharp disagreement with one another. He saw his own path as that of the "middle course"; he did not want to fall "either to the right or to the left."[79]

Such a middle course is admittedly not very wide. Instead, Luther's path is a dangerous walk along a mountain ridge. One ought not to wonder that this way has been understood by only a few, when considering its theological way of thinking and its practical-existential aspect, and it has never become popular. For it is not even easy to understand; it is certainly not easy to live.

13.4.3. Ethics of Discipleship and Ethics of the Table of Duties

Before we consider the path Luther takes, we must consider carefully the task he set for himself and the manner in which he sought to think and to live, which is set forth already in the New Testament. No Christian discovers this for himself; it presents itself to the one who wants to be Christian.

With reference to the words of Jesus, the call to radical discipleship — with the expectation that one will leave everything, have no place to lay one's head, thus not even a house in which to spend the night — is described by New Testament scholars as a "radical call to wander."[80] This radical call to

---

78. What the Augsburg Confession, article 16, rejects (*BC*, 48-50), the "Schleitheimer Articles" (1527) affirm: *Der linke Flügel der Reformation, Glaubenszeugnisse der Täufer, Spiritualisten, Schwärmer und Antitrinitarier*, ed. Heinold Fast (Bremen: C. Schunemann, 1962), 60-71.

79. WA 18:112.33ff.; cf. LW 40:130 (*Against the Heavenly Prophets in the Matter of Images and Sacraments — Part One*, 1525). On Luther's understanding of the two or three paths, cf. chaps. 4.6 and 11.2 above.

80. Cf., e.g., Gerd Theissen, "Wanderradikalismus. Literatursoziologische Aspekte der Überlieferung von Worten Jesu im Urchristentum," in *Studien zur Soziologie des Urchristentums*, WUNT 19 (Tübingen: Mohr, 1979), 79-105 (= *ZThK* 70 [1973]: 245-72).

wander and the discipleship that was tied to it ceased to exist in later communities: it became "integrated into a middle class way of life" by adjusting itself to fit this world. Admonitions to husbands and wives, parents and children, masters and servants, detailing their relationships to one another, are found in the letters to the Colossians and the Ephesians; Martin Luther first named them; others still follow what he wrote and identify them in theological discussions as the Table of Duties. These admonitions — "Husbands, love your wives!"; "Fathers, do not provoke your children!" (Col. 3:18–4:1; Eph. 5:21–6:9), etc. — could be hung up as placards in the living room of the house, so that every member of the household could learn what they say and would know how life in the house was to be organized, how one was to interact with everyone else.[81] These admonitions have their sense, literally their place, in the home. For one who has no house, no dwelling, no possessions, no wife, and no children, they would play no role.

Some New Testament scholars have now come to the conclusion that life in discipleship, in radical wandering, cannot be reconciled, even today, with life in a household; one can take part in one or the other: either life within a household or the life of discipleship.

In light of this assessment, it is clear what Luther accomplished as an ethicist: he would not allow the alternative of household or discipleship to stand and thus pursued his own path of wandering along the mountain ridge. My view is that he got it right, both in terms of the subject itself and historically as well. For this reason the interpretation advocated by New Testament scholars, and the corresponding viewpoint of a social historian of someone of the caliber of Ernst Troeltsch,[82] is not on target.

Even the context of the words of the earthly Jesus does not suggest that one's task is to distinguish between house and discipleship. The same one who called some into discipleship, to leave house and family, sharpens the duties one has toward parents and teaches that there is to be no dissolution of marriage.

How do the two fit together? Or did Jesus contradict himself? This problem cannot be resolved easily if one considers Luke 14:26-27 and Mark 7:9-13 together. "Whoever comes to me and does not hate father and mother, wife and children, brothers and sisters, yes, even life itself, cannot be my disciple. Whoever does not carry the cross and follow me cannot be my disciple" (Luke

---

81. The concluding sentence of the Table of Duties in the Small Catechism (par. 15, in *BC*, 367) reads: "Ein jeder lern sein Lektion, / So wird es wohl im Hause stohn" [Let all their lessons learn with care, / So that the household well may fare].

82. Cf. Ernst Troeltsch, *The Social Teaching of the Christian Churches* (London: Allen and Unwin; New York: Macmillan, 1956), especially 745-52, 993-99.

14:26-27). That is the one side: discipleship in its most radical portrayal; "a life of radical wandering."

On the other side, Mark 7:9-13 states it most clearly: Moses said you should honor your father and your mother. Whoever curses father or mother should be put to death. But you — and now follows the impressive "Corban" saying of Jesus — when you rededicate elsewhere what you ought to give to your father and mother, giving it a new function in what is apparently a radical discipleship, when you want to give to God what you are responsible to give to your parents (and one could go on: what you are responsible to give your wife and children, brothers and sisters), then you are acting radically against the will of God.

When one compares the two passages cited from the words of Jesus, the task Luther held in tension as an ethicist is demonstrated: namely, to hold life in the household, in the world, in the world of work, family, and politics together with life in discipleship because of the call of Jesus Christ, which meant for Luther: based on obeying the first commandment, to fear God above all things, to love him and to trust him.

He undertakes his path of wandering along the mountain ridge when he distinguishes obedience to the first table of the Ten Commandments (commandments one to three) from obedience to the second table (commandments four to ten). If it deals with a matter of the first table, concerned with the validity of the first commandment, then everything is to be abandoned and everything is to be suffered: "And take they our life, Goods, fame, child, and wife, Though these all be gone!"[83] Who would not be deeply upset just by singing these words from the hymn "A Mighty Fortress Is Our God" — to such an extent that one might dare not to sing along, upset by its radical call, based on such a message — such an almost sinister faith and trust in God alone and his Word, which says: and take they our life, goods, fame, child, and wife, though these all be gone; but they cannot take God and his promise away!

We give attention to a longer passage from Luther's sermon that is the source for the disputation, so that we can better understand how he wanders along that mountain ridge.

> Come and follow me. . . . If we could achieve the kingdom of heaven by throwing away money and goods, it would not last long . . . until no one

---

83. *LSB*, #656, 4. Cf. the circular disputation on the three hierarchies, thesis 21 (WA 39II:40.16f.; 1539), and also the lecture on the psalms of ascent (1532-33) in WA 40III:62f., especially the connection between the way God reveals himself (62.4f.) to the second table of the Decalogue (62.12-14; 63.4-6).

would have anything to eat or drink. Christ did not do that. He did not sell everything, but he ate and drank and had clothes. And he took what was provided for him. Judas kept the money sack; he also gave [money] to the poor. And they had bread for times of need. If the viewpoint of Jesus matched that of what Saint Francis dreams, then one would have to say: . . . If one should sell everything, why do you keep everything: For this reason Paul was someone who worked with his hands, a carpet maker. He went to those who were masters of his trade, to their quarters, and earned his bread with [his own] hands. That would have been idle foolishness [on Paul's part, if Francis was right]. For this reason, the meaning of this commandment [come and follow after me!] is to be understood spiritually . . . : The heart should be distinguished from material goods — so that you pay even closer attention to God . . . and, if it is necessary, not only that you sell everything, but . . . on his behalf that you relinquish your body and life. . . .

"How?" someone will now say. "Shall I hang myself on a tree? Or shall I stick myself in the throat with a knife and commit suicide?" No, you are to value your life highly. But when [either] God is to be renounced, who gave you life, or instead your life is to be taken, then you should renounce life. For I ought to love nothing so much as God and should say: Before I will renounce my God, I would sooner relinquish my body and life.

[Thus one ought to understand the word] that Christ speaks concerning the correct . . . fulfillment of the commandments of God. . . . [But] otherwise marriage partners ought to stay together; father and mother ought to raise their children and ought not to go apart from one another. But if a tyrant would come and would say: Renounce God and his Word or else let everything you have be taken, or if a father and mother would try to keep their children from salvation, then one should let all be given over to the tyrant, [then one ought] to let all be given to the father and mother . . . so that one continues to have God's . . . grace and can say: "God gave me a father and mother, money and nourishment; if I need to relinquish it because of God's will, let it be gone!" But if such pressure is not put on you, you can stay with wife and child, father and mother, with your possessions, and you are not forced to renounce God, then certainly God does not begrudge you wife, child, goods, and even your life. Then I should stay by my wife and the two of us remain one flesh. [Then we should live in the world] and be subject to the authorities. Then I should not go and take a knife and stab myself in the throat. That would be a false understanding. But [only] when the matter involves matters concerning God should one leave father, mother, brother, sister.[84]

84. WA 47:353.10–354.15 (Matt. 18–24 interpreted in sermons).

This is what Luther says in the sermon. And in the corresponding theses, when distinguishing the first table of the Ten Commandments from the second, he speaks about what Jesus' call to discipleship requires, that

> everything is to be abandoned and to be sold in regard to the first table, the confession, the public matters connected with faith. As regards the first table [I am the Lord, your God; you should have no other gods besides me!], one must namely hold on to that costly pearl of the kingdom of heaven and buy it, whereas everything else is to be sold and everything is to be left behind and everything is to be lost. Everything that you rightfully have and possess as regards the second table of the law for this life is joyfully to be given up for the sake of the first table, which means for the sake of eternal life. But if it does not involve the first table and the confession to God, everything is to be acquired, held, distributed, and managed. For we are called to obey the second table, which means according to a godly and natural right to care for the body and this life, to nourish, to protect, and to manage it. If someone, beyond the scope of the first table or the confession, does not care for his own body, he then denies the faith and is worse than an unbeliever. Christ says: What God has joined together, man must not separate. That means: If someone in this case abandons his own family and sells what he owns, he sins at the same time beyond what involves the second table and goes against the first as well.[85]

He does not obey God. Everything is to be abandoned; everything is to be kept — depending on which direction one is looking. This dialectic is hard to conceptualize and still more difficult to live out. Yet it provides a most helpful orientation by going to the heart of the matter about the relationship between Christian faith and life.

13.4.4. Appropriate Evangelical Poverty

In the sermon that was preached before the theses were developed, the dialectical relationship between letting go and holding on was explicated by using the example of money and goods. The question was: What does Christ mean when he says that a rich man cannot enter the kingdom of heaven? The rich man, who cannot come into the kingdom of heaven, does not seek God because he places his trust in his money and goods.[86] Christ calls him "a godless

---

85. WA 39II:40.16-31 ("Von den drei Hierarchien," theses 21-27).
86. Cf. WA 47:355.36f. (Matt. 18–24 interpreted in sermons).

person, for whom a penny is of more value than anything else. He holds onto that as his idol and lord, honors and venerates it, as all the greedy bellies do, who would rather let a poor person die of hunger than to give him a single penny."[87] The rich man who does not come into the kingdom of God is the rich man who serves mammon. Thus, in the Gospel, the person is not called rich who has lots of money and goods, but only the one who *relies on* his money and property. In this regard, Luther refers to Psalm 62:10: "If riches increase, do not set your heart on them! For riches are a gift from God. One ought not to throw them away, but one should thank God for them and use them in a Christian manner."[88] If one could actually use all one's money and property, fields and grain, house and home as God's gift and could give them to others, then things would not be any problem for us. And if we could enjoy all our property in this way, it would be good. But we make it into an idol, place our trust in the creature and not in the Creator, and therefore do not come into the kingdom of heaven. "It is impossible that God and mammon are in the heart of man at the same time. If God is there, the idol must go wander; if you wish to be saved, you are to have only one God. That is what the first commandment demands."[89]

It is surprising what great importance Luther attaches, not only in this sermon but also in many other sermons, to greed.[90] For him, greed is simply unnatural[91] — sin, which shows that the human being secludes himself and lives an unthankful life, because he does not give to others what he has received and thus interrupts the process of receiving and giving, cuts himself off from the course of life. Luther sees greed as the move toward making decisions for oneself, curving in on oneself, which ends up in demonic depths; "the devil commands the people to do this."[92] In greed the human being, by hardening himself into a position of being unthankful, turns away from his Creator, closes in upon himself, and closes his ear, his heart, and his hand at the same time toward the neighbor. That is the exact opposite of that type of possessing without which human existence cannot continue and is against what leads Paul to ask the question that Luther applies appropriately to the situation: "What do you have that you did not receive?" (1 Cor. 4:7).

87. WA 47:355.37-40.

88. WA 47:356.27-29. On the following, cf. WA 47:356.37–357.1.

89. WA 47:357.2-5.

90. Cf. chap. 5.2 above. On the subject as a whole, cf. Ricardo Rieth, *"Habsucht" bei Martin Luther. Ökonomisches und theologisches Denken, Tradition und soziale Wirklichkeit in der Reformation* (Weimar: Böhlau Verlag, 1996).

91. Cf. WA 47:357.12 (Matt. 18–24 interpreted in sermons).

92. WA 47:357.19f.

To understand possessions in this way means to live in poverty in the sense that is appropriate to the gospel. What do you have that you did not receive? This question deserves our attention, indeed that our heart might be changed — and along with it our existence and possessions, together with the distribution of the goods we have on this earth.

13.4.5. Appropriate Evangelical Chastity

Just as greed is a distorted relationship with that which one needs for this life, thus with a distortion of the goods that are used in service for life and to promote life, in the same way unchastity is the distorted relationship in sexual matters, a distorted relationship as regards what God has planted within us and what God judged to be very good in his creation. And just as the appropriate poverty is not some type of strained and hypocritical denial of all possessions, the right type of chastity is not a strained and hypocritical denial of sexual relations, but is its proper use — in mutual love and honorable recognition.

The truth about the chastity vow taken by monks was experienced by Luther in his praise of marriage, and was preached and taught to further generations by means of the catechism: "We should fear and love God so that we lead chaste and decent lives in words and deeds and each one loves and honors his spouse."[93] One ought to know that he or she has been called by God in this way — just as is true for the man who is called to refrain from marriage by means of a free decision who, as Luther says, "has within himself the desire," "to have more freedom for his profession,"[94] and thus because of one's service. The same holds true for the single and the married: you are called to freedom!

13.4.6. Appropriate Evangelical Obedience

The call to freedom determines the truth concerning obedience as well. If the monk follows the *regula* "not because of his own decision" but "because of the judgment and command of another person," obeying him and "not his own desires,"[95] Luther said, along with Karl Marx, that the monks and "clerics

93. Exposition of the sixth commandment (*BSLK* 509.1-5; cf. SC I, 12, in *BC*, 353).
94. WA 47:337.11f. (Matt. 18–24 interpreted in sermons).
95. *Regula sancti Benedicti*, cap. 5, 12 (CSEL 75:36).

Toni Zenz, "The Listener"
Bronze, 1957, Pax-Christi Church, Essen, Germany

have turned into the laity, because he has turned the laity into clerics";[96] the truth of obedience applies to everyone. Luther brings the truth of the monk's vow of obedience, which is hidden in darkness, to light. The human being can only be considered a person who listens, is only a human being when he is completely an ear — as the sculpture by Toni Zenz gives one opportunity to see and to consider.

The human being is thus human in that he is addressed. When listening, he can answer and speak for himself, but he also must answer; he must respond on his own. As one who hears he is free — admittedly not completely spontaneously, but also not completely as one who receives, but as both at the same time: between having something presented and using it for oneself, receiving and transferring, authority and critique.[97]

In this sense obedience is the basic structure of our relationship with one another, our ability to communicate, our social structure, the political existence with one another that goes all the way to shape world domestic policy. That the travel along the mountain ridge, which was discussed earlier, is particularly difficult is clear to everyone. But there is no alternative. Discipleship takes place in the world's house; if it is taken out of this house, it becomes enthusiastic and monkish. Stated the other way, the call to discipleship for the Christian — with direct appeal to Luther — protects one from acclimating to the world's house in self-satisfaction.

To summarize: Luther's accomplishment as an ethicist lies in the fact that he made the distorted truth of the monk's vow concerning poverty, chastity, and obedience to become something that could play its proper role. He articulated this truth in the form of the disputation, the sermon, and the catechism. He related, with utter clarity, the relationship between the first table of the Ten Commandments and the second and showed how the second table was related to the first — particularly impressively in the Small Catechism in which, as was shown earlier, the explanation of each individual commandment was always related to the first commandment: "We should fear and love God, so that we . . ." The first commandment, in the strict sense, "You shall have no other gods besides me," is not a commandment in and of itself, but is the flip side of the pure gospel, which states the promise as it frees one from self-glorification and assures one in the midst of doubt: "I am the Lord, your God!"

96. Karl Marx, *Critique of Hegel's "Philosophy of Right,"* trans. Annette Jolin and Joseph O. Malley (Cambridge: At the University Press, 1970), 138.

97. Cf. chap. 4.1 above.

This promise, in which the triune God gives himself, is what according to Luther gives a foundation for a Christian ethos and empowers one to live the life of one who has been freed — in the tension and yet in the intertwined relationship between the ethos of the Table of Duties and the ethos of discipleship.[98]

98. On the entire chapter, cf. Oswald Bayer, "Luther's Ethics as Pastoral Care," *Lutheran Quarterly* 4 (Summer 1990); Bayer, *Freedom in Response: Lutheran Ethics; Sources and Controversies* (Oxford: Oxford University Press, 2007), 119-37.

Chapter 14 Spiritual and Temporal Rule:
God's Two Realms

One, which makes pious, the other,
which creates external peace and hinders evil deeds.
Neither is sufficient in the world without the other.

14.1. Pastoral Care Ethics

If "ethics" is understood as "theory about how to conduct one's life,"[1] then a situation that Luther identifies as foundational is all too easily hidden: sin, under whose auspices human life in community takes place. Luther is cognizant of sin in everything that he writes, in which human beings turn away from their status as creature and turn to glorification of the self. Thus, in regard to his viewpoints concerning ethical questions — and he never dodges a topic — he does not formulate a general theory but seeks to teach the conscience in each concrete situation. "In each case, I must give guidance to the poor, bewildered conscience."[2] For him the issue is not about values-neutral observations and descriptions of human behavior and action, according to which one assumes that the conscience is already somewhat developed and a final decision is left to the private individual. Luther's ethical efforts — as his theology in general — is offered as pastoral care. It applies to the entire person as a physical being and within the overall framework of participation in society — concentrating on the person's conscience, as it is formed and shaped by God's Word in law and gospel.

Luther often responds to someone as a result of a request that was sent to him — as in the document titled *Whether Soldiers, Too, Can Be Saved,*[3] from 1526; he makes clear that he responds to the request of someone who is asking

1. Cf., for example, Trutz Rendtorff, *Ethik. Grundelemente, Methodologie und Konkretionen einer ethischen Theologie,* vol. 1 (Stuttgart, Berlin, Cologne, and Mainz: Kohlhammer, 1980), 11.
2. WA 10:275.9 ("Sermon vom ehelichen Leben," 1522).
3. WA 19:623-662; cf. *LW* 46:93-137.

for instruction for his conscience: "So that now, as much as is possible for us to advise the weak, despairing and doubting soul and so that the wanton ones can get better instruction," so he writes to an electoral field commander, the knight Assa from Kram, "I have consented to answer your request and have sent this little book."[4] Many of Luther's writings on ethical topics grew out of sermons and were thus directed from the outset toward a specific situation — so also the treatise on temporal authority, which is particularly insightful with respect to the theme of this chapter.

Luther's ethical instructions, as became apparent already in the description of his teaching about the three estates[5] and his understanding of "good works,"[6] are to be understood on the basis of the first commandment and thus to be assessed on the basis of the God who reveals himself and awakens and demands faith. The teaching about the two realms — or as it is often inaccurately called, teaching about the two kingdoms — can be understood appropriately only within this overall framework as well.

To be sure, the discussion about the "two kingdoms" as the identifying characteristic for his treatment is not completely unjustified, since Luther himself sometimes uses this terminology and moves within the Augustinian tradition and its teaching about the "two *civitates*," the city[7] of God or heaven and the earthly or bedeviled city. But one must take note that Luther turns Augustine's terminology into something dynamic: Luther does not speak in the main about two separated *regions*,[8] but rather about God's two *realms*.[9] Whereas Au-

---

4. WA 19:623.20-22; cf. *LW* 46:93.

5. Cf. chap. 6 above.

6. Cf. chap. 13 above.

7. Ulrich Duchrow, *Christenheit und Weltverantwortung. Traditionsgeschichte und systematische Struktur der Zweireichelehre* (Stuttgart: E. Klett, 1970), translates it as *Herrschaftsverband* (ruling alliance) so as to preserve the theological connections and to avoid equivocations with the actually existing state (245f.). Augustine himself uses the distinction to orient the biblical typology that contrasts "Jerusalem" (Pss. 46 and 48; Rev. 21–22) and "Babylon" (Rev. 17–18); *civitas* must then be translated first as "city."

8. Johannes Heckel, *Im Irrgarten der Zwei-Reiche-Lehre Luthers* (Munich: Kaiser, 1957), takes his point of departure from Augustine's idea of kingdoms and views Luther's reference to "regiments" [Trans.: "realms" in this translation] as derived from it. Unlike Paul Althaus (*Die Ethik Martin Luthers* [Gütersloh: Gütersloher Verlagshaus, 1965], 56-59), he stresses, to the exclusion of all else, that the Christian is in no way directly subject in the temporal realm (with *LW* 45:89, *Temporal Authority: To What Extent It Should Be Obeyed*), but only indirectly — for the sake of love. Thus, for Heckel the temporal realm becomes inauthentic, depraved; from the eschatological perspective he recognizes only one true realm of Christ — and thus tends to agree with Barth — whereas he treats earthly rule more as a juridical than a theological concept.

9. Note well: "of God"; the temporal realm is also the realm *of God*. The difference consists only in the manner in which he exercises his rule.

gustine uses a theology of history to describe two "cities," each of which has different individuals and groups of individuals, Luther maintains that every Christian takes part in both governing units; the differentiation between the two realms goes at the same time right through each Christian person.[10]

14.2. History of Application, Misunderstandings, and Contrasting Positions

A misunderstanding that is particularly connected with the terminology "two-kingdoms doctrine" originated at the beginning of the last century, as advocated particularly by Friedrich Naumann. It says that Luther divided the world into two static regions, two spheres: the one, inner and spiritual, is a matter for the conscience that is open to the sight of God; the other is external and temporal, which was supposedly surrendered by Luther to "making up its own laws," though it needs the inner conscience to give it balance.[11] This criticism, advanced primarily by philosophers such as Max Scheler[12] and Herbert Marcuse,[13] was also suggested by Karl Barth and other Reformed theologians; it found support in the mistaken judgments of Lutheran theologians during the time of the Weimar Republic and National Socialism. This view simply abandoned the temporal sphere in general to its own devices or else identified human law directly with the will of God.[14]

The Reformed side spoke out in opposition with its teaching about the "kingly rule of Christ": no realm is removed from the rule of Christ, neither the spiritual nor the temporal. The second thesis of the Barmen Theological Declaration of 1934 maintains that Christ is not only God's promise but, "with the same earnestness," is also God's "powerful claim on our entire life," which frees us from the "godless bonds of this world." Thus what is to be re-

10. Cf. Heinrich Bornkamm, *Luther's Doctrine of the Two Kingdoms*, trans. Karl H. Hertz (Philadelphia: Fortress, 1966).

11. Friedrich Naumann, *Briefe über Religion*, 3rd ed. (Berlin: Buchverlag der "Hilfe," 1904), especially the twenty-sixth letter, 82.

12. Max Scheler, *Von zwei deutschen Krankheiten, Gesammelte Werke*, vol. 6, 2nd ed. (Bern: Bouvier, 1963), 204-19.

13. Cf. Oswald Bayer, "Marcuses Kritik an Luthers Freiheitsbegriff," in Bayer, *Leibliches Wort. Reformation und Neuzeit im Konflikt* (Tübingen: Mohr-Siebeck, 1992), 151-75.

14. Thus the "Ansbacher Ratschlag" of June 11, 1934, essentially set down by Werner Elert (Kurt Dietrich Schmidt, ed., *Die Bekenntnisse und grundsätzliche Äußerungen zur Kirchenfrage*, vol. 2, *Das Jahr 1934* [Gottingen: Vandenhoeck & Ruprecht, 1935], 102-4), which accuses the Barmen Theological Declaration of antinomianism, and directly affirms the German government of that period.

jected is "the false teaching that there are certain areas of life where we are not under Jesus Christ, but under other lords,"[15] in which one is thus to respect the right of the state to pass its own laws independently.[16] A counterbalance to this second thesis is contained in the fifth thesis, of course, in which the teaching about the two realms is accorded its proper place — which was necessary to gain the support of the Lutherans who participated in the Barmen Confessional Synod and was likewise of decisive importance: "Scripture tells us that the state, using every possible measure of human insight and human capacity and according to divine institution, in the world that is not yet redeemed and in which the church also exists, is charged with providing for justice and peace under threat and the use of force."[17] The false teaching is what is advocated by a totalitarian state and by a church that accepts assignments dictated by the state.

With respect to the way Luther's distinction between the two realms affected history, it ought not to be ignored that his emergency measure, asking the lord of a territory to serve as an "emergency bishop," and the resulting expression of church government in which the sovereigns governed the church led to what at times was a fatal association between throne and altar.[18] It was only in 1918 that the rule of sovereigns in the church came to an end; until then, to take one example, the Prussian king was the head of "his" church.

A prominent example of how Luther's teaching about two realms was used to *criticize* authority and legitimized opposition against a totalitarian regime is offered by the document entitled *Kirkens Grunn* (1942),[19] which origi-

15. Alfred Burgsmüller and Rudolf Weth, eds., *Die Barmer Theologische Erklärung. Einführung und Dokumentation,* 6th ed. (Neukirchen-Vluyn: Neukirchener Verlag, 1998), 35. Most editions of the *Evangelisches Gesangbuch* (evangelical hymnal) contain the Barmen Declaration (Württemberg: no. 836).

16. Concerning the problem, cf. Ahti Hakamies, *"Eigengesetzlichkeit" der natürlichen Ordnungen als Grundproblem der neueren Lutherdeutung. Studien zur Geschichte und Problematik der Zwei-Reiche-Lehre Luthers* (Witten: Luther Verlag, 1971). In the current debate it is helpful to distinguish between relative and absolute autonomy.

17. Burgsmüller and Weth, *Die Barmer Theologische Erklärung,* 38.

18. But we should not refrain from mentioning that the Reformed court preachers in Prussia shared most vigorously in this development, whereas many Lutheran theologians (not the least of whom was Paul Gerhardt) were opposed again and again to the absolutism of the prince.

19. In *Norwegische Kirchendokumente. Aus den Jahren des Kampfes zwischen Kirche und weltlicher Macht 1941-1943,* ed. Laure Wyss, 2nd ed. (Zürich: Evangelisches Verlag, 1946), 29-36. In addition, cf. Torleiv Austad, "Der Grund der Kirche. Eine Bekenntniserklärung der norwegischen Kirche von 1942," in *Die öffentliche Verantwortung der Evangelisch-Lutherischen Kirche in einer Bekenntnissituation,* ed. Joachim Heubach, Veröffentlichungen der Luther-Akademie Ratzeburg, vol. 7 (Erlangen, 1984), 70-84.

nated in the Norwegian church dispute. Through it, the Oslo bishop Eivind Berggrav prevented the integration of the Norwegian church into the National Socialist system during the German occupation.[20]

This teaching had an impact on history also for the "left wing" of the Reformation. Just as some "Enthusiasts" at the time of Luther advocated a spiritualistic and rigoristic divine state, which led to, among other things, the catastrophe of the Münster Anabaptist Kingdom in 1534-35, others, including the Anabaptists, Mennonites, and other "dissenters," followed in the seventeenth and eighteenth centuries and among the established church bodies that called for a strict separation between the two realms and brought about — first in America and now also in Europe — the present separation of state and church, as a basic right of religious freedom and neutrality of the state with respect to its worldview.[21]

14.3. "Temporal Authority: To What Extent It Should Be Obeyed"

Luther's foundational writing on the theme, which comes from the Weimar sermon before the electoral household, carries the title *Temporal Authority: To What Extent It Should Be Obeyed.*[22] It was occasioned by correspondence with Johann von Schwarzenberg and the question of Duke Johann of Elec-

---

20. Cf. especially Eivind Berggrav, "Wenn der Kutscher trunken ist. Luther über die Pflicht zum Ungehorsam gegenüber der Obrigkeit (1941)," in *Widerstandsrecht,* ed. Arthur Kaufmann, WdF 173 (Darmstadt: Wissenschaftliche Buchgesellschaft, 1972), 135-51; Berggrav, "Staat und Kirche in lutherischer Sicht," in *Offizieller Bericht der Zweiten Vollversammlung des Lutherischen Weltbundes* (Hannover: Lutherhaus Verlag, 1952), 78-86. Further, cf. Torleiv Austad, "Die Lehre von den zwei Regimenten im norwegischen Kichenkampf 1940-1945," in *Zwei Reiche und Regimente. Ideologie oder evangelische Orientierung?* ed. Ulrich Duchrow (Gütersloh: Gütersloher Verlagshaus, 1977), 87-96.

21. In *Die Menschenrechte im Spiegel der reformatorischen Theologie* (Heidelberg: C. Winter, 1987), included in his *Gesammelte Schriften,* ed. Klaus Schlaich (Tübingen: Mohr, 1989), 2:1122-93, Martin Heckel persuasively argues against the thesis of Georg Jellinek, *Die Erklärung der Menschen- und Bürgerrechte* (1895), who traced religious freedom directly and exclusively to the English collateral wing of the Reformation. Heckel shows that the current distinction between religion and politics in essence goes back to Luther as well.

22. WA 11:245-281 (1523); cf. *LW* 45:81-129. Transcripts of only the third and fourth sermons that he preached at Weimar on October 24 and 25, 1522, were available (WA 10III:37-85). When Luther turned his attention to writing about the issue of temporal authority, he used these sermons, as best as he could remember them (cf. *LW* 45:77-80). On the correspondence with Johann von Schwarzenberg: Volker Mantey, *Zwei Schwerter — Zwei Reiche. Martin Luthers Zwei-Reiche-Lehre vor ihrem spätmittelalterlichen Hintergrund* (Tübingen, 2005), 235-45.

toral Saxony, who asked Luther to respond to the question of a spiritual responsibility for temporal power. Also, Duke George of Saxony, in the neighboring territory, just a few months before, had forbidden the dissemination of the New Testament that Luther translated and published — which was the real reason for this treatise. Even though it must be understood in light of the circumstances of that actual situation, as is true of every one of Luther's writings, he never really revised it significantly but used its framework to make wide-ranging observations on political ethics — admittedly not without making adjustments.[23]

a. In the first part, Luther begins with the question about how the Sermon on the Mount, with its call for *renouncing the use of force,* relates to those biblical texts that call for subordination under *temporal authority.* With regard to the biblical basis for temporal rule, he refers particularly to 1 Peter 2:13-14 and Romans 13:1-7: "For the Lord's sake accept the authority of every human institution, whether of the emperor as supreme, or of governors, as sent by him to punish those who do wrong and to praise those who do right." "Let every person be subject to the governing authorities; for there is no authority except from God, and those authorities that exist have been instituted by God." In addition to this, passages are cited such as Genesis 4:14-15 (Cain's fear that he will be punished for the murder he committed) and Genesis 9:6 (whoever sheds blood, his blood shall be shed as well); passages from the Covenant Code in Exodus; and finally Luke 3:14, where the Baptist allows the soldiers to remain in their calling as long as they do not act unjustly. In tension with this stands the fifth antithesis in the Sermon on the Mount (Matt. 5:38-40): "You have heard that it was said [Exod. 21:24], 'An eye for an eye and a tooth for a tooth.' But I say to you, Do not resist an evildoer. But if anyone strikes you on the right cheek, turn the other also; and if anyone wants to sue you and take your coat, give your cloak as well." Further passages in this vein are Romans 12:19, Matthew 5:44, and 1 Peter 3:9.

Luther was presented with what had been offered earlier as a way to resolve this issue: the two-level ethics, of "commandments" and "evangelical counsels" *(praecepta* and *consilia evangelica):*[24] according to this view, the "commandments" are applicable to all, whereas the "evangelical counsels" — thus the alleged "special" ethics of the gospel — are applicable only to those who are mature. Luther rejects this distinction, because in his view it has no basis in Scripture. The Sermon on the Mount, as an intensification of the Ten

23. Cf. nn. 27 and 50 below.
24. Cf. chap. 13.1 above.

Commandments, is to apply to *all* Christians, just as do the Ten Commandments themselves.[25]

What seems to stand in contradiction — renunciation of power (Sermon on the Mount) and the state's use of its monopoly of power (Rom. 13:1-7) — is kept together by Luther, even though in tension: he does not find any distinction within the church — between mature and less mature Christians — but does find such a distinction to be applicable to humanity in general: Christians are spiritual people, who as such do not need to be under temporal authority.[26] But since all people are not Christian, the temporal authority is still necessary.[27]

The two realms do not exist in contradiction to one another; both are necessary: "One makes a person pious, the other creates external peace and hinders evil actions. Neither is sufficient in the world without the other";[28] renunciation of all power is "actually" applicable only to the "beloved Christians."[29] "But since a true Christian on earth lives for and serves not just himself, but his neighbor, he acts according to the nature of his spirit to do what he does not have to do but to do what is helpful and necessary for his neighbor."[30] This can go to the point, according to Luther, that the Christian ought to be ready to be "hangman, jailer, judge" if one is not otherwise available.[31] In service to the neighbor and for the general welfare, the Christian is a "person in an office" and, as such, must threaten and act with force when necessary; but for himself, as a "Christian person," he ought to be ready to suffer everything — such as to refrain from vengeance and also to forgo the chance to sue for his own rights.[32]

If the "sword" — which means the just, orderly use of power — needs to be used in regard to the life of the neighbor and because of public order, then

---

25. The subject is dealt with more precisely in 14.4.

26. In the treatise on temporal authority Luther does not deal with the Christian as *simul peccator.* Cf. Volker Stümke, "Einen Räuber darf, einen Werwolf muss man töten. Zur Sozialethik Luthers in der Zirkulardisputation von 1539," in *Subjektiver Geist. Reflexion und Erfahrung im Glauben,* ed. Klaus-Michael Kodalle and Anne M. Steinmeier, Festschrift for Traugott Koch (Würzburg: Königshausen und Neumann, 2002), 207-28, here 225 n. 76.

27. In the treatise on temporal authority of 1523, Luther still interprets the temporal realm exclusively in terms of a compulsory order, as an order that is necessary to limit sin. Later, especially in the teaching about the three estates, he shows appreciation for the political dimension within the context of the household as an order of creation within the divine economy (cf. chap. 6.1 and chap. 3.2 above).

28. WA 11:252.12-14; cf. *LW* 45:92.

29. WA 11:252.26; cf. *LW* 45:92.

30. WA 11:253.23-26; cf. *LW* 45:94.

31. WA 11:255.1; cf. *LW* 45:95.

32. WA 11:259.7-16; cf. *LW* 45:101.

Luther can also describe participation in the temporal authority of God as "divine service."[33] The distinction of the two realms cuts right through the middle of the individual Christian's life — more or less distinctively, since not everyone assumes temporal responsibilities in the same way.[34] Luther explained that Jesus did not exercise the office of the sword because that was not part of his particular office, even though it was not essentially prohibited. To be sure: one must have a rare and particular grace to exercise the office of the sword as a Christian; Luther expects that the danger of misuse is quite high here.

b. In the second part Luther discusses "how far temporal authority extends."[35] He comes to the conclusion that the power of the state in fact includes having the right to expect obedience, but only to a certain limit. That this is the "chief point"[36] of what he writes can be seen in the complete title of the document: *Temporal Authority: **To What Extent It Should Be Obeyed**.*[37] The power of the princes and temporal rulers extends only as far as the physical aspects of life. By contrast, concerning faith and its foundation in the Word of God, it has no power. From this Luther developed the idea of the right of passive resistance in the form of a public protest. Duke George had no appropriate authority to demand that his subjects hand over their New Testaments, which he actually did demand; this controversy is spiritual and can therefore be waged only by spiritual means — with the Word.[38] "Because the way he believes or does not believe is upon the conscience of each individual, and because there is no detriment thereby to the temporal authorities, they should also be at peace and take care of their own responsibilities, and let one believe this way or that, as one can and desires, and oppress no one by

33. WA 11:258.1-3; 260.32-35; cf. *LW* 45:100; 45:103. By "sword" Luther understands "all that pertains to the secular rule, all secular rights and laws, customs and habits": *LW* 20:172 (*Lectures on Zechariah*, German, 1527). Luther argues in analogous fashion in his exposition of the prohibition against oaths (*LW* 20:172), but goes a little beyond his exegetical goal as he make systematizing statements, as Albrecht Beutel correctly notes in "Biblischer Text und theologische Theoriebildung in Luthers Schrift 'Von weltlicher Obrigkeit, wie weit man ihr Gehorsam schuldig sei' (1523)," in *Biblischer Text und theologische Theoriebildung*, ed. Stephan Chapman, Christine Helmer, and Christof Landmesser (Neukirchen-Vluyn: Neukirchener Verlag, 2001), 77-104.

34. *LW* 45:101.

35. WA 11:261.26; cf. *LW* 45:104.

36. WA 11:261.27; cf. *LW* 45:104.

37. Emphasis added.

38. So also Luther's vote on questions of associating with heretics (*LW* 45:114-15), from which he unfortunately deviated in part later on. On the variety of ways that Reformation theologians and princes dealt with the problem of heretics, cf. Paul Wappler, *Die Stellung Kursachsens und des Landgrafen Philipp von Hessen zur Täuferbewegung*, Reformationsgeschichtliche Studien und Texte 13/14 (Münster: Aschendorff, 1910).

force. For faith is a free activity, concerning which no one can force an-other."[39] Luther cites Romans 13:7, from the "chapter on authority," to clarify the *limitation* that is placed on responsibilities to the state: "Pay to all what is due them — taxes to whom taxes are due, revenue to whom revenue is due, respect to whom respect is due, honor to whom honor is due."[40] Luther offers another significant passage that refers to the limits of the state's power when he cites Matthew 22:21 ("Give therefore to the emperor the things that are the emperor's, and to God the things that are God's"); but his chief supporting text is contained in the famous *clausula Petri* from Acts 5:29: "We must obey God rather than any human authority." Whoever subordinates himself to the authority of the duke in matters of the Bible denies the authority of God and is no Christian.[41]

c. Finally, in the third section of this document, Luther offers a more specific treatment to explain the relationship: *instruction for the heart and the conscience of princes,* a "mirror for the prince." At this point he relativizes what he says about the way one is compelled to obey authority when he obligates the prince to be competent and responsible. Luther does not question temporal authority in any significant sense — since chaos would otherwise threaten — but such authority does damage to itself and to others if it acts in an inappropriate manner. If a Christian happens to be a ruler, then this "strange bird"[42] ought to trust God, rule with thoughtfulness and with reason, avoid war and guarantee a just peace, and above all act with propriety, fairness (ἐπιείκεια),[43] and insight.

What is most noteworthy is that all of these — except for fearing God — describe prudent behavior for every human being, and are thus not actions unique to Christians. Similar to Romans 12:1-2, a Magna Carta of Christian ethics, which uses terms common to the way the Greeks taught virtues, Luther accentuates fairness and insight and emphasizes healthy human reason. He expects that such reason will go beyond an exaggerated demand to be holy or a casuistic way of applying justice: *summum ius, summa iniuria.*[44] "I say this so

39. WA 11:264.16-20; cf. *LW* 45:108.
40. Rom. 13:7 NRSV.
41. Cf. *LW* 45:111-12.
42. WA 11:267.30f.; cf. *LW* 45:113.
43. Cf. Althaus, *Die Ethik Martin Luthers,* 113f., 139f. Cf. WA 19:632.8-24 (Ob Kriegsleute auch in seligem Stande sein können; 1526) and WA 47:365.28f. (sermons on Matthew 18–24, 1537-40): "ἐπιείκεια means that one can close one's eyes to and does not always deal in the harshest way, puts up with, endures.
44. "Strictest law, greatest injustice" (cf. WA 17II:92.11: Rom. 13:8ff., the Epistle for the fourth Sunday after Epiphany, a *Fastenpostille,* 1525; *LW* 46:100, *Whether Soldiers, Too, Can Be Saved).*

that no one thinks it is enough, and sufficiently worthy, if one follows justice and juridical recommendations as prescribed. There is more to it"[45] — namely, the fairness that has been mentioned, the ἐπιείκεια: Solomonic wisdom, being able to feel with one's fingertips, being able to measure with one's eyes.

In summary: God rules in the temporal as well as in the spiritual arena; both are his, and both types of authority belong to him alone. But the art and manner of the way they are exercised are different for each. In the *temporal* arena God rules through "police [i.e., polity, through the justly ordered state] and temporal authority," as formulated briefly and succinctly in the Augsburg Confession, article 16:[46] "in such estates Christian love and appropriate good works are to be practiced by each one according to his calling."[47] As in the treatise on temporal authority, Acts 5:29 offers the criterion here for setting the limit for the authority in the realm of the power exercised by humans in the world. In the *spiritual* realm, by contrast, the basic concept applies: *sine vi humana, sed verbo* — "not by human power, but by means of the Word of God alone," as this is articulated in the famous phrase from the Augsburg Confession, article 28.[48]

14.4. A Person Who Is a Christian and a Person Who Holds an Office

Concerning the question about the exact way to demarcate the boundary between being "a person who is a Christian" and "a person who holds an office," Luther offers his opinion in different ways. In the treatise about temporal authority from 1523, Luther leans in the direction of a "martyr ethic": the Christian ought to be ready to suffer in his own person — even if it would result in burdens for his family. Injustice is to be endured with humility, because God's hidden rule can be experienced therein.[49] But one must ask Luther whether the existence of a "Christian person" can ever take place apart from that of "a

---

45. WA 11:272.22-24; cf. *LW* 45:119.

46. *BSLK* 70.9; cf. CA XVI, German text, in *BC*, 48.

47. *BSLK* 71.17-20; cf. CA XVI, German text, in *BC*, 50.

48. *BSLK* 124.9.4f.; cf. CA XXVIII, 21, in *BC*, 95. Cf. *LW* 20:172 (cf. n. 33 above): "By the sword, however, I understand all that pertains to the secular rule. . . . By the Word I understand all that pertains to the spiritual rule."

49. Cf. the scandalous fourth stanza from "Ein feste Burg," cited above (chap. 13, n. 83), in *EG*, #362: "Nehmen sie den Leib, Gut, Ehr, Kind und Weib: lass fahren dahin, sie haben's kein Gewinn, das Reich muss uns doch bleiben" [Literally: "Let them take the body, goods, honor, child, wife: let all be gone; they have not won a thing, the kingdom must remain ours"].

person who holds an office," since his concept of office is so wide-ranging; to take one example, it would even include being a parent. But a good point is certainly being made when one distinguishes between a "person who is a Christian" and a "person who is an officeholder" with respect to one's calling in life and interpersonal relationships; I ought no longer to seek justification for my existence in these relationships. This presents difficulties only when one must decide if one has to act as a "person who is a Christian" or as a "person who holds an office."

In his disputation *Concerning the Three Hierarchies* of 1539, which has been examined already in connection with the three estates, Luther changed his opinion:[50] he was also willing now to allow the Christian to protect himself and to defend himself when necessary — and that by using theological argumentation. He plays this out by using the example of an attack in a robbery, in which it is the responsibility of the authorities to act against evil; the Christian who is subject to them has to act against evil as well. Later in Luther's life, it gradually became clearer to him that categorical suffering could also become flight from the world and that it would thus correspond to the ideal of the mendicant friar, which could never be attained; true Christian living is engaged in a battle for order in the tumult of the world as it seeks to benefit life.[51]

14.5. Luther's Exposition of the Sermon on the Mount

In the preface to his interpretation of the Sermon on the Mount,[52] Luther starts once again by contrasting the two-level ethical system of "laws" and "counsels."

The Scholastics appealed to Matthew 5:48: "Be perfect, therefore, as your heavenly Father is perfect." In their opinion such a requirement could not be reasonably attained by ordinary Christian people. For this reason, they isolated from the Sermon on the Mount twelve *consilia Evangelii*, evangelical "admonitions," which applied only to the monks and nuns, "which one could fulfill, whoever desired to do so, so that he could become somewhat advanced and more complete than other Christians";[53] among these "admonitions" one

---

50. Stümke, "Einen Räuber darf, einen Werwolf muss man töten," 209 n. 11, harshly criticizes the cited verse (cf. n. 49 above), as well as the 1526 treatise concerning soldiers, in which Luther still advocated this "martyr ethic" (*LW* 46:108).

51. WA 40III:207.36f. in context (on Ps. 127:1; 1532-33).

52. *LW* 21:3-5 ("Luther's Preface to the Sermon on the Mount").

53. WA 32:300.5-8; cf. 300.15ff.; cf. *LW* 21:4.

could count love of the enemy, avoidance of vengeance, readiness to lend every-thing, etc. But in this way, according to Luther, the Scholastics explain these works as unnecessary additions and in actuality suspend them.[54] In opposition, he states that Christ, in the Sermon on the Mount, "threatens angrily that those who relax in the matter of even the least of such commandments should not be in heaven, those who empty the word 'commandments' of any meaning."[55] In brief: as far as Luther is concerned, the sermon deals through and through with commandments that apply to each and every person, not with recommenda-tions for just a few. That is one front against which Luther directs his polemic.

On the other side, the "new jurists and sophists, namely, the Sectarians and Anabaptists,"[56] fall off the horse as well "when they teach that one ought to have no possessions, ought not to take an oath, ought not to serve in a position of au-thority or in a court, ought not to protect or defend, should run from wife and child."[57] In this way the devil mixes and mingles everything together, so that "they do not know the difference between the temporal and godly [i.e., spiri-tual] kingdom, much less what various things are to be taught and to be done in each of the kingdoms";[58] this is what unites the Enthusiasts with the monks. The devil uses both extremes, "so that he can thus suppress good works com-pletely, as took place under the Papacy, or else he arranges for false good works and imagined holiness, which he has begun to do at present through the new monks, the Sectarians."[59] Each wants to arrange for something that is "different or special or better than what God has commanded,"[60] and errs thereby.

What is important is not the external work, but the mind-set, the spirit in which a person lives and believes:

> For one finds some beggars who take the bread in front of the door, who are as proud and evil as is no rich person, and some shabby farmers, with whom it is harder to deal in the right way than with any lord and prince. Therefore, in terms of your physical and external existence, be poor or rich, depending on what has been provided for you — God doesn't ask about this — and know that each one must be poor before God, meaning in the

54. *LW* 21:4.

55. WA 32:300.3-5; cf. *LW* 21:4. Cf. 45:101-3. Jesus' "But I say to you" does not abolish but in-terprets the law — as applicable to everyone.

56. WA 32:300.34f.; cf. *LW* 21:5.

57. WA 32:301.1f.; cf. *LW* 21:5. For this reason Augsburg Confession, article 16, is also di-rected explicitly against the Anabaptists (chiefly against the Schleitheim Articles; cf. chap. 13, n. 78 above).

58. WA 32:301.3-6; cf. *LW* 21:5.

59. WA 32:301.19-22; cf. *LW* 21:5.

60. WA 32:301.26f.; cf. *LW* 21:5.

spiritual sense and in matters of the heart. One ought not to set his confidence, trust, and dependence on goods that pass away, nor set his heart on such things and let mammon be his idol.[61]

14.6. Ecclesiastical Law

The teaching about the two realms offers a rule of thumb for distinguishing what is temporal from what is spiritual, concerning the two ways in which God rules in the world and the church. The situation is more difficult when the church is viewed with respect to its temporal side: How is the relationship between the temporal and spiritual appropriately applied in terms of ecclesiastical law?

In the first place, the formula *non vi, sed verbo* ("not with human power but by the Word"), which comes from the Augsburg Confession, article 28, spoke in 1530 against the way the Roman Church mixed the two realms, against the fact that bishops also waged war, had temporal offices, and, to take another example, selected the German emperor in their role as electors. In the second place, it rejected the right that bishops claimed to issue spiritual laws — ceremonial laws — and thus to burden consciences. The "power," the authority of office for the bishops, is rooted according to article 28 in that which identifies the church, as mentioned already in article 7: in preaching the gospel, in administering the sacraments, and in the office of the keys (which includes the right to excommunicate, but which ought not to be exercised with undue harshness).[62] "But that the bishops otherwise claimed power and legal authority in other matters, such as marriage and the tithe, went beyond their authority since they have these only on the authorization of *human* authorities."[63]

But how then, within the church according to its proper power and rights, is the church to act appropriately? Melanchthon concedes in the Augsburg Confession "that the bishops or pastors can establish order, so that everything in the church takes place in an orderly way [1 Cor. 14:40], not in order to obtain the grace of God" but "because of love and peace."[64] Even the

---

61. WA 32:307.26-34; cf. *LW* 21:12-13.

62. CA XXVIII, 21, in *BC*, 95: "[B]y divine right, this jurisdiction belongs to the bishops as bishops (that is, to those to whom the ministry of Word and sacraments has been committed): to forgive sins, to reject teaching that opposes the gospel, and to exclude from the communion of the church the ungodly whose ungodliness is known — doing all this not with human power but by the Word."

63. *BSLK* 125.3-6; cf. CA XXVIII, 29, in *BC*, 95 (*humano iure*, "by human law," italics added).

64. *BSLK* 129.13-16.28f.; cf. CA XXVIII, 53, 55, in *BC*, 99.

argument frequently cited by the Roman side concerning the apostolic council (Acts 15:20, 29) did not apply, since it did not result in spiritual laws, but dealt only with matters appropriate to the time, which could go out of date. The commandment to refrain from what had blood and was choked was issued to avoid "scandal," and was valid "for a time."[65]

This argument opened up a wide space for formulations, which the evangelical church bodies have used with great vigor. There is no single way that Protestants are organized. Whether with bishops, with synods and presbyters, as Congregationalists do, or, as is most common, with a mixed form — everything is conceivable, all can serve the gospel, but all can also be misused.

To consider ecclesiastical law as a "form of the gospel," as is often demanded by the Reformed wing, means that one makes too much of the temporal elements by making spiritual demands. The gospel is a matter of the Word alone, not a matter of how human beings conceive ways to exercise authority by coercion because they demand the right. But with respect to the rule and administration of the church, it would be inappropriate that its only proper function is the "political use of the law" *(usus politicus legis),* which is accorded validity in the state.[66] The structures of the church and what happens within it exist in actuality under a special justification, if it is really true that Christians actually no longer need the external law. This requirement has a basis in reality. One should thus continue, within the church, to seek for ways to improve such things as regulations about one's service and the quality of pastoral interaction. When Luther describes the nature of the office of bishop as being that of service as a pastor,[67] this does not work in contradiction to the function of a bishop as one who serves in a leadership capacity, but it certainly gives an indication in what spirit — which, like every office, is unavoidably bound up with the exercise of human power — his office is to be administered.

14.7. Current Application and Open Questions

In the "world that has not yet been redeemed" the state and the Christians who are actively involved in supporting its constitutional principles have the divine mandate to stand up against evil, in that they take care of "justice and peace."[68] Kosovo, Macedonia, Afghanistan, the Near East — the challenges are more ob-

65. *BSLK* 131.21; cf. CA XXVIII, 65, in *BC,* 101.

66. One sign of this is that in Germany the territorial churches of today take a "third way" in their legislation beyond bureaucracy of civil service and tariff legislation.

67. *LW* 45:117. Cf. n. 62 above.

68. Cf. n. 17 above.

vious than ever. In the past years it has become apparent that talk about human rights and freedom remains empty and unreliable unless a certain amount of "force for implementation" is there as well. That is true even in pedagogical matters, it is true when one parks in the wrong place, and it is especially true in international politics. Reforms and actions that bring help to others cannot only be demanded, but must also be watched over as they are implemented and protected — when necessary, with the military — if they are to have a chance.[69] Complete pacifism as a political program is just another form of enthusiasm.

Luther primarily dealt with the temporal exercise of power from the perspective of the "sword," since there were very few opportunities in his time to have democratic participation.[70] It is well-known — and Luther was aware of it as well — that his views had problematic consequences in the Peasants' War. They can be explained to some extent by the unique dynamic of the events, because it took Luther time to get any response into print. But Luther also placed high value on the legal order that existed already for communal existence; *the main point of Luther's political ethic is standing for what is right*.[71] He feared nothing so much as a *bellum omnium contra omnes,* a war of everyone against everyone else; all private feuding had been forbidden throughout the empire since 1495; that served as his backdrop. He did in fact see the injustices of the ruling princes, though he feared that absolute chaos would result if there was an overthrow: "The populace hates authority by its very nature."[72] Even if the way the rulers carried out the duties of their offices often left much to be desired, their office was still ordained and instituted by God — which one could never say about anarchy. Thus, for Luther, an uprising against the princes could be carried out only passively. In any case, the path of justice was to be maintained; to take matters into one's own hand was not a matter for a private citizen against his authorities. But the power of the ruler was limited by the power of God.[73]

69. Cf. Stümke, "Einen Räuber darf, einen Werwolf muss man töten," 227 n. 82: in years to come the question "as to the legitimacy of active resistance to dissolving the constitutional state relationships in other countries" will become even more acute.

70. Cf. chap. 6.3.2 above.

71. Cf. Reinhard Schwarz, "Christusgemeinschaft und Rechtsgemeinschaft — Theologie und Gesellschaft in Luthers Rede von 'Zwei Reichen,'" in *Herausforderung,* ed. Fernando Castillo and Heinrich Fries (Regensburg: Pustet, 1980), 9-27.

72. WA 40III:268.18f.; cf. lines 19-23 (on Ps. 127:5, 1532-33). Cf. especially Luther's sharp turn of phrase against the "mob" in the treatise on *Kriegsleute* (1526): WA 19:635.14-16; 639:30–640.2.

73. Whether the conviction that temporal authority is instituted by God has served more to criticize temporal authority or to legitimate it is still under dispute (Stümke, "Einen Räuber darf, einen Werwolf muss man töten," 219f.). It was Luther's concern to separate what he thought was a peace-loving emperor from a warmongering pope (219 n. 55). Later, a particularly difficult issue

For us today, working together politically is more than merely "an order of necessity against the sin." Political life in community can be designed to give the human being a chance to unfold the gifts given to him in creation.[74] But if one sees what is going on beyond Europe and in our own land in opposition to democracy, it would be irresponsible to deny that the questions about power are still being posed.

14.8. Concerning the Relationship between the Teaching about the Two Realms and the Teaching about the Three Estates

According to Luther's own judgment, the teaching about the three estates was more significant than the teaching about the two realms. That latter subject does not appear in summaries of his teaching and in the testaments that he composed, though the three estates are dealt with.[75] What he teaches about each topic is not identical, but each can complement the other. Even here one must observe that Luther himself changes his views about these matters more than is noticed by those who try to articulate the essentials of what he taught.

Above all, two factors are significant:

a. In the teaching about the two realms, Luther thinks about this as a critical *distinction* — God deals in each realm in a different way. When Luther explains the three estates, he presents a positive *arrangement* — it is always God who works in each person in all three estates, within the world.

b. The teaching about the two realms does not provide a static and permanent distinction. It applies only as an interim arrangement — now, in the rupture between ages, when different time periods are treated as one; at some time, however, when the world is consummated, it will be removed. This distinction takes into account the fact that not all people are Christians and that even the Christian himself, as a new man, must still be in relationship with the old, sinful man within himself — until the time of his death — as one who still needs the law. *Luther's distinction between God's two realms serves to orient the Christian who believes that the world is consummated but who cannot see it yet.*

By contrast, the teaching about the three estates goes beyond this, in that its

---

was posed for him as to the relative weight to be given to theological and legal arguments in connection with whether "lower persons" (princes) could resist the "higher" person (the emperor) with military force (220f.). In addition, cf. Eike Wolgast, *Die Wittenberger Theologie und die Politik der evangelischen Stände. Studien zu Luthers Gutachten in politischen Fragen,* Quellen und Forschungen zur Reformationsgeschichte, vol. 47 (Gütersloh: Gütersloher Verlagshaus, 1977).

74. Cf. chap. 6.3.2 above.

75. Cf. chap. 6.1 above.

existence is rooted in Paradise, and will not be voided, even in the eschaton, but will be fulfilled. This applies not only to the church but also to relationships in the second estate that involve marriage and family. That what is taught about the three estates envelops what is taught about the two realms and has an impact on it is clear from the disputation of 1539, which has been mentioned already: in addition to anarchistic elements and political authorities that are antagonistic toward God, Luther mentions a third opponent as well, against which complete resistance is commanded, not just in a measured way — namely, the Antichrist.[76] The Antichrist stands forever in opposition to the estates that have been made holy by the Word of God. He destroys not just temporal order but all estates, and thereby also the faith and God's creation in general. For this reason, it is not sufficient to oppose him simply with words, as one could basically go against the heretic or use just means to oppose the authorities. Only because he "is to be accorded no estate and thus stands completely outside the divine order, Luther can call for comprehensive, active opposition against him."[77] The polemic in the title of the disputation concerning the three estates against the pope as the enemy of the three estates, and thus as the enemy of all human beings, is no merely casual, sarcastic remark, but states the very goal of the entire argumentation, with obvious political consequences.

The present papacy no longer functions in this sense as the enemy of the gospel and as a usurper of political power, as was the case in Luther's time; it would be a mistake to identify it with the Antichrist. Luther's dispute at this point correctly concentrated on the ecclesiastical level — at least on the basis of the theological side — and is carried out *sine vi, sed verbo*. But if one looks away for the moment from the concrete identification of the Antichrist with the Roman papacy of his era, Luther's eschatological perspective remains important. As was articulated at the beginning, theological ethics is not an abstract system of teaching, to be isolated from the concerns with which theology must deal: concerning sin, God's intervention, the end of history, and the consummation of the world.

The ethic based on the two realms is limited in time; by contrast, the three estates, if one can look beyond the pressure of the moment in the political realm, will be altered but not done away with altogether. A form of community — a completely intensive community — is to be expected in the eschaton that will correspond to what was intended originally in the creation. But the distinction between the two realms, together with the distinction of law and gospel, will be eliminated in the eschaton.

---

76. WA 39II:42.1-44, 6 (theses 51-91).
77. Stümke, "Einen Räuber darf, einen Werwolf muss man töten," 216.

Chapter 15   Consummation of the World
and God's Triune Nature

> *We are such creatures*
> *with whom God will speak,*
> *eternally and immortally,*
> *whether it is in wrath or whether it is in mercy.*

15.1. Consummation of the World

15.1.1. A Double Termination or Reconciliation for All?

"As the final point, I believe in the resurrection of all the dead on the Last Day, both the righteous and the wicked, so that then each one will receive in his body what he deserves, and thus that the righteous will live forever with Christ and the wicked will die forever with the devil and his angels. For I do not believe what others do, who teach that the devil will come to salvation on the Last Day as well."[1] Augsburg Confession, article 17, corresponds exactly to this conclusion to Luther's *Confession* of 1528, together with the rejection of those who taught universal salvation and those who taught a reign of one thousand years "before the resurrection of the dead."[2]

Article 2, on original sin, is presupposed thereby, which begins by discussing sin within the context of the final judgment. Thus the matter of sin does not merely involve the present conflict between the human being and God as such, but is also connected with damnation "under the eternal wrath of God" that comes as a consequence.[3] The conflict between humanity and God thus remains determinative; it excludes one from eternal participation with God, which keeps one from being in his kingdom. By the power of God's judgment, the sin-

---

1. WA 26:509.13-18; cf. *LW* 37:372 (*Confession concerning Christ's Supper*, 1528).

2. *BSLK* 72.1-18; cf. CA XVII, in *BC*, 51. Cf. also the differentiation between "will raise me and all the *dead*" and "will give me with *all believers* in Christ eternal life" in the explanation of the third article in the Small Catechism (cf. chap. 11.1.2.c above; italics added).

3. *BSLK* 53.11f.; cf. CA II, in *BC*, 38.

ner remains under wrath, so long as he "has not been born again by baptism and the Holy Spirit."[4] At the judgment, Christ will give to every person what he or she has become in the here and now, in faith or else in unbelief.

This reformational confession is still opposed today by those who seek to speak about a double predestination — whether for eternal salvation or for eternal damnation. This view is to be understood and rejected as the way someone projects a personal desire for vengeance onto a Christian way of thinking when one has not yet arrived at a mature understanding of God. Another way to look at it would be from the positive side, which asks: Based on the gospel, is it not more correct to believe, to hope, and also to *teach* that *all* human beings will be saved in the end, along with all creatures, after passing through death and judgment?[5]

It would not be theologically defensible to be forced to decide between these alternatives. One can find biblical arguments and arguments throughout the history of theological inquiry offered on both sides — in which the predominant stream of tradition opts for double predestination. But the question is unavoidable: Can one *teach* one or the other of these possibilities? Or is the salvation of all — against the real threat and fear that human beings can be lost — not rather a topic of faith and hope in the strictest sense and a matter to be taken up in *prayer*? This is articulated in the last petition of the Lord's Prayer: "And lead us not into temptation, but deliver us from evil." The hope for the deliverance of all is *not a statement* that is appropriate *as teaching* in the sense of a proposition, but rather is appropriate to *prayer*.[6] Specifically within the realm of eschatology, as one teaches about the last things, one must examine most carefully whether at all — and if so, in what sense — one can dare to articulate a teaching in the sense of making definitive statements as propositions. Correspondingly, Luther and Melanchthon are to be criticized at this point.

15.1.2. The Consummation of One's Own Life and the Consummation of the World

When Luther confesses with the New Testament that the relationship with God does not come to an end at death, this does not include some notion about a continuity that is somehow rooted in the framework of a human dis-

4. *BSLK* 53.12f.; cf. CA II, 2, in *BC*, 38.
5. Cf., e.g., J. Christine Janowski, *Allerlösung. Annäherungen an eine entdualisierte Eschatologie,* 2 vols. (Neukirchen: Neukirchener Verlag, 2000).
6. Cf. Oswald Bayer, *Gott als Autor. Zu einer poietologischen Theologie* (Tübingen, 1999), 198-205 ("Wann endlich hat das Böse ein Ende?").

position, no matter how that might be conceptualized. For Luther the continuity is not found within the person of the individual — in the sense of the immortality of the soul;[7] in a much different sense he expects the continuity only because of the actions and speech of God. As human beings who are called into life by God alone, we are addressed in such a way that one purely and simply cannot undo; we are "such creatures with whom God will speak, eternally and immortally, . . . whether it is in wrath or whether it is in mercy."[8] No human being can remove this responsibility — the empowerment and the necessity to give an answer. God's address to human beings remains in force, even through death and beyond.

From the very beginning each individual is embedded within the totality of humanity and among the rest of the creatures. The question about the salvation of the individual cannot be isolated from the question about the consummation of the whole world. Luther makes a significant number of statements about individual eschatology — such as those that speak of death as sleep: "We are to sleep, until he [Christ] comes and knocks on the little grave and says: Doctor Martin, arise! Then I will come to life in an instant and will be happy with him forever."[9] But still, Luther does not pose egotistical questions about his own salvation, but about the consummation of the *promissio* of the love of God for the whole world, for all who believe and thus at the same time for the individual as well. "This is my faith; for this is what all Christians believe."[10]

Based on God's love, which as such forms community, the possibility of a private happiness and of an egotistical form of salvation is excluded from the outset. This can be explained better than by using the picture of "being awakened," which can be misunderstood individualistically, as one considers the promise that applies to all, such as that in the Lord's Supper.

---

7. On this point the interpretation of Luther is admittedly controversial. Cf. Paul Althaus, *Unsterblichkeit und ewiges Leben bei Luther. Zur Auseinandersetzung mit Carl Stange* (Gütersloh: Bertelsmann, 1930); Fritz Heidler, *Luthers Lehre von der Unsterblichkeit der Seele*, Ratzeburger Hefte 1 (Erlangen: Martin-Luther-Verlag, 1983); Aleksander Radler, *Unsterblichkeitsgedanke und Auferstehungsglaube*, Veröffentlichungen der Luther-Akademie Ratzeburg, vol. 11 (Erlangen: Martin-Luther-Verlag, 1988), 25-39 (the literature on pp. 38f. is important); Christian Herrmann, *Unsterblichkeit der Seele durch Auferstehung. Studien zu den anthropologischen Implikationen der Eschatologie* (Göttingen: Vandenhoeck & Ruprecht, 1997).

8. WA 43:481.32-35; cf. *LW* 5:7 (on Gen. 26:24-25; the sentence structure has been reversed).

9. WA 37:151.8 (sermon on Luke 7:1ff., September 28, 1533). "Just as someone falls asleep and comes to the morning in no time, without knowing how it happens, so we will rise suddenly on the Last Day not knowing how it came about that we died and how we came through it" (WA 17II:235.17 [on John 8:46-59; *Fastenpostille* 1525]).

10. WA 26:509.19; cf. *LW* 37:372.

It is not by chance that the Gospels often depict the reign of God as a wedding banquet and the joyous celebration that accompanies it or some unspecified celebratory meal. At a decisive juncture in the Revelation to Saint John (Rev. 21:4; cf. 7:17) the Isaiah Apocalypse is cited: "On this mountain the Lord of hosts will make for all peoples a feast of rich food, a feast of well-aged wines, of rich food filled with marrow, of well-aged wines strained clear. And he will destroy on this mountain the shroud that is cast over all peoples, the sheet that is spread over all nations; he will swallow up death forever. Then the Lord God will wipe away the tears from all faces" (Isa. 25:6-8).

The communal meal provides a depiction of the reign of God that cannot be interchanged with another concept: as gift, communion, and joy. Such communion, in which separation, aloneness, and isolation are overcome, is not achieved through effort and is not acquired, and it is not produced within world history; instead, it is guaranteed, given as a gift, and "prepared beforehand" by him, as it is described most clearly in the story of the judgment of the world (Matt. 25:34). Luther paraphrases this most impressively: "The kingdom . . . will not be prepared; it is prepared; but the sons of the kingdom will be prepared; they do not prepare the kingdom. This means: the kingdom serves the sons, not the sons the kingdom."[11]

Eschatology cannot provide answers outside the framework of God's actions as the one who rules as the triune Creator, Redeemer, and Consumator[12] throughout the world and within the entire world, since in such a case the reformational teaching about justification would be understood in too narrow a sense. That must be maintained over against the common view of how to teach about justification that narrows it down in an individualistic way, which misses the point about its cosmic and universal dimensions. The very way in which the Augsburg Confession is arranged, with its overall framework that provides an arch from article 2 (universal sin) to article 17 (final judgment), shows paradigmatically how the universal and individual, the cosmic and personal perspectives are brought together: on the one side, the work of God for the individual and for that person's justification is taken into account within the wider context of the world as a whole (articles 2-6); the other end of the arch depicts the deliverance of the individual once again, but within the wider framework of the universal dimension of how God deals with the world (articles 7-17).

This same observation holds concerning the way we can apply the judi-

---

11. Martin Luther, *The Bondage of the Will,* trans. Henry Cole (Grand Rapids: Eerdmans, 1931), 191. Cf. chap. 13, n. 50 above.

12. Cf. 15.2 below.

cial background of the term "justification" for today. We know the term at present only in its reflexive sense: "one can justify oneself" in response to an accusation. By contrast, the judicial regulations of the sixteenth century "use the term in order to deal with carrying out or executing justice against a person who committed a wrong. Torture was implicit when one spoke of a 'sharp justification'; when one spoke of 'painful justification,' it involved being delivered over to the hangman."[13]

The emphasis on public responsibility must be heard as well, an emphasis that in the final analysis includes reference to the final judgment, which includes salvation and judgment. To speak of justification thus does not mean that the demands of God are set aside; gospel does not mean that the law is minimized, as if the curse of the law is set aside and the wrath of God is simply removed from the scene. That sin, "even still now" *(nunc quoque)* "brings eternal death,"[14] even after Christ, excludes the possibility that this eschatological consequence can be relativized with christological abstractions, as if we might say: we *would have been* lost and condemned sinners without Christ, but since he died and was raised, sin no longer has its power to bring damnation in and of itself. The judgment of God is not simply behind us because of Christ's cross; all of us go against him through life and death. One can speak of justification only as that of the sinner who is really lost and condemned, related to a world that is radically sinful, and set within the framework of the last judgment.

15.1.3. End of Time

As was demonstrated in the introductory chapter, Luther lived in a rupture between ages; he thought within a time frame that was apocalyptic. It was impossible for him to think of time as that which encompasses only the present dimension. He presents his *Confession* of 1528 as a very specific response, which is offered not simply before human beings, but from beginning to end as what he declares before the judgment seat of God: "Since I see that uproar and error gets worse the longer it goes on and that the raging and raving of Satan does not cease . . . , I wish to use this document to confess my faith be-

---

13. Otto Hermann Pesch and Albrecht Peters, *Einführung in die Lehre von Gnade und Rechtfertigung* (Darmstadt: Wissenschaftliche Buchgesellschaft, 1981), 135, with reference to Werner Elert, "Deutschrechtliche Züge in Luthers Rechtfertigungslehre (1935)," in *Ein Lehrer der Kirche. Kirchlich-theologische Aufsätze und Vorträge von Werner Elert*, ed. Max Keller-Hüschemenger (Berlin and Hamburg: Lutherisches Verlagshaus, 1967), 23-31.

14. *BSLK* 53.8f.; cf. CA II, 2, in *BC*, 39.

fore God and the whole world, point by point, in which I expect to remain until death, in order that by it, for which God will help me, I will be cut off from this world and will come before the judgment seat of our Lord Jesus Christ. . . . I am at this point neither drunk nor indiscreet; I know what I am saying" — I am able to offer testimony, in full possession of my spiritual powers — "also feeling confident about what it means for me as regards the return of our Lord Jesus Christ at the Last Judgment."[15]

The theological-eschatological character of the statement of the reformational faith, which appeared in public in the political realm as well, can be seen clearly, to take one example, in the "Appellation and Protestation *(protestatio)* of the Evangelical Imperial Estates" in Speyer (1529), which is where the name "Protestants" first appeared: "in matters that deal with God's honor and the salvation and blessedness of our souls, each must stand before God on his own and give an account [Rom. 14:12], so that in that way no one can excuse himself because of the actions or decisions of a minority or majority."[16] Correspondingly, Melanchthon also views the confessional situation at the time of the Augsburg Confession in 1530 within an eschatological framework: "For your royal majesty will certainly graciously observe that these matters do not deal with temporal goods, lands, or people, but with eternal salvation and damnation of souls and consciences; and as [we have] dealt with it here, so God will demand an account concerning this on Judgment Day."[17]

For Luther, the alternative to a view of life that is solely connected with this world is certainly not that one should flee the world and concentrate on that which is to come. As shown by the proverb about the apple tree,[18] which did not see the light of day until 1945 but which is certainly appropriate for understanding Luther's way of thinking, Luther's affirmation about the creation is narrowed down to unique courage about life that expects that this world will pass away. That the world will pass away is treated by Luther neither as a dispassionate diagnosis nor as something to be feared. Instead, it is anticipated by faith. It is indeed the "distorted world" that is passing away, the world that "is drunk with its own blindness."[19] The way the distortion of the

---

15. WA 26:499.2–500.5; cf. *LW* 37:360-61.

16. *Deutsche Reichstagsakten, Jüngere Reihe,* vol. 7/2, ed. die historische Kommission bei der Bayerischen Akademie der Wissenschaften (Munich: Walter Kaemmerer, 1963), 1277, 29-33. Cf. chap. 14, n. 21 above on the origin of the idea of religious freedom.

17. *BSLK* 136.6-9; cf. 83c.11-15; cf. Augsburg Confession, Melanchthon's first draft of the conclusion, *Bekenntnisschriften der lutherischen Kirche,* p. 136, lines 6-9. Cf. Augsburg Confession, conclusion of part 1, German text, pars. 1-2, in *BC,* 58, 60.

18. Cf. the introduction, n. 28 above.

19. *BSLK* 649.26-28; cf. LC II, 21, in *BC,* 433.

world is overcome is found already in the story of the flood in Genesis.[20] The complete conquest of this distorted world will bring about the victory of grace for all to see.

The consequence for our life in the here and now, in the tension between promise and fulfillment, admittedly does not state that for faith everything fragmentary has already been sketched out to become clear and that every breakdown can be understood as necessary. That which opposes and is at enmity with life cannot be figured out logically even if one confesses that the consummation of the world lies ahead. Guilt and forgiveness do not take effect in a way that already becomes clear in this world; continuity is expected only because of the faithfulness of the one who does not allow the work of his hands to go for naught. Because of faith, I can refrain from wanting to perceive the inner workings of the world. At the same time, I am delivered from having to utter the final judgment about myself and others.

At this point we embark once again on a journey through most difficult waters. Luther thought he was living in the last days; "it is certainly true that all is coming to an end" and "the Day of Judgment stands before the door" — that is how it reads in his introduction to the book of Daniel.[21] In a certain sense the sixteenth century was an apocalyptic time; apocalyptic is not so much a question about chronology as it is of the quality of the era. In virtually no other age, since the great Germanic migrations from the fourth to the sixth century after Christ, was order in Europe endangered as it was then — externally by the Turkish wars, internally by the Peasants' War and the split because of various confessional groups; Luther could not conceive the possibility that settled and less apocalyptic times would follow once again. The battle for the correct understanding of the gospel was carried out right in the open; the fronts were easily identified. Luther was thus not reticent about calling out the enemies of the gospel by name. In the preface to the book of Daniel,[22] and often in other places as well — already from 1519 on[23]

20. The fact that the creation is preserved through the judgment (through the flood as the *annihilatio mundi* = destruction of the world) is the action of God alone, who concludes a covenant with Noah (Gen. 6:18) and extends his promise universally (Gen. 9:1-17). It is true already for the Old Testament: only through judgment is the world perceived as creation; this stands against a naive piety about the cosmos.

21. Heinrich Bornkamm, ed., *Luthers Vorreden zur Bibel*, 3rd ed. (Göttingen: Vandenhoeck & Ruprecht, 1989), 121f. (= WA DB 11II:124.20; cf. *LW* 35:315-16).

22. WA DB 11II:50.1–124.20. (This portion, including that in n. 21 above, was inserted in 1541, and contains a lengthy exposition of chaps. 11:36–12:12, dealing with the pope as Antichrist and signs of the end).

23. Cf. Volker Leppin, "Luthers Antichristverständnis vor dem Hintergrund der mittelalterlichen Konzeptionen," *KuD* 45 (1999): 48-63.

— he identified the pope as the Antichrist. It can be stated once again that one cannot make that identification today, on the basis of the present papacy.

Luther risked interpreting his era within the framework of the apocalyptic texts of the Bible and thus erred at times as well. A particularly dark chapter involves his late writings and sermons against the Jews.[24] They ought not to be explained away on psychological grounds as matters that were irrelevant faux pas or as the obstinate actions of an old man; Luther's interpretation of the texts, which makes them applicable to things of this world, is bound up with the basic statements that he makes concerning his "battle theology." For him, the issue is always about the honor of Christ. His apocalyptic view of time, in a sad way, caused him to step back even from his teaching about the two realms, so that — precisely in his opinion concerning the Jews — he arrived at conclusions that could not be justified.[25] There is little that can be explained away here, hardly anything that can be made clear, and nothing that can be excused. When it comes to Luther and Holy Scripture, one must say here, against Luther: the Christian is delivered from the pressure of having to utter a final judgment about oneself and about others. Christ alone is the judge.

15.1.4. Not the Last Thing, but the Last One

With Revelation 22:20 — "Indeed, come, Lord Jesus" — Luther prays that the Day of Judgment will come. It is the *extremus dies laeta;*[26] "we . . . wait for the arrival of the Lord and say: 'Come, Dear Lord Jesus.'"[27] The Day of Judgment that one awaits is thus not to be understood in a neutral sense, but rather in a personal sense: it is the Lord who is expected. We do not wait for an anonymous Last Thing, but for *the Last One,* whom we know by faith already.[28] The

24. Cf. Heiko Oberman, *Wurzeln des Antisemitismus. Christenangst und Judenplage im Zeitalter von Humanismus und Reformation* (Berlin: Severin & Siedler, 1981); Johannes Brosseder, *Luthers Stellung zu den Juden im Spiegel seiner Interpreten* (Munich: M. Hueber, 1972); Reinhard Schwarz, *Luther,* 2nd ed. (Göttingen, 1998), 248-54. Cf. the introduction, n. 9 above.

25. In light of the way his writings were used in the nineteenth and twentieth centuries, it should of course be emphasized that a racist point of view plays no role with Luther.

26. The "happy last day" (WA 49:731.5). Cf. Otto Hermann Pesch, "Im Angesicht des barmherzigen Richters. Lebenszeit, Tod und Jüngster Tag in der Theologie Martin Luthers," *Catholica* 42 (1988): 245-73.

27. WA 49:742.11, but most especially the conclusion to the preface to the first Genesis volume *ennaratio:* WA 42:2.30-35 (1543).

28. Cf. Axel Wiemer, *"Mein Trost, Kampf und Sieg ist Christus." Martin Luthers eschatologische Theologie nach seinen Reihenpredigten über 1 Cor. 15 (1532/33),* TBT 119 (Berlin and New York, 2003).

anticipation of the beloved Day of Judgment is thus identical with the anticipation of the "beloved Lord." The last verse of the hymn "Beloved Christians, Now Rejoice,"[29] written by Erasmus Alber, a student and friend of Luther's, speaks pregnantly about this expectation:

> Oh dear Lord, hurry to judgment!
> Let your glorious face be seen,
> The nature of your triune being,
> Oh, help us God in eternity.

15.2. God's Triune Nature

15.2.1. Setting and Way to Speak about the Triune God

Can anything follow after the "consummation of the world"? Does the fact that the teaching about the Trinity is purposely placed here suggest that it is a simple supplement, an addendum? Absolutely not! One should remember at what point the Trinity has been discussed in specific terms already: in connection with the teaching about creation and concerning the Holy Spirit, but particularly with reference to the overthrow within God himself that led from wrath to grace, from death to life, which took place once for all on Good Friday and Easter. This overthrow is made particularly clear in Luther's hymn of liberation, "Dear Christians, One and All, Rejoice" — an overthrow that takes place within the dramatic interchange between Father and Son, which the Holy Spirit imparts to us by means of the *promissio.*

The teaching about the Trinity clearly has its proper place with reference to the deliverance from sin, death, and the devil, through what happened in Christ, together with the removal — admittedly only in the eschaton — of the temptation to explain matters by using theodicy and predestination. Speaking about the Trinity is rooted in the events connected with Christ and continues toward the final revelation of the triune God at the end of time. It is thus properly located neither as a bland addition nor in the middle as just one dogmatic theme among many, but correctly in the middle and correctly at the end: in the middle by faith and at the end by sight — corresponding to the difference articulated in 2 Corinthians 5:7 ("we walk by faith, not by sight"). Because of this perspective, the discussion about the Trinity has coursed through the second half of our discussion of Luther's theology like a major

29. *EG,* #6, 5 (1546).

artery, because the Christ event has to be explained. To be sure, even the article concerning creation, as an article of faith, can be understood only from the perspective of a trinitarian theology.

But does the teaching about the Trinity thereby need to be relegated to a "theoretical framework about the Christian faith"[30] — as an introductory note before the bracket that includes every other theme? In any case, this continues to happen today, as many follow the example of the dogmatic writings of so prominent a theologian as Karl Barth; this is the pattern that is followed by an ever-increasing number of dogmatic theologians throughout the world. But my analysis suggests that this does not correspond to Luther's theology. The teaching about God's trinitarian nature is not a dogmatic proposition, with which one can begin and then derive and unfold all the other themes — in such a way that the theologian can at the same time survey the unfolding plan of salvation with a bird's-eye view. If one proceeds in such a way, one will come dangerously close to what Luther continually rejected as a brand of speculation that ignores time and the situation.[31] In addition, one would not be able to determine the way one has to distinguish the general teaching about God from specific teaching about the Trinity — which Luther considered to be a necessary endeavor.[32]

A dogmatic study that begins with the teaching about the Trinity ignores or minimizes the problem of unfaith. But the triune nature of God can be comprehended only as an unfolding of the pure gospel — and disagreement about the gospel will continue until the end of the world. The gospel is a topic for faith, which cannot use speculative activities to provide one with insight. In this sense, the discussion about the triune nature of God most properly has its place in connection with eschatology, since it is only at this point that all

---

30. Cf. Christoph Schwöbel, "Trinitätslehre als Rahmentheorie des christlichen Glaubens," in *Trinität*, ed. Wilfried Härle and Reiner Preul, MJTh 10 (Marburg, 1998), 129-54, as well as Schwöbel, "Trinität IV. Systematisch-theologisch," in *TRE* 34 (2002), 110-21, here 118f.

31. Cf. his polemic against the speculation found in commentaries on Peter Lombard's *Sentences*, which, in the first book, *On the Trinity*, "bore with their heads through the heavens and look around up there," but "when they find no one there, since Christ is lying in the crib and in the bosom of the woman, they crash down again and break their necks" (WA 9:406.17-20 [sermon on Gen. 28:12; ca. 1520]). "God the Father wanted to do away with disputes about the article of faith by saying about God his Son: Listen to him [Matt. 17:5]" (WA 39II:287.5f. [first thesis of the Disputation at the Promotion of Georg Major, 1544]). At the same time, this does not prevent Luther from working intensively in this disputation and several others on the teaching about the Trinity as teaching about God's eternity during his last years. On the subject, cf. Christine Helmer, "God from Eternity to Eternity: Luther's Trinitarian Understanding," *HTR* 96 (2003): 127-46.

32. Cf. chaps. 6.2 and 10.1 above, and 2.2 below.

controversial aspects of the Trinity will be removed. Many hymns of the church make this point; they end with a trinitarian verse.

In many senses the liturgy provides a good criterion for the arrangement and importance attached to theological statements. God is addressed in the worship service as the triune God. This calls attention to the doxological character of these statements: the trinitarian nature of God is the subject of praise and worship. Since the triune God will be visible for everyone and will be beyond dispute only at the eschaton, we speak in the here and now about the Trinity in a way that is always linked to songs of lament and in a protest against death. We cannot act at this point in life as if we are already in heaven. As long as we are not yet at the point of seeing, our song of praise always takes shape in a battle against the agonizing challenges of life.

What does this contribute to the understanding of Luther's theology? We can make this clear by looking at Luther's discussion about the horrible hiddenness of God, the *Deus absconditus*.[33] Theologians who presuppose the triune nature of God attribute the dark side of God to the person of the Father and speak of the wrath of God as the other side of his love. But that results in rendering impotent what Luther identified as demonic, what is experienced as completely incomprehensible, and what is also discussed specifically in Scripture — as for example in the story of Jacob engaging in battle at the Jabbok with the unknown and anonymous one during the night. *The incomprehensible hiddenness of God does not imply that there is a Trinity; its clarity indicates the exact opposite.* Only the one who flees from the hidden God, who looks away, and who by the power of the Holy Spirit looks to Christ will recognize that he is Father as well.

God's love is not something that is obvious in and of itself; it can be experienced and conceptualized only in the dynamic action of God to provide redemption, which tears the sinner away from judgment "as if through fire" (1 Cor. 3:15). His mercy and love is that which we have no right to claim, that which is completely secret and wondrous: that *he* turns to go the other way and repents (Hos. 11:8-9). God does this because we cannot; he turns back and takes his judgment away. That is the gospel. *The triune nature of God is nothing other than the God who reveals himself to us in the gospel.*

---

33. Cf. chap. 9 above.

15.2.2. Teaching about the Trinity, Distinguished from
General Teaching about God

Based on the observations concerning Luther's hymn of liberation, "Dear Christians, One and All, Rejoice,"[34] certain elements are decisive with respect to the teaching about the Trinity. It considers nothing other than the *gospel,* the event that brings deliverance: the freedom that "Christ achieved for us and has given,"[35] and which he promises and imparts to us in the Word through the Holy Spirit.

If teaching about the Trinity considers the pure gospel, and nothing but the gospel, it is then the "summary of the gospel,"[36] in which case one cannot attribute to the triune God only the law that kills. Whoever confesses that the one who speaks against me in the law and the one who speaks for me in the gospel, who indeed intercedes on my behalf, is one and the same being, articulates the paradox of a miracle, which cannot be softened somehow by assuming that it is clear that God is always the same. Luther's hymn of liberation identifies a problem — in the radical break between the third and fourth stanzas — that gives theology a problem to wrestle with that is unprecedented.

This problem is commonly minimized by those who suggest that the law that kills, that God "hates" me and allows me to sink "into hell,"[37] is taught as something that is unquestionably the action of the triune God. But when the teaching about the Trinity, as one sees it described in the second part of the hymn of salvation,[38] is considered only and specifically within the framework of the gospel — nothing other than God's mercy and his love — and when the destiny of the lost human being is not to be attributed only to the perversion of his own freedom, but that this perversion affects his relationship with "God" as well, then it is *unavoidable that one must differentiate the teaching about the Trinity from a "general" teaching about God and about anthropology* and that the two cannot be allowed to be part of the same discussion; the break between stanzas 3 and 4, if it proves adequate for explaining the situation, makes such a differentiation necessary.

The way Luther goes about distinguishing the teaching about the Trinity

---

34. Cf. chap. 10.1 above.

35. WA 7:20.26f.; cf. *The Freedom of a Christian,* trans. Bertram Lee Woolf, in *Reformation Writings of Martin Luther* (London: Lutterworth, 1952), 357. Cf. *LW* 31:344.

36. Jörg Baur, "Die Trinitätslehre als Summe des Evangeliums," in Baur, *Einsicht und Glaube: Aufsätze,* vol. 1 (Göttingen: Vandenhoeck & Ruprecht, 1978), 112-21.

37. Stanza 3.

38. Stanzas 4-10.

from "general" teaching about God is demonstrated, to take one example, in the Large Catechism — in fact in a most prominent position: as a summary at the end of his interpretation of the confession of faith, in one of the most important texts by Luther that teaches about the Trinity: "The whole world, even though it has observed what God ought to be and what he has in mind and is doing . . . still has not [been able to] get anywhere with trying to achieve understanding."[39] This is true for all human beings, even for monotheists: even though they "believe in and worship the [one] true God, they still do not really know his mind toward them; they cannot expect from him either love or good things, so that they will remain in eternal wrath and [eternal] damnation."[40] Even the Ten Commandments "do not make any Christians; for God's wrath and displeasure remain over us, since we cannot accomplish what God demands of us."[41]

"But here," in the creed, "you have everything in the richest measure. For in it he has revealed himself and disclosed the deepest level of his fatherly heart and his purely inexpressible love in all three articles. For he made us, just so that he could redeem and sanctify us." In addition, in order to give us everything "that is in heaven and on earth, he also gave us his Son and the Holy Spirit, in order that he would bring us to himself through them. For we can never get to the point that we can recognize the Father's favor and grace" except "through the Lord Christ, who is a mirror of the Father's heart, apart from which we see nothing but a judge who is wrathful and terrifying. But we cannot learn anything about Christ either, if it is not revealed by the Holy Spirit."[42]

"[A]part from him [Christ] we see nothing but a judge who is wrathful and terrifying!" The God who comes to us apart from being the triune God, who is purely and completely love, "looks on," and has for us the grimace of the devil. *Extra Iesum deum quaerere est diabolus*[43] — to seek God apart from Jesus is the devil. *The "general" teaching about God, to be distinguished from the teaching about the Trinity, describes the non-Christian person:* it poses the

39. *BSLK* 660.23-27; cf. LC II, 63, in *BC*, 439.

40. *BSLK* 661.10-15; cf. LC II, 66, in *BC*, 440.

41. *BSLK* 661.30-33; cf. LC II, 67, in *BC*, 440.

42. *BSLK* 660.27-47; cf. LC II, 63-65, in *BC*, 439-40. Parallel to this, it says about the teaching concerning the trinitarian faith: through its knowledge "we love and delight in all the commandments of God; because we see that God, with all that he has, gives himself to us — the Father, with all creatures; the Son, with his entire work; and the Holy Ghost, with all his gifts — to assist and enable us to keep the Ten Commandments" (*BSLK* 661.36-42; cf. LC II, 69, in *BC*, 440).

43. WA 40III:337.11 (on Ps. 130:1; 1532-33); cf. chap. 9, n. 28.

question about what it means for one to have something to do with "God" apart from Jesus and thus apart from the love of the triune God, who through the Son, in the Holy Spirit, revealed and opened "the deepest level of his fatherly heart and pure inexpressible love";[44] it speaks about what Luther articulates in the second and third stanzas of his hymn of liberation.

But the "general" teaching about God and about anthropology, which is to be differentiated from the teaching about the Trinity, does not simply involve the experience of the law that accuses and kills, as this is described in Luther's hymn of liberation. It also deals with the much larger issue of what is experienced in the setting Luther identifies as the *primus usus legis,* the *usus politicus.* But last, not least, it refers to the experience of every single one of us, the incomprehensible, terrorizing hiddenness of God, in which he hides his power in a dark, unendingly distant and yet unendingly close way — coming as one who is consuming, scorching, oppressing.

It is one of the grandiose blunders of the more recent history of both philosophy and theology that the attempt has been made to conceptualize this almighty nature theologically as trinitarian. This blunder results in a darkening, in fact in a dislocation, of the gospel, which can be conceptualized only from the perspective of the doctrine of the Trinity. Whoever tries to use teaching about the Trinity, which should be treated separately — to describe "general" teaching about the Trinity and anthropology — by speaking about the Trinity and calling for reflection about the essence of the Trinity, must of necessity turn the teaching about the Trinity into a general teaching about God. This has actually taken place for those who have followed post-Christian natural theology, as it has been developed since the time of Lessing and Kant and as it is to be found in full form in the speculative philosophy of Hegel.[45]

The distinction between what is involved in the teaching about the Trinity and "general" teaching about God and anthropology, which is to be applied appropriately against the move to elevate it to the speculative realm, is encountered in faith and in the hope that this distinction will be removed, along with the distinction between law and gospel, in the eschaton. Then the *triune* God — *he alone* — will be all in all (1 Cor. 15:28). Then we also will no longer be assailed by the oppressive, incomprehensible hiddenness that weighs us down even to the point of our death. It will be consumed by open

---

44. *BSLK* 660.29-31; cf. LC II, 64, in *BC,* 439; cf. n. 42 above.

45. Cf. Oswald Bayer, *Theology the Lutheran Way* (Grand Rapids: Eerdmans, 2007), 193-98 ("The Problem of Natural Theology").

love, which itself cannot be comprehended, which will free us from its power and which comes to us conclusively already now in the gospel.

This end that we believe in and hope for, because of the love that has come to us and has been promised to us — the consummation of the work of creation by the triune God — is misinterpreted with regard to its true character when it is claimed that it exists as a timeless principle of knowledge and existence. Its universality cannot be demonstrated in the abstract, not even with theoretical means linked to the Trinity; one cannot apply its truths to every circumstance one can postulate and treat it as an a priori — as one might do with something like transcendental thinking.

The liturgy and its poetic nature precludes a premature and impatient application of the confession about God as triune; it allows for time to pass and it marks the rupture in time between the new and old world, as well as the break between faith and sight (2 Cor. 5:7) — handling it verbally: holding it at a distance and keeping it open. A doctrine of the Trinity that is presented in such a setting allows the logic of poetic formulations to be taken into account. Statements can be constructed with particular attention paid to the liturgical forms, along with the poetry that is used paradigmatically as proclamation in Luther's hymn of liberation; such will not fall into the realm of speculation that forgets about time and situation. It will not try to articulate verbally what continues to be an open wound in the life of faith, until we see the face of the triune God without agonizing struggle.

15.2.3. The Triune God as Speech Event

Luther does not think about the triune God in a speculative way but in a way that speaks theologically. This can be seen most clearly in his reformational commentary on the prologue to the Gospel of John: God is the Word, that by which he speaks in, with, and to himself, that which remains in him, and that which in no way can be separated from him: "His Word is so much like him that the entire divinity is completely within, and whoever has the Word has the entire divinity";[46] the "Word is not merely wind or noise, but brings with it the entire being of the divine nature."[47] Thus one can speak of God's "be-

46. WA 10I/1:188.7f.; cf. *LW* 52:46 ("The Gospel for the Main Christmas Service").
47. WA 10I/1:186.15f.; cf. *LW* 52:45. The situation is, "as we said above in the Epistle [Heb. 1:1ff.] where we dealt with the brightness of his glory and image, divine nature is formed to accompany the image and it becomes the very image itself. The brilliance also radiates the glory so that it merges with the glory. Accordingly, in this passage, too, God of himself speaks his word so that the godhead follows the word and remains with its nature in the word and is there in its essence."

ing" only insofar as it is "Word," as a power to communicate, which from its side makes communication possible.

We encounter once again Luther's unique concept of the Word, which is clearly differentiated from the normal use of language — insofar as for him the word is conceptualized as an expression of inner nature — and thus not just as sound and fury. If God is understood as Word, then the Trinity is to be comprehended as dialogue: God, within himself, is communication, relationship, a relational "three-ness," as Luther says; he never found any positive connection to the word "Trinity" or "threefoldedness": "Threefoldedness is not very good German. In the Godhead there is the highest unity. Some call it three-ity [*Dreiheit*], which has too much of a mocking tone. Augustine complains as well that he did not have an adequate term. . . . Call it a three-ness [*Gedritt*]. I cannot assign it a name."[48] If the Trinity is a dialogue, if God, within himself, is communication, relationship, a relational three-ness, then he does not allow himself to be conceptualized in any way as a monad, as a monarchical being or subject. Instead, within himself he is in motion: speaking and hearing, speaking and answering, as Father and Son, to whom the Spirit listens, so that what is heard can be communicated to us.[49] Thus the entire being of the triune God is a unique communication to me and to all creatures, an event of complete giving and a trustworthy, reliable promise. One last reference will be made to Luther's *Confession* of 1528: Father, Son, and Holy Spirit, "that they are the three persons and one God"; the following subordinate clause describes what God is according to his nature: "who has given himself to us absolutely completely, along with all that he is and has."[50] The *Father* gives himself to us absolutely completely in the creation; the *Son* gives himself to us in the redemption and opens for us thereby once again the access to the Father; finally, the *Spirit* gives himself to us in the *promissio*, which constitutes faith, and at the same time gives us the Son and the Father. The triune God reveals himself in the *promissio*. *The trinitarian nature of God is the inner structure of the* promissio.

---

48. WA 46:436.8-12 (sermon on Matt. 3:16-17, of June 16, 1538). Cf. Emanuel Hirsch, *Hilfsbuch zum Studium der Dogmatik*, 4th ed. (Berlin: De Gruyter, 1964), 17: "Luther does not yet know the term 'Dreieinigkeit,' which — just like the Latin formulation *triunus*, e.g., in Dannhauer, 1697, and Hollazius, 1707 — might have come into existence later because of what he had said against 'Dreifaltigkeit.'"

49. "The Holy Spirit is the Listener from eternity" (*LW* 24:365, "Sermons on the Gospel of St. John: Chapter 16," 1539; to John 16:13).

50. WA 26:505.38f.; cf. *LW* 37:366. Cf. chap. 5, n. 11, and chap. 11, n. 49, above.

15.2.4. Time and Eternity

If the triune God is conceptualized as a communicative speech event, both internally and externally, a consequence follows that is paradoxical from the perspective of philosophy, and for some also from that of theology: the apparently sharp dividing line between eternity and time blurs, as does the dividing line between subject and object. God is not something like the monarchical subject of reconciliation; no: because Christ identifies himself with the sinner, reconciliation takes place *within* God as well.

The hymn of liberation, "Dear Christians, One and All, Rejoice," can also be sung and understood as a confession of the Trinity. Because the eternal God takes time to create the world; because he identifies himself absolutely completely with the destiny of Jesus of Nazareth that takes place within time; because he ventures forth in an inner drama that takes place as we exist within time — whether that takes place through faith or through the contrary experience of unbelief: for this reason his eternal truth is not beyond the bounds of time. God "laments in eternity my [time-related!] suffering."[51] This implies an inner conversation within the Trinity: "He said to his beloved Son: 'The time is here to be merciful; go forth, my heart's worthy crown'";[52] finally, the summary: "there you have become happy."[53]

This corresponds exactly to the concept of eternity formulated by Boethius: "Aeternitas igitur est interminabilis vitae tota simul et perfecta possessio" [Eternity is thus the entire and also complete possession of indeterminate life].[54] Eternity is not time stretched out or unending, but is the fullness of time, its unity. Eternity is not timeless, it is time-filled. As stated by the Luther scholar Johann Georg Hamann: we know "of no [other] eternal truths" except what is "unendingly time-related."[55] That, to be sure, is a paradoxical way of speaking, but it protects one from the false path of speculating, on the one hand, about the Trinity in a sense that is unbound by time or, on the other hand, assuming that there are epochs of the Father, Son, and Spirit that follow, one upon the other.

---

51. "Dear Christians, One and All, Rejoice," in *LSB*, #556, stanza 4.

52. Stanza 5.

53. Stanza 8.

54. Boethius, *The Consolation of Philosophy*, trans. Richard Green (New York: Bobbs-Merrill, 1962), 115.

55. Johann Georg Hamann, *Golgotha und Scheblimini! Von einem Prediger in der Wüsten* (1784), in *Sämtliche Werke*, ed. Josef Nadler, vol. 3 (Vienna: Herder, 1951), 303, 36f.

15.3. Almighty God — Heavenly Father[56]

God, whom we must experience in ambiguous ways as almighty as long as we are still on our journey (2 Cor. 5:7), but whom we are able to address already now as a good and merciful Father, can be addressed only in the certainty that is declared in the *invocatio* of the Lord's Prayer. The complete teaching of the Trinity is implicit when one addresses God as Father.[57]

The identifying characteristic that precedes all the petitions in the Lord's Prayer is the *invocatio* at the beginning, addressing God as "Father" in a way that is full of confidence and is sure of being heard — better yet: as "Abba!" This word that is used by little children in their playroom suggests addressing "papa" with full confidence: the name that connects what is nearby, home territory, and safety from danger.

To address God with this name, as demonstrated in the history of religions as well as in systematic and theological settings, is by no means a given: against his almighty nature, death and life, in short: against absolutely everything that works in our life to say "Abba!" is either the expression of a delusion and an infantile illusion, which cannot stand the test to be considered a principle of reality, or the expression of that unprecedented confidence — which overcomes the world — that Paul brings to expression: "For I am convinced that neither death, nor life, nor angels, nor rulers, nor things present, nor things to come, nor powers, nor height, nor depth, nor anything else in all creation, will be able to separate us from the love of God in Christ Jesus our Lord" (Rom. 8:38-39).

Clarity is not yet ours, since we cannot yet distinguish everything as being completely good or completely evil. What oppresses us with great force and makes all of life less than certain seeks to bring us down whether we are filled with pride or in despair; it seeks to destroy us. In spite of this, God is addressed as "Abba!" with the confidence that evil has been defeated and that we are redeemed from the evil one. That is the monstrous message of the New Testament — which provokes one immediately to see it as contradictory: evil has been overcome already through the cross and resurrection of Jesus Christ, the world has already come into a situation of complete peace (John 19:30), so that one can dare to sing: "Now is great peace unceasing, all warfare now is at an end."[58]

---

56. This section is based upon Luther's explanation of the Lord's Prayer. For a discussion of the subject in detail, cf. Albrecht Peters, *Kommentar zu Luthers Katechismen*, vol. 3, *Das Vaterunser*, ed. Gottfried Seebass (Göttingen: Vandenhoeck & Ruprecht, 1992).

57. Cf. also chap. 16 below.

58. *EG*, #179, 1 (Nikolaus Decius: "Allein Gott in der Höh sei Ehr" = "All Glory Be to God on High," *LSB*, #947).

Such confidence about peace and salvation is the work of God himself, of his presence as the Holy Spirit whose mission and commission consist in bringing to remembrance everything that Jesus said (John 14:26). For this reason, if the Lord's Prayer is prayed with earnestness in the present time, it is because this happens only by the power of the Holy Spirit: "For all who are led by the Spirit of God are children of God. For you did not receive a spirit of slavery to fall back into fear, but you have received a spirit of adoption. When we cry, 'Abba! Father!' it is that very Spirit bearing witness with our spirit that we are children of God" (Rom. 8:14-16).

The state of affairs that is wrapped up within the *invocatio* of the Lord's Prayer, which is clear to see in this text as it moves one to theological reflection upon the Trinity — that one addresses the Father through the Son by the power of the Holy Spirit — can be seen in a particularly clear way in Galatians 4:4-6: "But when the fullness of time had come, God sent his Son, born of a woman, born under the law, in order to redeem those who were under the law, so that we might receive adoption as children. And because you are children, God has sent the Spirit of his Son into our hearts, crying, 'Abba! Father!'"

The believer who is confident about the love of God when uttering the *invocatio* of the Lord's Prayer will find anything that contradicts this love to be intolerable. The believer who is filled with trust and can speak "Abba!" with confidence and can add the "Amen!" at the end of the prayer, to give further emphasis to that trust, allows for the obvious tension that comes with problems that bring suffering; the confidence of salvation permits one to lament about the evil that threatens. The lament, which is uttered as a petition in its sharpest form, with the assurance of being heard, lives unashamedly with persistence (Luke 11:8), pressuring and assailing God with the request to deliver us and our fellow creatures from evil and thus to bring to justice all the foes of the creation — including the last enemy, death.

> Make an end, O Lord, make an end
> Along with all our troubles![59]

This is the way Paul Gerhardt gives expression to "Maranatha!" (1 Cor. 16:22; Rev. 22:20; *Didache* 10.6), which — as is also true of the petition for the coming of the kingdom of God — is the positive way of articulating the double petition formulated in the negative at the end of the Lord's Prayer.

The one who has already delivered us from the evil one and who can thus be addressed as Father is assailed with the petition: "and deliver us from the

---

59. *EG*, #361, 12 (Paul Gerhardt: "Befiehl du deine Wege" = "Entrust Your Days and Burdens," *LSB*, 754, stanza 6 [not all stanzas are translated]).

evil one." That is because the confidence expressed in the *invocatio* is attacked right up to the end of our life — to the point of the end of the evil one, which comes at the same time as the consummation of the world.[60]

To see God in an eschatological sense comes with being one with his righteousness. The "light of glory . . . will demonstrate at that time that God, whose judgment [now] seems to be based on righteousness that one cannot comprehend, is the most righteous one and completely manifest righteousness."[61] This *lumen gloriae* will be manifest not just in the light of nature but most properly in the light of the grace of the incomprehensible hiddenness of God. Identical with the final judgment, that will bring the dispute with God to an end and will resolve the question about theodicy: "On that day you will ask nothing of me" (John 16:23).

This final justification comes within the indisputable self-revelation of the triune God — as love.

60. If *Didache* 10.6 is a prayer for the arrival of grace (as the arrival of the Lord), as well as for the death of this world, this aeon, then it is a prayer for the death of the old world as fallen creation and thus for the restoration of the original creation as the consummation of the world through the last judgment.

61. WA 18:785.35-37; cf. Luther, *The Bondage of the Will*, 389. In its context (cf. chap. 9.3.3 above), this conclusion to *De servo arbitrio* (along with Luther's preface to the book of Job in *LW* 35:251-53 [1524]) is in my opinion the most telling articulation of the most striking aspect of the eschatology.

Chapter 16 Promise and Prayer

> *If there were no promise,*
> *our prayer would be worthless.*

Throughout this application of Luther's theology to the present time we have not attempted to present his thought as a world of thought in and of itself, which we could try to separate from its own original "setting in life." That is why we came again and again to the significance of prayer as a constitutive factor for Luther's theology. The chapter that draws the entire study to a close concentrates on the topic of prayer — as it follows Luther's outline for prayer in his sermon of May 13, 1520,[1] for Rogate [Pray!] Sunday. As nowhere else, this text documents in a pregnant way Luther's reformational understanding of prayer; it shows very clearly not only how Luther explained the Trinity in such a way that its theological character as promise was central, but also how his understanding of prayer itself had a trinitarian character. Whenever Luther preached in subsequent years on Rogate Sunday, he came back to the basic structure of what he articulated in this sermon. The same viewpoint is encountered in his explanation of the Lord's Prayer in the Large Catechism: prayer is constituted in the command *(praeceptum)* and the promise *(promissio)* that it will be heard, in that it comes from within a situation where there is dire need *(necessitas),* but also in that it takes place with earnestness and with passionate reliance on the promise that it will be heard *(desideratio).*[2]

The outline reads as follows:

---

1. On the question of dating, cf. Oswald Bayer, *Promissio. Geschichte der reformatorischen Wende in Luthers Theologie,* FKDG (Göttingen: Vandenhoeck & Ruprecht, 1971; 2nd ed., Darmstadt, 1989), 322f. n. 27.

2. LC III, 1-27, in *BC,* 440-44.

Every prayer [*oratio*] consists of five [identifying characteristics]; otherwise the prayer is offered in vain.

The *first* is the promise of God [*promissio Dei*], which is the foundation on which the entire prayer relies: if there were no promise, our prayer would be worthless; it would be unworthy of a favorable hearing, since it would rely on its own merit.

The *second* is that one states the specifics of the dire straits [*rei necessariae*] or else the substance of what is desired by means of the petition, so that the scattered thoughts can be focused on the godly promise, because I hope to acquire help; this is what one calls gathering one's thoughts [*animi collectio*]. Based on this, [self-]selected little prayers, rosaries, and the like are not priestly prayers, since they do not gather one's thoughts, nor do they summarize the matter on the heart that seeks resolution.

Third: Faith is necessary [*fide opus est*], by means of which I believe in the God who makes promises, that I can expect that what I pray for is possible without having any doubt. To be sure, God ensures that all things are guaranteed not because of you and your prayer, but because of his trustworthiness [*veritas:* truthfulness, faithfulness], by means of which he has promised that he [the one who has been asked] will give it. Thus, only trust [*fiducia*] can expect that the faithfulness [*veritas*] of God is at work to ensure it will happen.

Fourth: [The prayer] is uttered with earnestness, not with a vacillating spirit and not as if one does not urgently desire the thing for which one prays [*magnopere desiderante*], as if on an adventure, where whatever happens happens, as if one throws something at a pear to knock it out of a tree. This would be a mockery of God, as if he were not willing to guarantee what he had promised. Such [adventures] not only fail to achieve what they seek, but they provoke God instead, with evil results.

Fifth: Such prayer takes place in the name of Jesus, by whose command [*iussu*] ("If you ask anything in my name" [John 16:23]; additionally: "Ask and you will receive" [Matt. 7:7]) and by whose authority we can come confidently before the Father of all things. Thus it cannot happen that the prayer goes without being heard [*non potest non fieri exauditio*]: the Father has promised an answer through the Son, as through an instrument [*instrumentum*]. And our sins hurt Christ; he prays concerning them in heaven, as if they were his own. Tell me now: What could cause a rejection here? The Son prays in heaven in my name; I pray on earth in his name. Thus the righteousness of Christ is my own, my sins are Christ's: this is admittedly an unequal exchange [*inaequalis permutatio*]. And both come to purity, connected together: my sins vanish in Christ and his holiness washes me clean, so that I become worthy of eternal life.[3]

16.1. "Thus It Cannot Happen That the Prayer Is Not Answered"

The final section answers the decisive question: How can I have any right to address the one who has power over all things, and furthermore, how can I be confident that I will be heard?

Freedom from such uncertainty and from our sins comes to us only in connection with that event in which God himself comes to us and brings us to himself: in the way God comes as the triune one. For only in the differentiation and yet mutual connection between Father, Son, and Spirit can we be certain concerning the speech and action of God, as those who believe and as those who pray — concerning his revealed will and his action that causes his will to take effect, his promise and the way it comes to realization, his mercy and his faithfulness.[4]

In the words of the *human* Jesus — "ask and you will receive!" — one can comprehend the command and promise of God himself. Stated the other way around, the word of Jesus as a human being can lead one to have confidence only because it is the command and promise of *God:* "Thus it cannot happen that the prayer is not answered: The Father has promised, through the Son, as through an instrument." The Son is the instrument; he stands in for the one who holds all things within himself, standing in the presence of humans. This took place once for all, and it still takes place today: the Son stands by with the Father, against the unfaith of human beings, to effect the will of God that was revealed once for all and that continues to have power even now — and thus stands by for the possibility and reality of faith and prayer. He thus acts in the same way as what is on the heart of the Father because of his own Word. Since he intercedes in prayer on our behalf, he identifies so intensely with our sins that he demolishes them.

We comprehend the unceasing prayer of the Son as the enduring, valid Word of the Lord. For — in the intermediary office of Christ — both are one: standing in with us before God and with God on our behalf. Since thus, in

3. WA 4:624.8-32. In the text that follows, citations lacking more specific reference are from this outline. It is analyzed and interpreted in detail in Bayer, *Promissio,* 319-37.

4. Luther refers to Ps. 85:10 ("that steadfast love and faithfulness will meet; righteousness and peace will kiss each other") in the parallel sermon entitled "Rogationtide Prayer and Procession," 1519 (*LW* 42:89).

such an interwoven way, the Son and the Lord are one and the same, our prayer and God's response are one as well — if our prayer corresponds to the Word of the Lord and if God is responding to the prayer of the Son. Prayer that is uttered in the name of Jesus can be certain of being heard. In that we call upon the Word of Jesus, claim it as valid, and "clothe"[5] ourselves with it — as Luther says in one of the later Rogate sermons — we have already received the response: in the name of Jesus God never refuses.

"Tell me now: What could cause a rejection here? The Son prays in heaven in my name; I pray on earth in his name." This intertwining of the two aspects of a single event can best be understood as corresponding to what happens when a human being speaks a word of forgiveness and divine forgiveness takes place at the same time, as Luther explains when he interprets Matthew 16:19 as a "statement of holy justice."[6] That which is reformational in Luther's theology does not suggest a general possibility that a human statement can be identified as divine; instead, in an *identifiable* human Word — in the Word of absolution — the saving presence of God can be believed. In the same way, human prayer is not to be considered a sure thing in and of itself; only such a prayer in which I come *through him*[7] to the Father has the assurance of being heard, because at the same time he is coming before the Father *on my behalf*. We treat his coming before the Father on our behalf as true when we ourselves come confidently before the Father.

From this vantage point it makes complete sense that Luther rejected Christology as teaching about the two natures of Christ in his Rogate sermon of 1525, if such teaching were to be reduced to a rigid formula, identifying little more than a state of affairs and no longer as a living relationship, namely, that movement in which God brings himself to us and us to him. Only in this way can the teaching about the work and office of Christ as intermediary be articulated appropriately according to Scripture — namely, as this corresponds to the text in John.[8] Luther uses a chiasm to depict the situation with utter clarity:

---

5. WA 15:548.3f. (Rogate sermon, 1524). Whoever "puts on" the promise, puts on Christ himself: "for I do not pray to the 'Father' because I could consider myself worthy . . . but rather because the Son, Jesus Christ, has passed on to me his name and all that he is, so that I can stand blameless before you [God!] by virtue of all his blessings, and I take these blessings onto myself and stand in his merit" (546.26-30).

6. Cf. Bayer, *Promissio*, 200f., on the subject; cf. also chap. 3.2.2 above.

7. Cf. *LW* 24:393 ("Sermons on the Gospel of St. John: Chapter 16," Rogate sermon, 1538, printed in 1539).

8. Cf. chap. 10.3.2 above. The person of Christ is comprehended through his work, his work through his person — by which metaphysical speculation concerning his person is rejected, as is an understanding of his work that merely treats the impact he made.

> And here we see as well that to believe in Christ, that *Christ is a person,* who is God and man, would not help anyone at all, but that *this same person is Christ,* which means that he went forth from the Father on our behalf and has come into the world and has once again left the world and returned to the Father, that means the same as: *That* is Christ, that he became man and died for us and that he has been raised and has gone forth to heaven. On the basis of this office he is called Jesus Christ, and those who believe about him that it is true, for them it means to be and to remain in his name.[9]

The mediation that took place through Christ as the content of the *promissio* matches exactly the way the "happy exchange"[10] is described by that well-known articulation in *On the Freedom of a Christian.* "Thus the righteousness of Christ is my own, my sins are Christ's: admittedly, an unequal exchange." What human beings gain through Christ is what God loses through Christ; God acquires the human beings with his loss, the loss of his purity. Only in this way can he come with them "into purity." The "unequal exchange" implies a concept about God, which thereby identifies the nature of God as that which participates in the troubles of human beings.[11] His authority is not distant from the world, without emotion; instead, it is of the type that encourages and empowers one to pray in Christ: "In the name of Jesus, based on his command . . . and authority, we are to come forth confidently before the Father of all things." By this authority of Christ, "order" or "command" and "promise" become one unity — because it is an authority that guarantees, that gives, and that delivers. Only God himself, on his own, can guarantee this, as the one who has power over all things, which means that "he hears."[12] Thus the claim to be God lies within that specific Word that promises that it will be heard, "Ask, and it will be given you!" The divinity of Jesus Christ is thus not the presupposition that guarantees the promise, but it directly im-

9. WA 17I:255.11-18, italics added. A lucid and pregnant formula, which embraces the doctrinal topics of Trinity, Christology, and soteriology, appears in the exposition of Luke 2:49 in the *Fastenpostille* of 1525 (WA 17II:24.18f.): "Thus Christ is present in that which is his Father's when he speaks with us through his Word and thereby brings us to the Father."

10. WA 7:25.34 (*Von der Freiheit eines Christenmenschen,* German version, 1520); cf. chap. 10 above. The fact that the last section of the Rogate sermon is a brief articulation of what is treated in a more extensive way in significant portions of the first part of *On the Freedom of a Christian* is examined in greater detail in Bayer, *Promissio,* 330f.

11. On the criticism of the concept of God in Aristotelian metaphysics that is connected with this point, cf. chap. 10.1 above and Oswald Bayer, *Theologie,* HST 1 (Gütersloh: Gütersloher Verlagshaus, 1994), 21-27 and 49-55, especially 54. Cf. above, chap. 5, n. 58.

12. As far as we are concerned, equating "making certain" with "hear and answer" still implies the difference between faith and sight.

plies it. In the indissoluble unity of person, work, and Word, the divinity of Jesus Christ is either believed *along with* his promise or denied *along with it.*[13]

That the sermon being discussed here does not — as do later Rogate sermons — mention the Holy Spirit does not alter anything concerning the trinitarian character of the intercessory event that is described. For Luther the teaching about the Holy Spirit is implicit within Christology, since "the Holy Spirit does not go forth as the body of Christ, since he is the Spirit of Christ."[14] He gives public witness to Christ's own words in his testament, which take effect after his death through his resurrection — and it is as a testament that Luther understands the Johannine farewell discourse — "how it is between me, you, and the Father."[15] The Spirit does not teach "about how things are within the Godhead";[16] instead, his activity is specifically directed toward us — by freeing us from being under our own power: "Whoever is to pray in the name of Christ ought not pray in his own name."[17]

Briefly: *For Luther prayer is a trinitarian speech-action, which draws us into itself:* whoever desires to speak with God "is to hear the Holy Spirit, who says that everything is comprehended in Christ."[18] As regards the teaching about the Trinity, Luther consequently would say only that faith in the Word has to do with God himself, certainly and completely: "As the Word is, so is God."[19]

16.2. Promise, Dire Need, Faith, Earnestness

It is clear from the closing section of the Rogate sermon why the *promissio* is the first identifying characteristic for prayer, why it alone is its "basis and power."[20] Prayer that is rooted in one's own will and one's own strength, by contrast, would be empty and worthless. Permission and empowering for prayer are found in the fact that God calls for prayer through Christ and at the same time promises that the prayer will be answered.

Luther calls the second important point about prayer the *dire need (necessitas)*. It does not constitute the prayer on its own,[21] but it belongs to it

---

13. Cf. WA 28:60.12-30 (*Wochenpredigt* on John 16:25-28, July 18, 1528).
14. WA 20:381.20f. (Rogate sermon, 1526).
15. WA 28:60.9f.
16. WA 28:60.31f.
17. WA 28:60.32f.
18. WA 34I:385.4f. (Rogate sermon, 1531).
19. WA 9:329.31 (sermons on Genesis, 1519-21).
20. WA 17I:249.15 (Rogate sermon, 1525).
21. Cf. the striking reference to Judas and Cain in the sermon on the Lord's Prayer of

in that the command and promise address the dire need. Necessity does not teach that it is necessary to pray — it can also drive one to doubt or move one to attempt to overcome the dire need on one's own. It is necessary to offer the petition not because of the necessity; in this case the command is a promise. Even more so: necessity actually allows itself to be recognized and identified only in light of the promise, in confrontation with the promise that the dire need will be overcome: "Place his promise and your dire need opposite one another!"[22] For this reason the concentration, the "gathering of one's thoughts" that involves the dire need that is identified and the help that is expected, is actually concentrating on the "divine promise."

This concentration on the promise is the *faith* that works in the prayer. The third identifying characteristic is understood by Luther as the courage that pressures God to stand by his Word and to resolve the issue. This "pressure" is a decisive moment for the faith that trusts the *promissio*.[23] Faith can do this because God pressures one to act thus. As the Rogate sermon of 1526 expresses it, the "amen" of the Son provides certainty: "This is the greatest promise, that he says 'amen, it shall be so' and thereby swears by his eternal faithfulness. For this reason you must begin the prayer so that you challenge God with his own words: 'God, you spoke an oath twice, by your dear Son, that I should pray and that I would be heard. Because of this assurance, which you have promised through the mouth of your dear Son, I come and pray.' And this is the foundation of prayer."[24] The faith that is identified is determined completely by its content, by the *promissio;* the certainty that puts the "lid on the top of"[25] the prayer with its "amen" is based upon the "amen" of the Son and is nothing other than its echo; that the prayer will be heard is verified in the Word alone, "experienced"[26] only by it. This promise that it will be

---

March 9, 15 23: "If this promise is not there, the dire need is not removed. For Judas and Cain had dire need, but they had no faith in the promise" (WA 11:56.21f.).

22. ". . . oppone promissionem suam et tuam necessitatem" (WA 20:380.9f., Rogate sermon, 1526).

23. The sermon of 1519 speaks of "admonishing" God of his promise (*LW* 42:87, 90). Cf. WA 17I:249.30 (Rogate sermon, 1525): "take the promise for yourself and use it as well to get God in your grasp." In addition to the Rogate sermons, cf. the idea of "holding God to his own words" in the famous sermon on the Syro-Phoenician woman (Matt. 15:21-28) (WA 17II:200-204, here 204.2, *Fastenpostille,* 1525).

24. WA 20:379.24-29.

25. WA 27:130.27 (Rogate sermon, 1528).

26. WA 27:130.27-33: "When you have prayed, you must feel something move in your heart to tell you that your prayer is heard. 'You [God] have commanded us to pray and have promised. I know that the prayer is accepted and heard.' You cannot base this feeling on your uprightness, but only on the command and promise of Christ. If you do not say this, your prayer has no

heard is more certain than life and death.[27] Since faith that trusts in the promise of God moves about within prayer and makes it certain with the "amen," which is anchored in the faithfulness of God, faith claims the power of the Word over all the powers of the world. For this reason, Luther can boldly state in his Rogate sermon from 1531: "Our prayer is God's power."[28] "What are all powers against that word 'amen'? The prayer of petition is a great power, a power of God, which the power of the pope, of Satan, of the Turks is not, for the whole world against the Word of God is, as Isaiah says, 'as a fleck of dust' [Isa. 40:15]. All the power of the world is just a little thing. Thus say: I trust the promise of God."[29] In Elijah "you see a single man praying, and he rules, with this prayer, over clouds, heaven, and earth, so that God lets us see what kind of power and force a true prayer has, so that nothing is impossible for him."[30]

By means of the power of the *promissio* of Christ, prayer is almighty, since it has been heard by God already.[31] But the certainty that is wrapped up in the Word that it will be heard is experienced with anguish when the eschatological fulfillment is so different when compared with the present dire need.[32] Since this discrepancy remains, the desire of the one who grasps God by his

---

Amen. Then everything will seem as if the prayer is true. Whether it is heard in the time you want — that does not matter."

27. WA 15:548.6 8 (Rogate sermon, 1524).

28. WA 34I:389.21f.

29. WA 34I:389.9-13.

30. WA 17I:251.19-22 (on 1 Kings 18, Rogate sermon of 1525).

31. Cf. *LW* 24:394: "By no means be in doubt or uncertain when you pray; but believe confidently that your prayer has come before God, has reached its goal, and has already been granted. For it has been offered in the name of Christ and has been concluded with the amen with which Christ Himself here confirms His Word."

32. *LW* 24:400: "Our joy cannot be full until we see Christ's name hallowed perfectly, all false doctrine and sects abolished, all tyrants and persecutors of Christ's kingdom subdued; not until we see the will and the designs of all godless people and of the devil checked and God's will alone prevailing; not until the cares of the belly or hunger and thirst no longer assail us, sin no longer oppresses us, temptation no longer weakens the heart, and death no longer holds us captive. But this will not take place until the life to come. There we shall feel nothing but perfect joy; there we shall no longer have even a droplet of sadness. In this life, however, all is imperfect, as St. Paul declares in I Cor. 13:9. In faith we have only a droplet of this joy; this is the beginning or foretaste which includes the comfort that Christ has redeemed us and that through Him we have entered God's kingdom. At the same time we are weak in showing the power that comes from Him and in our obedience to Him; progress is slow and cannot be perfect either in faith or in life. Again and again we fall into the mire and are weighed down with sadness and a heavy conscience, which prevent our joy from being perfect or make it so slight that we can hardly feel this incipient joy."

promise experiences utmost tension between the dire need and the promise. The tension felt, as one desires what is promised, makes for the earnestness of the prayer; its essence and impact are thus a *desideratio,* which is what the fourth section of the Rogate sermon addresses. Such earnestness keeps one from foundering in fear, as well as from merely going on a frivolous adventure ("as if on an adventure, where whatever happens happens, as if one throws something at a pear"). It is much more the case that prayer takes place as a bold venture, firmly rooted and oriented toward its goal — in which the cause and the goal are one.[33]

This is not contradicted by the Rogate sermon of 1525, in which the *desideratio* appears with the catchword "sighing of the heart" (*suspirium cordis;* cf. Rom. 8:23).[34] Since this sighing means in fact that fear, necessity, and temptation are not to be treated with quiet acceptance or with resignation, but are to be suffered with a most dynamic desire and yearning because of the promise that they will be overcome, Luther does not view the dire need of the one who is praying in and of itself, but in light of the one "who has promised that he will provide."

In this regard it ought not to be overlooked that the *desideratio* created by the *promissio,* in opposition to the dire need, does not involve a possibility and ability that are within the human purview, but remains the work of God himself as the unutterable sighing of the Spirit, who stands in on our behalf (Rom. 8:26-27):[35] as with the origin, so also the use of the *promissio* is an event of the trinitarian God; it also occurs "only from the unfathomable depth of divine goodness, before whom come all petitions and desires, through his gracious promise and encouragement that move us to pray and desire, so that we learn how much more he cares for us and is more ready to give than we are to take and to seek."[36]

33. See 16.1 above. Cf. *LW* 42:89 ("Rogationtide Prayer and Procession"): you are worthy and fit to pray when "you proceed with bold courage, trusting in the truthful and certain promises of your gracious God."

34. WA 17I:251.8–252.3; 251.36–252.22.

35. The *desideratio* as a transsubjective power is thus described: "Yearning exceeds all words and thoughts. This is why it is that the human being himself does not sense how deep his sighing or yearning is" (WA 17I:252.11-13).

36. WA 2:175.13-17; cf. *LW* 42:87.

Index of Names

Index of Subjects

Absolution, 52-53, 57-58, 269-70

Academic theology *(bonarum artium cognitio)*, 18, 26-27; and creation as speech act, 103-5; and disciplines (grammar, dialectic, rhetoric), 27; distinction between "academic task" and "world-oriented task," 18-19; and language-learning, 26-27; and teaching about the church/three estates, 139

The Address to the Christian Nobility of the German Nation concerning the Reform of the Christian Estate (1520), 274

Adoptionism, 237

Against Hans Wurst (1541), 260, 261

Against the Heavenly Prophets in the Matter of Images and Sacraments (1525), 246

Anabaptists, 243, 256, 313; enthusiasm of, 298-99; and Luther's exposition on the Sermon on the Mount, 320; and Luther's teaching about the three estates, 140; and the two realms, 313

Antichrist, 4, 325, 332-33

Antinomianism and nomism, 65-66

"Apocalyptic," defining, 9

Apology of the Augsburg Confession (Melanchthon), 279-80

Apostles' Creed: explanation to the first

article (how the human being is placed into the world as a creature), 163-74; explanation to the first article (regarding creation/justification), 95-96; explanation to the second article (and faith in Jesus Christ), 230-34; summary of the three articles in the *Confession* (1528), 99

"Appellation and Protestation *(protestatio)* of the Evangelical Imperial Estates," 331

Assertio omnium articulorum (Affirmation of All the Articles of Martin Luther That Were Condemned in the Most Recent Bull of Leo X) (1520), 73, 187

Atheism, 55, 137

Augsburg Confession: (article 2), 192, 326, 329; (article 5), 90, 249, 251, 255, 257-59, 260, 266, 273-76; (article 6), 288; (article 7), 244, 259-61; (article 8), 280; (article 11), 185; (article 14), 257-58, 273-76; (article 16), 318; (article 17), 326, 329; (article 18), 158; (article 19), 195; (article 28), 318, 321; on the call of God and church, 244; and the church, 244, 255, 257-61, 266, 273-76, 280; and command to love, 153; and the consummation of the world (final

359

God-given skill *(habitus)*, 27-28; *gratis Spiritus* (the grace of the Spirit), 17-20, 24; and meditation *(meditatio)*, 19-20; *occasio* (opportunity/the temporal moment), 22-24; and the *oratio* (prayer), 19, 24; *sedulo lectio* (constant, concentrated textual study), 25-26; *tentatio* (the agonizing struggle), 19, 20-21

Theological anthropology, 39, 184

Theology (topic of), 29-43; experiential wisdom *(sapientia experimentalis)*, 30-37; history and time, 31-32; Luther's contrast to the Aristotelian system, 30-32; *meditatio* (meditation on the text), 34-35; *oratio* (prayer), 32-34; *promissio,* 53-54; subject of the sinning human being and the justifying God, 37-42; as taking place within three elements/settings, 41-42; *tentatio* (agonizing struggle), 35-37; "three rules" for the correct way to study, 32-37; *vita passiva:* faith, 42-43

Three estates (church, household, state), 120-53; and certainty/uncertainty, 136-39; and the church as order of creation, 122-23, 125-39; and *Confession concerning Christ's Supper,* 121-26, 152-53, 158; and distinction between what is "holy"/and what is "saved," 158; distinguishing the fundamental estate from the other two, 125-26; estate of the household *(oeconomia)*, 123, 142-47; and explanation of the first commandment, 128, 129, 138, 139, 153; and first rule of scriptural interpretation as found in Genesis lectures, 122; and God and idol, 130, 135-36; and language's role in characterizing the changeable nature of human beings, 121; and love, 152-53; and Luther's reformational understanding, 124; and natural reason/reasonable knowledge of God, 127-35; and older concept of estate and "standing," 120-21; and original sin, 135-36; the political state, 123, 147-52;

question about justification and creation, 138-39; and question of natural theology, 126-36; significance for discussion/dialogue with the world religions, 139; and the spiritual importance of the temporal, 140-41; and teaching about the two realms (spiritual/temporal), 124-26, 324-25

"Three lights," 211-13

Time: consummation of the world and end of time, 10, 330-33; and creation (history and the ages), 116-19; in the modern age, 118; and *occasio* (opportunity/the temporal moment), 22-23; and teaching about the Trinity, 342; as topic of theology, 31-32. *See also* Eschatology

To the Councilmen of All Cities in Germany That They Establish and Maintain Christian Schools (1524), 23

Treatise on Good Works, 282-90

A Treatise on the New Testament, That Is, the Holy Mass (1520), 271

Trinity/God's triune nature, 334-42; and consummation of the world, 326-45; and "Dear Christians, One and All, Rejoice" (hymn of liberation), 222-25, 334, 337-40, 342; and discussion of eschatology/consummation of the world, 334-36; as distinguished from general teaching about God/anthropology, 337-40; and eschatological sense of God's righteousness, 345; and God's incomprehensible hiddenness, 336, 339-40; Holy Spirit and gift of the triune God, 254; the invocatio of the Lord's Prayer (addressing God as Father), 343-45; and the Large Catechism, 208, 338-39; and the law that kills, 337, 339; and the *promissio,* 341; setting and way to speak about, 334-36; as speech event (dialogue), 340-41; time and eternity, 342

Tübingen statement on Roman Catholic theological understanding of Scripture, 86-88

Index of Scripture and Other Ancient Literature